821.8 ARN

MATTHEW ARNOLD AND THE

CLASSICAL TRADITION

Matthew Arnold

and

the Classical Tradition

WARREN D. ANDERSON

Ann Arbor Paperbacks
The University of Michigan Press

VXORI

CARISSIMAE

Library of Congress Cataloging-in-Publication Data

Anderson, Warren D.
     Matthew Arnold and the classical tradition / Warren D. Anderson.
          p.   cm.
     Bibliography: p.
     Includes index.
     ISBN 0-472-09177-8 (alk.paper)   ISBN 0-472-06177-1
(pbk. : alk. paper)
     1. Arnold, Matthew, 1822–1888—Knowledge—Literature.
2. Civilization, Classical, in literature.   3. English poetry—
Classical influences.   4. Classicism—Great Britain.   I. Title.
PR4024.A48   1988
821'.8—dc19   88-23050
                                                                              CIP

Preface

Matthew Arnold remains a Victorian poet and literary essayist whose works command attention outside the classroom. On many occasions they have proved their ability to rouse a storm of controversy that is no mere tempest in an inkpot. This claim may seem strange. For one thing, not many of his poems have the power to touch us. Except at rare moments, they lack the thrust of language and the uncanny psychological portraiture that amazed Pound in Browning's *Men and Women*. Neither do they possess the varied music of which Tennyson showed such mastery.

Yet the most discussed short poem in English, rivaled only by Hopkins's "Windhover," has been "Dover Beach." Beyond the academic fact of bibliographical lineage, it has had a remarkable success with undergraduates. In it they encounter — unrealized perhaps, but indisputable — what is only erratically present in Browning's work and conspicuously absent from Tennyson's: a controlling intelligence. Or if we turn to the field of prose, where Arnold faced no opposition from either of these challengers, *Culture and Anarchy* continues to call forth both agreement and disagreement, as if it were a product of our own anarchical time. Mill on the meaning of liberty, like Newman on the nature of a university education, deserves our attention and respect. It is Arnold, however, who takes concepts such as these and plays them off against each other. If he does so less nobly, less majestically, the result nevertheless has proven to be uncommonly capable of holding its place in the to and fro of current argument.

We come back to an intelligence exercising control, even to a fault, over its material and itself. Chief among the influences that formed it was classical literature, especially the poetry and philosophy of Greece. In this book I have attempted to show the process of formation, and its results. Since the poetry bespeaks a developing relationship with the classical, one that might be summarized in terms of approach and with-drawal, a chronological treatment of the material has seemed appro-priate. By contrast, the prose works are for the most part written from a defined position. They therefore lend themselves to discussion in terms of an author, field, or concept. Two chapters have been devoted to the role of Stoic and Epicurean philosophy. The extent of scholarly writing on Arnold's classicism since 1965, shown in the additional bibliography prepared for this present edition, suggests that the original undertaking may have had some justification. Many of the avenues on which I set out have now been explored further with good results, making possible a larger view. This "broad prospect," for which Matthew Arnold tire-lessly sought, is welcome indeed.

As the late Kenneth Allott rightly said, Howard Lowry was "the 'onlie begetter' of modern Arnold scholarship" (*The Poems of Matthew Arnold*, Preface, p. xv); it was he who proposed that I write this book. During the writing he made rare materials available from his own li-brary with characteristic generosity. I honor him as scholar, Christian humanist, and friend. The College of Wooster, of which he was presi-dent, granted me research leaves in 1958 – 59 and 1963 – 64 that made the writing and revision possible. It is a pleasure to acknowledge the kindness of Professor Allott and of Professor Geoffrey Tillotson. At the public schools which Arnold attended, the headmaster of Winchester College, Mr. H. D. P. Lee, and its archivist, Mr. J. C. Harvey, took pains to help me on a number of points; and I remember the friendliness that the staff of Rugby School showed to a visitor. I benefited much from the resources and special services of the Bodleian, the Reading Room of the British Museum, and the libraries of the College of Wooster, Stanford University, and the University of London. To the University of Michigan I owe a special debt for unfailing good counsel from the readers and editors of its Press and from Professor R. H. Super, a great source of help, responsible for the emphasis on Stoic and Epicurean ideas. My wife's unerring critiques improved the style, and she contrib-uted much to the labors of reading proof and compiling an index. Whatever errors and infelicities escaped the vigilance of so numerous and excellent a company of helpers must be laid at my doorstep.

Acknowledgments are gladly made to the following: G. Bell & Sons, Ltd., for permission to quote material from R. J. Cholmeley, ed., *The Idylls of Theocritus;* Harvard University Press and the Loeb Clas-sical Library, for passages from the Loeb translation of Aristotle's *Poetics* by W. H. Fyfe; Oxford University Press, for passages from C. B. Tinker and H. F. Lowry, *The Poetry of Matthew Arnold: A Commentary;*

Princeton University Press, for a passage from J. E. Baker, ed., *The Reinterpretation of Victorian Literature;* Putnam's & Coward-McCann, for a quotation from E. P. de Senancour, *Obermann,* translated by A. E. Waite; and University of Chicago Press, for passages from R. Lattimore, tr., *The Iliad of Homer.*

W.D.A.
1988

Contents

I

The Student Years

For Thomas Arnold the Christmas of 1822 marked a special joy:
December 24th had seen the birth of his first child, a son. The boy
was to be christened Matthew, a family name, with John Keble
standing as godfather.[1] Despite these excellent auspices, orthodox
Christianity would never keep a firm hold upon Matthew Arnold's
thought; but there was another tradition which claimed him once
the infant years were past and held him through more than fifty
years. It was the tradition of classical literature, embodiment of
Greek and Roman civilization and accepted pattern for Victorian
culture. The ways in which Arnold responded to it form the subject of this study.

To be born into the middle or upper classes in England during
the earlier decades of the nineteenth century was, in a sense, to be
born into the classical tradition. All serious education gave the
chief places of honor to Latin and Greek. Young Matthew, however, had a special position as the son of Thomas Arnold. His
father, a product of the old school of close textual searching into
the poets, had begun to follow new paths of his own even during
school days at Winchester. As an Oxford undergraduate he bent
his mind to Greek philosophy, preferring it to all ancient poetry.
Later he became increasingly devoted to classical history, although
his delight in Aristotle never lessened, and at the time of his pre-
mature death in 1842 he had been appointed Regius Professor of
Modern History at Oxford.[2]

This final honor was wholly fitting. Thomas Arnold used his
profound knowledge of the events of antiquity to illuminate the
present, which he saw as a reflection of the past. "So far as we see
and understand the present," he said with characteristic absolutism,
"we can see and understand the past: so far but no farther." After
completing the first broadly conceived edition of Thucydides to

appear in England, he wrote that he lingered round "the subject of what is miscalled ancient history, the really modern history of the civilization of Greece and Rome." This was no academic posture but a part of the man himself, the same man who on holiday evenings would read to the children his favorite stories from Herodotus.[3]

Some importance attaches to the fact that Matthew's earliest years were spent under the influence of such a personality. Quite probably there was no other home in England where a boy could have received so vivid an impression of the classical past viewed comparatively, as a paradigm of the present. The lasting tendency to see not deep but wide, an approach that was to vary from mere eclecticism to genuine insight, may have been instilled during these first ten years of childhood.

In the earlier nineteenth century it was still common for boys to receive their education at home until they were ready to enter a public school. Thomas Arnold was uniquely equipped to undertake such teaching, and the regimen he established by 1826 was no less unique. The older children, Matthew among them, studied scripture, arithmetic, history, and geography in addition to five languages—Greek, Latin, French, German, Italian. Schooling began as soon as the child could walk; by the age of five he was learning Latin, French, arithmetic, and scripture. Although much of the teaching was done by a governess, Dr. Arnold took part of this burden besides supervising and examining his little pupils. In 1828 he accepted the headmastership of Rugby; two years later Matthew went to Laleham as a pupil of the Reverend John Buckland, his father's brother-in-law.[4]

The nature of the syllabus at Laleham can be gathered from the experience of John Duke Coleridge, future Lord Chief Justice of England, who had entered the school early in 1829. By December of that year he writes, "I am pretty well up with my class with my Virgil and Greek Grammar." [5] Coleridge was then not quite nine years old. At the close of the first school year he memorized seven of Vergil's *Eclogues;* so quickly and so intensively did schoolboys stock their minds with classical poetry. Beginning with such comparatively easy tasks as this, they went on in some instances to learn incredible quantities of Vergil or Homer. Coleridge's reference shows that he had already acquired considerably more than the rudiments of Latin before going "to Buckland's." Such previous training must have been a regular preliminary for the preparatory schools, of which John Buckland's was not the most demanding.[6] Certainly the eight-year-old Matthew Arnold should have come well prepared in 1830, yet he proceeded to show a laziness that vexed his teacher and his father equally. The Arnolds had already felt grave concern at their eldest son's rebelliousness and tendency towards illness or accident during his first years. One senses that with his father at least he was never a favorite, and his poor showing at Laleham cannot have eased the relationship.

By 1833 Matthew had returned ingloriously to the family home at Rugby. He now studied privately with Herbert Hill, a Fellow of New College. In October of that year Dr. Arnold writes approvingly, "The boys go to him every day to their great benefit." [7] Two years later the tutoring produced Matthew's earliest extant verses, written for the second birthday of his little sister Frances. Hill had assigned this as the subject for an exercise in Latin verse composition, and the twelve-year-old brought his tutor four stanzas of four lines each. They bore the title *Natalis Dies Bonzensis;* "Bonze" was Frances' nickname in the family. These verses he wrote not as poetry but, in his mother's words, "as his task" or regular assignment. "He brought it up," she writes, "without the least idea of its being better than his ordinary productions." Herbert Hill thought otherwise and made a copy of it.[8] As Latin verse the poem has its faults, but the fact that it was composed quite without literary self-consciousness gives it a special place among Arnold's juvenilia. A line-for-line translation of the relevant portions runs somewhat as follows:

Bonze's Birthday

Now swiftly, little sister mine,
The days of the year have fled away: chilling frost
Has twice come hastening, and radiant warmth
Has passed away on speeding foot.

Birthday time is here, and everyone
Brings you gifts and many rewards:
(The next six lines describe the presents: a ball, a toy kitten, a picture-book, and so on.)

With happy cries you take them all;
You clap your hands and keep running everywhere,
Hurrying to show us the wonderful presents
With a kiss for each of us.

The first stanza owes its substance almost entirely to the Augustan poets, and the second and third are thoroughly prosaic; but the closing lines, despite their mishandled participles, picture the happy, excited little girl with a simple charm that would be difficult to equal. There are no mythological allusions or instances of alliteration. Except for the stock images of the opening lines, the poem has nothing about it that could be called "classical" or even essentially poetic. Its great virtue is a striking lack of affectation. In this it differs from Matthew's first known attempt at English verse, the lines written eight months later by the sea at Eaglehurst; [9] for here he writes of the Naiads and Thetis with a high degree of conventionality. At this stage conventional expression was only to be expected; nevertheless the problem, still unrealized, of his relationship to the classical tradition had begun to appear.

With all its shakiness, the Latin birthday ode suggests that Herbert Hill had schooled his young pupil uncommonly well. This was proved when Matthew and his brother Thomas enrolled at Winchester in the autumn of 1836.[10] Concerning their placing in the school Mr. Joseph H. Harvey, Archivist of Winchester College, has very kindly supplied the following facts and comment:

> The College Long Roll (list of boys in the school) for (autumn) 1836 ... shows that Arnold senior (Matthew Arnold) was then in "Quinta Classis Senior Pars", while his brother, Arnold junior (Thomas Arnold, junior) was in "Quinta Classis Media Pars".
>
> There were at the time six real classes in the school as a whole ..., viz. Sixth, Fifth Senior, Fifth Middle, Fifth Junior, Fourth Senior, and Fourth Middle. The fact that Matthew Arnold had entered the school in the next class to the top shows that he must already have reached an advanced stage of study in Latin and Greek before he entered Winchester.

It is difficult to realize what the experience of beginning school life must have meant in this period. One such beginner wrote many years later that as soon as a boy passed within the College walls, he plunged straight into the Middle Ages. The statement will not seem extreme to anyone familiar with the various accounts of conditions at Winchester in the early nineteenth century. Even more drastic, in its different way, is a generalizing comment by M. L. Clarke:

The English grammar school as it was established in the sixteenth century, and continued for some three centuries after, was essentially the grammar school of the ancient world, or, to be more precise, a combination of the ancient schools of grammar and of rhetoric, with the former predominating. Its curriculum and methods were not very different from those of the Roman Empire, and an Etonian under Keate would have felt quite at home in the schools of the time of Quintilian or Ausonius.[11]

Evidence of the personal meaning of his entrance into Winchester comes from the thirteen-year-old Matthew himself. On August 31, 1836, he had set out for his new school; during the first days of September he set down his loneliness in verses which included these lines:

> And if a moment's space we stay
> The world around seems all forsaken
> And we—deserted and alone.[12]

While the poem has no particular distinction, the portion quoted here and the phrase "to fight our fight" may remind readers of the tone and imagery that would later characterize "Dover Beach."

There exists no record of the Greek and Latin authors studied by the Senior part of Fifth form in 1836. We come closest through a partial schedule which probably relates to the period 1824–35. Since the public schools were extremely slow to change in this or any other respect, it may be taken as probable that Matthew Arnold's "set books" included Vergil's *Georgics*, the *Satires* of Horace, and Sophocles' *Electra*. The sole existing list of books for Senior Part Fifth that seems complete dates from 1757; it mentions Homer, Vergil, Horace, Juvenal, Velleius Paterculus, and Dionysius of Halicarnassus. Homer's is the only name that can be added to the other three as presumably a part of Arnold's studies. Together with Vergil and Horace, the *Iliad* and *Odyssey* were required of every English schoolboy.[13] The lower forms also would have read these authors; it is the presence of a play of Sophocles that marks Arnold's advanced place in the school. Greek and Latin dominated the curriculum. Little else was studied; nothing else was considered important.

Of the three principal methods employed in teaching, translating constituted only one. Latin composition took up at least fifteen hours a week, and the institution known as "Standing-up" was solemnized periodically throughout the school year. On each such occasion boys would publicly recite from memory massive quantities of Greek or Latin verse.[14] In the 1840's Henry Furneaux, the future editor of Tacitus, recited 1,600 lines for each of the eight so-called "lessons." A generation earlier Thomas Arnold himself, just turned thirteen, wrote from Winchester that he was about to "say without book 3000 lines of Homer." In a postscript he adds, "I have said 16000 Latin lines." "The case for Standing-up," says A. K. Cook, "was that it supplied the mind, at a time when the memory is most retentive, with perennial sources of refreshment and delight." He mentions also that Matthew Arnold supposedly was sent to Winchester for a year "that he might have the experience of a Standing-up." According to another source, however, Sixth form and Senior Part Fifth were exempt from this requirement.[15]

One supposes this high standing to be a recognition of the thoroughness of Matthew's tutoring; at any rate he publicly told the Head Master, Dr. Moberly, that he found the burden of school work light.[16] It was the first known display of that real or seeming superciliousness which was to annoy so many. He paid for it at "cloister peelings," a student ceremony at which unpopular boys were pelted with the soft inside portions of rolls. The inward effect of this on a proud and sensitive child can only be conjectured, but one who sat next to Matthew in the classroom at Rugby remembers him as "very reserved, and he seemed to have brought with him from Winchester College . . . a singular constraint which he showed even towards his father." There is nevertheless no reason to believe that the incident caused young Arnold's withdrawal at the close of the school year. His brother Thomas states clearly that their father had always intended Rugby to be their principal school, after a year at Winchester.[17]

Under "Entrances in 1837" the *Rugby School Register* lists "Arnold, Matthew, son of Dr. Arnold, Rugby, aged 14, June 26." Then in its ninth year under Thomas Arnold, the school had experienced changes which brought about a new Rugby and eventually a new, enduring concept of the English public school. These changes extended to the teaching of classics, as was necessary if real innovations were to be effected. The increasing stress upon Greek authors reflected a more general movement, though Dr. Arnold held a chief place among the small group of educators who gave it their powerful support. On the other hand, bringing Plato and Aristotle into the curriculum marked a new step. "His choice of books for school reading," Clarke notes, "was largely determined by his own interests"; [18] the headmaster of a public school had autonomy in such matters, as he still does. Nevertheless the Doctor did not allow personal inclinations to unbalance the syllabus, even though he himself preferred the philosophers to the tragic poets.

A striking feature of the new régime was translation of passages entire. Laborious, word-for-word parsing had prevailed time out of mind in the public schools. Since the seventeenth century Winchester had refused to employ this piecemeal method, which gave students nothing more than the cadaver of an author, and it was apparently from his old school that Dr. Arnold brought the more liberal procedure to Rugby. He himself set the example, his pupil Dean Stanley tells us:

> In the common lessons, his scholarship was chiefly displayed in his power of extempore translation into English. . . . In itself, he looked upon it as the only means of really entering into the spirit of the ancient authors; and, requiring as he did besides, that the translation [by his pupils] should be made into idiomatic English, and if possible into that style of English which most corresponded to the period or the subject of the Greek or Latin writer in question, he considered it further as an excellent exercise in the principles of taste and in the knowledge and use of the English language, no less than those of Greece and Rome. . . .
>
> The simple language of that early [Homeric] age was exactly what he was most able to reproduce in his own simple and touching translations. . . .[19]

In 1833 he writes to Archbishop Whately of his painstaking efforts to "make the boys vary their language and their phraseology, according to the age and style of the writer whom they are translating." It is in this respect that his way of using the Winchester method seems to have been unique.[20] An article in the first volume (1835) of the *Rugby Magazine* gives a detailed account of what was involved.[21] The schoolboy author cites three rules, clearly Thomas Arnold's, for translation from Latin or Greek.[22] According to the third of these an acceptable rendering

> should use such a style of English, as most nearly corresponds with the original; . . . it should use the phraseology of such English writers, as have lived contemporary with the writers

we are translating; contemporary, that is, in the age, not of years, but of taste, feeling, and knowledge.... Homer should be translated in the simple language of our old ballads, Aeschylus in that of Milton....

One may recall what Matthew Arnold was to say about Macaulay's *Lays of Ancient Rome* and Maginn's translation of Homer "in the simple language of our old ballads." [23] It is nonetheless true that at Rugby he first learned a comparative literary approach to the classics. The seed had fallen on good ground.

Dr. Arnold's poetic sense had never been really keen; it could not match his feeling for historical and moral values. Stanley's statement is eloquent: "He was the first Englishman who drew attention in our public schools to the historical, political, and philosophical value of philology and of the ancient writers, as distinguished from the mere verbal criticism and elegant scholarship of the last century." This value he believed to be meaningful for men as social and ethical beings. It was not information he sought from the past, but guidance. During his earlier years as Headmaster dissatisfaction with the traditional role of Greek and Latin had led him to moderate their tyranny over the curriculum.[24] Later he restored certain features of the old system, and according to Stanley the changes in his views resulted mainly from a growing conviction of "the value of the ancient authors, as really belonging to a period of modern civilization like our own." In them, he once stated, "the great principles of all political questions, whether civil or ecclesiastical, are perfectly discussed and illustrated." [25]

In short, his considered attitude was that of the type of reader whom Thucydides had expressly hoped to find, one of those "inquirers who desire an exact knowledge of the past as an aid to the interpretation of the future, which in the course of human things must resemble if ... not reflect it." So Dr. Arnold in his edition of Thucydides' *Histories* describes that mighty work as "a living picture of things present, fitted not so much for the curiosity of the scholar, as for the instruction of the statesman and citizen." His final phrase parallels the introductory statements of the *Nicomachean Ethics*—a reminder of the central place Aristotle held, with Thucydides, in his thought.[26]

Thomas Arnold's lack of sympathy with the classical poets was accompanied by a conviction (altered somewhat during later years) that schoolboys seldom could grasp the real nature of such material; they might better be dealing with prose. "I stand in amaze," he wrote sorrowfully, "at the utter want of poetical feeling in the minds of the majority of boys. They cannot in the least understand either Homer or Virgil." Actually his own attitude was shaped by an ethical bias that hindered a true appraisal of much classical poetry. Aristophanes, Juvenal, even Horace left him uneasy, though he could admire their brilliance: aesthetic and moral judgment were out of balance. "In the subject of lessons," Stanley recalls, "it was not only the language, but the author and the age which rose before him; it was not merely a lesson to be got through and explained, but a work which was *to be understood, to be condemned or admired*." Neither the Dean nor his famous teacher would have sensed any internal contradiction in the last part of this statement: it bears witness to the tensely moral atmosphere of Rugby during the 1830's.[27]

Though Matthew Arnold fell considerably below the standard of a model Rugbeian,[28] the school years proved to have a more profound effect on him than on any of his fellows; in time this influence was to alter the shadings of English thought. Clough's sensitive temperament could not withstand the intellectual chaos of Oxford; Arnold rode out the storm. The lofty coolness marking his manner from the beginning gave not merely concealment but protection to deep concerns that were to emerge in his writing. One of these was the ethical approach, whereby any work of literature—including his own poetry—was "to be condemned or admired" according as it seemed dispiriting or fortifying. The comparative view of literature also figures importantly among these concerns. Arnold sees Homer in perspective among the world's supreme writers; less successfully, he sets a hymn of St. Francis beside a Theocritean *Idyll*. Whether triumphant or mishandled, the method is characteristic of him. Together with the criterion of morality in literature it embodies his debt to Rugby.

The extent of Arnold's schoolboy reading in the classics can be gathered from the list that his immediate predecessor, Clough, set down for American readers. "I went to Oxford from the sixth form (the highest class) of a public school," he writes, looking back on his matriculation in 1837.

> I had at that time read all Thucydides, except the sixth and seventh books; the first six books of Herodotus. . . . I had read five plays, I think, of Sophocles, four of Aeschylus . . . four, perhaps or five, of Euripides, considerable portions of Aristophanes; nearly all the "Odyssey"; only about a third of

the "Iliad", but that several times over; one or two dialogues of Plato . . . not quite all Virgil; all Horace; a good deal of Livy and Tacitus: a considerable portion of Aristotle's "Rhetoric", and two or three books of his "Ethics" . . . besides of course other things.[29]

The chief advance over Winchester's syllabus lay in the attention given to the major historians and philosophers. Also to be remarked is the greatly increased amount of reading in Attic tragedy. Certain authors were little read; some, such as Tibullus and Propertius, were omitted altogether. Nevertheless, the amount of classical reading that a Rugby boy got through in the 1830's is awesome by any present-day standard.

In a letter of October 15, 1841, Dr. Arnold writes, "Our eldest son is gone up to Oxford this day to commence his residence at Balliol," and some weeks earlier, "I wish [my sons] to do well at the University, which will be an arming them in a manner for whatever may happen to them." The reference evidently is to Matthew and Thomas, whose future calling their father now found "very hard to determine"; their lack of diligence had caused him lasting concern. For a time he thought Cambridge might be the place for Matthew, but a letter written from Fox How shows that by early summer of 1841 he had decided otherwise:

> I could not consent to send my son to an University where . . . his whole studies would be formal merely and not real, either mathematics or philology, with nothing at all like the Aristotle and Thucydides at Oxford.[30]

As Michaelmas Term began Matthew Arnold entered three worlds: the University of Oxford, Balliol College, and the Honour School of Literae Humaniores. The first of these was a remote administrative entity and remains so today. The brief Latin ceremony of Matriculation, the long ordeal of Examination Schools, the final degree-granting are University functions; in all other important respects power rests where it did more than a century ago, with the colleges. Dr. Arnold's wish to have his son at Balliol was a natural one: Rugbeians of his new régime had made a name for themselves there, so that the distinction of being "Rugby and Balliol" was already real.[31]

The Honour School *in Literis Humanioribus*, which had existed since 1807, took precise form only in 1830. Its subject matter as then defined was Greek and Roman history, rhetoric, poetry, and moral and political science "in so far as they may be drawn from writers of antiquity, still allowing them occasionally as may seem expedient to be illustrated by the writings of the moderns." [32] Oxford's classical Honour School still follows, with little change, this definition of humane letters. Instead of an official syllabus of classical reading there was a tacit understanding: an Honours man, or "classman," of Arnold's time was expected to familiarize himself with works in moral and political science, history, and poetry.[33]

Aristotle ruled the first of these fields. His *Nicomachean Ethics* and *Rhetoric* were regarded as essential; the *Politics* or *Poetics* might also be read. It was thought advisable to offer at least one dialogue of Plato, and usually the *Phaedo* was chosen. Jowett's powerful advocacy had not yet established the *Republic* in the central place it still holds. History meant Herodotus and Thucydides above all, with Xenophon's *Hellenica* sometimes added. The first ten books of Livy and three books of Polybius were read, while with Tacitus one had a choice of *Annals* 1–6 or the *Histories*. The accepted list for poetry began with Aeschylus and Sophocles but gave Aristophanes as an alternative to Euripides; at least four plays of each were required. The only other mandatory authors were Vergil, Horace, and Juvenal, with a wide option available from Homer, Pindar, and the bucolic poets (Theocritus, Bion, Moschus) on the Greek side and Plautus, Terence, and Lucretius on the Latin.

In this unofficial list only two or three Latin authors of the first rank are required; Cicero does not appear at all. Greek had become, and would remain, the center of interest. A cultivated Englishman of the nineteenth century, moreover, was for the most part concerned very specifically with Periclean Athens, a civilization which he could compare with his own. Even Homer could be omitted from the canon, and the study of Demosthenes ceased altogether. These and lesser figures of Greek literature were now schoolboy tasks; the Oxonian might dispense with them.

In all but a few instances text and critical apparatus were the student's only available guides. Copies of classical texts used at Oxford by Clough show numerous marginalia, almost all of them concerned with problems of textual criticism.[34] Considering the undeveloped state of systematic scholarship at that time, the intensity and thoroughness of Clough's approach must be thought remarkable. There is no trace of a larger view in these annotations, however, and almost none of any personal reaction. The use of plain texts nevertheless had one great merit: it compelled the student to address himself directly to the authors. An acquaintance with commentators was not allowed to take the place of knowledge gained at first hand. Frederick W. Robertson, who matriculated in 1837, has described the system: "Four years are spent in preparing about fourteen books only for examination.... These are made text-books, read, re-read, digested, worked, got up, until they become part and parcel of the mind." [35] A serious student would carry through this program devotedly; the concerned tone of Clough's letters suggests that Matthew Arnold was less dedicated.

Arnold's tutor was W. R. Lingen, a good friend in later life. Although we do not know what lecturers he heard, during his first year he probably attended A. C. Tait's lectures on Aristotle and Bishop Butler. In 1842, after Thomas Arnold's sudden death, Tait left Balliol to become Headmaster of Rugby. That same year saw the arrival of a new Balliol tutor, Benjamin Jowett. Only a little older than Matthew himself, Jowett was already a phenomenon and undoubtedly exercised a considerable influence upon him. That he converted young Arnold to Hegelian doctrine, however, is no more than conjecture.[36]

At Oxford in the 1840's men such as Jowett were rare indeed. The quality of lecturing and tutoring tended to be unsatisfactory even at Balliol; an outstanding Rugbeian actually dropped to a lower academic level upon entering Oxford. When the brilliant young Arthur Stanley went up to Balliol in 1834 he found the study of ancient history less advanced than at Rugby. A few years later, the failure of classical studies in general to provide anything new and interesting profoundly discouraged Clough. Even Thomas Hughes, who betrayed no intellectual leanings either at Rugby or afterwards, felt that Oxford had failed to move beyond the curriculum and standards of the Lower Fifth form at Rugby. By the time Matthew Arnold came up to Oxford matters had improved. The lecturers were less inadequate, and modern authorities no longer went unrecognized; Dr. Arnold's edition of Thucydides, for example, had come into use. But Winchester also used it around this time, and the most that can be said for Oxford is that in a field of signal importance it had managed to draw even with the best public schools.[37]

The scattered references to Arnold's undergraduate career by his contemporaries at the University have to do almost entirely with nonacademic matters. His "Olympian" looks and manner are recalled, or his charm, or the leap over Wadham's railings that made him remembered by many who never became readers of poetry or criticism. Here can be seen the side of Oxford life that really mattered to him, the chief influence during this period of first maturity. Prolonged religious controversy had cast over the University an unsettling influence, so that many brilliant tutors and undergraduates never realized their evident promise—one thinks of the disturbing, unpredictable W. G. Ward and his un-happy pupil Clough; this contagion never affected Arnold. It was his good fortune to become one of a group of undergraduates, principally Balliol men, whose minds were as lively as his own. Moreover, he was invited to join the "Decade," a private debating society which numbered Jowett, Stanley, and Clough among its membership of less than twenty. John Duke Coleridge describes the meetings:

> There was a Society called the Decade in those days . . . which I think did a good deal for the mental education of those who belonged to it, of those of us, at least, who came from public schools. . . . We met in one another's rooms. We discussed all things human and divine. We thought we stripped things to the very bone, we believed we dragged recondite truths into the light of common day and subjected them to the scrutiny of what we were pleased to call our minds.[38]

Coleridge's words go a long way towards showing what Ox-ford meant to Arnold.[39] For the rest, we think of his countless rambles and river excursions with his few closest friends. It was said of these young men that they passed their years at Oxford as in a great country house, and Arnold seems to have come as close to perfect happiness as his nature ever permitted. This was a time of intellectual awakening that tempered, however incompletely, a critical mind forged at Thomas Arnold's Rugby. It was also a time of awakening to the natural world.[40]

In this twofold sense Oxford set the tone of Matthew Arnold's responses to classical literature and civilization, though its influence was neither absolute nor wholly enduring. Beyond these limits it does not appear to have determined his classicism. The authors who meant most to him—Homer, Sophocles, Aristotle, Marcus Aurelius—had already been encountered or else were a part of later reading. A possible exception is the Aristotle of the *Poetics*, a work which underlies the 1853 Preface; but we have seen that it was not included among the "set books" essential for Literae

Humaniores. Moreover, Arnold's references to the study of Aristotle at Oxford seem to be concerned with the *Ethics*. Though his classicism has been called distinctively Oxonian, there is no evidence for this beyond what we have mentioned.

Arnold's one undergraduate success was winning the Newdigate Prize with "Cromwell." The fact that he was second for the Hertford Latin Scholarship, a highly valued classical award, indicates unusual ability in Latin and perhaps a greater diligence than ever became apparent to his friends. He certainly was not diligent in reading for his final examinations, which he took in the autumn of 1844. He came out in the Second class; Clough had predicted it, remarking that this would perhaps be better than he deserved.[41] Today, when a Second in the difficult Honour School of Literae Humaniores is thought very creditable indeed, we may not be able to take altogether seriously the lasting dismay aroused by Arnold's showing. His place in the University, however, does much to explain this. Oxford saw him as the son of a great educator and clearly gifted in his own right. Above all, perhaps, it saw him as the product of a famous school from whose sons uncommon achievements were expected. His failure to get a First must have seemed a betrayal of evident promise. The same fate had earlier befallen Clough, who went back to Dr. Arnold and said, "I have failed."

Such self-accusation never became evident in Matthew. When he returned to Rugby to teach the Sixth form for a few months he had as much apparent insouciance as ever.[42] His blithe ways certainly were not chastened by a removal to Oriel, which elected him a Fellow in March of 1845.[43] For the next two years he remained in residence, occasionally travelling for pleasure on the Continent, and then became private secretary to Lord Lansdowne. The long years of formal association with the classics and Oxford came to an end. Ahead lay the far longer period of their influence.

The Earlier Poems

In 1849 *The Strayed Reveller, and Other Poems*, by "A.," revealed a poet who acknowledged his classical training but was not sure what role it ought to play. Arnold's uncertainty at once sets him apart from eighteenth century writers. Unlike Pope and Johnson he did not turn unhesitatingly to a Horace or a Juvenal; his lyricism owes nothing to the "pindaric" cultivated by earlier poets. To take for granted the time-honored preconceptions of classical values was no longer a possibility. The writer's task was now to define these values anew for his own purposes and establish what seemed to have a continuing significance.

When such rediscovery of the literature of Greece and Rome is systematic one may fittingly speak of classicism. This term, with its regular attributes of balance, lucidity, and restraint, does not apply to the thought of Matthew Arnold before 1850. It is of course possible that he had been seeking a formulation ever since he turned seriously to poetry. We know that his concern goes back at least as far as 1843, for when "Cromwell" was newly completed he wrote to John Duke Coleridge confessing faults in the structure. "I should think," he added concernedly, "that the construction of a Prize Poem ought to be conducted on certain fixed principles," and his words may contain a faint foreshadowing of the 1853 Preface.[1] The shape of things to come is still far from apparent, nevertheless. A half-dozen years later the first volume of poems shows that for Arnold the classical has not yet become doctrine. He is seeking a relationship with it through trial and error, and it is these varied experiments that claim our attention.

One such experiment, "Horatian Echo," remained unpublished until the close of Arnold's life. He called the poem "a relic of youth," and a note in the 1890 edition gives the date of composition as 1847. It is thus among the very first of all his works to contain marked classical elements. It is also a trivial effort by any standard, and in this very triviality lies its interest; for here we see the author's one experiment with light verse modeled on Latin poetry. The previous history of this genre goes back as far as Alcuin and his fellow scholars at Charlemagne's court; a large and honored company of English poets have practiced it. Among classical sources the most favored has usually been the Horace of the *Odes*—incisive rather than deep, poignant at times yet unfailingly urbane. It is he whom Arnold recalls here and then dismisses from serious consideration.

When he had at last consented to the publication of "Horatian Echo" the author was questioned on his choice of a title: would not the plural be more appropriate? Modern readers may well think so; yet the title as it stands represents Arnold's meaning, because it accords with the total impression Horace had made upon him. Neither the patriot of the "Roman Odes" nor the advocate of the middle way appears here; a decade later both aspects will be omitted from the eloquent sketch of Horace that brings "On the Modern Element in Literature" to a close. The lecture, however, actually shows fewer Horatian themes than does the poem. In addition to its Epicureanism the latter touches upon the madding crowd, dislike of politics, the demands of erotic and convivial verse, consolation for the lover scorned by a courtesan, and the final *memento mori* with its "crumbling bones and windy dust"—*pulvis et umbra sumus*.

Taken subjectively these lines do recall Horace; they are the lasting reverberation of the *Odes* in Arnold's mind. Yet they are not Horatian, nor are they meant to be. We tend to interpret the adjective here as "like Horace." It is much more likely that "(Echo) of Horace," a Latinate usage less familiar now, gives the meaning actually intended. The difference at any rate is evident, and nowhere does it appear more clearly than in the structure. When an ode of Horace contains any strongly reflective element it sometimes replaces an initial theme or mood by a second one, contrasting but related. The opening ode of Book 1 illustrates this: "Some prize success in sports or politics or commerce; I, success in lyric poetry." If Arnold had omitted the last two stanzas of his poem it would have the binary structure and the very themes of Horace's dedicatory ode. Actually he employs these stanzas to introduce a quite new pattern which is in itself binary.

Against the temporary triumph of the scornful fair one he sets her irrevocable, swiftly approaching defeat at the hands of old age and death. The theme is familiar enough in Horace, but not as an addendum; it demands separate treatment.

Other differences are less obvious—the moralizing distich in lines 25–26, the repetitive end-line "When dawns that day, that day," the evocation of Helen and Juliet in the manner of Villon. If none of these points succeeds in being Horatian, that is no great matter. The difficulty is that in none of them does Arnold find his own voice. They have far less significance, consequently, than the reference to those who "cloak the troubles of the heart With pleasant smile," where the thought bears on poetry. Horace would never have said this, but it is highly revealing of Arnold.

"Horatian Echo" represents a possible path which Arnold chose not to travel again. The choice was perhaps inevitable: in poetry at least, badinage was never to be his strong point.[2] Another path taken once and abandoned can be seen in "A Modern Sappho." The poem has none of Sappho's passion, none of her longing for a beloved girl who has left her. Arnold brings before his reader not the ruthless Eros that strikes its victims down, but a strategy modulated within a setting of balustrades and Biedermeier. Only the "quick lilac-shade" flickering on the grass recalls Sappho's vignettes through its delicacy of perception. The difference is well illustrated in line 7: "Let me pause, let me strive, in myself make some order." Such emotional disarray is unthinkable in Sappho, whose power lies in the ability to discipline her passion; she can even smile at her own anguish.[3] This is the heart of the true classical, a secret that Matthew Arnold had yet to discover and make his own.

Probably he had no deep concern with the classical here. The poem makes even less of an effort than "Horatian Echo" to suggest its supposed inspiration. His themes of emotion and experience are to sound again, and far more effectively, in other poems. Here an incongruous title only impairs any effectiveness which their setting possesses. A kind of passion is sought for if not achieved; but it is romantic passion, and it cannot be reconciled with the classical by an allusion.

With "Mycerinus" Arnold turns from classical poetry to the *Histories* of Herodotus, whose tale of Menkeres serves him as a point of departure. He endows the Pharaoh with a modern skepticism and rebelliousness against the course of fate, adding the Puritan's guilt that blights pleasure. Commentators have thought

of Job, and not without reason; but it is misleading to argue that
the figure of Mycerinus is predominantly Hebraic. To suppose a
conflict with Hellenism is no less erroneous, for Hebraism here is
opposed not by Hellenism but by the Hellenistic and Roman ethic
of Stoicism. In the ruler who inwardly "Took measure of his soul,
and knew its strength," who was "calm'd, ennobled, comforted,
sustained" by that knowledge, this philosophical element becomes
obvious. We recognize most immediately the austere ethic of
Arnold's hero, Marcus Aurelius, who found happiness possible
"even in a palace," but also the martyr's faith of those Stoics whose
courage Seneca and Tacitus record. To all this the first conjecture
regarding Mycerinus' secret thoughts forms a violent contrast:

> It may be that sometimes his wondering soul
> From the loud joyful laughter of his lips
> Might shrink half startled, like a guilty man
> Who wrestles with his dreams. . . .

Here is the burden of guilt, the sense of sin in which Arnold later
found Hellenism deficient. The Stoic's determination to grant
pleasure neither more nor less than its due importance is shadowed
by the pall of Hebraic and Puritan conscience, triumphing over
pleasure by making it joyless.

"It may be . . .": this one phrase, at the same time forced and
tentative, embodies the weakness of Arnold's approach. Having
traced out the main outlines of Herodotus' narrative, he does not
find it possible to work within them. The suggestion of Mycerinus'
inward state ought to have followed naturally from the aspect of
outward circumstances, as in "Empedocles on Etna," instead of
being superimposed.[4] Arnold had yet to learn that he could not
deal seriously with classical subjects by standing off from them,
adding a touch of moral awareness when it suited him. This is not
to say that he has written a wholly unclassical poem. Herodotus'
vagueness regarding the ways of God to man leaves a wide field of
speculation open and Arnold enters upon it vigorously, suggesting
Epicurean gods whom human suffering cannot move. He speaks
also of the possibility that gods no less than men may be "slaves of
a tyrannous necessity," the *anangkê* known to us as unalterable
Fate. Here he has turned to one of the most ancient springs of
Greek thought, raising a question familiar to Homer and
Aeschylus. The Pharaoh's speculations undoubtedly have much of
the Greek manner; yet they end in blasphemy, counter to
Herodotus' narrative and all accepted Greek practice.

Considered as an attempt to refashion and endow with inwardness the Herodotean original, "Mycerinus" achieves at best a dubious success. Judged as a self-sufficient work, it suffers inescapably from disunity: by accepting Herodotus' narrative Arnold makes his alternative interpretations ineffective. No amount of ingenuity can reconcile Stoic serenity with revelling that turns night into day for the pretense of cheating death. As a key to one of the lasting moods and doctrines of its author, however, "Mycerinus" is a valuable document.

Thoughtful readers have seen many sources in "Resignation." Classical origins play a considerable part, especially the positions taken up by the Stoics and Lucretius. Apart from classical factors, "Resignation" brings together a remarkable diversity of themes: the vanity of human wishes, the Westmoreland march up-country to "the sea" where so many of the later poems will debouch, a Wordsworthian preoccupation with gipsies, and the role of the poet.[5] From a classicist's point of view this work is to be placed among Arnold's experimental poems. It constitutes in part a notable example of his attempts, frequent until mid-century, to devise a working relationship between his own times and antiquity. Later he will be smoother, more Parnassian; seldom will he be more moving.

Certain of the early poems, such as "In Utrumque Paratus," "Courage," and "In Harmony with Nature," relate to classical thought in an important degree but are not comparable with the poems discussed in the present chapter. Their classical derivation is largely or wholly from the ethical background of Stoicism and Epicureanism, and it is necessary to see them against that background. They will therefore be discussed in a separate chapter; this is also to include a more detailed discussion, stressing philosophical elements, of "Resignation" and certain other poems already noted.

"To a work of his youth, a work produced in long-past days of ardour and emotion, an author can never be very hardhearted." [6] With these words Arnold, from the vantage of his fifty-third year, described a poem he had written in his middle twenties, "The New Sirens." Many of his contemporaries had been less indulgent when it appeared. They found it puzzling at best; even Clough could make out no more than the concluding portion, and Arnold drafted a long précis for his benefit. This key, however, unlocks fewer doors than might have been expected; some comment on the poem seems necessary, especially with regard to certain hidden or half-disclosed elements.

The identity of the New Sirens can hardly remain in doubt. They represent the appeal exerted by Romanticism and the Romantic mode of life. As the précis explains, they are "really something better and more lawfully attractive than the old Sirens": their love "is romantic, and claims to be a satisfying of the spirit." The entire poem amounts to a denial of this claim. If countless details remain obscure, it is at least clear that in Arnold's opinion Romanticism does not satisfy the spirit.[7] What it offers, he explains to Clough, is "*alternation* of ennui and excitement," a life of questionable value which will leave the spirit wearied.[8]

The poet, then, speaks as a critic of Romanticism. What is not clear is whether his criticism reveals a countering position. It might have been expected that he would also speak as a champion of the classical. A number of passages may contain clues bearing on this point. So at the opening of the second stanza the poet, who had begun by addressing the Sirens (4–5), suddenly is speaking to the Graces. "For," he continues (10), "I dream'd they wore your forms." That is, they were endowed with the charms that the *Charites* or *Gratiae* had in their keeping—a harmless conceit, nothing more than surface decoration.

Suddenly all is confusion. The Sirens with the look of Graces are, it seems, a strange compound of Lorelei, malevolent storm-spirits, and wreckers who lure ships to destruction (11–16). But these were dream-creatures. Now the wakened poet gradually perceives them to be quite different. They have abandoned the sea, and to their splendid palace come a multitude bearing tribute like the Magi (17–24). The Sirens' primal savagery is gone: their faces, once so cruel, now glow with love; they seek no longer "The delight of death-embraces" (49–56).

Two stanzas follow the palace description (25–40):

> And we too, from upland valleys,
> Where some Muse with half-curved frown
> Leans her ear to your mad sallies
> Which the charm'd winds never drown;
> By faint music guided, ranging
> The scared glens, we wander'd on,
>   Left our awful laurels hanging,
> And came heap'd with myrtles to your throne.
>
>
> From the dragon-warder'd fountains
> Where the springs of knowledge are,

> From the watchers on the mountains,
> And the bright and morning star;
> We are exiles, we are falling,
> We have lost them at your call—
> O ye false ones, at your calling
> Seeking ceiled chambers and a palace-hall!

Here is the characteristic Arnoldian topography of mountain and lowland symbolizing exalted and debased, intellectual (the spiritual is a later antithesis) and sensual.[9] Classical references embellish it, as in other poems; nowhere does any intimate or necessary connection exist. A quizzical highland Muse listens to the Siren song from afar with mixed emotions. The poet, and others with him, have left their laurels hanging to come to the Sirens "with myrtles"; thus the Muse is a Muse of poetry (perhaps of lyric poetry), as we might have supposed, and in a reversal of the usual pattern she has been deserted by her protegés. The laurels they have left behind are the emblems of Apollo, "awful" because of the awe he inspires; it is such a bough that Empedocles casts down when he renounces his service to the god. The myrtle branches which they bring instead to the palace in supplication—"your throne" emphasizes the queen-suppliant relationship—are of course equally traditional as sacred to the queen of love, Venus. Through this substituted symbol Arnold seems to provide an implicit commentary on the claim that the Sirens' love satisfies the spirit.

The "dragon-warder'd fountains" of the springs of knowledge must belong to the symbolic mountain landscape, but in themselves they are utter fantasy with no relation to the classical background. While the image lends a heightened color, it seems to contribute nothing to the larger design. As for the nature of this design, the first seven stanzas [10] may provide the needed clue. They show the poet trying once again to work out a coexistence of the classical with immediate reality. This he could not manage to do. His questioning and condemnation of Romanticism throughout the poem cannot entirely cancel out a deep sympathy towards Romantic aims, and the classical counter-position becomes thoroughly obscured as a result of his muddled strategy. It does not really exist, in fact, for the poet has not got his bearings. Much later in the poem (168) he refers to his doubts and objections as "this sobbing, Phrygian strain," clearly without expecting that he can oppose anything sound or positive to the enchantments of the

Sirens.[11] His opening stanzas indeed have offered no grounds for such a hope: the Graces and the anonymous Muse find themselves near neighbors of Caspar, Melchior, and Balthasar thanks to a phrase (20–21) even more gorgeous than the dragon fountains and quite as alien to the context. The symbolic contrast between laurel and myrtle has unusual significance, for it provides the only indication that Arnold's real concern is the poet's experience and that he himself is involved; but he has masked both the meaning and the importance of his antithesis all too successfully.

According to the prose abstract "the speaker, a poet," tells the New Sirens "he has dreamed they were - the [sic] Sirens the fierce sensual lovers of antiquity." The concluding phrase contains a surprising error. Although obscure comic writers of the Hellenistic period did portray erotic Sirens, there can be no doubt that the Sirens of antiquity and of literary tradition are the creatures described in the *Odyssey;* Arnold refers explicitly to the Homeric setting (41–44). The lure of these Sirens was intellectual: they sought a response of the mind, not of the flesh. The Hebraic serpent promises awareness of good and evil, the Sirens promise *knowledge of all things.* Moreover, as Professor W. B. Stanford has pointed out, their words are given added charm by the most intellectual of all arts, music.[12] It is by the unremitting use of active intelligence—knowledge as power—that Odysseus, who as Homer says "came to know the ways of thought of many men," manages to escape death and prevail over his enemies; the quest for knowledge drives him even to the lower world. For such a man, the hope of omniscience has far greater allure than any version of the Mohammedan's erotic paradise.

It is not at all unlikely that the literary inspiration for ,"The New Sirens" came from George Sand's startling autobiographical novel *Lélia,* as a noted Arnold scholar has recently suggested. "The germ of the distinction between the old and the new Sirens," we are told, "is to be found in the prolonged debate in *Lélia* (1833) between Pulchérie (the type of the classical siren, who stands for sensual appetite) and Lélia (the type of the modern 'romantic' siren with her alternations of passion and ennui)." [13] There is the further point that the reprinting of this poem was in the first place an act of sentimental homage to George Sand's memory. Pulchérie is a courtezan; she is also sister to Lélia, and the sensual-spiritual distinction sometimes gives way to a strong implication that the two are actually indistinguishable. This ambivalence must be taken into account when one attempts to contrast the two sisters.

Lélia, written after a time of severe emotional shock, is the novel in which George Sand portrayed herself most completely. Hardly her best work, it has importance as a fictional statement of the obsessive *moi* of Romanticism. It will surely receive close attention when that sorely needed work is written which establishes the significance of George Sand's writing for Matthew Arnold. In the absence of such a study we cannot entirely grasp either his classicism or his Romanticism.

Since one may not properly speak of the classical Sirens as representing sensual appetite, Pulchérie ought not to typify them in modern terms; and yet she does seem to have inspired Arnold's conception of the Sirens as they were known to antiquity. Writing as he did, he ignored Homeric and general classical precedent. We do not know the reason for this, but it is possible that around the years 1845–47 the "Milton jeune et voyageant"—George Sand's own description of Arnold—experienced a good deal of emotional turbulence. An overriding concern with personal problems may have been precisely what prevented him from arriving at some classical formulation in "The New Sirens." The antique details proved ineffective because Arnold's mood was still attuned to Romanticism, a circumstance which delivered him into the hands of the beloved enemy. He could do nothing more than question and deplore the attractions of Romantic attitudes, which are set forth with the greatest fulness.

The classicism of the poems noted thus far has been an attempt to establish a working arrangement with antiquity. Classicism can also mean decorous and lifeless imitation; to his lasting credit Arnold never settled for this, least of all in the later 1840's. Taken from one point of view the poetry of this period constitutes a series of experiments, approaches to the classical that fail to achieve their goal. In structure, style, and philosophy "Horatian Echo" bears little relation to the *Odes;* on the other hand, the poet has not yet set the stamp of his own personality on his lines. The resulting impression is one of colorless writing, if also of deftness and energy. The distinctively Romantic emotion of "A Modern Sappho" places it in another world from that of the poetess who sang on Lesbos, a world so different that the poem's title succeeds only in appearing incongruous. With "Mycerinus" the poet undertakes a classical theme at greater length than before. By choosing to retell Herodotus' narrative, however, he has committed himself to a character portrait in which the added Stoic ethical touches have an inescapably jarring effect. Finally, "The New Sirens" shows him still affected by the Romanticism he rejects, still unable to find an alternative such as classicism would notably provide.

In these years preceding 1850 Arnold had still to settle upon a fitting poetic use of the writers who had dominated his education and become part of his thinking. Successive attempts had shown the various errors that might be avoided in future. His purpose was not to be gained, it appeared, by grouping characteristic themes, or by forcing illegitimate parallels, or indeed by taking in hand an original that might prove intractable. Neither would it help matters to introduce bits of the antique as occasional decoration, without a master plan of any kind. His first unsuccessful approaches had cleared the ground: the time had come for an effort to build solidly on the foundations that twenty years of academic training had provided. This effort was made, consciously or unconsciously, in "The Strayed Reveller."

The fact that "The Strayed Reveller" was chosen to be the title poem of the 1849 volume shows an author's satisfaction in what he had created. It has delighted many, and it continues to give delight. Nineteenth-century reviewers were hostile to it as often as not; in our own day critics have usually approved. The brief interpretation in the *Commentary* forms a convenient introduction:

> This symbolic poem seems to suggest a similarity between the intoxication of the Bacchic revellers in their ecstasy and the experience of poets in the act of creation. From the latter the gods demand a suffering proportioned to the knowledge of active life, communicated to poets by them in visions. The young reveller, who has paid neither the price that Circe receives for her cup nor that which the gods exact for song, but who is under the immediate protection and inspiration of Dionysus, is contrasted with Ulysses, the much-enduring man, the type of active experience, somewhat as Callicles in the later dramatic poem was to be set over against the philosopher Empedocles.[14]

In order to consider these remarks we must summarize what happens to the youth. He rises at dawn, takes up his Dionysiac ceremonial wreath and thyrsus, and hurries "to join The rout early gather'd" at Dionysus' temple in the town. On the way he enters Circe's palace and drinks the liquor that he finds in a bowl on the altar. Overcome, he sleeps the day through; at evening the goddess discovers him when she returns from a day's hunting with

Ulysses. She is indulgent rather than angry, and at her bidding the youth drinks again. Ulysses enters; he surmises that this sweet-voiced youth has "follow'd Through the islands some divine bard...taught many things [by] Age and the Muses." If so, he is welcome and honored.

The youth has already told Circe that he is a "strayed reveller"; now he does not answer directly. "The Gods," he begins, "are happy. They turn on all sides Their shining eyes, And see below them The earth and men"—Tiresias, the Centaurs, the Indian and Scythian, the Chorasmian ferry bearing merchants fearful for their silks and jewels, the Heroes "At sunset nearing The Happy Islands." These things, he says, "The wise bards also Behold and sing. But...what labour!...what pain!" For the Gods exact a price for song: "To become what we sing."

How has the reveller come by his knowledge? Had the poem ended with the magical lines "Or where the echoing oars Of Argo first Startled the unknown sea" (258–60), one would suppose Dionysiac inspiration. The poem goes on, however: "The old Silenus...told me these things," the youth adds.

> But I,...
> Sitting on the warm steps,
> Looking over the valley,
> All day long have seen,
> Without pain, without labour,
> Sometimes a wild-hair'd Maenad—
> Sometimes a Faun with torches—
> And sometimes, for a moment,
>
> .   .   .   .
>
> The desired, the divine,
> Beloved Iacchus.

The forms of the goddess and her consort waver, begin to fade before his eyes. He asks for the cup again; in words first used at the beginning of the poem, he again seeks to have "the wild, thronging train, The bright procession of eddying forms" sweep ever faster through his soul. His cry brings "The Strayed Reveller" to a close.

To understand the youth's request it is necessary to recall his words after he has first demanded the cup (7–13). They describe Circe as she stands before him, and they call to mind the Pensive Nymph of eighteenth- and nineteenth-century art. White-robed, she negligently holds a wine cup, one arm leaning against a column and propping the cheek. We know her sisters if not her self, for we have met them many times in statuary, frieze, and painting; they formed an established part of the Victorian scene.

But Arnold has not merely conventionalized his classical subject and made it Victorian. He has sought unconsciously to weaken its force, as in so many other instances, and thereby he reveals a characteristic which is primarily personal. These lines suggest what is to come: Circe's cup will endow the reveller with a dreamlike perception instead of turning him into a beast. Several critics have remarked upon this particular weakening of the original; [15] none has noticed the change embodied in the portrait of the reveller himself. We are shown a youth, impulsive and impressionable no doubt, who nevertheless remains clearly on the side of decorum. He sets out for the temple of Dionysus at dawn like a dutiful young Anglican going to early Communion.[16] This restraint is not unlike the sobriety that had come to characterize Dionysiac worship at Athens by the earlier fourth century; it bears very little resemblance to the sudden fierce rapture, unpredictable in its coming and unearthly in its effects, that fell upon the women of Thebes in Euripides' *Bacchae*.[17]

Moreover, when the youth turns aside into the empty precinct of Circe, his "straying" removes any possibility of Dionysiac inspiration. By absenting himself from the revel he elects not to be possessed by the power of Dionysus. Then, taking the chalice (another Arnoldian refinement), he places himself under Circe's spell instead.[18] The result is a strange state halfway between dreaming and waking which he has become too transported to analyze. He speaks first as if just awakened from day-long sleep, but he tells Ulysses of listening to Silenus at noon and sitting "Looking over the valley, All day long." Strict logic suggests that this final vision of Dionysus with his Bacchantes and satyrs is a part of the larger dream, not a separate and real epiphany.

Silenus had said that "the wise bards" must pay for having the all-seeing eyes of the Gods by sharing men's labor and pain: their splendid visions are bought with a price. The youth carefully distinguishes from this the things he himself has seen "Without pain, without labour." Silenus' wise bards are such as Sophocles and Apollonius; since it would be absurd to hint at Homer in a speech addressed to Ulysses, the most obvious example of all is passed over. The Scythian "On the wide stepp, unharnessing His wheel'd house" comes apparently from *Prometheus Bound*, though Indian and merchant were found in a travel-book. Arnold's

Orientalizing in these two vignettes foreshadows his retelling of Firdausi; they embody personal preoccupations, and it may be that they are included to show in what company he himself hoped to be ranked. At all events a number of his references single out poets of unquestioned greatness, though Sainte-Beuve did well to point out to him the real difference in merit between Apollonius and Vergil. We are concerned with the truth as Arnold saw it, not with objective truth, and we can hardly doubt that for him the "wise bards" of Silenus represented all that is deepest and most majestic in poetry. Here may be seen one view at least of what the classical ideal meant to him.

The intended meaning of the reveller and his visions is less easy to determine. His intoxication, lulling and exhilarating by turns, is not Dionysiac but Circean. This has been paralleled by a succession of moods, first and last by the desire to have one's spirit caught up in a vortex of rushing, brilliant inner experience. Unfortunately no clear line has been drawn between the world of the psyche and the external real world. All we know about either is what the reveller tells us, and his impressions waver between reality and hallucination. The next to last stanza shows him saying, in effect, that only a third draught from Circe's cup can prevent all that his senses grasp from dissolving, like Prospero's vision of the great globe itself. "Ye fade, ye swim, ye waver before me— The cup again!"

Confused and inconsistent, all this nevertheless seems clear in its larger outlines. It is the intoxicating Romantic vision that the reveller seeks when he calls once more for Circe's wine. The characteristics noted in the preceding lines are Romantic: they are designed to contrast with the classically conceived figure of the wise bard, taught by age and the Muses, the poet whose knowledge of suffering has enabled him to identify himself with the beings and experiences of which he sings.[19] Arnold's skeleton key to "The New Sirens," a work generally accepted as dealing with Romanticism, reveals similarities to "The Strayed Reveller": "A lawn . . . in front of the palace of the New Sirens. . . . Time evening. The speaker (one of a band of poets) stands . . . , newly awakened from a sleep." Near its conclusion the abstract twice mentions the "*alternation* of ennui and excitement" which has come to characterize the life of the New Sirens; the reveller's Circean moods embody something of this alternation. It might be argued that the two poems deal with differing aspects of the same broad theme.

"The Strayed Reveller" suggests no clear similarity between

the ecstatic intoxication of Dionysiac revels and the act of poetic creation. In fact, it makes a certain effort to keep them separate. Since systematic antithesis was never Matthew Arnold's forte, only a partial scheme of his intentions can be drawn up. The reveller's personal experience, for example, is Circean in its origins but becomes concerned with Dionysus; the levels of representation have overlapped.[20] As for the thesis that the reveller is contrasted with Ulysses somewhat as Callicles with Empedocles, a more compelling contrast is the one propounded by the youth himself: his own almost Epicurean *securitas* set against the laborious knowledge of the bard who must feel life's thousand pressures.

In these respects at least, it appears that no unitary vision of poetry underlies the early poems. They are a series of attempts to penetrate two profound mysteries, the act of poetic creation and the poet's relationship to the world about him. "My poems are fragments," Arnold wrote.[21] It is true; but the truth it embodies has a good, even a splendid aspect. The reveller's visions and the wisdom of Silenus, the rapture of Callicles and Empedocles' brooding take their place with the Stoicism of "Resignation," and with much else besides, among these successive attempts.

If "The Strayed Reveller" seems in some measure a successful evocation of antiquity, assuredly this is not because of the stage equipment. Palace and altar, distant temple and wooded hills add more formality than brilliance.[22] The secret is rather that Arnold has put aside his concern for nobility of character. He does not demand the elevation that he attributed to Homeric epic and Periclean tragedy. For once he is content to portray—to feel and to communicate feeling.[23] This sensitiveness does not pervade the entire poem. Until the youth begins his long reply to Ulysses Arnold has been classicizing, posturing gracefully among the props and flats of the artificial antique. Then the reveller begins: "The Gods are happy...." This and what follows are a new heaven and a new earth. Only once, in certain of the lyrics of Callicles, will Arnold again rise thus to a sheer awareness of life, to the truly classical summing-up of passion resolved. His untroubled gods with their shining eyes are not the all-too-human Olympians of Homer. They remind one, perhaps, of the round-eyed, strangely smiling *kouros*-figures of archaic Greek art— "Apollo or a youth," the placard will say. Their impersonality is not repellent, as in the bitter speculations of Mycerinus; here it seems natural, it convinces.

Again, the picture of Tiresias is bleak, colorless, heavy with silence and doom. Only T. S. Eliot can match it: "I Tiresias . . . who have sat by Thebes below the wall And walked among the lowest of the dead." Then the Centaurs enter, and there follows a richly orchestrated change to color, movement, sound, all the impact of sheerly physical existence. The poet's initial debt is probably to Maurice de Guérin's *Centaure*, a strange, compelling work. Not merely by chance, then, does the statement of the gods' price exacted for poetry conclude this particular section. Though modern critics have tended to write him off, de Guérin enters into his subject to a remarkable degree, becoming what he sings, and this identification may have been strongly in Arnold's mind.

The description passes on to a vision of struggle and agony. "In wild pain" the poets "feel the biting spears Of the grim Lapithae, and Theseus, drive, Drive crashing through their bones"; for them too Heracles' arrows redden the water with blood. The ferocity of expression, unparalleled in Arnold's poetry, marks the presence of the Dionysiac fury which repels him but which he does not ignore. These lines are no more serene or statuesque than the *Bacchae*, and they are no less a part of the classical experience.

In a manner that recalls Miltonic simile, Arnold proceeds to use Oriental coloring along with classical. Unlike Milton, he even mingles the two in his picture of the Scythian nomad. Then, the Argonauts in their dark ship, and here is added, very beautifully, the Romantic note of endless and magical vistas, of "the foamless, long-heaving Violet sea" near the Islands of the Blest "Or where the echoing oars Of Argo first Startled the unknown sea." It is difficult to think of any lines that more hauntingly embody the Romantic in a classical setting.[24] On the other hand, we err if we interpret the youth's entire speech as Romanticism, genuine or simulated. This approach may come from an unreal conception of the classical, which is not cut off forever from a common area with the Romantic.[25]

Taken as a whole "The Strayed Reveller" proves uncommonly rewarding to anyone concerned with Matthew Arnold's place in the classical tradition. It shows him working out the possible relevance of that tradition, not merely to poetry in general but specifically to his own situation as a poet. His evident success in giving the broader view a place beside the personal one —even a place of greater honor—distinguishes this poem from its companion piece "The New Sirens." In this respect at least "The Strayed Reveller" possesses the classicism that is absent from the other work. We have maintained that the reveller's intoxication may be thought to represent the Romantic vision. It would be extreme, nevertheless, to suppose that this element dominates the poem as a whole. Unlike the one-sided debate in "The New Sirens," the meeting of opposing forces here is a real one.

Arnold has partly externalized this conflict for his readers through the procession of "eddying forms," already encountered as the modern Siren-figures. Yet even these are mere visions within the reveller's consciousness, and it is there, to speak truly, that the entire lyric drama is played out. We are not warranted, therefore, in looking for a counterpart of Callicles or Empedocles. The youth's long speech, to which the entire first part of the poem (1–129) has carefully led up, constitutes an attempt to decide between the claims of classicism and Romanticism. These claims moreover bear manifestly and urgently upon the poet's calling; their relevance is not hinted at by the appropriate classical allusion, as in "The New Sirens."

Arnold succeeded in putting the question squarely enough. No mean achievement, it was the only one he could manage at this stage in his search for a viable classicism. An answer to the question is not forthcoming; neither alternative has been chosen, neither rejected. For the reveller it is no small thing to gain a place among the "wise bards," and yet what sets a special mark upon the poet is not wisdom but the fate of becoming what one sings.

This concept suggests a basis of theory in Romanticism. It is difficult to see on what other grounds Arnold could hold fast to the idea, unless he were to interpret it as the immediacy of Dionysiac experience. Just such immediacy, we have maintained, fills with life and beauty the descriptions in the reveller's long speech. But the shock of the immediate disconcerts certain temperaments unduly, and although the youth is a votary of Dionysus and claims visions of the god, Arnold makes no effort to develop these possibilities.[26] Unlike Nietzsche, and less wisely, he failed here at least to acknowledge the true double nature of the classical at its most vital and creative, which is to say the Hellenic. "The Strayed Reveller" embodies his dilemma as no other early poem does before "Empedocles on Etna." It also shows him unable, or unwilling, to resolve that dilemma by choosing between alternatives. The enigmatic figure of the final stanzas, who claims that "Without pain, without labour" he has looked upon Dionysus and the frenzied Maenads capable of tearing men to bits, may suggest the poet, wishfully thinking that the bard's godlike insight can be had without paying the inward price.[27]

When he was writing "The Strayed Reveller" Matthew Arnold came closer than at any other time in the whole of his life to the possibility of possession by the classical at the height of its power.[28] This force cannot invariably be bounded within the accepted aspects of classicism: its inevitability is not the rightness of decorum, its tensions do not betoken a mannered restraint. It moves at a level of intensity where literary categories no longer seem important and opposing tendencies are fused together. This motion moreover is no discursive, logical sequence but the essentially poetic, self-contained equipoise that Coleridge had termed "esemplastic" [29]—the vital stasis of Keats' Greek vase-painting and Eliot's Chinese jar, the interlocked rhythms of Lapith and Centaur in the sculptures at Olympia. It was too great a challenge for any Victorian.

The last poem of the 1849 edition with which we shall deal is "Fragment of an 'Antigone.'" Bonnerot considers it one of the four lyric poems which employ classical themes, freely reworked, to catch and intensify the reverberations of personal emotion, and which employ mythological allusion for symbolic rather than merely decorative purposes.[30] "Reading this fragment," he continues, "one feels that the author has been victorious over himself, and that this victory, which is the triumph of classicism, consists in rendering passion purer, not in extinguishing it." Thus (he maintains) the passion is transcended and shown under its general and timeless aspects, as also in "Philomela."

It is difficult to comment on these aperçus. When one is dealing with Arnold's early lyrics the phantom of Marguerite reappears continually, and who can be sure whether to exorcise it or to summon it nearer? Yet a poem should stand on its own merits, and by this criterion "Fragment of an 'Antigone'" proves stately and interesting, not highly polished or deeply moving. The metre remains iambic, though with many variations; there has been no attempt to match the variety of a Sophoclean lyric passage. The syntax presents some difficulty, and in the first half of the poem compound epithets stud the diction. Both features presumably reflect the poet's desire to reproduce the tone of Sophoclean tragedy; but such externals, like the strophic correspondence, are at best a veneer.

If the poem's form is conventionalized, its content is not. The chorus first praise a philosophy made up of Epicurean hedonism, Stoic indifference to windfalls, and finally an enlightened self-interest that suggests nineteenth-century Utilitarianism. Seneca's choric odes may come to mind here; those of Attic tragedy, hardly. Antistrophe and second strophe deal with the changes and chances of man's life: "Voyages, exiles, hates, dissensions, wars," and at the end "The all-hated, order-breaking . . . Death." These lines have an undeniable majesty, the majesty of a St. Paul using Koine more than that of a Sophocles.[31]

"Self-selected good" is termed less laudable than "obedience to the primal law Which consecrates the ties of blood." The poem goes on to develop its new theme impressively, preparing the reader for Haemon's lament. Yet it is an abrupt change of direction, for this second antistrophe denies the doctrine of the opening strophe. Considered in itself, obedience to the duties imposed by blood ties forms the central impulse of Sophocles' *Antigone*. It stands at an extreme from the obedience to self-selected good that Creon so disastrously chooses, sophisticating himself into the belief that he is acting solely for the good of the state.

We soon realize that Arnold does not see the matter thus. His Haemon says of Creon's death sentence that "he, at least, by slaying her, August laws doth mightily vindicate"—this of a *kêrugma*, an extraordinary emergency decree not recorded in the tables of law but proclaimed by a herald. Misunderstanding the true nature of Creon's proclamation means that one almost certainly misses the contrasts in the great ode venerating the unwritten laws, laws that are not momentary creations but exist immortally, beyond the reach of men. Apparently Arnold misconceived the *Antigone* as a conflict between individual and state, and he would seem to have been influenced also by Hegel's argument that both Creon and Antigone were right in a partial sense.[32] The confusion brought about by these two notions has been enormous.

The "Fragment" concludes with a long meditation on the power of fate even over the immortals. Here Arnold handles myth with skill and beauty, though he is overly fond of place-names. His particular theme was made famous by Horace in an ode (4.7) which may have helped to suggest this whole section. He has taken pains at any rate to maintain independence of Sophocles. Borrowings are of the most general kind, and the main sources prove to be three choruses of the *Antigone*.[33] In these Sophocles has treated a variety of related themes. He celebrates the astonishing ability of man to overcome all things save death; the strength of ancestral evil and the belief that to live greatly is to suffer greatly; resistless Eros that grips both men and gods with madness as Aphrodite works her will; and finally the imprisonments of Danaë, Idaea, and Lycurgus as parallels to Antigone's entombment.

Arnold, by contrast, dwells on the helplessness of man. He is deliberate in ignoring the idea of a family curse, which Sophocles himself normally kept in the background; the Introduction to *Merope* makes clear his feelings on this point. More significantly, he ignores the companion view that equates the heroic with suffering, a doctrine vital to our understanding of Sophocles. Love is no longer the maddening, overwhelming force of Sophoclean tragedy: with the altered Horatian aspect we have noted, it has been made firmly subordinate to fate. Into this thought is woven the theme of imprisonment, which becomes a meditation on the ultimate powerlessness of love to stay the course of destiny.

Despite its flashes of skill and beauty, "Fragment of an 'Antigone' " seems an unsatisfactory attempt to draw upon classical sources. The comparatively rigid demands of Greek tragic form could not be relaxed sufficiently to allow Arnold's temperament free play, and some of the changes he did make were merely damaging.[34] The vividness of the mythology, moreover, is offset by the objectivity with which the individual stories are presented.

"Fragment of Chorus of a 'Dejaneira,' " first published in 1867, has been plausibly assigned to the same early period as the "Antigone" fragment. It differs markedly from its companion, for there is no strophic correspondence or variety of line length, no use of myth or even of place names. The very diction suffers from this bleakness: it has become noticeably less lyrical and at times falls to a prosaic level. Arnold has used three passages from Sophocles' *Trachiniae*, or *Women of Trachis*, whose tragic heroine Dejaneira unknowingly dooms her husband Heracles to an agonizing death.[35] With these sources, limited in themselves, he has done little. While the "Antigone" fragment seeks to match the tone of its original, the present work creates an atmosphere radically different from that of the *Trachiniae*.

In this play, which scholars tend to place among Sophocles' later writings, the chorus make a notably ineffective showing. The tragedy is a private one in which they cannot share; it offers no themes for generalization. Yet what Arnold has done is precisely to generalize, and despite the poem's title its broad statements cannot be supported from the *Trachiniae*. For the most part he does not follow the practices of tragic lyric, so that by Greek standards what he writes is not choric material. The two final stanzas, however, escape this charge. Their foundation is genuinely Sophoclean, and they build upon it vigorously, concluding with a justification of the death that cuts off life in its prime. Like Pindar's victory odes these lines capture the individual at his *akmê*, the highest pitch of his powers. The underlying horror of senility is genuinely Hellenic, besides being a factor in the poet's thought.[36]

On balance, the poem seems to separate into two parts which a classicist might think infelicitous and more or less successful, respectively. The first of these has come so completely adrift from its classical moorings that judgment must be left to the literary critic. Broadly, however, we may surmise that "Fragment of Chorus of a 'Dejaneira' " and its companion piece constitute the final type of classically derived expression that Arnold tried and found wanting during the later 1840's. Throughout this period he was testing his capacities, seeking to combine them with classical modes of poetic statement. Limitations of temperament and understanding become apparent, and failures easily outnumber successes; yet "The Strayed Reveller" proves that the Victorian world had been granted a poet whose image of antiquity could move with a strange life of its own.

By comparison, the poems published in 1852 frequently disappoint. The Muses and Tiber and Helicon that figure in "Consolation" matter neither to the poet nor to his readers. "The Second Best" cites moderation as the ideal so seldom attained. Although the intellectual's weariness is here, one cannot readily say whether this poem exemplifies the "Alexandrian pessimism" noted in Arnold's private agenda; it ends on a note of optimism that combines Stoic ethics with Arnoldian ideals of culture.[37] "Self-Deception" derives partly from the Platonic myth of Er, but it presents "a Power beyond our seeing" who has left us with "Shreds of gifts which he refused in full." In Plato's account of souls preparing to enter mortal existence, each chooses his lot and does so with complete impartiality. "God is not responsible," Plato points out. "The responsibility is his who has made the choice." [38] The determinism of "Self-Deception" has no classical origins; Bonnerot may be right in connecting it with the marked fatalism, "less antique than Christian," of "Sohrab" and "Balder Dead."

Arnold's note-book entry for January 4, 1852, contains the remark, "Finished Wordsworth's pindaric." If this accepted reading of the entry is correct,[39] the reference may be to "The Youth of Nature," and it is usually so interpreted; but a dozen lines of classical allusions cannot turn a poem more than ten times that length into a "pindaric." During the eighteenth century, and throughout at least the first half of the nineteenth, this term was applied somewhat indiscriminately to English odes. It nevertheless tended to presuppose a fair degree of length, a marked varia-tion in the number of feet making up a line, classical allusions, and at least an attempt at elevation—often accompanied by a pretense of bardic rapture. "The Youth of Nature" does not seem to meet these requirements adequately. Its twin, "The Youth of Man," is also called a pindaric in the note-book entries for 1852. Both instances are beyond our ability to explain convincingly.[40]

The poems discussed in this chapter show a notable variety of approaches to the classical. They do not, however, give evidence of any common element. Matthew Arnold's long apprenticeship in Greek and Latin, a training then unsurpassed outside Germany, evidently had included no detached consideration of the nature of classicism or the classical. Any impressions he had gained were acquired unconsciously, perhaps the best way if a sound founda-tion is to be built. Once he had taken up the writing of poetry, however, some attitude became increasingly necessary. Sooner or later he had to decide for himself.

Two ways of avoiding the decision were possible. He might have declared his poetic independence from antiquity; at the other extreme, he might have joined the ranks of its conventional imi-tators. But like every Victorian poet of substance he scorned a mere imitative classicism; and as for breaking with the past, he possessed neither the temperament nor the visionary powers of a Blake. In poem after poem Arnold sought a means of reunion with antiquity. It seemed that the goal might be realized in "The Strayed Reveller"; and here he turned away, apparently lacking the resolve for a final decision. The poems which followed are an anticlimax. Their splendor, real enough at moments, is at best a fitful one. The fact that they show a good deal more concern than earlier poems with the element of myth suggests that they belong more properly with "Empedocles on Etna," the remarkable work to which the next chapter will be devoted.

In summary, it appears that thus far Arnold's poems lacked a common factor in approaching the classical. It follows that he had not committed himself to any ordered principle which could be termed classicism. He continued nevertheless to search for a viable relationship with antiquity, and the record of the crucial phases of his search may be found in his double portrait of Empedocles and Callicles.

III

The Poetry of Decision

The title poem of Arnold's 1852 edition has been variously assessed ever since it first appeared. In 1853 an anonymous reviewer called it "an utter mistake" and protested that everything about it was modern. Sixty years ago Saintsbury judged it faulty "not because the situation is unmanageable, but because the poet has not managed it." More recent critics have approached the poem with a good deal of respect. T. S. Eliot called it one of the finest academic poems ever written, and scholarly journals during recent years have reflected the growing conviction that "Empedocles on Etna" should be taken seriously.[1] We shall deal with it here primarily as a classical frame for Arnold's thought, secondarily as an intricate composite of classical and other sources. The inquiry will seek to determine whether, and for what reasons, this poem displays or fails to display the decisive classicism missing from earlier works.[2]

In its most immediate origins the larger structure owes a good deal to Romanticism. Parallels with Byron's "Manfred" are too numerous and important to be accidental, and it has been plausibly argued that Arnold simplified and rearranged some of Byron's materials to get a pattern for his poem.[3] The demonstration can be taken one step further: "Manfred" is a descendant of *Prometheus Bound*. Instances of structural and textual correspondence make clear the relationship, which Byron himself declared to be real though unintended. Thus "Empedocles on Etna" is Aeschylean at two levels—directly, through Arnold's knowledge of the Greek play, and also indirectly, through the use he apparently made of Byron. Yet its structure is not a cobbling together of Byronic and Aeschylean scraps. Arnold planned his poem with the greatest care, as if determined to produce the major work that critics now recognize it to be.[4]

Callicles' opening speech keeps in one vein until Pausanias appears. It is of the earth earthy; he rejoices over the physical beauty of life. "Apollo! What mortal could be sick or sorry here?" (1.1.19–20). For Arnold this came to epitomize what he saw, many years later, as the Greek insensitiveness to inward pain; he thought it an immaturity of soul.[5] Although the later reference should not simply be read back into the early poetry, it suggests a way of looking at the young lyre-singer, whose serenity seems almost frightening.

The first portion of the conversation between Callicles and the physician Pausanias is sham classical; once they have begun to speak of Empedocles the scene gains intensity. Callicles finds "a settled trouble" in the philosopher's mood and would allay it with music if he might. Pausanias urges him to do so unseen from a lower part of the mountain, and he goes on to speak of Empedocles' miraculous powers: they have swelled with "the swelling evil of this time" (1.1.113) when he is in exile, robbed of philosophical ascendancy by the sophists. The resurrection tale is no miracle at all, Callicles replies. Moreover (1.1.150–53),

> 'Tis not the times, 'tis not the sophists vex him;
> There is some root of suffering in himself,
>
> .   .   .
>
> Which makes the time look black and sad to him.

This evidently is no unreflecting child of nature, as some have tried to make out, but a psychologist and rationalist.[6] Callicles realizes the vulnerability of man's mind, whether to superstitious delusions or to a morbid subjectivity. Here he speaks in the iambics of blank verse dialogue, the metre used in ancient drama for portions recited without musical accompaniment. After twenty lines of transition (1.2.36–56) his utterances change to pure lyrics. They were reprinted as such under separate titles, and one wonders whether Arnold felt that the singer appeared under two successive and separable aspects.

The question may be narrowed: either the time is out of joint, as Empedocles and Pausanias maintain, or inner discord makes it "look black and sad" to the philosopher. If Callicles is right, Empedocles' complaints are not meant to be entirely convincing. This is very difficult to believe, since Arnold stated in an advance précis of the poem that Empedocles sees "the truth of the truth."[7] The 1853 Preface takes the same line: its opening paragraphs speak of one who was of the line of Orpheus but lived too late, among men who preferred delusive sophistries. Yet it also speaks of Empedocles as akin to Faust and Hamlet, with their doubts and despairs voiced in the mind's soliloquy. Callicles' explanation has not been wholly ignored.

Arnold has already established the alternatives, and thus the central dilemma, with which the poem as a whole is concerned. The Empedoclean-Pausanian mind, the mind of the modern intellectual, turns from an infected world inward upon itself and scorns any other recourse. Callicles, symbol of the classical ideal expressed through its most perfect medium, accepts the world about him as sound and beautiful. At the same time he realizes that some may have a distorted vision of it. One attitude is self-absorbed, the other unconscious of self. On the question of that which is more than mortal, the first of these embraces extremes of skepticism or again of superstition. The other gives a synthesis not easily explained; it combines lucid rationalism with a joyous acceptance of ancient tradition, the *muthoi* or "stories" that modern man calls myth. Finally, we use poetry for self-expression, whereas the Greek poet often sought to restore and strengthen wholeness of spirit in those who heard him. Callicles sings his serene airs, which often seem so remote from ordinary human feeling, out of pity and affection for Empedocles. As the second scene opens, then, the issue has been joined. The remainder of the poem must display the strengths and weaknesses of either side and seek a final assessment.[8]

The ground-plan of "Empedocles on Etna" indicates that Callicles' songs regularly follow, and are related to, the speeches of Empedocles.[9] In this respect the opening lyric that tells of Chiron and Achilles (1.2.57–76) offers some difficulty, for as yet the philosopher has made no statement of belief except for the few lines on "mind" as our sovereign resource (1.2.27–29). If, however, the first conversation between Callicles and Pausanias is recalled, the purpose of this Pindaric vignette begins to appear. Empedocles' personal bitterness has distorted his view of the world, and he realizes this ever more clearly during his introspections. What fascinates him as the one saving reality is the indeterminable potential of man's mind. By taking thought a man can devise his own safety, can help himself.[10] With this self-concerned knowledge the vision of Chiron and Achilles has nothing in common. It speaks of the timeless, super-personal wisdom of the Centaurs, whose mythical origins are interwoven with the brute creation as well as the human. Its themes are to sound again, more spaciously, in Callicles' hymn to Apollo at the conclusion of the poem. Underlying them all is the affirmation of life, not as a doctrine but as a primal impulse.

Classical borrowings, especially from Lucretius, are frequent in the 350 lines of bleak alexandrines that follow.[11] The full list of sources includes Horace, Epictetus, the historical Empedocles, and possibly Apollonius Rhodius. None of these figures importantly. A phrase or two has Horatian overtones, a few lines suggest Apollonius. Fragments of Empedocles' actual teaching are slightly more prominent, but essentially Arnold borrowed nothing but a name and a collection of miscellaneous biographical details. Regarding the Empedoclean Leitmotiv of a cosmic struggle between Love and Strife he has nothing to say; yet in a sense this may be the master symbol of the entire poem.

These hundreds of lines occasionally reveal Stoic origins. When Pausanias complains that "we feel, day and night, The burden of ourselves," Empedocles answers (1.2.129–31, 142–46):

> Well, then, the wiser wight
> In his own bosom delves,
> And asks what ails him so, and gets what cure he can.

> Once read thy own breast right,
> And thou hast done with fears;
> Man gets no other light,
> Search he a thousand years.
> Sink in thyself! there ask what ails thee, at that shrine!

One is reminded of the Stoic teaching that our true possessions are inward. The Epicurean scorn of religion, a scorn not shared by Stoics, is likewise strong here; stronger still is Epictetus' doctrine of an inner life. These attitudes belonged to the world of Hellenistic and Roman thought. They did not come into being until after the close of the Hellenic age, late in the fourth century. Greece was indeed their place of origin, but the great names most frequently associated with them are Roman: Lucretius, Seneca, Marcus Aurelius.

We do not usually hesitate to apply the term classical either to this age or to its ethical beliefs. For Matthew Arnold, on the other hand, the classical was the Hellenic. In one of his letters he says he feels like a Roman—not a Greek—who has been born in the uninvigorating times of the later Empire.[12] Hellas was the ideal; Rome was the actuality through which one is compelled to make his way. The codes of practical ethic that gave Arnold a measure of comfort were shaped by post-Hellenic or Judaeo-Christian thought; the world which seemed too much with him was that of the megalopolis whose feverish pace he knew from the *De Rerum Natura,* from Tacitus and Horace, and from the acid-bitten descriptions of Juvenal, applied to London itself by Samuel Johnson. In 1852 at least, Matthew Arnold had found no solution for the individual's feeling of barren isolation except withdrawal into the self. For him this was a modern problem, whatever its roots in Graeco-Roman philosophizing, and the solution Empedocles expounds is a modern solution.[13] What the poet wishes to say about the classical will only be found elsewhere, in the songs of Callicles.

The second of these must be accounted one of the most exquisite achievements of Victorian poetry. It is the *muthos* of Cadmus and Harmonia, transformed into "bright and aged snakes" basking among the green valleys of Illyria (1.2.427–60). Like the songs which precede and follow it, this derives in a considerable degree from Pindar's victory odes.[14] It makes no attempt either to follow Pindar's manner or to be a "pindaric"; its purposes are quite different from those either of the derivative form or of the Greek originals. When he celebrated temporal and individual victories Pindar incorporated timeless myth without a change of tone. He soared constantly, exalted, intense beyond all other poets; his stanzas blaze with the gleam of gold and fire. But intensity and brilliant images could not serve Arnold's purpose. He was seeking to contrast the serenity of Hellenic poetry and its acceptance of the world with the strain borne by modern men who feel the constant burden of themselves, a burden from which Callicles is free.[15] Empedocles has dwelt upon the suffering life brings and the unreasonableness of expecting to be happy in an existence after death. Callicles does not counter these arguments. Moved simply by the impulse to console his distraught friend, he sings of a mortal couple to whom the gods had granted escape and forgetfulness of cares after extreme unhappiness.[16]

It is not a satisfactory answer, of course. The error lies in supposing that Arnold meant the myth to be an answer at all. "Empedocles on Etna" must be accepted for what it is: not a contest of philosophies but an alternation between two different worlds.[17] We can say of the myth nothing more interpretive or more profoundly true than simply that it is.

As the second act begins Empedocles stands alone on the summit of Etna. "The world hath the day, and must break thee, Not thou the world," he reflects (2.17–18). He is now resolved to plunge into the crater, but as he advances to the rim Callicles' singing is heard once more. The song has become less disengaged: it touches upon present happenings and moods, taking on such importance that the philosopher's following speech amounts to little more than commentary. "The lyre's voice is lovely every-where," the youth begins (2.37). Only to the rebel Typho does it sound hatefully; "an awful pleasure bland" comes over the counte-nance of Zeus when the music rises to Olympus (2.41–42, 67–69). The main sources of Callicles' lyric are evident: Pindar's famous ode on the power of music has been supplemented from the *Prometheus Bound*, perhaps with "Manfred" as a mediate source for Aeschylus. The nature of these borrowings from the Greek indicates that Arnold is specifically concerned here with lyric poetry; thus in a sense the 1853 Preface touches on lyric when it weighs and rejects "Empedocles on Etna."

Empedocles proceeds to muse on the song in lines no less irregular than those he has just heard.[18] In a noteworthy instance of structural symbolism uniform line length now passes to the lyre-singer and remains with him almost exclusively throughout the remainder of the poem. When he sings again his theme is Apollo's contest with the satyr Marsyas, Hellenic lyre against Asiatic auloi (double pipes of reed, Oriental in origin, that Vic-torians miscalled flutes).[19] Under Arnold's imaginative treatment the myth takes on not merely added color but a new development. The Maenad followers of the defeated Marsyas desert him and throng about Apollo; the radiant god disdainfully turns away to watch Marsyas being flayed alive. The young aulete Olympus stands "Weeping at his master's end" and covers his eyes "Not to see Apollo's scorn." The Maenads and satyrs are followers of Dionysus, as "The Strayed Reveller" has shown.[20] The double aulos had particular associations with this god, and Phrygian was considered the aulos mode par excellence, inseparable from the Dionysiac dithyramb. It is with this larger background that Arnold contrasts Apollo and the Hellenic lyre. As they symbolize all that is serene and rational, so the god from Asia and the Asiatic pipes are symbols of emotion, of irrationality.

It is not clear why the myth of the lyre's victory should have been inserted at this point rather than at some other. Empedocles' act of stripping off his robe may have some analogy with the flay-ing of Marsyas, but it hardly seems important. From 2.109 on, the philosopher is caught up in the flux of his own thought; when the song is done he continues as if unaware of any interruption. The injunctions of 2.118–20, "Lie there, My golden circlet, My purple robe!" are completed seventy lines later with "And lie thou there, My laurel bough!"

When connection appears so slight and separation so marked, one may wonder whether the myth has not been included for a private reason, as embodying some private dilemma of the poet. Possibly the description of Apollo's triumph over Marsyas and the satyr's forfeit of his life forms a more meaningful part of Arnold's poetry than has been realized. It may symbolize his decision to reject the Dionysiac element in Greek poetic tradition, looking instead for inspiration to the Apolline serenity and control that he saw in Homer and in the tragic drama of Periclean Athens. The 1853 Preface does not first work out and then definitively state a point of view; it seeks to justify a point of view already worked out. Its thesis is not one to have been adopted hastily; debate and decision could fittingly be reflected in these agitated, non-Pindaric lines of "Empedocles on Etna" taken as "an allegory of one's own mind." What is certain is that the years which followed brought a "Sohrab and Rustum," a "Balder Dead," a *Merope;* they brought nothing to equal "Empedocles on Etna" or the long speech in "The Strayed Reveller." [21]

If the myth here reflects a crisis in Arnold's attitude towards classical poetry (and perhaps poetry in general), presumably it objectifies the sense of pain and loss attendant on his decision. This could be the reason for stressing Apollo's deliberate cruelty and the mourning of Olympus over former joys. The latter speaks much as does Empedocles in the speech which follows (2.235–57), and it is possible that both speak with Arnold's voice. This is not of course the later figure—Professor of Poetry, widely followed essayist, and established critic of the Victorian age—who has accepted a truce with necessity. It is the young man, leaving his twenties now and entered upon a choking routine, who begins to grasp the terms on which he made that truce. For the statuesque classicizing of Persian epic and Norse myth a price was exacted: the poet failed to become what he sang.

Empedocles' final speech combines diverse elements in its alternation of blank verse with lyrics: passages from Lucretius, Parmenides, and the historical Empedocles all are identifiable. Arnold has used them for his own purposes, fitting them with great skill into his portrait of an intellectual obsessed by alienation of the self. The portrait is not that of Empedocles, however. The Empedoclean mask drops away when he speaks of the struggle that will weigh down future existences throughout the cycle of rebirth (2.383–85):

> And we shall fly for refuge to past times,
> Their soul of unworn youth, their breath of greatness;
> And the reality will pluck us back....

Coming from a pre-Socratic philosopher this would have no relation to any conceivable historical reality. It is Matthew Arnold who speaks, and in his words we see emerging a new attitude towards the Hellenic tradition, an attitude never to be greatly altered or long abandoned during the remainder of his life. Flying for refuge to past times well describes his classicism after 1853, providing it is realized that he was not an escapist. The classical place of refuge was for him a stronghold, an outpost of light from which he could fight against darkness.[22] Yet his way of speaking suggests detachment—it is as if the Greek world were becoming externalized. This impression comes most strongly of all from the reference to antiquity's "breath of greatness": the phrase is not quite at home in Arnold's poetry, but his critical essays show a wealth of comparable expressions.

Knowing the nature and extent of borrowings from Oriental philosophy in this speech would greatly further any investigation of its sources.[23] Hellenic accounts of cyclic reincarnation can be traced back to the Orient, so that certain details which seem to suggest Empedocles or Parmenides or Plato may prove to have been misleading. The belief that to be true to our real self is to be "one with the whole world" recalls Stoic doctrine; so does the self-reproach for having failed to keep up a courage and strength like that of the elements—a marked change from the passiveness of Nature in "Resignation."[24]

Empedocles' words, "The numbing cloud Mounts off my soul...," recall the third and fourth lines of Callicles' prelude to the myth of Apollo's victory over Marsyas, "The music of the lyre blows away The clouds which wrap the soul." This echo suggests first of all a struggle for supremacy, a conflict unresolved or doubtfully resolved. For Empedocles, what frees the soul from oppressive cloud is the hope of some partial escape from going "astray for ever" in the cycle of being. Thus the seeming annihilation of suicide actually seeks complete absorption into the All of the cosmos (2.353), "That general life, which does not cease," described in "Resignation," "The life of plants, and stones, and rain." Paradoxically, Empedocles nurses this hope because he feels that he has merited it through an unremitting intellectual integrity. The mind and its workings fascinate him; his thought spirals incessantly inwards. Callicles has a different answer: the unclouded soul owes its liberty to "the music of the lyre," the serene outward vision of poetry.[25] This vision accepts the world; feeling no estrangement, it discovers none. It acknowledges loveliness, whether in the mountain glens or in the naked breasts of the Maenads. It does not altogether turn away even from the horror of flaying: the Dionysiac element remains powerful in defeat, and Apollo's victory is not secured without an effort.

These two views of the world cannot have equal validity. One or the other must predominate, even if the ultimate truth should prove to include both. Empedocles has rejected life, in deed now as well as word, but Arnold has not yet given a clear answer to the dilemma. There will be one further opportunity, the final song of Callicles. Its lines, set to the marching-rhythm of a Greek chorus,[26] have become the best-known and most frequently quoted portion of the entire poem. "Not here, O Apollo! Are haunts meet for thee," the youth sings, as even the lower slopes of Etna tremble; the lyre-god must seek out Helicon. A succession of lulling lines is followed by a sudden epiphany (2.437–48): Apollo "comes leading His choir, the Nine." The god has manifested himself in his character of *Mousagêtês*, leader of the Muses.[27] The immortal company bathe at a roadside spring; they journey towards Olympus, their "endless abode." But this is the god of song, joining antiphonally with the Muses in an amoebaean refrain. This indeed is Apollo much as Western literature first described him, the Homeric god playing the phorminx and singing with his nine attendants to delight the feasting immortals; and the Muses are unmistakably those of Hesiod's *Theogony*. What then is the theme of the Apolline, the Muse-born song?

> What will be for ever;
> What was from of old.
>
> First hymn they the Father
> Of all things; and then,
> The rest of immortals,
> The actions of men.

> The day in his hotness,
> The strife with the palm;
> The night in her silence,
> The stars in their calm.[28]

This final hymn (for it is to be taken as such) starts in the traditional Greek manner. *Ek Dios archômestha* was the time-honored introductory formula: "Let us begin with Zeus." What is remarkable is what follows (2.463–68), for the themes have already been encountered. They are the wisdom that Chiron taught young Achilles, the closing burden of Callicles' first song (1.2.71–76):

> He told him of the Gods, the stars,
> The tides;—and then of mortal wars
> [And of the life which heroes lead
> Before they reach the Elysian place
> And rest in the immortal mead;]
> And all the wisdom of his race.

While the bracketed lines relate principally to the immediate context, the others form a part of Arnold's larger design: they enable the Calliclean philosophy of "Empedocles on Etna" to come full circle, sounding before and after the Empedoclean counter-themes.

When one looks back over the entire poem, It nowhere becomes evident that Arnold has discovered and clearly stated a final answer. Two opposed outlooks have been set forth by means of a dramatic device, not at all classical but thoroughly Victorian, which rules out any possibility of set debate or philosophical dialogue. Arnold deliberately chose this method of presentation, and it may be suggested that he did so to demonstrate the impossibility of communication between the inner worlds represented by Callicles and Empedocles. The introspective man of thought brooding upon his wrongs and the barrenness of the time, ill at ease in solitude as in society, has no common language with the poet, whose thought radiates outward. Arnold himself embodied this dilemma. He lacked the power of systematic exposition and belittled its value; his critical method remained essentially intuitive. Possibly this lack ultimately explains the poem's distinctive structure.

It was a discerning critic, therefore, who pointed out that

"Empedocles on Etna" is what you make of it when you have read the whole poem.[29] The assessment to which the reader has looked forward, the final reckoning, is not forthcoming; incommensurables have no calculus. But while Arnold may not arrive at any rationale, he clearly makes a choice between the two ways of responding to life. It speaks ill for mid-nineteenth-century criticism that he felt compelled to dissociate his own views from those of his protagonist. Empedocles' beliefs, he pointed out, ought not to have led to suicide. The point is baldly stated and disregards the Stoic justification of suicide, but there is truth in it. Callicles embraces life, Empedocles death. The latter view may prevail in the end: of his youth Empedocles says (2.250), "The smallest thing could give us pleasure then." What took away his Calliclean delight in life was too great contact with men in a world grown hostile; this is the contagion of which Arnold's works so often show an awareness. A Calliclean spirit may not be able to retain its serenity in the midst of the jarring shocks of existence. Nevertheless, it is the way of Callicles that Arnold chooses as an ideal.[30]

We have conjectured that "Empedocles on Etna" contains a further choice. The classical-Romantic antithesis does not come in question here; the poet has already revealed his feelings, particularly in "The New Sirens." The question is rather how he will employ classical form and content—whether they are to penetrate him and become embodied in poetry such as the great passages of "The Strayed Reveller" or to serve instead as graceful external ornament.

If the interpretation we have proposed is a valid one, an answer to this question can already be discerned. The emotional agitation of Greek lyricism must give way to an impersonal Apolline serenity even as Callicles' themes, at first inspired by Pindar, conclude within the range that Homer assigned to the bard.[31] Marsyas is beaten, his music stilled; the Dionysiac notes that sounded so clearly for a time in Circe's palace are rarely to be heard again. Arnold's classicism now begins to take refuge in externals—first Homeric and then tragic form, but always form of some kind.[32] It is within the frame of classical convention that his restless melancholy and sense of isolation must find expression henceforth when he deals with the past; often they cannot do so without incongruity. Nevertheless they demand expression, as the Empoclean elements of his nature that cannot be merely wished out of existence. The tension created by their presence removes some of the chill from this hieratic classicism, but it remains cold. Arnold in fact cannot realize within himself the Calliclean ideal of the remarkable poem we have been considering. He is determined to circumscribe it with Aristotelian formalism, with the doctrine of Longinus that great writing bespeaks a great soul, and with the moral consciousness of a son and pupil of Thomas Arnold.

This poem has rightly been called the most ambitious of Matthew Arnold's works, because the most filled with tensions; [33] but it also signalizes his turning away from personal involvement towards a Parnassian objectivity. Despite its many splendors it reminds us of what might have been, for at some time after "The Strayed Reveller" and before the 1853 Preface Arnold decided against sacrificing everything in the effort to reach that place, all but inaccessible, where he knew Excellence dwells among the rocks.[34] The decision was reasonable enough; nevertheless, once that step has been taken limitations are imposed, certain intensities of feeling will not be granted again. "Empedocles on Etna" marks the close of a period in Matthew Arnold's development and indicates what his classicism is to be.

IV

The Poetry of Parnassus

By 1853 Matthew Arnold had crossed the boundary between two worlds. "The Strayed Reveller" and "Empedocles on Etna," with their companion poems, lay behind him. Ahead was a lifetime of prose—*On Translating Homer, Culture and Anarchy*, the critical essays, the theological works—and only rare triumphs in poetry. He was newly married, and for the sake of the security that his marriage seemed to demand he had taken an uncongenial routine post. Itinerant school-inspecting, often literally from morning until night, replaced the hours of leisured reading at Winchester, Rugby, and Balliol.[1] Except for the summer holidays he had only the margins of his time to use as he wished.

Although few writers have achieved so much under such harassing circumstances, what Arnold did accomplish was nevertheless shaped by forces which bear no very great relation to outward disadvantages. His first important prose work was the Preface to the 1853 edition of his poems; nowhere else does he attempt to deal systematically with the formal problems of classical and Romantic attitudes. Previously he had written of the estranged self and the world's multitudinousness in "Empedocles on Etna." The 1853 Preface is a recoil from this earlier subjective approach. We have already seen the new attitude foreshadowed; now it is documented.

The results of Arnold's altered thinking appear in his description of the age of Empedocles, an age that had reached its close not long after the middle of the fifth century, to be followed by the incomparable glory of Athens under Pericles:

> What those who are familiar only with the great monuments of early Greek genius suppose to be its exclusive

characteristics, have disappeared; the calm, the cheerfulness, the disinterested objectivity have disappeared; the dialogue of the mind with itself has commenced; modern problems have presented themselves; we hear already the doubts, we witness the discouragement, of Hamlet and of Faust.[2]

The claims expressed in this superbly written passage will reappear again and again through the next three decades; yet it is difficult to see any striking relevance to the Greeks of the period preceding the Peloponnesian War. Perhaps calm and cheerfulness and objectivity have their true relevance to Arnold himself. These, it may be, were qualities which he felt he needed, after the turmoil and self-consciousness revealed not only in "Empedocles on Etna" but in "The Strayed Reveller" and the early letters to Clough.

Against this supposed historical background Empedocles stands out clearly, an alien figure in a world of weakened morality and Sophism. The poem that dealt with his estrangement is now to be rejected. It belongs, says Arnold, to that class of situations

from the representation of which ... no poetical enjoyment can be derived ... in which the suffering finds no vent in action; in which a continuous state of mental distress is prolonged, unrelieved by incident, hope, or resistance; in which there is everything to be endured, nothing to be done.

A certain morbidity and monotony characterize such situations, he adds; they are painful rather than tragic.[3]

This suggests a new criterion. Its origin becomes evident when Arnold speaks of it directly, in his statement concerning serious poetry. Everything, he tells us, depends on the subject. If it has been fittingly chosen and thoroughly understood, everything else will follow from it. "Theory and practice alike," Aristotle's *Poetics* and the works to which it applies, combine to teach us this lesson. The words of Aristotle that Arnold has in mind are the following:

(There are six parts ... of every tragedy, ... a fable or plot, characters, diction, thought, spectacle and melody). ...

The most important of the six is the combination of the incidents of the story. Tragedy is essentially an imitation not of persons but of action and life, of happiness and misery. All human happiness or misery takes the form of action; the end for which we live is a certain kind of activity, not a quality. Character gives us qualities, but it is in our actions—what we do—that we are happy or the reverse. In a play accordingly they do not act in order to portray the characters; they include the characters for the sake of the action. So that it is the action in it, i.e. its fable or plot, that is the end and purpose of the tragedy; and the end is everywhere the chief thing. . . . The first essential, the life and soul, so to speak, of tragedy is the plot.[4]

Nothing in the above justifies the inference that from a happy choice of subject everything else will follow. Here we are conscious of having stumbled against one of those half-concealed boundary markers, tokens that we are passing into Matthew Arnold's private domain. This is the same Arnold who looked back on his undergraduate study of the *Nicomachean Ethics* and smiled at the pious efforts of tutors and tutored to justify every syllable of Aristotelian doctrine. If his skepticism does not extend to the treatise on poetry there must be good reason. It would seem to lie in an abandonment of uncontrolled lyric feeling for a faith in the saving power of form.

This conjecture accords with the fact that the 1853 Preface lists the finest of the Greek literary techniques as "clearness of arrangement, rigour of development, simplicity of style," the manifestations of a "severe and scrupulous self-restraint." We are told further that the Greeks kept to the most rigid standards regarding "the adaptability of the subject to the kind of poetry selected, and the careful construction of the poem." Here context shows that Arnold was concerned with the need for unity, a total impression rather than a random aggregate of "striking" passages. What chiefly dictates his position is in fact a reaction against this very capriciousness, so emphatically condemned in the closing words of all three of his prefaces written during the 1850's.[5]

Another passage in the 1853 essay makes this point clear: As the individual writer "penetrates into the spirit of the great classical works," says Arnold,

as he becomes gradually aware of their intense significance, their noble simplicity, and their calm pathos, he will be convinced that it is . . . unity and profoundness of moral impression . . . at which the ancient poets aimed; that it is this which constitutes the grandeur of their works, and which makes them immortal.

The reference to "calm pathos" seems to involve Arnold's belief that Greek tragedies ended on a subdued note, and this depends in turn upon a now discredited notion of the function of a tragic chorus.[6] "Noble simplicity" combines the moral with the formalistic, but we learn at once which factor predominates: the impression made by Greek poetry is essentially moral.

The fourth and fifth paragraphs unite moral, aesthetic, and intellectual elements in a statement of the aims of poetry. It should not only interest but also "inspirit and rejoice the reader"; its duty moreover is to "convey a charm, and infuse delight," adding to men's happiness as well as their knowledge. The use of "inspirit" has already suggested the nature of Arnold's deepest concerns. They become still clearer when the Preface continues with a statement of Schiller's: "All art is dedicated to Joy, and there is no higher and no more serious problem, than how to make men happy." [7] Moral needs have the place of first importance; aesthetic needs are never discussed. This single-level analysis forms a revealing contrast with Aristotle's requirement that each art should provide the pleasure proper to it.

Schiller's enthronement of *die Freude* here consorts oddly with received impressions of tragedy, not least with those which Aristotle had set down. Aware of this, Arnold reminds the reader beforehand of Hesiod's claim: the Muses "were born that they might be a forgetfulness of evils, and a truce from cares." Having quoted Schiller on joy, he apparently turns back once more to the *Poetics* as a starting point for further analysis:

> In presence of the most tragic circumstances, represented in a work of art, the feeling of enjoyment, as is well known, may still subsist: the representation of the most utter calamity, of the liveliest anguish, is not sufficient to destroy it: the more tragic the situation, the deeper becomes the enjoyment.[8]

In these opening paragraphs Arnold assumes a general equivalence of terms and concepts when no such gratifying harmony exists. The relevance of Hesiod here is specious. Moreover, Arnold ignores Aristotle's description of the specific pleasure afforded by tragedy—the katharsis through pity and fear—and departs still further from him by separating pleasure into ethical and nonethical levels. As for the doctrine of joy taken from Schiller, the awkwardness of its presence in the 1853 Preface suggests its alien position generally.

The katharsis of the *Poetics* does appear briefly in Arnold's correspondence five years later, when *Merope* and Greek tragedy are much in his thoughts. He feels the greatest admiration for Aristotle's definition of tragedy, but he cannot wholly accept its essential feature. Pity and fear are therefore altered to "commiseration and awe," a significant change to which we shall recur.[9] The 1853 Preface, however, which owes more to the *Poetics* than to any other source, emphasizes only Aristotle's thesis that the "action" or subject dominates the other factors.[10] To this Arnold adds a strong moral concern, ignoring factors of aesthetics and style. From a literary point of view, his interest seems to be centered henceforth in the structural aspect.[11] The critical canons that he cites in rejecting "Empedocles on Etna" are meant to apply only to epic and tragic form. It is epic and tragedy that now claim his attention, as the main body of the essay demonstrates. They are for him the vehicles of the greatest subjects, those which "most powerfully appeal to the great primary human affections" inherent in the race.

The display piece of the 1853 edition, "Sohrab and Rustum," was designed to illustrate the principles of the Preface. Although Arnold did not give it the status of a title poem, he must have known that readers would compare it with "The Strayed Reveller" and "Empedocles on Etna," and there is no indication that this prospect caused him misgivings. The poem creates an impression of having been worked on with uncommon care: the occasional prosiness and wavering focus that mark its earlier rivals are no longer present. In fact, Arnold's approach to the classical as a frame of expression has ceased to be experimental. He seeks now to be objective, to deal in terms of form. With very few exceptions, the classically derived poems published from 1853 on have a resulting quality that warrants the term Parnassian.[12]

"Sohrab and Rustum" has the subtitle "An Episode." In Greek drama the *epeisodion* was the action between choric songs, and it is not impossible that this original sense may have relevance here. The famous closing description of the Oxus has reminded more than one commentator of a tragic chorus, and the poem opens with a reference to the river. It is far more probable, however, that Arnold used the term to mean simply a more or less self-contained portion taken from an epic. Thus he begins as if in the midst of narrative, making the first word a connective. His device is justified, since the poem relates a chapter (so to speak) of Persian epic, adding material from travel-books.[13] Details and incidents from the French translation of the original were rejected if they seemed to lack dignity; the same kind of selectiveness later went into the shaping of "Balder Dead."

The poem's most obvious indebtedness to classical sources lies in its repeated use of Homeric simile, although passages taken from

Homer actually express narrative or discourse much more often than simile. The influence of Vergil and Milton is clearly present as well,[14] and distinctions must be drawn among these three sources. In Homer comparisons spring from a unitary world-view, and they possess surprising naturalness. Our picture of man in an alien universe represents the complete opposite of this outlook, for which the phenomenal world contains no manifestation of life that is estranged from any other.[15] Vergil, living in an age of anxiety, could not match Homer's elemental robustness. His similes imitate those of his predecessor, but differences are evident. The subjective element enters into his use of simile; so does personification, which had never been a part of Homeric comparison, and particularizing now may reach an extreme. For Milton the simile served a new purpose, suggesting the tremendous dimensions of the universe by what was distant and marvellous in the known world—Ormuzd and Ind, Ternate and Tidore.[16]

Such are the major tendencies which underlie the carefully elaborated comparisons so prominent in "Sohrab and Rustum." Despite the many formal resemblances, they differ from Homer basically and inevitably because they cannot match his wholeness. World-weariness and melancholy fill the entire poem, causing critics to comment repeatedly on the strong Vergilian tone; but Vergil contributed a mood and not a technique. Arnold, who was partially aware of what he owed to Milton,[17] followed the Miltonic tradition in making so many of his similes richly exotic. This was a tactical error; "Sohrab" seeks the level of Homeric narrative, and on this level the particularizing simile can add no larger perspective. Its exoticism has an effectiveness that is largely self-contained, since the main setting is already exotic.

Arnold claims to have taken pains to "Orientalize" his similes; this suggests that he looked on them as decoration.[18] He aims at striking effects, despite all his warnings against this in the 1853 Preface, and not at a true unity. The result was just what he had indicted: a kind of patchwork brocade, tricking out the substance of Firdausi's tale rather than honestly adorning it. This exoticism could be wonderfully effective: the "cunning workman, in Pekin," with his porcelain vase, the lamplight on "studious forehead and thin hands," will be remembered as long as English poetry endures. Yet here, as in all major respects, "Sohrab and Rustum" draws its power from the sense of hopeless, unequal struggle that is Matthew Arnold's *cri de coeur*.

No vital involvement with the classical can be found in this poem, which Clough privately described as "pseudo-antique." [19] Greek and Latin literature make little use of its theme, common to folklore—mortal combat between a father and son ignorant of their relationship, a foreshadowing perhaps of the clash by night.[20] Its conception of fate is clothed in an image which seems to recall the *Aeneid*, the image of swimmers suspended in a wave; yet that conception itself is neither Vergilian nor Homeric. Arnold's fondness for the imagery of water appears here as it does at various moments of particular significance within the poem, nowhere so memorably as in the closing description of the Oxus. Few would deny that the fame of these lines has been deserved; the relevant point is that they represent a triumph of something other than the classical.[21]

Arnold did not lack a precedent here. Homer had in the most literal sense personified a river, matching it against the strength of Achilles. Yet Homer's Scamander does not cease to be a force of nature even when it has been reinterpreted in an aspect that can be related to the heroic absolute. By contrast, the Oxus is personified because it represents not so much the larger and continuing rhythm beyond human circumstance as the stages of man's life.[22] Arnold's awareness here of the individual's estrangement from nature sets him apart from the unitary Homeric view. He writes as a modern, and it is from this fact that "Sohrab" derives its measure of real pathos.

Again, the tragic situation of Achilles as a social being lies in his enforced association with men who could not comprehend the uncompromising imperatives that drove him on. Far from being the plaything of fate he has actually been allowed to decide the manner of his death—in the midst of youth and fame or at the close of an obscure old age—and during much of the brief action of the *Iliad* the decision seems still to be open. There can be no reversals or recognitions, no piquant denouement. Except for the attempt to mistreat Hector's body the issues are drawn in advance; the attitudes have already been taken up. With Rustum and his son it is far otherwise. Both display a pride and a fierceness that belong as much to the *Iliad* as to the *Shah-Nameh*, for these are indispensable common properties of epic; here the parallel ends. Father and son have been joined in single combat by an unforeseen, unforeseeable turn of fate.[23] Their relationship becomes known only in the last moments of Sohrab's life, a deeply affecting scene. Such discoveries are essential to Greek New Comedy and its Roman inheritors, and they were thought suited to epic or even to tragedy provided the level of intensity was relaxed. Neither Homeric nor Hellenic poetry, however, used them to portray the more sombre aspects of existence.

Despite what ought to follow from the 1853 Preface, this reworking of Persian chronicle brings before us no "great and excellent human action." We see instead a rushing seaward of the wave of fate which had held father and son suspended. Sohrab claims that the time and mode of his death were predestined from the beginning: this represents a conscious link with the usual course of Homeric fatalism. Like the similes and the formulaic diction, it establishes an external relationship; any inward, essential affinities with Homer will be sought in vain.[24] These results follow logically from the decision reflected in "Empedocles on Etna." If "Sohrab and Rustum" today has any claim to serious consideration outside the schoolroom it is despite such embellishments, not because of them.

"Philomela," scarcely more than thirty lines long, actually provides a more instructive example of the Parnassian classicism that marked Arnold's ways of thought after 1852. Any danger of becoming rapt, intoxicated like Shelley and Hölderlin with the wine of Hellas, was precluded by the terms of his truce with necessity. He was now a discreet, disengaged Hellenophile; in the symbolic decision that we have conjectured, he had chosen Apollo and rejected Dionysus. "Empedocles on Etna" showed him still superimposing his own experience upon the classical past, and many have heard a personal note in "Sohrab and Rustum"; the present poem is the work of one who has succeeded in dissociating this past from any immediate concern. His first draft had contained no reference to the singer as a "wanderer from a Grecian shore" and "the Thracian wild," none to "the sweet, tranquil Thames" or the "English grass." Their appearance in the published version accords with the poet's altered perspective: he now wishes to fix the boundary between the two worlds as promptly as possible in his lyric.

"Philomela" assuredly does not lack power. The Greek maiden's "hot cheeks and sear'd eyes" contrast poignantly with the cool serenity of an English summer night. The intensity of that "wild, unquench'd, deep-sunken" grieving may bear witness for a moment to the involvement revealed in "Empedocles," but if so it is only for a moment. Arnold adds to the three epithets a fourth, substituting "old-world" for the "old" of his original version, and thus makes clear his essential disengagement. The reference to

"Lone Daulis, and the high Cephissian vale" recalls a similar passage (99–100) in "Fragment of an 'Antigone,'" published four years earlier. This statuesque use of geographical reference repeatedly strikes an impersonal note in the poems. At a more intense level—"Sophocles long ago Heard it on the Aegaean," "Nor Thebes, nor the Ismenus, any more"—Arnold tends to omit epithet.[25] His device of direct address to a woman companion prompts a comparison with "Dover Beach," where it had greater success. In the present poem Eugenia has survived from "Horatian Echo," but by this time no trace of the *Odes* can be felt: she is simply a name. Finally, when the poet describes the nightingale's song to her as "Eternal passion! Eternal pain!" we hear again the shepherd in Circe's palace:

> These things, Ulysses,
> The wise bards also
> Behold and sing.
> But oh, what labour!
> O prince, what pain! [26]

The difference is that these lines from "The Strayed Reveller" are rooted in a serious concern with the meaning of classical experience and derive strength from it. When the same thought recurs in "Philomela" there is no rootedness: the poem characteristically strikes an attitude, seeks an effect.

The structure and tone of "The Scholar-Gipsy" owe something to Keats' "Ode to Autumn"; they also have a debt to the *Idylls* of Theocritus.[27] Arnold acknowledged the influence of these sketches on "Thyrsis," and their example has formed the pastoral elements of this earlier work no less importantly. Yet both poems have ignored Theocritean precedent, and Keats as well, in the localizing of their country scenes. This applies with greater force to "The Scholar-Gipsy," where the world of nature suffers less intrusion from the world of men. Arnold particularly loved the Oxford country; his poem is an avowal of that love, an elegy not for Glanvill's eternal wandering scholar but for the magical Oxford years that Arnold himself had known. Names of hill and village and wood have the force of incantations; they call up the past that the poet finds again only when he makes it timeless. The fact that it is a profoundly unclassical way of distilling experience does not alter its effectiveness or its merit. One must be cautious about assuming that either the present poem or "Thyrsis" seeks to embody a quest for the classical vision of life.

The elaborate image of the Tyrian trader may well come from a brief comment in Thucydides. Its detail and color, which are absent from the historian's words, show that the main source was poetic imagination combined with an awareness of ancient history.[28] For more than four centuries after Troy's overthrow Mediterranean and Aegean commerce was under the control of the Phoenicians, whose ships went out ceaselessly from the great cities of Tyre and Sidon. They early established trading stations on Sicily, but only as stopping-places along the way to the Mediterranean's outermost western limits. Their first colony, Gades (Cadiz), was founded on the farther side of the Pillars of Hercules "where the Atlantic rages Outside the western straits." During the eighth century this commercial hegemony was increasingly threatened as Greek city-states began their own colonization; by 700 B.C. the Tyrian trader was no longer master of the sea-ways.[29]

Whether the comparison is intended symbolically or analogically, and whether it can be termed successful on either interpretation, are questions not likely to be settled here. Their relevance to Arnold's conception of the classical is doubtful in any case. For a relationship to Hellenic thought we must look rather to his unfavorable portrait of the Greeks. The coaster is merry, its crew lighthearted, its cargo of delicacies appeals to the senses. Yet the entire picture is Arnold's chosen image of "the strange disease of modern life" (203). The rejection cannot be denied, but it should be seen in its true proportions. The Hellenism branded as a contagion here is that of sensuous experience, from which Arnold has now turned away. Henceforth his classicism, which could not attain to a Calliclean wholeness, will look instead to Periclean ideals. He will stress formal excellence and moral or intellectual elevation, setting aside one entire aspect of classical experience. We are given to understand that our concern is not to be merry but to be serious; and here the Hebraic Tyrian better reflects Arnold's thought, for he is already weighing the antitheses that will find definitive expression in *Culture and Anarchy*.

A minor but effective element is provided by the shepherd, whom Arnold urges to leave and "begin the quest." His presence, conveyed in a distant echoing of Theocritus' and Vergil's country dialogue, stresses the nature of the poem as true pastoral. "Thyrsis," more specifically elegiac, employs no such device; Corydon speaks only to the dead. Yet the evocation of pastoral seems as unobtrusive as the Theocritean opulence in the nature descriptions, and this is perhaps the result intended. The excellence of Arnold's techniques throughout "The Scholar-Gipsy" deserves our admiration, but the poem shows no deep concern with classical thought or feeling. In these techniques Arnold classicizes. Except through history, he does not use the past to voice his preoccupations. He has created a moving and felicitous work; nevertheless, it does not echo the inner world that found utterance in "Empedocles on Etna."

Dominating the 1855 volume of Arnold's poetry is his second attempt at epic narrative, "Balder Dead." Minor classical borrowings, according to the authors of the *Commentary*, are too numerous to cite in detail; "the whole spirit of the classics is what really transforms 'Balder' from a Norse poem into something vastly different. As in 'Sohrab,' of course, much of Arnold's care went into his elaborate similes." [30] These statements, concerned as they are with the essential questions of influence, suggest one way of entering upon an examination of "Balder." The poem is longer than "Sohrab and Rustum," yet it borrows less frequently from the classics and uses less than half as many similes. Again, the similes that it does incorporate are non-Homeric in every case but one, and the one exception undergoes a remarkable change; nor does any other ancient author figure in them, save for a brief appearance by Vergil. Clearly Arnold has discarded the methods adopted for "Sohrab." His suggestions of classical epic are more diffused, and they are no longer connected with the particular epic device of comparison.

This change of plan appears to recognize the changed nature of the material. In its background Firdausi's narrative shows a certain likeness to the setting of the *Iliad*, yet it is free from peculiarities of coloring; both circumstances make appropriate the attempt to infuse Homer's tone. Its inevitable exoticism does not clash with that tone, for East as well as West lies within Homer's knowledge. The region he does not know, or knows only very uncertainly through sailors' stories, is that of the North. A distance that no map can measure separates the sunlit, graceful, childlike Olympians from the ponderous Vikings in their Valhalla. Nectar and ambrosia, mead and messes of boar's flesh: *man ist, was er isst*. Yet among these heavy-footed Norse gods may come sorrow and death, unknown upon Olympus. Here the merrymakers of Homer's pantheon would be wholly irrelevant. Parallels with the *Iliad* must derive from the suffering world of mortals where an Achilles knows isolation, a Hector meets death.

There is a particular respect in which Arnold's altered approach shows his awareness of the new problem presented by Icelandic saga. Its ethos is boisterous, energetic, crudely powerful, and he has been accused of failing utterly to do it justice; yet he made a clear attempt to do so. By taking all but one or two of his similes from the world of his own thought rather than from Greek and Latin literature, he sought to come to terms with his signally unclassical material. He failed because his temperament was set towards other ends, as the similes show. Some are neutral in tone; others prove more revealing. Thus the blind Hoder brushes by his brother (1.230–34)

> ... as a spray of honeysuckle flowers
> Brushes across a tired traveller's face
>
> .   .   .   .
>
> And starts him, that he thinks a ghost went by;

and Hermod, returning from Hell without Balder, is likened to a farmer who has lost his dog. The alarm and muted desperation in these passages color much of Arnold's poetry, and one wonders whether the impulse which prompted their expression was entirely literary. Clearer still is the note of frustration. We hear it in the lines which close the poem, the "long complaining cry" of the tethered stork who strains uselessly to join the southward flights at autumn. It comes no less unmistakably when Arnold speaks of the bitter despondency of the gods at their failure to ransom Balder, when they had so nearly succeeded (3.357–67): they are like seafarers who sight their home port but are driven out to sea —"the glimpse Of port they had makes bitterer far their toil." Here the poet has taken a Homeric concept of long-deferred joy and, by a typical addition, turned it into one of disappointment. Only thus can Homer serve him when his thought shapes any deep feeling.[31]

Classical borrowings are proportionately fewer here than in "Sohrab," yet their presence is noticeable. The cleverness with which Arnold has inserted them shows a singular familiarity with the *Iliad* and *Odyssey;* what he has not done is to make them integral.[32] Their fundamentally decorative nature becomes apparent in a passage (1.76–80) describing Hoder's sorrowing departure from the feast in Odin's hall:

> Though sightless, yet his own mind led the God.
> Down to the margin of the roaring sea

> He came, and sadly went along the sand,
> Between the waves and black o'erhanging cliffs
> Where in and out the screaming seafowl fly. . . .

Here, after a momentary evocation of Sophocles' Teiresias, Arnold recalls two figures of the *Iliad*, Chryses and Achilles, who walked distraught "by the edge of the loud-roaring sea." But the echo has no significance. We go on at once to cliffs and seafowl, with still more natural description to come, and we realize that what predominates is not the human situation (as in Homer) but the physical setting, that it is in fact the essential meaning of the passage.[33]

Other instances, no less obvious, are far more acceptable to the reader who has some acquaintance with Homer—the sort of reader, not at all uncommon a century ago, for whom "Balder Dead" was written. Generally speaking, such instances prove successful in one of two ways, either as formulaic insertions or as portions of sections which are in themselves added material not found in the prose *Edda*. Insertions are employed, by no means without skill and taste, when Norse custom approximates to Homeric; the added portions appear when Arnold's inventiveness has contrived a passage or scene which is congenial to such borrowed material. Initial references to Hela's realm and the episodes which take place there make up the major part of the second category. Except for its place-names, this version of the lower world derives from the two great classical accounts of a journey to the dead, *Odyssey* 11 and *Aeneid* 6, and more especially from Homer. In a setting thus prepared Balder may fittingly speak the words of Achilles (2.265–67):

> Better to live a serf, a captured man,
> Who scatters rushes in a master's hall,
> Than be a crown'd king here, and rule the dead.

The poem's classical materials, so predominantly Homeric, are without doubt its most important secondary source. Their presence, however, does not suffice to give it a Homeric spirit. Arnold is no longer in the grip of antiquity; Homer and the mighty contemporaries of Pericles and Augustus have now become a means to effectiveness. They may reinforce the mood, but that mood has already been fixed by the poet's temperament. Perhaps its deepest expression comes in the words of Balder (3.503–6):

... I am long since weary of your storm
Of carnage, and find, Hermod, in your life
Something too much of war and broils, which makes
Life one perpetual fight, a bath of blood.

Here are the imagery and tone of the closing lines of "Dover
Beach," lines which may already have been written when Arnold
was completing his saga episode for the 1855 volume.

Such power as "Balder Dead" possesses comes from its elegiac
mood, from the sense of sorrow and tenderness, anguished struggle
and inevitable defeat that is Arnold's own. At times his classical
interpolations serve to deepen this sense, and they need no further
justification. The classicism remains an addition nonetheless: it is
integral neither with the poem nor with the poet. Had it been a
natural pattern of expression, instinct would presumably have directed the writing along different paths. More probably the work
would not have been written at all. In actual fact devotion to an
artificial classicism prompted an eclectic approach, and for Matthew Arnold eclecticism was more than a technique; it was a basic
impulse. With the greatest diligence he picked and chose not
merely from Homer and Vergil but from the *Edda* itself. Osten-
sibly this was to ensure the dignity postulated in the 1853 Preface;
instinctively the poet was making visible the sombre shapes of his
inward vision. Working thus at cross-purposes with himself, he
could not properly achieve either goal.

The lines published among the 1867 *New Poems* and there
entitled "Early Death and Fame" originated a dozen years earlier,
as part of "Haworth Churchyard." They retain an air of having
been excerpted, and the 1888 edition places them after "Fragment
of Chorus of a 'Dejaneira,'" presumably with the author's approval. There is undoubtedly a surface resemblance between the
two poems, but the deeper dissimilarity makes it unimportant.
The "Fragment" at least has a point of departure in the opening
lines of Sophocles' *Trachiniae,* which tell us to count no man
either fortunate or ill-fortuned until his life has ended. "Early
Death and Fame," originating perhaps in the same passage, takes a
very different course. It begins with praise of the life passed in
calm obscurity, which is to say, without the "toil and dolour un-
told" mentioned in the "Fragment" as a part of the common conception. The poet then passes to a plea for those who must die in
youth. To such a person should be granted a compensating intensity of experience and achievement (15–19):

> Fuller for him be the hours!
> Give him emotion, though pain!
> Let him live, let him feel: *I have lived.*
> Heap up his moments with life!
> Triple his pulses with fame!

This is the Romantic thirst for life that cannot be slaked; it is Faust, with the knowledge of death heavy upon him, clutching at the passing hour. No such fever burns in the famous *carpe diem* of Horace or in Martial's still more emphatic *ille sapit quisquis . . . vixit heri*, much less in any Greek lament over early death. Achilles' choice may be the origin of these lines; if so, a far different spirit informs the modern poetic conception that has come from it. Not intensity of experience but adherence to an inner absolute, an imperative that will admit no compromise, gives the meaning of heroic existence for Homer's tragic hero. If any part of "Early Death and Fame" can be said to embody a classical precedent it is the first stanza, with its quietism that may echo Horace on the perils of eminence.

While the *New Poems* of 1867 include a number which cannot be dated, all but one might reasonably be placed after 1860. The last of the three sonnets entitled "Rachel" very probably was written no earlier than the summer of 1863 and not much later. It claims our attention with the concluding lines of the sestet:

> In her, like us, there clash'd, contending powers,
> Germany, France, Christ, Moses, Athens, Rome.
> The strife, the mixture in her soul, are ours;
> Her genius and her glory are her own.

Whatever the poetic value of these verses, they have importance as an index of the author's classicism. His thoughts are turning now to the eclectic nature of Western culture, more specifically to its dualism. One notes the first line of the sestet: "Ah, not the radiant power of Greece alone." At length they will find expression in the chapters called "Hebraism and Hellenism," possibly Arnold's most influential prose. The concept even as it occurs in this sonnet may be termed prosaic; certainly there seems to be no personal note. The poet himself was no longer torn by the strife of which he speaks here, though he never ceased from interpreting it and attempting its mediation.

One of the *New Poems* which cannot be dated is "Bacchanalia: or, the New Age." There is no reason to consider it an early work appearing belatedly, for it contrasts sharply with the poem with which it is always compared, "The Strayed Reveller." Dionysus' followers reappear, and with them another dreaming poet-spectator. What does not return is the questing spirit and unmoralized immediacy of the 1849 title poem. There Arnold was attempting to clarify the poet's role through classical symbols; and though his equations may have become confused, his attempt seemed the first token of a vital connection with antiquity, a new path of the mind. By the time of "Bacchanalia," when he had ceased to command any mood except the elegiac, he showed no doubts about the nature of poetic sensibility. In fact, he devotes his closing distichs to defining it as the ability to feel not merely the present but the past as well. These didactic verses, so typical of Arnold's less inspired moments, conclude the poem logically enough; yet they assort oddly with the pastoral loveliness of the first half. Their prosaic quality suggests the author's already established province. Professors Tinker and Lowry have well said, "In 'Bacchanalia' the development of [his] critical function is plainly disclosed. . . . The reader is here rapidly moving towards the later work of Arnold as a critic of both literature and life"—and, it need scarcely be added, a prose critic.[34]

Dionysiac experience figures very rarely in the poems; yet "The desired, the divine . . . Iacchus" and his train of satyrs and maenads supposedly appear to the young shepherd of "The Strayed Reveller," and their manifestation cannot be merely decorative. On the other hand, its significance is difficult to determine. The visions granted by Circe's wine seem to represent the fitful raptures of Romanticism, but the final stanzas may imply a relationship of some kind between the Romantic and the Dionysiac. This perplexes, since the reveller is not under the influence of Dionysus.

"Bacchanalia" brings no such problems with it. The scene of its delightful opening stanza is rural England, as unmistakably as the scene of "The Strayed Reveller" is Greece, and "the wild Maenads" with "Youth and Iacchus Maddening their blood" display scarcely less decorum than a group of English schoolgirls hiking with their games mistress. They "Fill with their sports the field," and apparently their Dionysiac excess consists in scattering hayricks and trampling the grass. One cannot take them seriously: Part I of the poem is in its entirety nothing but a pretty picture, designed to hint at a mocking allegory of the age. Previously "The New Sirens" had sought to do something of a similar kind for Romanticism and had failed. Arnold did not commit the same error twice; this time he carefully explains the meaning of his image. Though readers can hardly fail to understand, they may wonder whether the trouble was worthwhile. In terms of its actual poetry "Bacchanalia" neither achieves nor seeks any meaningful contact with the past, and the total impression is somewhat that of a joke which fails to come off.

The tone of the work is in the end not humorous, as a matter of fact, but mordant and satirical; and the images for which we now remember it, especially the "one or two immortal lights" of genius mounting the heavens, prepare the way for a critical judgment. This domination by the critical intellect sharply distinguishes "Bacchanalia" from "The Strayed Reveller," which has a prevailing note of aesthetic experience. It is questionable to hold that the two poems display a common conception of the poet as one who should unite past and present, and not "take refuge in the Hellenic dream." [35] The contention has an element of truth, for Arnold was not advocating escapism. One notes, however, that "Bacchanalia" evidently regards an understanding of the past as fundamental to the total view which a poet must command. What can be said is that Arnold's attitude towards the past has become increasingly external; the comparative approach of his critical essays grows more and more apparent.

"Thyrsis," first published in 1866, does not refute this, although it is a very different work. "The diction of the poem," said Arnold, "was modelled on that of Theocritus, whom I have been much reading during the two years this poem has been forming itself." As various critics have seen, the poet must not be taken literally here. His diction was in general that of his age: the originality derives rather from his mood. "It is not line, phrase, or epithet that Arnold has imitated," R. T. Kerlin notes, and rightly. This critic goes on, however, to claim that "it is the Greek tone and spirit that he possesses. The subtle repetitions in 'Thyrsis' will be recognized as Theocritean." [36] In point of fact these repetitions seem a part of Arnoldian idiom, with hardly more than chance resemblances to the *Idylls*. The typical bucolic refrain does not appear at all. "*The bloom is gone, and with the bloom go I!*" sounds at the close of the sixth stanza, but there is no other echo. As for the Greek quality of tone and spirit, Kerlin was writing in 1910, almost the end of an age. A few years more, and such attitudes would hold only historic interest.

Except for Miltonic echoes the one clear borrowing in "Thyrsis" comes from a pastoral elegy formerly attributed to

Moschus, the *Epitaphium Bionis* or lament for the poet Bion. What, then, was Arnold's meaning when he said its diction had been "modelled on that of Theocritus"? Probably he meant "to confess nothing more than the influence upon him of the straight-forward, unadorned style of the rural idylls," according to the authors of the *Commentary*. This strikes very near the heart of the matter. Theocritean pastoral has a predominating simplicity of expression, although its actual dialect is an adaptation of Doric with noticeable Homeric additions; in the letter already quoted Arnold says: "I meant the diction to be so artless as to be almost heedless." [37] Moreover, Theocritus avoids on principle the pedantic mythologizing which Callimachus and his fellow Alexandrians thought indispensable to poetry. Arnold likewise avoids it, not so strictly as the Greek poet: his stanza on Lityerses and Daphnis deserved Robert Bridges' charge of irrelevance.

In attempting to estimate the qualities of "Thyrsis," and "The Scholar-Gipsy" as well, we may first note one account of how pastoral developed from Alexandrian to Victorian times.

> Song has nothing essential to do with the pastoral. . . . But song is generally introduced because one of the most salient features of Greek peasant life was the singing-match, and this afforded at once both an easy and a graceful subject for composition . . . .
>
> The result was fatal for the pastoral; the charm of form became the essential; the truth of the representation to country life became of secondary importance, and finally was left altogether out of sight. Theocritus himself must be held responsible in part for the change.
>
> The shepherds of the beautiful first idyll are shepherds in name rather than in vocation; in [*Idyll*] vii we have . . . an imitation of the country singing-match, in two poets who disguise their names but not their personality. Yet here there is nothing to offend: nothing to disgust us by its hopeless unreality. It is only when we come to the imitators of Theocritus that we see that the pastoral has become merely a fashionable setting for any incongruous thought. There is no trace of any study of the country in Bion and Moschus; Vergil's *Eclogues* are echoes of Theocritus, exquisite in sound, but signifying anything rather than Italian peasant life. . . . Kings, statesmen, and poets must all be shepherds . . . in their shepherd dress and under their shepherd names they must discourse of affairs of state or church, as in Milton's *Lycidas*

and in the *Shepheardes Calendar*.... The plaint for Daphnis leads easily to the plaint for Bion; that to Vergil's "Gallus," to "Lycidas," to "Thyrsis." The form developes, but does not change materially; but the matter changes from the simple "rural ditty" to the "strain of higher mood." Meanwhile real pastoral poetry as Theocritus made it—the mirror held up to country life—found but little favour. If one wrote in the style of Theocritus he did not represent life as it was in other lands than Greece; if he wrote of life as he saw it, he had to desert the sacred classical form and still more sacred diction.[38]

Arnold comes off a little better than these remarks seem to imply. He has not clung to classical form or to any great measure of classical diction; he has, in a sense, written of life as he saw it. "Thyrsis" remains a living part of our literature, ranked among our very few great elegies, because it voices with almost perfect adequacy an intense personal experience of life's passage and meaning. It is not a lament for Clough; the charge that pastoral could not do justice to his complexity misses the point. It is a lament for the golden years when Matthew Arnold knew as much happiness as was ever granted him—or so it seemed, at a remove of twenty years. The classically derived elegy had finally become his one natural vehicle for deep expression, and perhaps he knew this. At the time of the publication of "Thyrsis" he wrote that when he began it he was "carried irresistibly into this form." [39]

A form, a frame of expression, is very nearly the sum of what he intended to borrow from antiquity. It would appear that in his own way he endeavored to make this fact clear. The poem contains no classical references at all until the ninth stanza showers them in a pretty confusion, and then immediately afterwards we hear:

> O easy access to the hearer's grace
>   When Dorian shepherds sang to Proserpine!
>   For she herself had trod Sicilian fields,
>   She knew the Dorian water's gush divine,
>   She knew each lily white which Enna yields,
>   Each rose with blushing face;
>   She loved the Dorian pipe, the Dorian strain.
>   But ah, of our poor Thames she never heard!
>   Her foot the Cumner cowslips never stirr'd;
>   And we should tease her with our plaint in vain!

Thus the poet gracefully makes clear that his setting is and must be wholly English, even though he has adopted the conventions of elegy. No such statement was needed for the much earlier "Scholar-Gipsy," which dispensed with them. This thoroughly English picturing of nature is the poem's great glory, and also one of its least classical qualities.[40] From the tradition rooted in Theocritus' *Idylls* Arnold has taken the outlines of a literary form, together with such occasional details as realization of that form requires; the indebtedness goes no further. His relationship with the Greek and Roman past remains external, a position from which there will be no change. "Thyrsis" does not suffer thereby, but it is the intensity of the poet's own feeling which animates his work and makes the classical embellishment enhance a total effectiveness. As in a few passages of "Sohrab and Rustum" and in one or two other poems published after 1852, the interplay between detached classicizing and personal emotion embodies a tension that gives strength.

Such a work is "Palladium." Professor Douglas Bush thinks it the most compact and perfectly finished of all Arnold's poems in which "morality is tinged with emotion." [41] Without disputing this, the course of argument just now suggested moves us to deal with the poem as classicism and emotion in equipoise. The two elements remain distinct, although the fighting before Troy becomes a symbol of that incessant clash to which Arnold's thought so often recurs. "We shall renew the battle in the plain Tomorrow": there is a powerful effort to draw past and present together. The technical mastery and expressiveness of the fourth stanza cannot be praised too highly; it moves with the inevitable tread of perfect poetry. Throughout the poem, moreover, the imagery which contrasts the soul's steadfastness with fluctuating emotions shows in an unusual degree not only clarity but control.

While "Palladium" draws upon a heroic context, it is not heroic. Against the critics' comparisons with Clough one must point out a distinction: the blind struggle here is indeed unavailing, for only the soul's aegis avails anything. Arnold is as far from the *aretê*, the heroic self-realization, of Homer's warriors as from that of the Sophoclean protagonist. This does not mean that he is preaching cynicism and hopelessness. The theme here is nothing less than the central concern of his maturity: the "buried life" of the spirit (to use only one of its names), in comparison with which all outward things are meaningless. The soul's "ruling effluence" (22) may owe something to the Stoic *hêgemonikon*, the ruling or guiding principle familiar to readers of Epictetus and Marcus Aurelius; otherwise no connection with classical thought is likely for this concept. If such a connection with Hellenistic philosophy does exist, the derived concept has characteristically been softened and made more remote. As one of our foremost Victorian scholars has pointed out, Arnold and Clough both "thought of man as possessing something within himself enormously precious and at the same time highly delicate and fragile." [42] This they called the Palladium, or the good in the depths of oneself, or the buried life, or individuality, but most commonly the soul. By whatever name it is known, it must at all costs be kept from the world's contaminating touch. To do so is the true struggle—a point that Arnold has omitted to make clear.

On the basis of this somewhat rarefied personal doctrine, he has fashioned a poem which he makes universal and timeless through the evocation of a Homeric background. His sources, however, are not principally Homeric. Other and later tradition brought the stories of Pallas Athena's statue, stolen from the citadel of Troy by Diomedes and Ulysses so that it would no longer keep the city safe. While the Palladium is important in the *Aeneid's* narrative of Troy, Arnold does not follow this Vergilian source. The fourth or "Messianic" *Eclogue*, contains a passage (35–36) that may well have been recalled:

> ... *erunt etiam altera bella*
> *atque iterum ad Troiam magnus mittetur Achilles.*

> "War, too, shall come again,
> And once more shall mighty Achilles be sent against Troy."

The fact that it forms part of the lighthearted description of a Golden Age would not have deterred Arnold from elaborating the thought towards a very different end-effect. One notes that Vergil's conception is markedly cyclical here, though again in a different way from Arnold's.

"Palladium" remains a remarkable achievement. "Le chef-d'oeuvre des poèmes classiques d'Arnold," says Bonnerot: he sees in it the perfect blending of moral profundity with the "magical" element that comes from evocative names.[43] We must, however, remember two things: the poem represents a particularly skilled expression of a classicizing attitude which uses the past without being drawn into its field of force; also, the singularly effective talismanic names constitute just such a use. The poetry of Parnassus has its triumphs, and "Palladium" must be counted among them.

Of the works first published in 1867, none has become more celebrated than "Dover Beach." For a great many modern readers Matthew Arnold's reputation rests chiefly on this poem. Unique in its fame, it is also uniquely difficult to date. What appears to be the first draft of lines 1–28 ends "And naked shingles of the world. Ah love &c." This certainly suggests, though it does not prove, that lines 29–37 had already been written or at least conceived. The two sections would thus embody a difference of chronology as well as imagery and tone, with an increasing likelihood that two distinct attitudes towards the classical are involved. The authors of the *Commentary* believe that "Dover Beach" was composed much earlier than 1867. Their view perhaps gains support from the fact that lines 1–28 are "pencilled on the back of a folded sheet of paper containing notes on the career of Empedocles," [44] though this in itself can prove nothing with certainty. It remains to determine what modes of classicism appear in the poem, and how they relate to this proposed dating.

A preoccupation with the allegory of river and ocean characterizes so wide a range of Arnold's poetry that it is practically useless in marking off one period from another. Tidal imagery is another matter. It occurs only once in the 1849 poems but at least a half-dozen times in those published during or after 1853, especially in the *New Poems* of 1867.[45] So far as this limited evidence has any validity, it suggests that the first 28 lines of "Dover Beach" belong to the middle or later periods of Arnold's poetic development, after he had objectified his relationship to classical thought and feeling.

> Sophocles long ago
> Heard it on the Aegaean, and it brought
> Into his mind the turbid ebb and flow
> Of human misery. . . .

The answer may be in these lines, if anywhere. There is in any case the clear task of seeking to determine their place in Arnold's thought. They cannot be explained in terms of any Greek original; the various choric passages of Sophocles to which they have been referred show that their origins are notably vague. Only the author's way of dealing with the tragic material can perhaps prove helpful here. A later discussion, in which "Dover Beach" is again taken up, will attempt to show that there were actually many such ways, having their common basis not in Sophocles but in Arnold's own complex nature. The present poem, however, is unique by virtue of its pessimism. All other references associate some form of serenity or joyousness with Sophocles: so for example the 1849 sonnet "To a Friend." To show him brooding on man's unhappiness constitutes an anomaly that hardly admits of being dated. The fact of its subjectiveness offers little aid, for there was no period of Arnold's literary career during which his preconceptions could not occasionally prevail over his desire to see things as they really are. This characteristic, however, rarely became evident before 1853. All in all, lines 1–28 appear to suit a date not earlier than 1853 and perhaps much later.

"... We are here as on a darkling plain, Swept with confused alarms of struggle and flight, Where ignorant armies clash by night." So end the nine lines not included in the penciled draft, and there referred to merely by the *aide-memoire* "Ah love &c." The surmise that they constitute the original portion of "Dover Beach" would be strengthened if we could link them with Arnold's earlier thought. Since he used the image of life as a battle throughout his poetic career, the mere fact of its use neither demonstrates nor disproves such a link. "Palladium" and a few other poems combine it with the imagery of tidal flux and recurrence; in "Dover Beach" the two have been kept separate, though both are present. The implicit nature of their relationship gives the poem a subtle unity that is not always perceived.

The specific use of the battle image consists, as is well known, in a borrowing from Thucydides. Thomas Arnold, editor and fervent admirer of the *Histories*, had made the account of the night fight at Epipolae familiar to Rugbeians, and Clough drew upon it at some length in "The Bothie." Tennyson's "Passing of Arthur" describes an eerie battle in the mist, largely an addition to Malory, but we need not suppose that this was in Arnold's mind. As Professor Geoffrey Tillotson has pointed out, the image seems to have been widely diffused in Victorian literary thought. Often the struggle would be consciously associated with contemporary questioning of Christianity—Clough and Tennyson illustrate this most notably—and in intention if not in fact this connection further unites the two seemingly unrelated tropes of "Dover Beach." [46] Nowhere has Arnold used a classical source more unobtrusively than in the poem's concluding lines. Taking a minor incident of the Peloponnesian War, he raises it to the stature of a universal modern symbol with such success that its original identity is neither evident nor important. His approach can be reconciled with the early 1850's more readily than with any later period, and taken together with the tidal image it lends some support to the belief that lines 1–28 were written later than the rest of the poem.

Many reasons account for the remarkable success of "Dover Beach": the subtle rhyming, the variety in line-length that derives ultimately from classical models, above all perhaps the brooding tone. Considerable credit, however, must be given to the handling of imagery. Abandoning his usual concern with rivers or the open sea, the poet walks by the waves' edge where Homer first had heard "the eternal note of sadness." [47] The sea-tide at length gives way to the tide of battle, described with a vividness unparalleled elsewhere in Arnold's poetry. His portrait of Sophocles may reflect nineteenth-century tendencies [48] but the Thucydidean image cannot be faulted, and in neither case does moralizing or determined cheerfulness blunt the effectiveness. One finds no statuesque classicism at any point: the poem in fact defies categories and remains a superb anomaly.

By 1867 Matthew Arnold was already more of an essayist than a poet, with the Homer lectures and the initial volume of *Essays in Criticism* to his credit. After that date he devoted himself wholly to prose for more than a dozen years; not until the period 1880–82 did he take up poetry once again, composing three elegies on a dachshund, the Dean of Westminster, and a canary.

"Geist's Grave" speaks of "That liquid, melancholy eye, From whose pathetic, soul-fed springs Seem'd surging the Virgilian cry, The sense of tears in mortal things" (13–16); *Sunt lacrimae rerum!* is added in a footnote. Poets since Vergil himself have been chary of disproportioned comparison, but here it does not really seem out of place to use the most haunting phrase in the entire *Aeneid*. The Arnolds made much of their dogs—too much, some thought; the affection that lends such charm to these verses is perfectly real, not the pretty pretense of a Catullus who writes of Lesbia's dead song-sparrow but thinks only of Lesbia.[49] *Et mentem mortalia tangunt:* the remainder of Vergil's line goes unspoken, but "Geist's Grave" is pervaded by a Vergilian preoccupation with death.

"Poor Matthias" does contain some of the phrasing and tone of Catullus. This will not be thought surprising in an elegy on a canary, especially when the poet makes it plain that he had never been particularly interested in Matthias. He uses the occasion to take up many themes; among them the thought of his own death is once more prominent. Acknowledging what fifteen years had seemed to prove, he writes that "as age comes on ... Poet's fire gets faint and low." Yet there were embers still:

> Was it, as the Grecian sings,
> Birds were born the first of things,
> Before the sun, before the wind,
> Before the gods, before mankind,
> Airy, ante-mundane throng—
> Witness their unworldly song!
> Proof they give, too, primal powers,
> Of a prescience more than ours—
> Teach us, while they come and go,
> When to sail, and when to sow.
> Cuckoo calling from the hill,
> Swallow skimming by the mill,
> Swallows trooping in the sedge,
> Starlings swirling from the hedge,
> Mark the seasons, map our year,
> As they show and disappear.
>
> No, away with tales like these
> Stol'n from Aristophanes!

This airy and beautiful stanza derives its poetic materials very largely from the parabasis or central chorus interlude of the *Birds;* its tone may come from the Hoopoe's lyrics.[50] The description has deliberately been given an English setting of "mill" and "sedge," but the total impression is delightfully Aristophanic. Stitching together of sources never becomes apparent; these verses triumph in their own right. Like his father, Arnold recognized the brilliance and sane humor of Aristophanes. We could wish he had drawn more often from the master of Old Comedy, for this stanza is worth pages of Browning's Greek scholarship.

The last serious poem to bear a classical stamp is "Westminster Abbey," written a year before "Poor Matthias." Arnold designed it as an elegiac tribute to his old friend Arthur Stanley, Dean of Westminster, yet it seems less an elegy than a variety of pindaric.[51] Like the victory odes, it makes the immediate occasion a point of departure rather than a center of interest; it gives myth a prominent place; and it is dominated by the very symbol which we especially associate with the Theban poet. It is hardly probable that these similarities are accidental. At thirty Arnold (so the theory goes) described his "Youth of Nature" as "Wordsworth's pindaric"; on the threshold of sixty he had apparently come to know what this form of poetry should be.

Three myths appear in "Westminster Abbey": a Christian miracle tale of Anglo-Saxon London joins with the story of Demeter and Demophoön and with a tradition concerning the deaths of the master builders Agamedes and Trophonius, who raised Apollo's temple at Delphi.[52] Such eclecticism would have been inconceivable in the early poems; now Arnold carries it off without faltering. From this point of view at least, the work ranks among his most finished. With only the faintest jar—for "to my mind there came how, long ago . . ." seems a little self-conscious —the monastic legend of Saint Peter coming to hallow the Abbey is succeeded by a retelling of fifty lines [53] from the *Homeric Hymn to Demeter*, an account of the goddess' attempt to render a mortal child deathless. Then follows Plutarch's story of how the two temple-builders sought a reward for their task, and how heaven gave them the reward of death as the perfect meed. The tale of Agamedes and Trophonius takes less than a single stanza, but Arnold elaborates the other myths to a degree without parallel in the entire range of his poetry.[54] Here is mythologizing in its own right, if not for its own sake.

The Hellenic and Christian stories nevertheless are held together, as the entire poem is held together, by a unifying symbol: the symbol of light.[55] The word occurs almost a score of times, always with the greatest deliberateness; the repetitious rhyme pattern that resulted was a price Arnold clearly had decided to pay. In this motif one sees the poem's most Pindaric trait, for the victory odes blaze with images of light. Pindar, however, made full use of the remarkable resources of Greek, which is particularly rich in words that flare and gleam and dazzle with the intensity of fire, the magnificence of gold. By contrast, Arnold almost completely avoids synonyms for his main symbol. The poem consequently loses more in dimension and visual suggestiveness than it gains in emphasis. There comes to mind the essayist, champion against the hosts of Philistia, repeating his cherished phrases with a wearying purposefulness.

The sixteenth stanza, known for its examples of extreme and archaic Latinate diction, is really worthy of attention because of its opening statement. "For this way and that swings The flux of mortal things, Though moving inly to one far-set goal"—a tidal image combines with that of a river making its way to the sea. At the end of his life Arnold denies final meaning to the world-view he had set forth in "Dover Beach." He credits the recurrence with a purpose, much as Clough had countered passages of "The Bothie" by "Say Not the Struggle Naught Availeth." Classical and Christian have been juxtaposed here no less than in the use of myth, though perhaps with less conscious intent, and their unresolved relationship mirrors a dualism within the poet's nature. These lines, the last significant statement of his poetry, offer no true synthesis. They embody his dilemma, and in that considerable measure they form a fitting testament.

The poem as a whole bears a different kind of witness, making plain the ultimate nature of Arnold's classicism. Except for the detailed mythologizing it contains nothing unexpected.[56] The attitudes of thirty years and more are here: periphrases, genteel revisions, sonorous Greek names, an eclectic manner, all employed by 1849; detachment from the Greek past, seemingly first adopted in "Empedocles on Etna"; even a momentary revelation, through images unequally combined, of that subjectivity which can enter the poems at any moment to complicate the task of understanding them. We shall meet many of these qualities again in the following chapters, devoted to Arnold's prose writings.

"Westminster Abbey" proves ineffective when it deals with Dean Stanley directly or stresses too vigorously its symbolism of light, but there are passages which rise above these constraints (34–40, 83–90):

> Lo, on a sudden all the Pile is bright!
> Nave, choir and transept glorified with light,
> While tongues of fire on coign and carving play!
> And heavenly odours fair
> Come streaming with the floods of glory in,
> And carols float along the happy air,
> As if the reign of joy did now begin.
>
> To my mind there came how, long ago,
> Lay on the hearth, amid a fiery ring,
> The charm'd babe of the Eleusinian king—
> His nurse, the Mighty Mother, will'd it so.
> Warm in her breast, by day,

> He slumber'd and ambrosia balmed the child;
> But all night long amid the flames he lay,
> Upon the hearth, and play'd with them, and smiled.

At such moments the comparison with Milton's Nativity Ode is not altogether ludicrous. The poem has a fitful splendor, Victorian perhaps rather than Pindaric, but real. Massive and ornate, strongly built if not deeply inspired, it stands as a unique poetic memorial to the latter decades of Matthew Arnold's thought.

In the long retrospect that a summary demands here, such imposing poetic architecture seems an unexpected development to come from the simplicity and childish sweetness of the Latin verses that an eleven-year-old had written for his little sister's birthday. To the schoolboy Arnold classical literature was the accepted substance of his labors, related to poetry essentially through "verse tasks"—exercises in Greek and Latin verse composition on set themes. His dealings with it were practical and simple; questions of artifice did not arise. Once he had begun to attempt English poetry the situation altered. Now the alternatives were to reject the Greek and Roman tradition, a course that he never contemplated, or to come to terms with it.

Just at this point, when a relationship between the traditional and the contemporary is being sought, the artificial begins to be a threat. For proof, one may recall the conventional mythological references in lines Matthew had written at Eaglehurst when he was thirteen. The allusions are apt, skillful, and eminently natural. It is precisely in their naturalness that the danger lies, for the classical can mean nothing more than this sort of embellishment. The young author went on to write a good deal of poetry, none of it extant, that may be taken as preparation for his Rugby prize poem, "Alaric at Rome." Despite the obvious opportunities which its subject offered, the poem contains literally not more than a single line (114) of classical reminiscence; the Oxford prize poem, "Cromwell," shows almost as great a dearth.

It appears that as a Rugbeian and Oxonian Arnold had taken the first step necessary in forming a positive classicism: he had rejected the conventional, unimaginative deference that manifests itself through imitation. The "A." who published *The Strayed Reveller, and Other Poems* in 1849 was seeking a truer relationship with the past. Through his poems he experiments, in effect if not always with conscious intent. He tries various ways of relating antiquity to his modern themes, aware that the two areas of ex-

perience are different (as in the title "A Modern Sappho," with
its stress on the adjective) and uncertain how to bring them together. These repeated experiments in fact fail to do so; the incongruity always becomes apparent. Arnold had never before
seriously considered the classical in a detached manner, as an element of possible importance to his own poetics; and only when
this further step is taken does the classical become classicism in
the usual sense of doctrine. Otherwise one is dealing with an impulse which can assume many isolated forms, as indeed happened
with a number of the 1849 poems. "The Strayed Reveller" almost
escapes the general indictment through its richness and sweep and
sense of poetic tradition. At its conclusion, however, neither impulse nor doctrine has taken a firm, enduring grip on the poet.

During the years immediately preceding 1850 the idea of the
classical seems to have presented itself to Arnold under a variety
of guises. It appeared as counterpart and paradigm of the present,
as the imperfectly defined antithesis of Romantic weakness, and,
in agreement with Goethe's dictum (*Das Classische nenne ich das
Gesunde*), as the element of soundness and strength generally. It
had no marked influence on his style, unless it may account for
the inverted word order. No distinctively Arnoldian manner of
poetic diction ever developed; the more notable individual strat-
agems, such as a frequent colorlessness and the use of short lines,
usually relate to contemporary factors. When Arnold directly
parallels or elaborates upon the writers of antiquity, we find that
his interpretations of the original do not usually commend themselves to present-day scholars. One note seldom sounds in these
early poems: the demand that poetry act as a therapeutic. This
concept, the theme of John Keble's lectures on poetry delivered
at Oxford between 1832 and 1841, will appear with some frequency in the essays. During the later 1840's only the famous
sonnet "To a Friend" comes near dealing with it. In this poem,
as we shall see, praise of the wholeness with which Sophocles saw
life represents still another view of the classical; and here it appears
in its most exalted manifestation, the Periclean.

Throughout these years Arnold was reading the *Discourses*
of Epictetus. His interest in Stoicism was not wholly uncritical,
and a comment in the canceled poem "Courage" reveals his awareness that the Stoic ideal needed to be supplemented by the Periclean. This work, published among the poems of 1852, praises
Cato's resolution in committing honorable suicide, permitted to a
Stoic when it was the only escape from degradation. Here Byron

too is mentioned with admiration: as in the figure of Empedocles, Titanic and Stoic qualities combine to produce the figure of the self-reliant hero, at once tragic and splendid. As Arnold looks to the past, however, he speaks of those who were less concerned than men of his own time with "the tendence of the whole" (10). It is clear that he refers to Stoicism, and his phrase indicates the analogy he felt between the Periclean achievement and the Victorian potential.

Two ideals appear here, one Hellenic and the other from later periods of antiquity. The first presupposes the city-state, while the second isolates the individual to a notable degree. Arnold's efforts to relate state and individual would later call forth his most powerful prose works. As he directed his attention finally towards problems of religion, he was to find the ethics of Epictetus and Marcus Aurelius increasingly more useful than Periclean ideals. Both figure in the poetry, and of the two Stoicism is noticeably more at home in this more private world. Neither, however, develops its full power until Arnold devotes himself to prose.

We have seen that the early poems, which sought ways of dealing with the classical, were succeeded by others indicating that a way had been chosen. Turning to prose follows naturally upon abandoning a view of poetry and of the classical which demanded personal commitment. To this rejection the 1853 Preface gives official status; it also announces the predominantly impersonal and external standards that Arnold now seeks to adopt. His attempt does not meet with complete success, for at times inner concerns find a voice in the later poetry, but they do not usually gain expression through a classical medium. The final contribution of Greek and Latin literature to Matthew Arnold's poetry is characteristically a greater effectiveness of formal characteristics. If one applies to these later works the accepted standards of dignity, lucidity, restraint, and proportion, an undeniable classicism becomes evident. The goal, so long sought, has now in some sense been attained. For the poet the price of attainment is to stay always at a prudent distance from the forces that might possess him, among them the power of classical antiquity.

Arnold had neither the means of ignoring that power nor the wish to do so. In prose he saw a sphere of immense future usefulness for the two aspects of antiquity that had meant most to him: the Hellenic, quintessentially classical literature of the Periclean era, and the Hellenistic philosophy of behavior. To these much else would be added, notably Homer and Plato, but the fifth-century writers and the Stoics were always to be at the center of his concern with the past. This was also a concern for the present, to be sure. It had been so from the time the earliest published poems were written. The difference is that in the later 1850's Arnold began to direct the major part of his energies to the long task of bringing before the reading public these literary and philosophic ideals as fundamentals of culture.

Subjective elements are now supposedly to be put aside. In fact this does not happen; their interplay with classical themes demands consideration throughout the remaining chapters. The Arnold with whom we must henceforth deal is no utter stranger: his nature will reveal characteristics already familiar. Now, however, he addresses himself openly to society, and the lyricism of his early poetry is succeeded by the agile rhetoric of prose. In these new circumstances the classical still can serve Arnold's needs, expressing through its varied aspects both the public and the private worlds of his mature thought.

Homer

None of Arnold's dealings with the classics has had so widespread and continuing an effect as his lectures *On Translating Homer.* They won outspoken praise from A. E. Housman, that most savage of all critics among classical scholars; the learned Sir Richard Jebb adopted their characterizations of Homeric style in his handbook on the poet; and rare today is the discussion of the theory of classical translation that does not consider them.[1]

These lectures to Oxford undergraduates are in fact of greater interest now than at any time since they first were delivered, just over a century ago. We find ourselves in the midst of a renaissance of translation: Greek and Latin literature is becoming increasingly accessible, not least the *Iliad* and *Odyssey.* Prose renderings of Homer by Dr. E. V. Rieu and the late W. H. D. Rouse sell in their thousands and their tens of thousands; Professor Richmond Lattimore's verse *Iliad* has received high praise; and it is becoming steadily more evident that in Robert Fitzgerald's poetic version of the *Odyssey* we have one of the rare and great translations. What the present age strikingly lacks is a Matthew Arnold to give these works their due. Until such a critic appears, there is still something to be gained from considering what Arnold himself had to say.

He neither possessed nor claimed to possess a scholar's special acquaintance with Homeric poetry. Even by amateur standards he was much the inferior of his contemporary, Gladstone—a recent scholarly survey of Homeric criticism ignores him completely, while devoting several pages to Gladstone's work. Such treatment works no injustice on Arnold; he might have accepted it as a kind of compliment. The important fact is that a strictly literary criticism constituted the beginning and end of his service to Homer. His inability to venture safely outside this province was a weakness; for certain matters, particularly matters of philology, it proved to be an undeniable handicap. Nevertheless, it did not disable him or seriously compromise his main contributions.

Arnold's right to be heard has the simplest basis imaginable. Unlearned though he may have been, he knew Homer's text. One can say of him what Hogg said of Shelley: "It would be curious to know how often he had read the whole of Homer through." He never paraded this constant reading and rereading to impress the public: his life with books remained a private thing where classical literature was concerned. Here his personal correspondence can help us. In 1849 he writes, "I have finished the *Iliad*, going straight through it, that is, I have within this year read through all Homer's works, and all those ascribed to him. But I have done little, though more than most years. . . ." Once he had taken up the exhausting life of an inspector of schools, it was a struggle to find time for anything outside the demands of routine. Writing late one evening in 1862, he says, "I shall . . . read about a hundred lines of the *Odyssey* . . . and go to bed about twelve"; during the hour and a quarter left before midnight he also planned to draw up a school report and write two or three letters.[2] Homer proves relatively easy for anyone with a good foundation in Greek, but it is clear that Arnold could get through the *Odyssey* as rapidly as many professional scholars.

His decision to deal with Homer was not a sudden one. The theme, and the wish to develop it, had long been in his mind;[3] the public lectures required of an Oxford Professor of Poetry offered a welcome chance to realize that wish. The choice should not surprise us, for no more congenial topic can well be imagined. Homer's reputation, insecure during the eighteenth century, had risen in the nineteenth. It is true that there was still a controversy over the authorship of the *Iliad* and *Odyssey*. This had originated in the establishment of textual criticism by Alexandrian scholars, and it gained vigorous new life when Friedrich August Wolf published his *Prolegomena ad Homerum* in 1795. The dispute continues today, apparently an eternal issue. Arnold saw, however, that the translator of Homer could ignore it as a tempest in an inkpot. He approved of the position taken by Goethe, who invoked the *Zeitgeist* when Homeric scholars changed from the separatist belief in multiple authorship to a unitarian view.[4] If Goethe's acceptance of a historical mystique does little to explain what is actually a very intricate problem, its attractiveness for Arnold is understandable. In any case, literary criticism remained safely within a separate province of Arnold's thought.

As a literary figure Homer stands out clearly; his historical position has never been certain. Herodotus, writing shortly after the middle of the fifth century b.c., placed him four hundred years earlier. On this point modern scholarship speaks with many voices, suggesting various later periods. It was precisely the uncertainty of the whole matter that suited Arnold's purpose so well; for once, the weakness of his historical sense could not handicap him. He was free to consider Homer as a timeless phenomenon, a discrete force which could be assessed from the standpoint of the nineteenth century and the history of post-Elizabethan English literature.[5] The brilliance and ease of these lectures, the sureness of touch that even T. S. Eliot has praised, could hardly have been so well realized if Arnold had not found his ground already cleared. The task in short, lay ideally to his hand: it brought out his virtues without seriously emphasizing their attendant defects.

Arnold himself considered the lectures to be a summing up of previous opinion rather than a new approach. "That Homer is plain, noble, etc., etc., is certainly the common-sense view of Homer," he writes in a letter of 1861, "and that hitherto generally received by the best judges." The justness of this self-criticism becomes clear when we examine Pope's treatment of Homer in the essays appended to his verse translations. More than this, we realize Arnold's modesty in claiming no more than he did. Actually he has achieved a greater success than any predecessor. Pope, for example, delivers a set piece with accustomed eloquence, and when the last majestic period has rolled into silence his reader might not find it an easy task to summarize the flowing argument. The procedure that Arnold adopts is the very different technique of the lecturer who organizes his remarks for systematic presentation, using every means to clarity.[6]

Homer is rapid in movement, plain alike in words and style, simple in ideas, noble in manner: these judgments are the heart of Matthew Arnold's position. In one way or another, everything that he has to say is an elaboration of them. We have seen that he privately considered them nothing more than common sense. It would be a little nearer the truth to say they represent critical sense, independent judgment that often recalls the thinking of predecessors. As for their being self-evident first truths, it remains to be seen whether and in what degree this may be true.

The first attribute, rapidity of movement, is explained as "directness and flowingness." This serves to give the definition a wider scope at the expense of sharpness. The tendency towards blurring arises out of a lack in Arnold's poetic equipment that cost him dearly, his inadequate grasp of prosody. For these discussions of Homer the result was uncertainty about the precise metrical nature of what he was discussing. Thus the lectures equate "rapid" with "flowing," although he had made a clear distinction between these two qualities in a letter of 1853.[7] His remarks also contain such a confused analysis as the following:

> ... *oute ken autos eni prôtoisi machoimên,*
> *oute ke se stelloimi machên es kudianeiran:* ...

says Homer; there he stops, and begins an opposed movement:

> *nun d'—empês gar kêres ephestasin thanatoio—*

In this line, Arnold continues, "Homer wishes to go away with the most marked rapidity from the line before."[8]

While it is entirely correct to point out an opposed movement beginning here, "rapidity" seems a singular term. The first two lines are strongly dactylic; the third is spondaic, and *nun d'* ("but as it is—"), which demands a pause, slows its movement even further.[9] There is indeed a change of tempo in these lines, one which entirely suits the movement of thought, but Arnold has characterized it very strangely. His failure to say anything further about Homer's rapidity can cause no regret. In treating such matters one cannot evade responsibility for a certain measure of scholarship, and when Arnold attempts to deal with them he is not on his chosen ground.[10]

Undoubtedly there are respects in which Homeric poetry seems rapid. Those who read it in the original will not need to be told how the hexameter bears one along. Yet it is most decidedly not the tripping stress metre of three-quarter-time verse music; we know that it was based on duration in a scheme of four beats. Unfortunately the schools of Victorian England did not observe this true principle. Like the average schoolboy of his time, Matthew Arnold read Homer and Vergil in triple rhythm, natural for the Englishman or American but false to the genuine rhythm of classical epic.[11] This preconception will account in part for his statements about Homer's rapidity, and it reveals their element of weakness.

Arnold's concern is with Homeric style generally, not with the special province of metre. This more general concern is the one that has meaning for the great majority, who know the *Iliad* and *Odyssey* only through translations that often are done in prose. Such readers may remain strangers to the hexameter and still sense the steady movement of Homer's narrative. We have noted that the lectures couple rapidity and flowingness, ignoring earlier distinctions; it now becomes evident that the latter term, so often overlooked, is for Arnold the truly operative one. This appears in the excellent distinction he establishes between Homer's straightforwardness and the involuted or checked movement of two styles famous in English poetry, the Miltonic period and the rhymed couplet of Pope's translations.[12] He correctly notes the "inversion and pregnant conciseness" of Milton (although these qualities are not wholly alien to epic) and the fatal tendency of rhyme to bring together elements which Homer carefully keeps apart.

Perhaps Milton receives less than his due on this occasion, for we cannot be carried along on his mighty current unless we read him by verse paragraph. It might be thought, also, that the lectures betray too partial a view of Homer's narrative. When the poet wished to pause he did so, whether to sketch a household scene or to tally the Achaean contingents sailing against Ilium. Yet on the whole it is true to describe his narrative style as flowing, and Arnold deserves credit for emphasizing this.

"Homer is plain alike in words and in style." With the claim of plain style there can be no quarrel.[13] The *Iliad* and *Odyssey* are the only mature works of Western literature to stand so near the bardic period of formulaic oral composition; their simplicity of style—*simplicité*, not the artificial *simplesse* Arnold disliked, nor yet *naïveté*—is to a great extent inevitable. But plain in words? Professor Highet has spoken to this point:

> Homer is often the very reverse of plain and direct in language, and seems undeniably obscure and odd.... Homer uses words which no other Greek poet ever employs; he is very free with strange verbal forms and combinations of particles and metrical tricks and relics of obsolete letters and combinations of disparate dialects and unintelligible ejaculations. Some of his phrases look really unnatural and distorted.

The Greeks themselves found it difficult to explain such parts of his language. . . . It is a splendidly flexible and sonorous language, but it is odd and difficult.[14]

These remarks overstate the case for Homer's difficulty, but they contain a good deal of truth. Realizing the awkwardness of his position, Arnold countered by appealing to authority. He invited several eminent classicists, among them Benjamin Jowett, to say whether they found Homer quaint and antiquated rather than unfailingly "simple and intelligible." As anyone else might have foreseen, these learned gentlemen did not feel moved to accept his invitation.[15] In fact, it was an unnecessary move on his part as well as a mistaken one. He realized clearly enough that Homer's verse is not an obstacle course for philologists: it is great literature and therefore truly meaningful only in its total effect, read fluently as he himself read it. But the lines of argument that he might have taken in the lectures were never really pursued; we are left with the appeal to scholarly authority.

Despite appearances this appeal is by no means an isolated, desperate bid for support. It originates rather in Arnold's conviction that the proper judge of any translation of Homer is a poetically "intelligent" classical scholar. Anxious to provide some objective standard, he shows his characteristic distaste for criteria wholly contained within literature. Here an anomaly results, for the central fact is his refusal to dissociate any literary work from man as a moral being, self-revealed through style and content. From this conviction comes his celebrated indictment of Shelley, and also his claim in the lectures that nothing so well fits a man for translating Homer as inward nobility. Neither intellectual nor aesthetic capacities are in question. Having recourse to the verdict of classical scholarship is therefore an anomalous procedure, and in their best moments the lectures themselves show it to be an invalid one as well.

"Homer is simple in ideas": one does not find in him the "union of idiomatic expression with curious or difficult thought" that characterizes Shakespeare. Since Arnold has little more to say on this point, presumably he considered it self-evident. One might have expected him to acknowledge the subtlety and inwardness of an achievement which, during our own time, has stirred such diverse artists as Joyce and Kazantzakis. Professor Trilling rightly draws our attention to Arnold's natural interest in Achilles.[16] What seems surprising is the lack of interest in Homer's other famous young man, Telemachus, shown in all his adolescent loneliness and turbulence and self-pity as he stands unaware on the threshold of manhood. Different eras come to Homer with different needs, but it is not easy to escape the feeling that Arnold's preoccupation with the fortifying qualities of epic has made him pass over other qualities no less valuable.[17] One thing, finally, can be said in his favor: he realized how roughly Homer was being handled by his countrymen. A statement in the lectures indicates a deeper view than the criterion of simplicity would suggest:

> When one observes the boistering, rollicking way in which his English admirers . . . love to talk of Homer and his poetry, one cannot help feeling that there is no very deep community of nature between them. [Homer would say to them,] "You do me a great deal of honour, but somehow or other you praise me too like barbarians." [18]

Fourth, "Homer is noble in manner." That manner, says Arnold firmly, "invests his subject, whatever his subject may be, with nobleness." His claim represents an impossible extension of the concept of the noble, by modern standards of criticism. It is meant to demolish Newman's contention that Homer rises and sinks with his subject. In Arnold's view—and here he gets onto solid ground—no poet can justly be said to do this "when all that he, as a poet, can do, is perfectly well done; when he is perfectly sound and good, that is, perfect as a poet, in the level regions of his subject as well as in its elevated regions." This, he maintains, is precisely what sets apart the great masters of poetry.[19] His judgment and the discussions which support it have lasting value; there are few finer passages in the lectures.

If Arnold's perceptions seem obvious today, they were not taken for granted a hundred years ago. Eighteenth-century fastidiousness, which never forgave Nausicaa for doing the washing, had passed away with the era of absolute aristocracies; but the attitudes which supplanted it were hardly an improvement. "Das Volk dichtet," Grimm had said, and men of the nineteenth century remembered his words. What they forgot was that he had also defended Homer as a great poet against the attacks of F. A. Wolf. Folk-poetry became a kind of learned craze, and Homer suffered fearful and wonderful misinterpretation in the light of its characteristics. His translators, with their ballad-metre versions, worked still greater havoc than the exegetes.

Perhaps the worst of these was Francis Newman, a man of

appalling erudition and no sense. Convinced that Homer's style was quaint, he determined to render it accordingly; he succeeded only in making it appear absurd. Nothing could have effaced more completely the clarity and compactness manifest in the original than Newman's lumbering assortment of philological oddities. His translation, with the preface which so fatally sought to justify it, made him the perfect target for Arnold's attacks. Many have felt that these were too closely pressed, and there is no denying that the lectures left a sense of lasting hurt in Newman. Nevertheless, the job needed to be done; all we can justly criticize is the polemical sharpness which marked its execution.

What Matthew Arnold achieved through his three Oxford lectures and later essay was the restoration of Homeric poetry to its proper place among the masterworks of Western literature. T. S. Eliot has acknowledged Arnold's service in ordering anew the canon of England's principal writers; *On Translating Homer* and *Last Words* show the same kind of accomplishment within a much wider field. His use of comparative criticism was eventually to become capricious, but here it has been employed with notable restraint. He claims no exclusive preëminence for Homer. At the beginning of the first lecture he refers to the *Iliad* and *Odyssey* as "the most important poetical monument existing," but this does not mark a general tone. Arnold intends us to see Homer as one of an immortal company, a figure most clearly understood when seen in their midst. Milton and Dante, he tells us, are of that company. They too are great, and it is by grasping the essential differences between their kinds of greatness and Homer's that we gain true insight. This principle applies equally well in the case of writers like Defoe, who must be ranked rather lower: their lesser measure can illustrate the scale of greatness.[20]

Such is the achievement which, for Arnold's time and for our own, constitutes the true justification of his remarks on Homer. He professes to be concerned with showing where previous translators of Homer have gone astray, and also with specifying the "right objects" to be borne in mind by future translators.[21] What he does in fact accomplish proves to be something considerably more important than the correction and instruction of translators. It is well that this should be the case, for many of his specific views on translation must seem unsatisfactory to modern readers.

To cite a major instance, he stubbornly defended and cherished that changeling of English prosody, the hexameter. In the modern period our most sensitive and accomplished translators have been able to use this metre only by relaxing its classical laws to a very great extent. The Victorians, however, assumed these laws to be basic. As a result they fell into a basic error: they supposed that they were dealing with some imperfect kind of quantitative scansion. This meant asking the wrong questions and seeking the wrong effects. Moreover, if Arnold's specimen hexameters are compared with the work of Clough and Kingsley, they prove to possess neither the flexibility and vigor of "The Bothie" nor the smoothness of "Andromeda." At Oxford they have been said to read beautifully as prose. Had the lectures been a defense of the author's own practices they would now be without general repute or influence.

To speak more generally, the entire conception of translation seems strangely out of touch with reality. It is reasonable to ask that a translator of Homer be "penetrated" by the poet's cardinal literary virtues. He is also, however, required by Arnold to possess inward nobility, and his version must please a jury of dons. When we find such views put forward in earnest, it is difficult not to deal with Arnold somewhat as he himself dealt with Francis Newman.

We do not do so, because these matters are unimportant. *On Translating Homer* continues to be read, not because it can give us any really useful or even reliable advice on translating Homer, but for the great and sufficient reason that it brings before us a giant of world literature. Only recently had the very concept and term *Weltliteratur* been originated by Arnold's revered master, Goethe: it is difficult for us, a century later, to realize what this new breadth of judgment meant in the Oxford lectures. From his point of vantage as a comparative critic Arnold grasped what Pope had not realized, the fact of Homer's maturity.[22] This enabled him to demolish the balladist interpretation, and with it Newman's view of the poet as a noble savage chanting verse "like an elegant and simple melody from an African of the Gold Coast." The effect of his discussion moreover discredited any strong belief in composite authorship of the *Iliad* and *Odyssey*. Avoiding scholarly debate, he stands on his chosen ground of literature and declares that the consistent nobility and grand manner of the *Iliad* offer the best proof of single authorship. These are all things worth saying; none of them is so important as the victory over parochialism. We honor Matthew Arnold above all for rescuing Homer from the distortions of narrow philologists and placing him where he belongs, among the masters of our tradition.[23]

It remains to ask the nature of Arnold's more personal responses to Homer. A portion of the evidence, often contained in letters to family and close friends, has shown that he read Homer's poetry throughout his life. This was no intellectual or aesthetic exercise, but a therapeutic discipline. In the shatteringly dull routine of correcting elementary school papers it kept his spirit from being suffocated; it cleansed his palate from the elegant sensualism of Daudet's *Sapho;* and always it provided him with a refuge from the multitudinousness, the narrowness, the material-ism of Victorian England. Homer, he tells us, was "the clearest-souled of men," always composing " 'with his eye on the object,' whether the object be a moral or a material one," and conveying it with immediacy rather than through a medium of self-conscious style. Moreover, he saw not only clearly but widely: a reader has "the sense of having, within short limits of time, a large portion of human life presented to him." [24]

These are just and wise appreciations; yet none of us comes to Greece empty-handed, nor is it given to us to see with the eyes of Homer. Subjective concerns first appear in the reference to moral objects. They are unmistakable in the claim that "what Homer has in common with Milton—the noble and profound application of ideas to life—is the most essential part of poetic greatness." [25] Arnold at once goes on to make his meaning clear: the most "essentially grand and characteristic things of Homer" are such passages as these:

> I have brought myself to do what no other man on earth
>   ever did:
>
> To kiss the hand of him who slew my son.
>
> You too, aged sir, were prosperous in former time, as
>   we have heard.
>
> For thus have the gods decreed that wretched mortals
> Should live—in misery; but they themselves are free
>   from cares.

A footnote to the second excerpt reads: "In the original this line, for mingled pathos and dignity, is perhaps without a rival even in Homer." [26]

Another passage, cited not only in the lectures but several times elsewhere in Arnold's writings, seems to have meant much to him. It is the address of Sarpedon to his comrade Glaucus:

> Man, supposing you and I, escaping this battle,
> would be able to live on forever, ageless, immortal,

so neither would I myself go on fighting in the foremost
nor would I urge you into the fighting where men win glory.
But now, seeing that the spirits of death stand close about us
in their thousands, no man can turn aside nor escape them,
let us go on and win glory for ourselves, or yield it to
others.[27]

Long after the Oxford lectures, and less than a year before
his death, Arnold contributed a few lines to an article in the *Fortnightly Review*, "Fine Passages in Verse and Prose: Selected by
Living Men of Letters." "I should say," he writes, "that no passages have moved and pleased me more than, in poetry, the lines
describing the pity of Zeus for the horses of Achilles (*Iliad*, xvii.
441–47), and the famous stanza of Horace, 'Linquenda tellus,' &c.
..." [28] The incident from the *Iliad*, with some lines added at the
beginning, has been translated as follows:

But the horses of Aiakides standing apart from the battle
wept, as they had done since they heard how their
    charioteer
had fallen in the dust at the hands of murderous Hector.

.   .   .   .

... Still as stands a grave monument which is set over
the mounded tomb of a dead man or lady, they stood there
holding motionless in its place the fair-wrought chariot,
leaning their heads along the ground. . . .

.   .   .   .

As he watched the mourning horses the son of
    Kronos pitied them,
and stirred his head and spoke to his own spirit: "Poor
    wretches,
why then did we ever give you to the lord Peleus,
a mortal man, and you yourselves are immortal and
    ageless?
Only so that among unhappy men you also might be
    grieved?
Since among all creatures that breathe on earth and
    crawl upon it
there is not anywhere a thing more dismal than man is."

All five of these touchstone passages come from the *Iliad*. It
is scarcely an exaggeration to say that for Arnold Homer meant
the tale of Troy. Even the great Odysseus appears but once, in

"The Strayed Reveller," and there the portrait has no depth. The Oxford lectures themselves could have been delivered, with only one word omitted, if the *Odyssey* had never existed.[29] This partiality, however strange, is not unaccountable. The forces that stirred beneath the surface of Arnold's life find their counterpart in the battle for Troy, the pathetic and magnificent figures moving towards death. To the poet of "Empedocles on Etna" and "A Southern Night," of "Mycerinus" and "Dover Beach," of Sohrab and Balder slain through mischance, Odysseus' rejection of immortality spoke less meaningfully than Achilles' choice of a swift, heroic death or Hector's refusal to cower before a hopeless future.

Commentators have noticed the tone of strain and sadness, at times almost morbid, in Arnold's touchstone verses and classically derived images. The Homeric touchstones cited earlier show it unmistakably, and with it a strong preference for the reflective and so to speak philosophical element. This element is not common in the *Iliad;* the *Odyssey* lacks it almost entirely. To anyone who had not read the poems Arnold's selections would give a one-sided impression. They may represent "the most essentially grand ... things of Homer"; despite his further claim, they do not represent the most essentially characteristic things.[30] The aspect of Homer they exemplify is the aspect that moved Matthew Arnold and seemed to embody "the noble and profound application of ideas to life."

The phrase embodies the same tendency as Arnold's more famous description of poetry, or again of literature generally, as "a criticism of life": it separates unduly from life the ideas of a writer, which are his criticism. To speak of "application" creates an impression that the poetry of Homer and Milton is synthetic rather than a fusion of inseparable elements. This was certainly not Arnold's considered view. Again, several of the "ideas" [31] of which he speaks represent nothing more systematic or didactic than a poignant mood—the pathos of Priam's lost happiness, or his supplication before the man who had killed his son.

Homeric poetry does not, of course, embody all the distinctive qualities which Arnold's convictions and temperament led him to seek in literature of the first rank. As he himself points out, it was greater than its age and thus not comparable with Attic tragedy. The tragedians he therefore terms more important, though less perfect. Few will doubt that Homer meets his pragmatic definition of a classic as what has not been bettered; but he realized that a critic must go further than this, and his other approaches take different lines. The idea of basing a course of lectures on Homer's essential characteristics was an excellent one. In its execution it marked a real and needed improvement over previous critiques, which had remained all too diffuse even in the hands of such a master as Pope; its eventual effect upon the whole field of literary criticism has been notable. Arnold's estimate nevertheless remains more subjective than he realized. The element of sad reflectiveness receives attention out of all proportion to its place in the great panorama of Homer. The same impulses that explain this preoccupation made Arnold ignore the *Odyssey*, which so many have felt to be an affirmation of life. "It contains everything," says Joyce, and he ends his own Dublin Odyssey with a repeated "yes." One cannot easily imagine Matthew Arnold doing so.[32]

The contradictory nature of Arnold's position appears most clearly of all in his elaborations of a remark by Goethe. Taken in its original context of the correspondence with Schiller, this proves to be nothing much more than a weary protest against the impossible conditions under which Goethe had to work at the time. No one reading it in context could mistake it for a serious comment on Homer; but we shall see what Arnold made of it. In the Oxford lectures Goethe's words follow a rather short-sighted criticism of one of Ruskin's interpretations:

> It is not true, as a matter of general criticism, that this kind of sentimentality, eminently modern, inspires Homer at all. "From Homer and Polygnotus I every day learn more clearly," says Goethe, "that in our life here above ground we have, properly speaking, to enact Hell":—if the student must properly have a key-note to the Iliad, let him take this of Goethe, and see what he can do with it. . . .[33]

The remark had already been in the writer's mind for several years at least. A letter of early 1857 mentions hopes of getting to the Continent:

> I shall be baffled, I daresay, as one continually is in so much, but I remember Goethe, "Homer and Polygnotus daily teach me more and more that our own life is a Hell, through which one must struggle as one best can." [34]

A later portion of *On Translating Homer* tells how Lord Granville on his deathbed quoted Sarpedon's fatalistic words, the fourth of the touchstone passages cited earlier. The story, says Arnold, seems to me to illustrate Goethe's saying which I mentioned, that our life, in Homer's view of it, represents a conflict and a hell; and it brings out, too, what there is tonic and fortifying in this doctrine.

The latter view recurs several times elsewhere. To Clough he writes that "Homer *animates*." "That divine poet," he says many years later, "is always in season, always brings us something suited to our wants." [35]

For Arnold there were three Homers, all of them Iliadic rather than Odyssean and each corresponding to a part of Arnold's own nature—suited, in fact, to his wants. First is the literary exemplar, a sure foundation for criticism; second, the realist, "clearest-soul'd of men," encompassing life's tumult and hellishness; and finally the bringer of solace, whose message holds strength as well as bleakness. These are not the objective dimensions of any real, dispassionately measured Homer. They are the length and breadth and height of Matthew Arnold's being. [36]

The Homeric image thus created is neither complete nor free from distortion. Much of its outline nevertheless has that vividness which comes only when the critic believes himself to be one with his subject. It has persuasiveness as well, for the particular critic with whom we are dealing was perceptive beyond all others of his age. Preconceptions narrowed his gaze; they did not blind it. If we ask what measure of accuracy was in that gaze no generality can meet the question, and those who particularize may arrive at other answers than have been suggested here. One thing can be said without hesitation: the Homer of Matthew Arnold is no remote academic portrait, but a living force.

VI

Tragedy

Man in a universe that is governed for good or ill by laws of more than human provenance, laws which he can only dimly comprehend but which inexorably summon him to judgment: such is the theme of Sophoclean drama. It has enduring power, and we have given it a secure place among the views which prefigure our dilemma. There is no need to single out Sophocles as the most modern of the Athenian tragic poets. The contemporary note sounds rather in Euripides, who saw men at the mercy of forces within themselves. Like Aristotle, however, we return instinctively to Sophocles as to a true center, a balance-point nearer humanity than either Aeschylean grandeur or the feverish Euripidean brilliance.If he is less close to the gods than Aeschylus, he seeks the meaning of existence within a wider context than Euripides' preoccupation with man can offer. In his seven tragedies he speaks to us deeply and, to some degree, intelligibly. The attempts at an answer may differ from ours; the questions often seem to be our questions.

The Sophoclean answer as Matthew Arnold interpreted it is best known from the sestet of "To a Friend":

> (But be his)
> My special thanks, whose even-balanced soul,
> From first youth tested up to extreme old age,
> Business could not make dull, nor passion wild;
>
> Who saw life steadily, and saw it whole;
> The mellow glory of the Attic stage,
> Singer of sweet Colonus, and its child.

Even balance of soul recalls the ethical vocabulary of Stoicism, yet there is some justification for applying it to Sophocles. In the judgment of antiquity at least, exemplified by Sophocles' own warning to call no man happy until he is dead, he had an unusually happy life. Born at Colonus five years before the battle of Marathon, he was so handsome and accomplished at sixteen—the time of "first youth"—that the Athenians chose him to lead the chorus celebrating their final victory at Salamis. Only eleven years later he won the first prize for tragedy, competing against Aeschylus, and began a swift rise to supremacy among the tragic poets. During his middle years he twice became one of the ten supreme commanders of the Athenian military and naval forces, elected to this post by his fellow-citizens.

In "extreme old age" Sophocles did not cease to serve the state, for he was appointed to a special mission of considerable importance when he had passed the age of eighty. These final years come before us in an anecdote from Plato's *Republic*. Asked if his sexual powers remained, the old poet answered spiritedly that he was thankful to be free from the power of physical desire, which he likened to a savage animal. Biographical evidence, perhaps of doubtful authenticity, suggests that he was not speaking from hearsay. According to still another tradition, he proved his mental competence by reciting in court a portion of the tragedy which he was then composing, the majestic *Oedipus at Colonus*. We do not need the story; the play itself completely proves its author's greatness during the last years of his life. At ninety he once again led a public celebration in Athens. This time the occasion was one of mourning: Euripides had died in Macedonia. A few months more, and Sophocles too was gone. As Aristophanes acknowledged soon afterward in the *Frogs*, Athens' great age of tragic drama had come to an end.

If the soul of Sophocles was tested from youth to old age, we know of no evidence for this. Was it, then, a nature that "business could not make dull, nor passion wild"? Arnold starts from the assumption that both forces did in fact assail the mind of Sophocles.[1] Where passion is concerned this seems a reasonable position; it becomes weaker when one considers the other factor. "Business," an unpoetic usage which breaks the tone of the sestet, may well have its ordinary meaning; but the fact that the poet's father owned a weapons manufactory is the only one which might suggest that he himself engaged in trade, and it does not suffice. More important by far is Arnold's honesty in crediting Sophocles with sensuality, though not with abandon. It seems all the more regrettable that readers so often take his words to mean ignorance of passion; yet part of the blame for this misunderstanding belongs to Arnold himself. His remarks have contributed to a view which still fights for survival even among classicists, the conception of Sophocles as a kind of Epicurean deity among tragedians, statuesque and serene.

Any comment on this central point must attempt to deal with the celebrated line, "Who saw life steadily, and saw it whole." The claim of steadiness has generally been allowed. Anyone who has read Sophocles can see its basis and can recognize the unflinching gaze of the playwright. That Arnold intended this meaning is not at all clear, however. If he did, a desire to justify the statuesque interpretation has often prompted a misreading. Far more difficult to interpret is the final claim of wholeness; it immediately raises large issues. One of these involves the difference between seeing life whole and seeing the whole of life. Such a difference may exist; the failure to realize this can lead to an attempt to show that Sophocles' plays are all-inclusive. Inevitably such an attempt ends in disillusionment, and Arnold comes to be unjustly discredited.

It seems reasonable to suggest that the famous phrase refers in fact to the grasp, not merely unitary but actually unifying, which marks a true poet's view of his world. More than once it has been taken as meaning that Sophocles saw integrally and with perspective the range of life within his vision.[2] This explanation seems highly plausible; actually it misleads us. The real point can be seen when we take into account three of Arnold's beliefs. First, poetry is truly "more philosophical" (that is, it has closer affinities with wisdom) than historical narrative, as Aristotle maintains. Second, because the poet discerns a larger pattern and higher significance in the limited portion of existence which enters his consciousness, he is able to suggest the meaning and design of all existence. Finally, his insight, being scaled to the higher truth, must inevitably be more true than any account which fails to rise beyond mere fact.[3]

Thus far we have been dealing with the concept of wholeness as with some exclusive objective quality, an excellence perhaps of focus and perspective. Arnold would never have remained content with such a limitation. Moralist rather than aesthetician in art, he took his stand not with Aristotle but with Plato. For him the good writer is the good man. So Quintilian had defined the orator as *vir bonus peritus dicendi*, "a good man skilled in speaking," and Milton had urged that the poet should himself be a poem.[4] The tradition originated in the awakening social consciousness of the Greek city-state. It achieved its last full expression among eighteenth-century English critics and thereafter came increasingly to be questioned or ignored. Arnold's determination to reaffirm it might appear to follow naturally enough from his intensely classical and moralistic upbringing; in terms of mature literary criticism his position represents a conscious expression of solidarity with those who, through twenty centuries, had preceded him.

This is not the entire story, to be sure. A fuller understanding means looking beyond Dr. Arnold's Rugby, beyond Plato and Longinus and the others who make up that fellowship of prophets. Arnold's quest for wholeness ended only with his death; his writings repeatedly witness to an awareness, by no means always conscious, that he had failed to achieve it. Sophocles, like Goethe, seemed to him to have succeeded, and the Sophoclean moral integration was linked with a creative genius that Arnold believed to be higher than even Goethe could claim. In Sophocles he saw the embodiment of all true greatness; to him he transferred his own unrealized ideal.

The concluding lines of "To a Friend" speak of "The mellow glory of the Attic stage, Singer of sweet Colonus, and its child." They have proved less harmful than what immediately precedes them, but they have done harm enough. This result surely was not intended, for Arnold's essays give us reason to suppose that "mellow" refers to something real, such as the avoidance of Aeschylus' grim and rugged outline or the much greater concern with subtlety and ambivalence in individual character. Had this been the whole of his meaning, no one who has read even a little in Athenian tragedy could fail to agree.

Unfortunately, it is difficult to avoid the feeling that he had also had in his thoughts the *Oedipus at Colonus;* "Singer of sweet Colonus" surely alludes to the graceful lyrics in which the aged poet paid a last tribute to the place of his birth. When we call to mind Arnold's lifelong delight in botanizing, we have no cause for astonishment at his choice of terms to describe an ode that sings so delightfully of ivy and crocus, narcissus and olive. "Sweet" is unfortunate only because it contributes to a false general impression. As for "mellow," the term hardly expresses a salient fea-

ture of the play, and it would apply even less happily to the protagonist; yet similar misrepresentations occur in all but recent
estimates of Sophoclean drama. While the great majority of classical scholars now hold more realistic views, the reading public
has been slow to awaken. That public derives its ideas of classical
literature from translations and critical opinion, but also from
the lines and phrases of a Tennyson or an Arnold. Whether or not
Tennyson ever felt misgivings about his portraits of Odysseus and
Vergil, it is demonstrably true that Arnold ignored the mischievous
consequences of his own phrase-making.

"To a Friend" suggests a positive, bracing attitude towards
life on Sophocles' part. Much later, in the essays, Arnold elaborates his suggestion. The Greek poet's response was one of joy,
we are told, because he had attained to a total view of life. That
is, he had come to see it not waveringly or with a partial understanding, but steadily and whole. Arnold explicitly bases his view
on the strong belief that wholeness of understanding always moves
us to affirmation, always gives rise to joy—a belief not yet worked
out in the early poems.[5] Here a cardinal principle of experience
combines with a vital part, if not the whole, of Sophocles' answer
to the riddle of man's existence. Of these two elements the theory
regarding experience proves to be much the easier to parallel from
Arnold's writings. It relates most importantly of all to his insistence
that one "see the thing as it really is." He believed that those who
truly come to possess an overview are not the men of widely ranging practical experience; they are the great poets.[6] It is the poet
who sees life unroll below him as "a placid and continuous whole,"
like the river which so often symbolizes it in Arnold's poetry.
"Placid" conveys the higher harmony in its inner calm, the awareness of ultimate peace and joy that can come only to a master
poet's understanding.

From Arnold's point of view it follows that the true realism
for a writer consists in showing the morally significant aspects of
experience. St. Paul exhorts the believers at Philippi to think on
"whatsoever things are true,... whatsoever things are lovely,
whatsoever things are of good report." It did not seem to him that
these things could be other than identical. So with Matthew Arnold: beneath the mannerisms of the aesthetician was always the
moralist. His morality derived only in part from the New Testament writings, but it certainly gained strength from them. If we
seek its philosophical rather than its religious bases, one of these

may be Plato's hierarchy of ideal archetypes culminating in the absolute good, source of all true reality. For Arnold as for Plato evil has no place in the real.

There is something splendid about this doctrine of perfect understanding casting out fear. Arnold's great contemporary Dostoyevsky came at last to a similar view, set within the very different frame of Orthodox belief. He would have understood the instinct, at least, that prompted such an interpretation of Sophocles. Whether the playwright himself would have approved is another question. Of the seven works which time has spared, only his *Philoctetes* sounds a note of joyous affirmation. The *Oedipus Tyrannus* closes with a sombre reflection on the steep and ruinous fall from greatness, and the final lines of the *Women of Trachis* contain Hyllus' words as he thinks on his father's agonizing death and his mother's suicide: "There is nothing of this that is not Zeus."

One cannot simply write off an attitude that so honest a man as Matthew Arnold maintained both in public and in private. Many will feel compelled to dissent from it; yet it is worth trying to understand. According to Professor Trilling, when Keats equated beauty with truth he was referring to that beauty which emerges from the whole experience of man, evil as well as good, the harrowing together with the charming; there is room for a Lear, and for an Oedipus. Perhaps Arnold held such a view. If he did, it is not easily reconciled with his distaste for realism in writers of his own time. Their writing, he maintained, made the soul say, "You hurt me." [7] A critic thus predisposed does not display quite the ideal capacity for seeing Sophocles steadily and whole.

It would appear more likely that predispositions are at the heart of Arnold's attitude. He took a certain defensive pride in being unsystematic, but no critic can well do without principles and writers who exemplify them. For the most part Arnold criticized inductively. It was not usual for him to make an author conform to any critical pattern. When he tries Chaucer or Shelley in his balances and finds them wanting, what we regret is his failure to have on hand an accurate set of weights; his honesty does not come under suspicion. In the case of Sophocles, however, there is reason to suppose that wishful thinking shaded Arnold's judgment. He found the seven plays grand in style, high and serious in tone; any other considered verdict is difficult to imagine. But he also claimed to hear the note of moral joy, and this is debatable at best.

It does gain a measure of support from the ode to Colonus, so typically suggested in "To a Friend" as representative of Sophoclean feeling. In actual fact these lines are anything but representative. Together with the later portions of the *Philoctetes* they send out a fugitive and gracious light upon the stark outlines of the tragic thought. Arnold himself recognized the beauty of Sophocles' plays for what it was, a "severe beauty."

Probably Arnold's belief derives not from the Colonus ode but from the presuppositions mentioned earlier. As was the case with so many of his views, the seed of the idea was Victorian and had its nurture from the Victorian moral climate. Although he affected to ignore criticism he paid a good deal of attention to his reviewers, who deplored the absence of healthy moral tone and sound spirits from his early poems.[8] Besides this pressure is the fact of Schiller's presence in the 1853 Preface, with his doctrine that joy constitutes the highest end of art. Arnold used this as a key to the thought of Sophocles, and here he seems to have laid aside "touchstones" in favor of what might be termed the validation of a moral law. We must acknowledge finally the poetic and personal influence of Wordsworth. This is suggested most clearly by a comment of Empedocles, lines often called the most Wordsworthian in all of Arnold's verse: "We received the shock of mighty thoughts On simple minds with a pure natural joy."[9] His upbringing, the pressures of his age, and his enduring inner conflicts all predisposed Arnold to find in Sophocles qualities that were not necessarily there.

Many years later, when these pressures had ceased or had taken different forms, he made a passing reference to Greek tragedy in *God and the Bible*.[10] It was, he declared, grand but joyless. The establishing of contradictions is poor sport, however, and we may turn with greater pleasure to Arnold's inaugural lecture of 1857, "On the Modern Element in Literature." The peculiar characteristic of Sophocles' poetry, he says,

> is its consummate, its unrivalled *adequacy;* ... it represents the highly developed human nature of that age ... in its completest and most harmonious development in all these directions, [namely political, social, religious, and moral], while there is shed over this poetry the charm of that noble serenity which always accompanies true insight. ... In Sophocles there is the same energy, the same maturity, the same freedom, the same intelligent observation [as in the Athenians

generally]; but all these idealized and glorified by the grace and light shed over them from the noblest poetical feeling. And therefore I have ventured to say of Sophocles, that he "saw life steadily, and saw it whole."

In "The French Play in London" Arnold again seeks to make clear the "peculiar value" of tragedy:

> Only by breasting in full the storm and cloud of life, breasting it and passing through it and above it, can the dramatist who feels the weight of mortal things liberate himself from the pressure, and rise, as we all seek to rise, to content and joy. Tragedy breasts the pressure of life.

It would be useless to look for any consistent, evenly developing pattern in these various remarks.[11] The most that can be said is that they are differing embodiments of one central attitude. Arnold came to see an affirmative element in tragedy, especially in Sophocles, but he could never decide whether this affirmation was joy or contentment or merely serenity. Yet he was certain that it constituted a moral experience, and a number of his difficulties result from insisting on this as an article of faith.

Thinking along similar lines, Arnold declared that the special value of Sophocles lay in the fact that he was concerned with the question of how man should live. What regimen the Greek poet may have suggested Arnold does not say; but this omission is merely typical, and the question itself bears more importantly on our inquiry. It is by no means an absurd question to attribute to Sophocles, whose plays contain many passages that could be taken as answers. Nevertheless, its real significance lies in what it reveals about Arnold. The tenacity with which he makes moral demands of literature indicates that in certain respects his predispositions were not Hellenic. As for his failure to recognize the Sophoclean answers, this may come from a realization of their variousness. At any rate, to say that the ancients considered poetry a complete *magister vitae* is much easier than to illustrate the point through Sophocles.[12]

The problem is well displayed in the *Oedipus Tyrannus*. Its three main characters make very different demands upon life. Jocasta frankly lives from day to day, scorning any human intermediary between heaven and earth. Creon, delighted to have wealth and high position without responsibility, displays a general tolerance joined with conventional piety. Oedipus is driven on by his unresting intelligence from eminence to ruin, and in that ruin he achieves the realization of his full greatness. Meanwhile the chorus of Theban elders have warned against the fault of going too far which is *hubris*. They come finally to that famed counsel, "Call no man happy until he is dead." In the course of the play they, like other Sophoclean choruses, have concluded that man must walk in the middle way of moderation, though fate may strike him down notwithstanding.

Which of these masks conceals the poet himself? For decades a controversy over this question has engaged classical scholars. A few hold that Sophocles sought primarily to create effective works for the stage. Ethical and spiritual complexities, say others, were his true concern. According to one view the piety of the chorus is meant to be respected, though the poet is not doctrinally liable for everything his choruses say. A recent interpreter believes the true facts to be that the chorus cannot transcend the common level of moralizing; figures such as Oedipus and Antigone do transcend it, thereby heroically challenging the gods, and are crushed.[13] On this view Sophocles was a "heroic humanist." Arnold might well have put forward a similar interpretation, since he eventually reached rather similar conclusions about the contemporary religious dilemma of the masses and of the sensitive individual.

One who knew Attic tragedy only through Arnold's published prose might well doubt whether it asks any questions at all, whether Sophoclean drama contains uncertainty as well as affirmation. Although readers may grant Arnold his claim that it considers the problem of how to live, they also recognize the clear affirmative note sounding throughout his discussions in the essays. "Dover Beach," however, has the blurred tones of uncertainty. At least four or five passages in the plays of Sophocles picture human misery by sea imagery. Arnold's thought may have responded to any one of them, most notably the lyrics from the *Antigone*, or to a composite association in which they all figured. This type of image early became a commonplace of Greek poetry, for the Aegean and Mediterranean have always menaced those who must face them in small craft. Yet Arnold speaks of a "turbid ebb and flow" not to be found in any of the Sophoclean sources. It is a tidal image of slow, persistent recurrence, whereas in classical thought disaster strikes swiftly and is compared to a sudden overwhelming wave. Tragedy accordingly has neither time nor fitting place for any more leisured concept. It seems likely that

Arnold here is concerned not so much with a classical theme as with an interpretive concept familiar in his poetry and prose, the theme of systole and diastole.[14]

Quite apart from the question of origins, there arises the problem of how these lines characterize Sophocles. A lone figure on the beach who hears insistent rhythms of man's misery in the shifting tide, he suggests the age of Byron rather than of Pericles. This withdrawal—the wish to be an isolated observer—has its earliest source in Stoicism, but critics have rightly recognized it as a part of Arnold's Romantic instincts. Loneliness and the sea are already associated at the very beginning of Western literature, when the solitary Achilles walks by the waves' edge. It is the conscious finding of a meaning, "a thought," that stamps Arnold's lines with the tone of the early nineteenth century.[15] Granting at once their intrinsic excellence, we should not assume that they are designed to say anything significant about Sophocles. In "Mycerinus" Arnold, with a show of diffidence, added a moral dimension to Herodotus' straightforward narrative by crediting the doomed king with a possible secret Stoicism of ennobling and sustaining power. His use of antiquity in "Dover Beach" is not very different, so far as the nature of Sophocles is concerned.

What has been said thus far indicates that the problematical, questioning, unresolved aspects of Sophoclean tragedy received little or no attention from Arnold. One might indeed read the whole array of his poems, essays, and letters without ever coming to suspect their existence. This one-sidedness has helped to form a misleading impression. "Sophocles is no philosopher or speculator on the deeper problems of life; he accepts the conventional religion without criticism": the words might have come from Arnold's pen. Actually they are cited from a recent and widely used guide to classical literature. This estimate is more than a little surprising; few Sophoclean scholars would agree with it. The conflict of laws in the *Antigone* is one of the facts which demolish such a view; another is the maddening of Ajax by a malicious goddess, together with the whole matter of divine intervention; and we have noted that strange summing up by Hyllus, "There is nothing of this that is not Zeus." [16]

No one can be sure he has discerned the master view of things, both human and divine, which informs the seven plays of Sophocles. What matters here is Matthew Arnold never attempted to discern it. The reason for this omission is bound up with his whole approach to Greek tragedy, an approach which sought to confirm his own principles rather than to explore the drama. Obviously a critic can never be free from all preconceptions in judging a creative work: it is a matter of choice and of degree, and we have seen how Arnold's attempt was shaped. Consciously seeking an affirmative view, he had shut his mind almost wholly to elements that would disturb his scheme. "Dover Beach," which so often upsets generalizations on Arnold's work, proves that he could rise to an awareness that such elements exist; other signs are wanting. The figure which emerges at last is that of the sweet singer and model citizen of Periclean Athens, cheerfully serious, incomparably adequate.[17]

Taken within a religious context such a description can only be called secular, and more than anything else it is a kind of secularism that limits Arnold's comprehension of Sophocles. His early insistence on the supreme value of structure in literature and the civic enthusiasm which colors his later writing have one thing at least in common: neither leaves any place for considering what Greek tragedy has to say about man's relationship with the gods. Though a humanist may perhaps claim the right to ignore such speculations, he does so at his peril. It is possible to read all of Arnold's many references to Sophocles without ever having to consider the fact that Athenian drama was part of a state liturgy. The absence of this element does not seem a point of strength.[18]

We may properly recall also the narrowness which neo-classicism brought to the study of tragedy. Critics anatomized it with impressive thoroughness and quite forgot that it had been a living part of a unique period in history. Few would now rank De Quincey among the major English critics; yet he pointed out what the neoclassics had forgotten, that a literature cannot be separated from its epoch. As inspector of schools and light-bringer to the Philistines, Matthew Arnold was well aware of this truth, learned from his father. The teaching of classics in England might be less embattled today if his suggestions had been heeded. As poet and critic he ignored the relationship between a period and its literature again and again, and the results of this treatment become apparent in his fragmentary, essentially incoherent portrait of Sophocles.

It is an eclectic portrait, and eclecticism may describe Arnold's attitude better than any other term. Sophocles served him variously, meeting various needs. Master of dramatic construction, model of the grand style, unique epitome of Periclean Athens, at one time cheerfully serious, at another brooding over human misery—the poet appears before us in all these aspects. A little ingenuity could no doubt fit them together plausibly enough, but the effort would be misdirected. The unity they possess is subjective, to be judged in terms of Arnold's complex nature. Viewed thus Sophocles will appear less *in propria persona* than as a projection of certain doctrines and emotions.[19] His relevance to Periclean Athens may be limited; not so his relevance to Victorian England. Though Matthew Arnold's dealings with antiquity cannot go unchallenged, it should not be forgotten that he sought to make a living use of Sophocles.

The place of Aeschylus in Arnold's esteem was high and secure. We encounter him as one of the four leading names of the hundred-year period that ended with the Peloponnesian War; a writer who adequately represented and interpreted an age of obvious preëminence; a writer moreover of depth, completeness, and naturalness in thought as in feeling, with the architectonic power of execution that comes only from a deep grasp of life. The recurring cry of the chorus in his *Agamemnon*, "Let the good prevail," represented for Arnold the master-thought of Sophocles, Dante, and Shakespeare—though also of Rousseau and George Sand.[20]

With all his high and excellent qualities, Aeschylus was very seldom a moving force in Arnold's thought. The small number of references does not in itself show this. What does lend weight to the claim is their lack of substance. For the most part they are too brief to be penetrating, and one looks in vain for the personal concern that led Arnold to search Homer and Sophocles with such manifest seriousness.

The refrain of the *Agamemnon* offers an evident opportunity to strike deep. This plea that good may win out has its proper significance not in terms of the first play, which comes back ominously to the same theme in its concluding line, but in relation to the *Oresteia* as a whole. Here Arnold's failure to reckon with trilogy form keeps him from seeing the supreme element of Aeschylean *architectonicé*. Fortunately this fact has only a limited bearing on matters of strictly literary judgment, the province in which Arnold is always most at home; thus from the *Oresteia* and the *Prometheus Bound* he has combined two famous phrases with a brilliant stroke. "The doer of a deed must suffer for it" and the "numberless laughter" of the waves are alike interpretive, he tells us. They illustrate the two ways in which poetry interprets, namely "by expressing, with inspired conviction, the ideas and laws of the inward world of man's moral and spiritual nature," and "by expressing with magical felicity the physiognomy and movement of the outward world." [21] His analysis ignores the distinctive nature of poetry, but in certain respects it would make a promising approach to Aeschylus.

He did not develop such possibilities, however. The honored place that he assigned to Aeschylus was distant from the centers of his own thought, and the incidental, illustrative nature of the references results naturally. Whatever value these may possess in themselves, they are used for the background of comparison. Apparently a closer relationship was impossible for Arnold. He ignored not only trilogy form but the social and religious conceptions which cannot be dissociated from it, least of all in the case of the *Oresteia*. To pass by these elements is to limit seriously the possibility of understanding Aeschylus, a difficult task under the best of circumstances.

It may be doubted whether Arnold sought such understanding. One who could dismiss the clash between Creon and Antigone as meaningless to modern man lacked inner access to Aeschylus' pondering of the ways of justice in heaven and earth. Again, Arnold's ideal in character portrayal was Sophoclean, the triumph of inwardness. Aeschylus sends his thought along other paths. Persuaded of a theocentric universe, he searches the personality of an Agamemnon, even a Clytemnestra, less deeply than the nature of superhuman beings—Zeus, Prometheus, the Furies—or of sin and its punishment. *Merope*, which will be discussed later in the present chapter, shows that this direction of inquiry had no meaning for Arnold.

Like Pindar, Aeschylus belongs to the first half of the fifth century, not to the succeeding generation which we term the Periclean age. It was this later period, the time of Sophocles and Aristophanes and Socrates, which moved Matthew Arnold's thought as no other age but his own had the power to do. His humanism was too discreetly modulated for any such Promethean outburst as Shelley's, and he had been born too early in his century to bow before the twin determinist Fates of heredity and environment honored in Eugene O'Neill's New England Oresteia. Working from an Aeschylean prototype, T. S. Eliot has dealt in *The Family Reunion* with the feelings of estrangement that haunt modern man like the Furies who avenged blood-guilt; such symbolic treatment Arnold declared to be anathema. Aeschylus did not speak to his condition, and it is only by doing this that any ancient writer can have true and meaningful influence.

Arnold gives Sophocles a place of high importance and shows

Aeschylus respect; Euripides he ignores. The absence of all mention from his published works and correspondence forms one of Arnold's strangest omissions. The balance is not adjusted by his entering a scant half-dozen Euripidean lines in the note-books. It does begin to alter, however, when one sees how regularly Euripides figures in the yearly or monthly lists of proposed reading. It is frequently impossible to know whether a given entry represents anything more than good intentions, particularly in the early years. Still, the final impression is that of a man who knew Euripidean drama more than casually and perhaps as well as he knew the work of Aeschylus. If the impression is valid, his silence calls for some explanation. We may ask, for example, why in his lecture "On the Modern Element in Literature" Arnold should have passed over Euripides when he was attempting to show the genuine modernity of classical poetry.

Possibly the answer lies in this same essay. As the conditions under which an "intellectual deliverance" becomes possible, Arnold postulates two things: "a significant, a highly developed, a culminating epoch" and "a comprehensive, a commensurate, an adequate literature." [22] On neither count was it possible to discuss Euripides. He stood apart from the civic life of Athens as neither Aeschylus nor Sophocles had done, and his work betrays a profound dissatisfaction with the accepted attitudes. To accuse Arnold of blackballing any writer who fails to champion the Periclean *status quo* would be unfair; his attitude is hardly so reactionary. It turns in fact upon the conviction that a genuinely comprehensive, commensurate, and adequate view of life will produce an attitude of "serious cheerfulness." Sophocles, we recall, was chosen as the supreme embodiment of this truth. Concerning Aeschylus, who had been coupled with Sophocles in the preceding sentence, we now find only a discreet silence.[23] How impossible a writer Euripides must have seemed, measured against such demands! The man was greater than the measure: one could wish to hear Arnold explaining why *The Trojan Women*, that terrible indictment of war's brutality, should be thought inadequate.

There can be no doubt, nevertheless, that Euripides was useless for Arnold's special purposes. Presumably it was no disqualification to have outlived the greatness of Athens. This was still more true of Aristophanes, yet Arnold found him to be fundamentally serious and took his "geniality" as a natural consequence of that *summum bonum*, adequacy. What made Euripides useless was the evident anomaly of his relationship to later fifth-century

Athens. Since he was not classical according to Arnold's accepta-
tion of that term, he could not receive canonical status. Because
this unsatisfactoriness was not discussed, we have missed what
would surely have been a worthy companion piece to the characterizations of Lucretius and Horace. Euripides may have been
too much like Arnold himself: troubled by the world, impatient
with the traditional limits of expression, reaching beyond them
towards the romantic where a portion of his spirit found its home.
It is possible that in these respects his tragedies were a silent force,
unacknowledged but more effectual than we can know.

Paradoxically, it was a lost play of Euripides that served as
the basis for *Merope*, published in 1858. The idea of writing an
original tragedy in the Greek manner had been with Arnold for
at least nine years. In a letter of early 1849 he speaks of "a tragedy
I have long had in my head" and adds, "I shall . . . try to get on
with my tragedy (Merope), which however will not be a very
quick affair." The prophecy proved true enough, but he perse-
vered. The 1853 Preface brackets the character of Merope with
those of Orestes and Alcmaeon, and within another five years the
work is done.[24]

Contemporary opinion was less than kind. Although *Merope*
found a friend here and there, most critics viewed it as Sainte-
Beuve did the *Argonautica: savant et mort*, learned and lifeless.
The passage of a century has confirmed the judgment. One or two
enthusiasts have praised the poem unrestrainedly, but all that can
honestly be said in its favor has been said by the authors of the
Commentary. Even this temperate summary records and analyzes
Merope's failure on many important counts, leaving no doubt
what the final verdict must be.

Several scholars have already discussed the poem so painstak-
ingly that any new attempt to examine it in detail must proceed
under restrictions. It occupies a unique place among Arnold's
works, moreover, for it represents an effort not to create but to
recreate. The result, if not the goal itself, is antiquarianism. Readers cannot hope to find vital attitudes set forth; the whole question
of Hellenic influence becomes meaningless here. Two things do
emerge from a study of *Merope:* its author's temperament and
his conception of Greek tragedy. Regarding the first we shall
have little to say; the second will be considered in detail.

Zealous for precedents and documentation, Arnold thought
it great good fortune that Euripides had written a lost *Cresphontes*,
of which some fifty verses were extant. Antiquity had thus set

the seal of approval upon the theme, or "action," of a tragedy in which the widow of the murdered Cresphontes figured importantly. Hyginus and Apollodorus had preserved the story: Merope, queen of Messenia, is forced to marry her husband's murderer, the usurper Polyphontes, but she manages to send away her infant son Aepytus. When he has grown to manhood he returns in disguise, seeking revenge. His story that the child of Cresphontes and Merope has been slain deceives not only Polyphontes but Merope herself, who imagines that this young stranger contrived her son's death. She enters the guest-chamber with an axe and is about to strike when an old retainer, formerly her secret messenger to Aepytus, recognizes him and averts disaster. Aepytus kills Polyphontes at a sacrifice of thanksgiving for his own supposed death; he then assumes his rightful place as king of Messenia.

The story bears certain resemblances to the *Electra* of Sophocles, especially in its final developments, and Arnold takes this play as his model. Following Aristotle's precepts, he endows Polyphontes with a measure of nobility; he further presents him as the unsuccessful suitor for Merope's hand rather than her second husband. Much is made of the climactic guest-chamber scene, which Aristotle praised for its great effect upon the Athenian audience.

Certain dangers inherent in Arnold's approach are already evident. He seems never to have considered the point that the extant dramas which Euripides staged as *tragôidiai* fall into a number of categories, generally distinct and sometimes strikingly dissimilar. We cannot know what type of treatment characterized the *Cresphontes*, though we may guess at some combination of the style of melodrama with the thesis of revenge tragedy. Certainly it would not be just to censure Arnold for his lack of interest in this question. His choice of Sophoclean treatment for a Euripidean theme is another matter. The two Electra plays show how differently these poets could present the same story, and to judge from Sophocles' extant plays the near murder of Aepytus by his mother makes sense only as a Euripidean device. Finally, the *Electra* was a singularly dangerous model. For contemporary critics of Greek tragedy it has proved the most difficult of Sophocles' works to interpret. Victorian opinion, by contrast, remained serenely assured about the propriety of the revenge killings and managed to discern an atmosphere of good spirits; [25] but this does not mean the problems they ignored were nonexistent.

Given these facts, one might expect *Merope* to be a pastiche.

In a sense it is, since its materials derive at various times from all three of the great Athenian dramatists.[26] Such a compilation runs the risk of having no character of its own, a risk Arnold sought to avoid by aiming at a Sophoclean tone. This meant concentrating on character, and he did so; but he failed to give his protagonists the inner strength that drives an Oedipus or an Antigone. To take the most relevant example of all, the Electra who lives for vengeance is replaced by a Merope who doubts and hesitates and counts the forces of conscience "the true avengers" (559–61). Aepytus, briskly confident that his plan of murder is righteous, shows far greater resoluteness. He does not, however, parallel the Sophoclean Orestes. The latter is clearly weaker than Electra; and so he must be, if the drama is to center upon her. Finally, Polyphontes stands (152) "upon the threshold of old age," afraid of becoming a tyrant, yet voicing a tyrant's threats in his final speech. His character is more complex than Merope's and more interesting. Though Arnold became aware of this, apparently it was not what he had intended. All these facts combine to make the scheme of relationships among the three main characters a different one from any to be found in Sophocles.[27]

The protagonists, moreover, uniformly lack the breadth of spirit and intense dedication that mark a heroic nature: they are closer to Prufrock than to Oedipus. It is essentially because of this that the tone of *Merope* so often proves to be Euripidean.[28] In Euripides mediocrity does not bar such characters from tragic experience if the situation allows some destructive impulse to have free play, shattering the group (Arnold's conception of course leaves no room for this). With Sophocles it is otherwise. Of him we may say what cannot be said of either Euripides or Aeschylus, that the tragic condition is inseparable from the heroic nature. For this reason *Merope* does not and cannot embody the Sophoclean view of tragedy, no matter what side we take in the continuing dispute regarding the nature of that view.

It does embody morality, to be sure. The ways in which it does so show how far Arnold had gone along his own path, ignoring not only Sophocles but Aristotle. His delicacy of feeling in setting aside the mythographer's tradition that Merope had married Polyphontes caused the introduction of a subplot: the slayer vainly courts his victim's widow. The device is as alien to Greek tragedy, in its different way, as the opening scene of the *Comedy of Errors* is to Roman comedy; but Shakespeare, unlike Arnold, did not claim to be reproducing classical form. As for Merope's belief that conscience is the true agent of punishment, this accords well enough with the unimportance of the gods in *Merope;* it has no relation to the dramatic world of Sophocles, where divine and human action often appear to be synchronized in a fateful relationship. One seems rather to have entered a quasi-Shakespearean world little concerned with the actions of divinity, a world which echoes the pleading of a Gertrude and the moralizing of a Polonius.[29]

No tragic poem thus conceived can become Sophoclean. The most painstaking structural archaizing will not achieve this, for such measures do not go deep enough. Arnold reproduced the formal divisions and subdivisions of his model, but he failed to provide, first of all, the unity Aristotle considered essential. In the choruses he sought to make antistrophe match strophe, and he devised lyric metres which he believed had an effect comparable with that of the Greek prototypes. Unfortunately his responsion proved decidedly erratic. Even Churton Collins, the devoted editor of *Merope,* sometimes admits defeat in his efforts to work out the metrical patterns.[30] The schemes he does set forth, moreover, contain a wealth of false quantities. Despite Arnold's claim, the metres themselves are modeled on Sophoclean rhythms.[31] Had they either followed the originals without compromise or else struck out on new paths, the result might have been happier; avoiding the issue was not a solution.

For Matthew Arnold, however, the most valuable quality in Sophocles was the "grand moral effect" of the poet's style. This he sought to reproduce by careful borrowings, by turn of phrase in discourse and dialogue, by any effect that might capture something of grandeur. Seeking elevation, he ended all too often by becoming stilted. The compound epithets that he was to bar from translations of Homer are here in full force. Sometimes the effect is that of the schoolboy's interlinear companion; on a few occasions the poem seems to be trying to parody itself. Syntax and diction twist into strange paths from time to time and take on a Latinate air or a pre-Elizabethan antiquity.[32]

These are matters of style in the narrow sense. The larger meaning of style extended for Arnold as far as the writer's whole nature, and in this instance he himself is the writer. The derivative nature of his poetic material repeatedly prevented him from speaking either in his own tones or with anything like the authentic note of Sophocles. Thus Merope's preoccupation with the power of an ancestral curse has no proper ancient source except

Aeschylus, while the lengthy speech-making about politics or psychology strangely combines Euripides and Matthew Arnold without being representative of either. Only once, perhaps, do we hear (177–80) the true, full note of Arnoldian melancholy:

> O Merope, how many noble thoughts,
> How many precious feelings of man's heart,
> How many loves, how many gratitudes,
> Do twenty years wear out, and see expire! [33]

Merope does not wholly lack virtues. There are passages of noble speech and vivid natural description, neither in the Sophoclean manner; a natural hesitancy about the widowed queen faintly recalls Deianeira in *The Women of Trachis;* [34] the choric prayer for peace in a surviving fragment of Euripides' *Cresphontes* has suggested a leitmotif which Arnold uses skillfully and with suitable irony. But the poem is assembled rather than created, so that it has no vital center, and in a number of important respects it is badly assembled.[35] From this laborious composite there emerges little that anyone would now acknowledge as Sophoclean. Possibly the chief service *Merope* can render is to put us on our guard against the common view of its author as a reliable interpreter of Sophocles and Athenian tragedy.[36]

VII

Gnomic and Lyric; Comedy, History, and Philosophy

During the fall of 1854 Arnold wrote to his wife that he had thought to refresh his mind by reading Kingsley's novel *Hypatia:* "That did not comfort me much, and I betook myself to Hesiod, a Greek friend I had with me, with excellent effect." There is no more winning reference to a classical author in the whole of Arnold's writings; one regrets that so little else was said about him. Despite a gnarled style, Hesiod offers vivid and charming moments that are uniquely his own. No other Greek writer has so well given us the chill of winter—the days with a cutting wind that "would flay the hide from an ox," when "the boneless one (the octopus) gnaws his foot" within the dark sea-cave and "the tender maiden, untaught in the ways of Aphrodite, sits warm by the fire." [1]

Even these few phrases reveal Hesiod as a countryman. He might be called the farmer's poet; actually he has a much better claim to the title than does his more famous imitator Vergil, a greater poet but not so close to the earth. It was the flinty earth of Boeotia that afforded Hesiod such a living as he could get, and the leanness of a poor farmer's life gives his verse its strength together with its bitterness. Such is the background to be remembered when we read in the 1853 Preface that "The Muses, as Hesiod says, were born that they might be 'a forgetfulness of evils, and a truce from cares.'" [2]

Many years pass before Arnold speaks of him again: we come to the period of religious essays that Saintsbury describes under the deadly chapter heading "In the Wilderness." "The influence which visited Hesiod," Arnold begins, "was a *real* one." Thus far, good; but he continues:

The spiritual visitant, indeed, which rejoiced the wise poet of Ascra, was not the Paraclete of Jesus. No, it was the Muse of art and science, the Muse of the gifted few, the Muse who brings to the ingenious and learned among mankind [relief from care]. The Paraclete that Jesus promised, on the other hand, was the Muse of *righteousness;* the Muse of the work-day, care-crossed, toil-stained millions of men,—the Muse of humanity.... That is why it is far more real, and far greater, than the Muse of Hesiod.[3]

He has forgotten the background, or ignored it, and thereby falsified half of his contrast. It is by no means the only instance of a curious handling of classical literature to occur in the theological works, but it provides the most striking example of an injustice. Hesiod is surely one of the most work-day, care-crossed, toil-stained figures in the whole of literature. Without any desire to be unjust, Arnold presents the details of his contrast precisely as they appear to him at the time of writing, colored not by con-scious design but by the demands of theme and temperament. Here Hesiod serves to illustrate an isolated point in *Literature and Dogma;* a study of the poet for his own sake might have produced different results.

It is not surprising that such a study never was undertaken. Hesiod, like Euripides, would have disturbed the proportions of Arnold's carefully adjusted classical panorama. The Hesiodic age was probably three centuries earlier than the age of Pericles, and it manifestly lacked the significant, culminating qualities that Arnold demanded of any period capable of producing great litera-ture. Hesiod himself is not notable for an impressive style, nor does his thought bear any strong stamp of moral nobility. For Arnold's purposes, in short, he will not do. A line or two about the Muses can be made to assort interestingly with Schiller and the third Person of the Trinity; the rest must be silence.[4]

In Arnold's ranking of the great poets, Pindar's place is not only assured but unexpectedly high. He appears as one of the four great names of the period between 530 and 430 B.C., which merely recognizes the obvious. To call him one of the "eminent masters of style" would be equally a truism, except that Vergil, Dante, and Milton are the only others so described. Pindar thus is more than canonical: he is one of the chief figures in world literature. Like Aeschylus and Sophocles, moreover, he contains thoughts as religious as those of Job or Isaiah, and like Socrates and Plato he shows a lofty concern with moral ideas. Once again in company with Aeschylus and Sophocles, he adequately interprets and represents his age.[5] These various claims are typical of a great many generic statements in which Arnold is stating something about a group of writers rather than concentrating on any individual. Such remarks are not to be pressed closely.

In much the same way, "A Speech at Eton" cites Pindar as one among many who used the terms around which Arnold's discussion is organized.[6] Here, however, we see the poet as more than the shadow of a mighty name. Of the command "Know thyself" Arnold says, "The words written up on the temple at Delphi called all comers to *soberness and righteousness*. The Doric and Aeolic Pindar felt profoundly this severe influence of Delphi." [7] The interpretation of the Delphic inscription comes from a minor dialogue attributed to Plato. It has often been overlooked in the many wilful renderings of this famous phrase, and Arnold deserves full marks for basing his judgment so soundly. Furthermore, the conjecture of Delphic influence—typically presented as fact—brings out an important side of the poet's nature.

Such a remark can be understood within the frame of reference provided by Greek religion. This is no longer possible when Arnold speaks of "the highest art, the art which by its height, depth, and gravity possesses religiousness,—such as the Greeks had, the art of Pindar and Phidias." The words embody both the breadth and the limitations of his concept of the religious, and we see his recurring tendency to interpret such matters in terms of style. The conscious linking of these two factors appears in a notable sentence from *On the Study of Celtic Literature:* "Style, in my sense of the word, is a peculiar recasting and heightening, under a certain condition of spiritual excitement, of what a man has to say, in such a manner as to add dignity and distinction to it." [8]

From this same work comes the choice of Pindar, Vergil, Dante, and Milton as "the eminent masters of style." The only Greek poet in the list is not likely to have been chosen at random. The larger context in fact suggests a reasoned choice, for we read shortly afterwards that "it is the simple passages in poets like Pindar or Dante which are perfect, being masterpieces of poetical simplicity." This happily describes such moments in the victory odes as that when the poet declares his intention to be great in great things and small in small. The most striking comment of all comes when Arnold says that Celtic poetry "has all through it a

sort of intoxication of style,—a *Pindarism*, to use a word formed
from the name of the poet, on whom, above all other poets, the
power of style seems to have exercised an inspiring and intoxicating effect." [9]

There is no fresh insight here, only the traditional view which
for more than two centuries had underlain varied and variously
successful attempts to write Pindaric odes. But Arnold was writing
for a new age with new aims in poetry, and it was perhaps needful
that Pindar's greatness should be recalled. The sum total of his
remarks might fittingly have been rather larger than it was, considering the rank he gave to this greatest of Greek lyric poets.[10]
What he did say was well said in most respects; few classical
authors have received juster treatment at his hands.

"There is a comic side from which to regard humanity as
well as a tragic one," Arnold declared;

> and the distinction of Aristophanes is to have regarded it from
> a true point of view on the comic side. He too, like Sophocles,
> regards the human nature of his time in its fullest develop-
> ment . . . : politics, education, social life, literature—all of the
> great modes in which the human life of his day manifested
> itself—are his subjects. . . . There is shed, therefore, over his
> poetry the charm, the vital freshness, which is felt when man
> and his relations are from any side adequately, and therefore
> genially, regarded.

These words from "On the Modern Element in Literature" [11] are
all that Arnold has given us about Aristophanes, and they are
concerned not so much with the poet as with the critic's own
views on standards of greatness in poetry. This may be their real
strength. The reader is given a perspective, encouraged to see
Aristophanes in the fifth-century setting that gives particular
meaning to him no less than to Sophocles.

When Arnold thus associates the masters of comedy and
tragedy he is leaving partly unexpressed the fundamental quality
of seriousness common to both. At one point in the full text of the
passage cited above, he maintains that a serious basis always
underlies Aristophanes' humor. Some pages later the full nature of
the comparison appears when he denies to Vergil "the serious
cheerfulness of Sophocles, of a man who has mastered the problem
of human life, who knows its gravity, and is therefore serious, but
knows that he comprehends it, and is therefore cheerful." While
one may well object to this interpretation of Sophocles, it is

possible to admire the attempt to find the common element uniting two great literary masters of a profoundly significant era. Whatever should be said of Sophocles, moreover, it is true of Aristophanes that he saw not deep but wide; and Arnold compels awareness that the comedies were written out of something more than a mere desire to amuse. During the present century scholars have stressed their nature as social commentary. This development accords with Arnold's attitude, although the excesses of the movement would have shocked him profoundly.

It is a little surprising that the frequent obscenity of Aristophanic comedy does not seem to have disturbed Arnold's chaste moral sense or qualified his literary verdict. His father, Dean Stanley tells us, never could wholly reconcile himself to the plays because of this element, despite his delight in their beauty.[12] But the actions and words that shelter under the broad term obscenity are of two very different kinds, as we know: they may either affirm or deny the richness of life. The one attitude manifests the mind's essential health; the other, its deep sickness. Aristophanes is unquestionably among the healthy who affirm, and in this matter Matthew Arnold may well have seen the truth more clearly than his father did. Certainty is hardly possible here, since Arnold, unlike Ruskin, never felt compelled to deal publicly with the relation of such problems to artistic morality.

Following the discussion of Aristophanes in "On the Modern Element in Literature," and linked closely with it, is the passage describing Menander. Twenty years later Arnold was to call him "a consummate critic of life" in the essay "Equality," which takes its very title from one of Menander's *sententiae* or moral sayings; until the twentieth-century discoveries and rediscoveries, these aphorisms were the only known remains of his comedies. The inaugural lecture itself, however, sounds a very different note:

> Between the times of Sophocles and Menander a great check had befallen the development of Greece.... It is Athens after this check, after this diminution of vitality,—it is man with part of his life shorn away, refined and intelligent indeed, but sceptical, frivolous, and dissolute,—which the poetry of Menander represented.... The instinct of humanity taught it, that in the one poetry [that of Aristophanes] there was the seed of life, in the other poetry the seed of death; and it has rescued Aristophanes, while it has left Menander to his fate.... If human life were complete without

faith, without enthusiasm, without energy, Horace, like Menander, would be the perfect interpreter of human life: but it is not. . . .

Only one passage of purely literary criticism can be set against this moral judgment. The simplicity of Menander's style is that of prose rather than of great poetry, Arnold maintains, and he sees in Goethe's style a like quality; "but Menander does not belong to a great poetical moment, he comes too late for it." [13]

The most immediate limitation of this estimate lies in the fact mentioned earlier, that the connected portions of Menander's surviving plays have come to us in papyrus manuscripts and fragments undiscovered or unheeded before the present century. Remarkable discoveries have been made even within the last few years. Arnold could hardly have been expected to see into the future; yet it is not evident that he walked altogether wisely, even by the limited light that was available.[14] He might have pondered the negligible influence of Aristophanes upon later literature of the first rank, compared with Menander's astonishing legacy. In this respect there can be no question which of the two poets has proved to contain "the seed of life." But the classical heritage as a process of historical transmission never held any interest for Arnold. According to his diagnosis, what the Victorian age needed was to come as nearly as possible into direct contact with the age of Pericles; intermediate influences could only be in the way.

We could wish, finally, that Arnold had sketched in a portion of the Periclean background and also given some idea of Athens in the late fourth century before he permitted "On the Modern Element in Literature" to appear in published form. Unlike the Oxford undergraduates who heard it as a public lecture in 1857, not all readers can have known beforehand that Aristophanic Old Comedy spoke with a public voice, Menandrian New Comedy with a private one; that the former presented individuals caught up in matters that concerned the state while the latter is peopled with stock types, individualized by Menander's genius, who expend their energies on domestic intrigue. Through indirect evidence these points had long been familiar to the scholarly world.

The strength of Arnold's estimate derives partly from the acuteness of his reactions to style. A very little reading of Menander's aphorisms demonstrates the stylistic simplicity imputed to him, the elegant and smoothly slipping verse that would very possibly have impressed Arnold as presenting man "with part of his life shorn away." In this phrase the Menandrian portrait is implicitly contrasted with the fully rounded, adequate representation of life given by Aristophanes and Sophocles. It is likely that Arnold has the same contrast in mind when, several pages later, he indicts Menander along with Horace for a lack of faith, enthusiasm, and energy. Taken in themselves the charges would be too severe; and recent discoveries, such as that of the almost complete *Dyscolus*, show that they are surprisingly wide of the mark. Like Jane Austen, Menander accomplishes superbly what he undertakes to do; but the range of human activities that each claims is deliberately limited. Arnold could never accept either one as an artist.

He might have been expected to set a disproportionate value on the didactic element in Menander, and his failure to do so may seem inconsistent with the large number of Menandrian *sententiae* copied in the notebooks. No real contradiction exists, however. It is a case of keeping private preferences strictly apart from literary criticism. "A large sense," he says, "is ... to be given to the term *moral*": thus "For ever wilt thou love, and she be fair" and "We are such stuff as dreams are made on" express moral ideas.[15] Though he never fully works out this position, it may be present in the estimate of Menander's worth.

Dr. Arnold had valued the historians of fifth-century Greece considerably above its poets; his eldest son held quite the reverse view. Throughout the published prose works and correspondence Herodotus makes four appearances in all.[16] Only one of them comes from Matthew Arnold's early life, and it shows the grounds for this continuing difference of opinion with his father. Writing to Clough in 1848 he says, "The difference between Herodotus and Sophocles is that the former sought all over the world's surface for the interest the latter found within men." In other words, as H. F. Lowry has noted here, the historian's survey of all action is less revealing than the tragic writer's insight into a single individual. Except for "Mycerinus" and an illustrative passage or two in *God and the Bible*, Arnold could make no use of Herodotus; his lifelong interests lay elsewhere.

With Thucydides, a more compressed and less objective writer, the case stands otherwise. Here was one who "applauded clear and fearless thinking, ... the resolute bringing of our actions to the rule of reason." To Arnold this is the true critical approach, and in Thucydides' words on the search for truth he discerns the modern note of a Burke or a Niebuhr assigning the real aim of historical inquiry. And yet, he continues, "Thucydides is no mere literary man" but "a man of action, a man of the world, a man of his time. He represents, at its best indeed, but he represents, the general intelligence of his age and nation." [17] We have found the same claim of representativeness made for Sophocles. In Arnold's eyes this quality had utmost importance: it is one of two chief reasons for praising Thucydides so highly. The other is his conviction that the Thucydidean view attempts to see "things in themselves as they really are." While the point is debatable, he did not question its truth.

Once again, as in the case of Aeschylus, he worships at a distance. Probably it is not exaggerating to say that the narrative of Thucydides had formed the center of his father's intellectual experience; he himself remained uninvolved. A great historian can show us what critical honesty means, but it is not his business to provide moral insights into the individual, and these alone could permanently hold Arnold's attention.

Critics have not failed to note Arnold's general dislike of philosophy, an attitude frankly acknowledged in his writings. It seems rather surprising, accordingly, that the classical author mentioned in them most frequently is Plato. There is no very great significance, to be sure, in the fact that Arnold places him among the "greatest and best Hellenic souls" and considers him one of those persons whose excellence, almost ideal along certain lines, makes them worthy spokesmen for man. These generalized eulogies occur all too frequently in Arnold's public utterance. By contrast, he indirectly reveals a part of his outlook when he writes to his mother (always treated as his confidante and intellectual equal) that Schleiermacher saw "really much more of Plato and Socrates than of Joshua and David" in Western Christianity. He goes on to say that his father had worked in a similar direction of belief; the tone of the context strongly suggests that he is thinking of himself as well.[18]

The way in which Arnold's genuinely unsystematic and unphilosophical attitude relates to a deep concern with Plato begins to reveal itself in his choice of quotations from Joubert. The following description, he thinks, has never been surpassed:

> Plato shows us nothing, but he brings brightness with him; he puts light into our eyes, and fills us with a clearness

by which all objects afterwards become illuminated. He teaches us nothing; but he prepares us, fashions us, and makes us ready to know all. Somehow or other, the habit of reading him augments in us the capacity for discerning and entertaining whatever fine truths may afterwards present themselves. Like mountain-air, it sharpens our organs, and gives us an appetite for wholesome foods.

Arnold's reservations are well expressed through a second quotation: "It is good to breathe his air, but not to live upon him." [19] The insights, the bracing clarity are what matter; the philosophical scheme is unimportant.

One might not guess from Joubert's tribute that the dialogues amount to more than a propaideutic. Arnold acknowledges their status as literature. Their form and treatment hold for him a dignity, an exquisiteness and charm unique among the works of philosophy; their style has a "varied cadence and subtle ease" that can only come from powerful, widely ranging thought. But, as always, the intellectual element receives less than its due. When Arnold calls Plato "at once a great literary man and a great philosopher" we know where he has his eye; and though he at once concedes the charm of the dialogues, in the same breath he denies "solidity" to them and even states that their theories are offered more in play than in earnest.[20] Despite his preoccupation with style he could never finally decide how it relates to content, nor yet how the element of form that he calls *architectonicé* fits into their relationship. The critical problem posed by a writer like Plato inevitably reveals this failure to arrive at satisfactory criteria.

At some point every student of the dialogues encounters the so-called "Socratic problem," in which the portrait given by Plato is matched against Xenophon's personal reminiscences in the *Memorabilia*. Few classical scholars have been persuaded to a belief in the Xenophontic Socrates. He seems as dull as his creator, offering sound, practical advice on every sort of problem to anyone who came along. It is this figure, however, whom Arnold rather uncertainly embraces. We are justified in speaking of uncertainty. "The true Socrates of the *Memorabilia*" who appears in *Culture and Anarchy* will not do for *Literature and Dogma*:

> Plato sophisticates somewhat the genuine Socrates; but it is very doubtful whether the culture and mental energy of Plato did not give him a more adequate vision of this true Socrates than Xenophon had.

A third statement shows that Arnold was confused in his facts even before *Culture and Anarchy*. The essay "Democracy," written in 1861, claims that Athenian shopkeepers and tradesmen took part in "the conversations recorded by Plato, or even by the matter-of-fact Xenophon." [21] It is true of the *Memorabilia* but untrue of the dialogues. Characteristically, Arnold was trying to support a dangerous generalization, in this case a claim that the middle and lower classes in ancient Athens achieved an unsurpassed development of their humanity. One can imagine no Hellenic author more eloquent in maintaining precisely the opposite view than Plato, aristocrat and reactionary.

Arnold's own portrait of Socrates proves to be surprisingly rewarding. He presents a man so filled with the new spirit of inquiry as to gain the name of Sophist, but actually seeking above all to recover "that firm foundation for human life, which a misuse of the new intellectual spirit was rendering impossible." Here was one who kept apart from the claptrap of current politics, yet called himself the only true politician alive—and rightly, for the actual politicians never sought, as he did, to show men the true nature of their condition. Plato himself, says Arnold in a letter, would have been less perfect had he not remained aloof from politics. As for the results of Socrates' efforts, they benefited the Athenians little. it is "for after times, and for the world" that they have proved so valuable. If he fails to inspire the love that Jesus calls forth, he has at least the inspiration of reason and conscience to offer. Besides,

> does not every man carry about with him a possible Socrates, in that power of a disinterested play of consciousness upon his stock notions and habits, of which this wise and admirable man gave all through his lifetime the great example, and which was the secret of his incomparable influence? [22]

To Arnold the political and social aspects of Platonic thought mattered only as they could be used to illustrate like aspects of his own time.[23] Audiences during the American tours may not have been altogether delighted by his reminder that Plato's gloomy picture of democratic Athens was justified, that "the majority were bad, and the remnant were impotent." It was nevertheless a natural part of the continuing attack on what he saw as menaces to the inner life of the two great nineteenth-century democracies. At home his paramount concern was for the middle class, which reminded him alarmingly of a "strong and

enormous creature . . . , surrounded by obsequious people seeking
to understand what its noises mean, and to make in their turn the
noises which may please it." Here Plato's image of the Athenian
masses recurs with powerful effect. On the other hand, when
Arnold describes the power-seeking portion of the middle class as
"wholly occupied, according to Plato's subtle expression, with the
things of itself and not its real self," he is adapting a philosophic
concept to political ends. In this instance he achieves neither power
nor clarity.[24]

Apart from direct quotations, the dialogues seem at times to
be echoing in Arnold's thoughts as he writes. This will become
more apparent in connection with education, but the field of
politics offers two possible instances. When he warns that "the
absence of the discipline of respect . . . a false smartness, a false
audacity" may threaten American democracy, his words recall
the indictment of *dêmokratia* in the *Republic*. For Plato the meaning of this term was rule by the masses (*dêmos*); it had strongly
unfavorable overtones. It is of some interest, therefore, that
Culture and Anarchy distinguishes "democracy" from "middle
class" and seems to make it identical with *dêmos*. Moreover,
Arnold classified the English in three groups, Barbarians, Philistines, and Populace. The latter are the unregarded masses of the
dêmos, in Roman terms not the *populus* but the *plebs*.[25]

"Literature and Science" shrewdly defends the ideals of
Platonic education. Arnold dismisses their historical setting as "a
primitive and obsolete order of things," but he seeks to show that
this setting cannot delimit them. His Platonic apologia thereby
turns into an implicit defense of the British school system, which
he may idealize for the moment. The defense itself embodies
realism as well as idealism:

> Education, many people . . . say, is still mainly governed
> by the ideas of men like Plato. . . . It is an education fitted for
> persons of leisure in such a community [as his]. . . . And how
> absurd it is, people end by saying, to inflict this education
> upon an industrious modern community!

Arnold knows that the shape of the world has changed. What he
does not believe for one moment is that Plato's paideutic aims have
become less valuable. As he sees it, "profound truth" marks the
claim that if thinking is to be useful it must be synoptic, capable
of dealing with a variety of factors simultaneously. The real
point, however, lies in the moral attitude underlying all that Plato

says. It is upon this that Arnold bases his reply to those who would abolish classical education:

> "An intelligent man," says Plato, "will prize those studies which result in his soul getting soberness, righteousness, and wisdom, and will less value the others." I cannot consider *that* a bad description of the aim of education.[26]

These ethical rewards, Arnold maintained, are essential for the spirit; and they will not come through science alone. Literature, and classical literature above all, brings them to us. The nineteenth century was highly content with them, although in Plato's own view they did not qualify a man to enter into the nature of divinity; this highest of all virtues is attained through pure intelligence, and thus reserved for such as love the things of the mind.[27] While Arnold recognized this, he saw also that in his own time the battle had to be fought on the level of moral virtues, a lower level from the Platonic and Aristotelian standpoint. It was a lasting belief. The voice that had spoken of the balance between literature and science in *Essays in Criticism* can still be heard beneath Jowett's claim, quoted in *Last Essays,* that moral and intellectual must reunite and in their highest conception are inseparable.[28]

One of the better-known passages of the *Republic* speaks of young men breathing in wholesome influences of right conduct from a proper educational environment. We can hardly doubt that Arnold, with his intense moral preoccupations, has this in mind when he argues for state-controlled schools of a national character. These, he maintains, would give the middle class the great advantage of "breathing in their youth the air of the best culture of their nation," an educational influence of supreme value. Elsewhere he says that in the "bracing air of the old religion of Delphi" the Athenians "imbibed influences of character and steadiness." [29]

Between education in its broader, Hellenic sense and conduct there is so intimate a connection that often the two cannot be kept separate. Arnold actually uses one to define the other, with the help of a major dialogue: "When Protagoras points out of what things we are, from childhood till we die, being taught and admonished . . . he bears his testimony to the scope and nature of *conduct,* tells us what conduct is." For conduct in itself the master concept is righteousness, variously regarded. It is the means of deliverance: "Plato and the sages, when they are asked what is saving, answer, 'To love righteousness.' " In meaning it approaches holiness: "Sophocles and Plato knew as well as [St. Paul] that 'without holiness no man shall see God,' and their notion of what goes to make up holiness was larger than his." For Arnold the Platonic *locus classicus* is an interpretation of "Know thyself" as a command to practice *sôphrosunê*, which is self-restraint or moderation, and *dikaiosunê*. The latter term he translates "righteousness" according to the notions of his age; we might consider "justness" a less colored rendering. On the question of sensuality he finds Plato's pureness a splendid quality, and twice cites his belief that dissolute behavior causes the lower side of our nature to overcome the higher. The truism takes on power when it is presented in the original terms: "The divine Plato tells us that we have within us a many-headed beast and a man, and that by dissoluteness we feed and strengthen the beast in us, and starve the man." [30]

All this remains at the level of moralizing. It deals with the goals which should motivate conduct but says nothing about our actual impulses. Here Arnold found his needs supplied by the words of Diotima reported in the *Symposium:* "Love, and impulse, and bent of all kinds, is, in fact, nothing else but the desire in men that good should for ever be present to them." [31] Plato and Aristotle develop this premise by showing how readily an apparent good may be mistaken for the reality. While Arnold does not explicitly set out the argument, it is implicit when he stresses the need to strike through the veils of appearance, and also the difficulty of doing so.

We recall that Plato believed the real could be apprehended, if at all, only by a leap of the mind after a long training culminating in dialectics. This is the Good-in-itself, and Arnold does not aspire so high. Dialectics cannot profit him: the arguments for the soul's immortality in the *Phaedo* are "over-subtle and sterile," indeed futile; and except for a half-dozen pages the *Theaetetus,* first of all treatises on epistemology, contains nothing but "barren logomachies." Such opinions do not mean that Arnold would wish to abolish dialectical activity.[32] Rather, he holds the exclusively ethical view that "the end and aim of all dialectics is, as by the great master of dialectics we have been most truly told, to help us to an answer to the question, how to live." It is a master-thought: his last year on earth finds him stating it anew and adding, "Our aim, [Plato] says, is very and true life." [33]

To sum up, Arnold managed to regard Plato as almost everything except a philosopher.[34] It is evident that he took pains to avoid a systematic approach, and also that he had no organized command of Platonic thought. Unfortunately for him, it was not until shortly after his periods of enrollment that the study of this author was properly begun at Rugby and Balliol.[35] Had he been born nearer 1830 than 1820 he would have studied the *Republic* as a set book both in Dr. Arnold's curriculum and in Greats; Benjamin Jowett's enthusiasm and rapidly mounting influence first secured for it at Oxford the central place it still holds in the Honour School of Literae Humaniores. But Arnold came upon the scene too early. The Oxford of his day actually required no Plato of its Greats men, a fact which shocked Continental observers. What Matthew Arnold knew of Plato—and it was not a great deal—came essentially from private reading.

As always, he read selectively and subjectively. No great degree of self-identification seems to have been involved, but a tendency to merge his nature with that of Plato or Socrates does reveal itself on a few occasions. We hear, for example, of spiritual nonconformists among the ranks of Philistines, Barbarians, and Populace. These are

> generous and humane souls, lovers of man's perfection, . . . and desirous that he who speaks to them should, as Plato says, not try to please his fellow-servants, but his true and legitimate master—the heavenly Gods.

More characteristic is the reading back of Arnoldian notions into Plato. This occurs in *Culture and Anarchy*, with references to "what Plato calls the true, firm, intelligible law of things" and "the law and science, to use Plato's words, of things as they really are." [36] Arnold is not making up supporting references out of whole cloth, for the concept of what truly exists beyond the world of appearance is genuinely and essentially Platonic. It is also doubtless one of the sources from which he put together the phrase that figures so often in his arguments. If, however, we employ his own criterion of having one's eye on the object, the area of emphasis becomes clear enough.

It must be concluded that Plato is useful as a source of quotation and illustration. No deeper dimension appears, nor was any intended. Within this limited sphere he served Arnold's purposes more successfully than any other ancient writer.

Oxford's chief remaining heritage from the Middle Ages is the study of Aristotle. The *Nicomachean Ethics* shares with

Plato's *Republic* the chief place in that portion of Literae Humaniores which deals with philosophy generally. Among the works of the ancient philosophers, these alone are offered by almost every student today. During Arnold's undergraduate years neither the *Republic* nor any other dialogue had to be offered for the final examinations in Greats, so that not even Plato challenged the importance of the *Ethics*.[37] As an introduction to ethical analysis it still deserves a place of honor, but nothing can justify the devout literal acceptance of its doctrines that cramped Oxford minds during the earlier 1840's. Late in life Arnold recalled this atmosphere of foolish faith:

> We at Oxford used to concentrate ourselves upon one or two great books.... Whatever was hard, whatever was obscure, the textbook was all right, and our understandings were to conform themselves to it. What agonies of puzzle has Butler's account of self-love, or Aristotle's of the intellectual virtues, caused to clever undergraduates and to clever tutors; and by what feats of astonishing explanation, astonishingly acquiesced in, were those agonies calmed! ... We at Oxford used to read our Aristotle or our Butler with the same absolute faith in the classicality of their matter as in the classicality of Homer's form.

Actually he esteemed Aristotle's treatise. His quarrel was with his fellow-students, his tutors, and not least himself. *Culture and Anarchy* reveals his feelings about the *Ethics* in a wry, quasi-apologetic sentence which the context shows to be a genuine tribute:

> Having been brought up at Oxford in the bad old times, when we were stuffed with Greek and Aristotle, ... my head is still full of a lumber of phrases we learnt at Oxford from Aristotle, about virtue being in a mean, and about excess and defect, and so on.[38]

We might have guessed the truth simply from the style, for when Arnold's prose takes on this tone he is writing about something that matters to him. The proof lies in his work as a whole: though the Aristotelian references are much less frequent than the Platonic, they strike deeper. Through them we get at the questions that he was trying to answer.

There is no doubt that Oxford left Arnold with a lasting sense of Aristotle's relevance. The *Ethics*, his "set book," steadies

his thought (though not the spelling or accents or breathing marks
of his Greek) as he writes to Clough in 1849: "... for God's sake
let us neither be fanatics nor yet chalf [*sic*] blown by the wind but
let us be ὡς ο φρονιμος διαρισειεν and not as any one else διαρισειεν."
Almost thirty years later he reaffirms this dictum: "the determination of how a thing really is, is ... 'as the judicious would determine.' " [39] Tone and outlook are changed: at twenty-five he could
not have spoken, as he does here, of the "admirable common-
sense" that Aristotle's remark displays. The dilemma of moral and
religious belief, however, remained throughout his life, and his
accord with Aristotle's verdict of the judicious represents a
typical humanist's solution.

The scrupulous analysis of virtue in the *Ethics* presented a
problem when Arnold sought to contrast the strict conscience of
Hebraism with the spontaneous consciousness of Hellenism. He
frankly recognized the difficulty and stated that Aristotle will
"undervalue knowing," that deliberate choice and perseverance in
what concerns virtue are vital to his ethical scheme. Yet such
seeming Hebraism amounts merely to "superficial agreement," we
are told, for Aristotle ranks the moral virtues beneath the intellectual. This last point cannot be disputed; the error lies in supposing that he undervalued knowing. He gave due importance,
we should rather say, to the inescapable fact that ethical attitudes
result from habituation. The passage of the *Ethics* which Arnold
had in mind leads up to this very point:

> A just and wise act is judged not merely in itself [like a
> fine work of art] but also according to whether the agent
> acted deliberately, choosing means to a good end simply be-
> cause it was good, and out of a constant and unchangeable
> disposition. The last two requirements are all-important with
> regard to the virtues, for it is the force of repetition which
> calls them into actualized being.[40]

Broadly speaking, out of all the vast Aristotelian corpus only
the *Nicomachean Ethics* and the *Poetics*, whose importance we
have seen in the 1853 Preface, could serve Arnold's purposes. One
of the few exceptions to this rule comes from a late work, *Literature and Dogma*. Here he quotes extensively from the *Politics* and
goes on to mention the distinction Aristotle makes between two
kinds of self-rule; involved here are the absolute rule of soul over
body and the "constitutional" rule of reason over the movement of
thought and desire. His comment on the passage is instructive:

> Aristotle (and it is a mark of his greatness) does not, in [this] passage . . . , begin with a complete system of psycho-physiology. . . . He here appeals throughout to a verifying sense . . . ; he does not appeal to a speculative theory of a system of things, and deduce conclusions from it.[41]

This verifying sense, Arnold says, resides within each of us. In critical judgments it constitutes his court of final appeal, a little superior to that appellate division where the "verdict of the judicious" is handed down. Here are the two great principles of his criticism, the first self-contained within the individual, the second a reference outward to authority. Arnold, who like Whitman could "contain multitudes," consciously combined both principles in his own person—or at any rate his critical *persona*—and had thus the best of both worlds. We cannot pretend that he arranged these particular worlds on an Aristotelian plan,[42] any more than we can credit him with fondness for system generally. Nevertheless, his quotations from Aristotle do not seem random, and they guide us to the concerns governing their choice.[43]

A second exceptional use of this author occurs in a book review dating from 1871. Here, for the first and last time, Arnold draws upon the *Rhetoric*. "The main element in our nature," he observes, "conquers at last; the steady, according to Aristotle's profound remark, becomes stupid, and the brilliant becomes non-sane." His translation is exactly right; his inference has no warrant at all in the line of argument developed by Aristotle, who had just offered a comparison with the alternation of good and bad crops.[44] This does not concern Arnold; for him the fact that a reference aided his argument was always more important than mere considerations of context. Given an evident broad similarity, he asked nothing more.

Arnold seems to have formed no general estimate of Aristotle. *Culture and Anarchy* shows a sense of something in common:

> Aristotle says, that those for whom ideas and the pursuit of the intelligible law of things can have much attraction, are principally the young . . . ; but the mass of mankind, he says, follow seeming goods for real, bestowing hardly a thought upon true sweetness and light; . . . "and to their lives," he adds mournfully, "who can give another and a better rhythm?"

There are several respects in which Arnold mistranslates or embroiders upon the original, even making wholesale additions.

More significant, however, are his insertion of "mournfully" and his later reference to the quotation as a "desponding" sentence: both are completely subjective.[45] Yet the advocate of Hellenism to temper Hebraism refuses to accept this supposed despondency as justified for his own time. He could himself provide a better rhythm for men's lives, or so he believed, and *Culture and Anarchy* was at least a noteworthy attempt to achieve this end.[46]

As Plato's pupils took their own directions a new type of thinker began to appear: the polymath. Aristotle provides the supreme example, and Arnold links him with the later research scholars who worked at Alexandria:

> The Greek spirit, after its splendid hour of creative activity was gone, gave our race another precious lesson, by exhibiting in the career of Aristotle and the great students of Alexandria, the idea of the correlation and equal dignity of the most different departments of human knowledge, and by showing the possibility of uniting them in a single mind's education.[47]

This is a passing comment, not a final view. Arnold neither possessed nor sought to acquire any unitary grasp of Aristotelian doctrine. Since that doctrine is presented in a singularly uninviting kind of lecture-note prose, the old familiar key of style for once could open no doors. Moreover, its extent demands capacities greater in their kind than he could claim. Its inexhaustible content, however, repeatedly brought before him issues and concepts of the highest importance. From his responses more can be learned about the man himself than he intended, and much concerning the tangled roots of his critical thought. Finally, the study of Aristotle, who closes the intellectual history of the Hellenic age, prepared Matthew Arnold to hear the only voices of ancient philosophy that could speak to his condition: the derivative Stoic and Epicurean systems of Hellenistic ethics.

VIII

Stoic and Epicurean:
The Poet's Universe

After Plato and Aristotle no strong continuing tradition kept alive the distinctively philosophic qualities of their thought. Systematic and metaphysical aspects would remain largely secondary until the Middle Ages. Both men had gifted disciples; neither had a true successor, as one can see clearly enough from the lackluster record of the Later Academy and Lyceum. The *Metaphysics* notes heterodox theories current in the Academy only a few years after Plato's death.

Neither Lyceum nor Academy controlled the central and powerful currents of speculative thought in the Hellenistic and later classical periods. This thought took its rise not in Platonic or Aristotelian doctrine but in the personality and teachings of Socrates, seen as Xenophon saw him, together with varied doctrines ascribed to several of his predecessors. A practical ethic, conveyed through exhortation and rebuke, now eclipses both the broader treatment undertaken by Plato and the elaborate theoretical patterns of his pupil's *Nicomachean Ethics*. The individual has become the center of attention. Plato's strongly social and political orientation no longer compels respect; the city-state itself has already passed into an unrealized obsolescence. Even Aristotle's *Politics,* one of the last pronouncements of the Hellenic mind, seems to reach out towards the coming age in its analysis of the aims of education.

Now the larger unit that matters is not the *polis* but the ecumene: *hê oikoumenê,* "the inhabited" areas of the earth considered for the first time as a unity rather than a meaningless aggregate of diverse local groupings. Like St. Paul's related and quite probably derivative concept of brotherhood in Christ, the common humanity of the ecumene recognizes neither free nor slave, king nor beggar. Certainly it had no use for a hierarchy such as that of philosopher-ruler, state police, and *Massenmensch*. The only meaningful kingdom is the mind, as Seneca was to point out. Although our rule ends at its borders, within them we have absolute power; to recognize this fact and face its consequences is thus to find the true grounds of being.

Yet the individual moves in a world of phenomena; only a solipsist can escape awareness of being part of a larger totality. One may either reject the testimony of one's senses or embrace an outright faith in them as the only modes of apprehending reality, taking a stand with Plato or Aristotle respectively. Again, one may declare belief in a universe pervaded by some kind of *logos*, a patterned force of reason that endows each man with immanent divinity and the scheme of things with meaning. Yet it is also possible to assent to none but a mechanistic universe of combining atoms, variable only by grace of a random declination in their course. The atomistic hypothesis, best known through Lucretius' vast poem on the nature and origins of the universe, was first advanced by the pre-Socratic thinker Democritus and his associates. The idea of a homogeneous cosmos knit together by a world-soul (see "Lines Written in Kensington Gardens," 37) has its earlier analogues in the attempts of Ionian pre-Socratics to find a single primary substance or principle underlying all things: water or air or fire, or mind, or the interaction of opposites.

Even the disagreement about sensory data goes back to a time when the Socratic revolution was still in the future. It recalls such men as Parmenides and Anaxagoras, whose cosmological theorizing Socrates dismissed when, in Cicero's phrase, he "brought philosophy down from the heavens to dwell among men." Not he but his great pupil, as most believe, raised anew the issue of sense perception and evaded its supposed delusions, arguing for proto-types remote from the phenomenal world of change. While the Platonic solution may draw philosophy once more towards the heavens, it differs radically from earlier theories.

We cannot lay any very great stress on the theoretical, for the main currents of philosophy that began during the Hellenistic period traced primarily the patterns of private awareness and responsibility. Their rhythms may have witnessed to a larger generative force, but what truly mattered about them, as men supposed, was their relation to individual behavior. This has not been any less true during succeeding centuries: structural theory tended to be ignored because other systems of thought could express comparable ideas more strikingly, while the precepts of late classical ethics have exerted a lasting force. Until very recently only Christianity has overshadowed them in sheer practical effectiveness, and they reappear throughout the New Testament. Yet they embody a humanist position; their central ideal of self-sufficiency can never be wholly reconciled with Christian self-negation.[1] The legitimate service of this ancient wisdom is to arm the thoughtful man, believer or unbeliever, with inward peace and even with joy.

In this brief and highly incomplete outline we have noted tendencies of thought which distinctively characterized Stoicism and Epicureanism. Other sects had come into existence after the close of the Hellenistic age, and two of them deserve passing mention as seed-beds of later Graeco-Roman thought. The Cynics had pushed to an unpleasant extreme the denial of worldly values; there were also the Cyrenaics, less determinedly conspicuous, who embraced the principles of pleasure with a thoroughness that left Epicurean orthodoxy far behind. Cynicism, however, has given us little except the anecdotes about Diogenes, and the Cyrenaics are only phantoms rustling faintly in the pages of *Marius the Epicurean*. During modern times post-Hellenic classical ethics has meant either Stoicism or, less often, Epicureanism.

According to Stoic views the wise man will be "free from passion, unsubdued by joy or grief," and "willingly submissive to natural law," as a very widely used source has it. This is not far off the mark, provided one remembers that freedom from passion means freedom from the tyranny of excessive feelings, not an absence of all feeling. Certain additional ideas demand recognition, and among them is the twofold conception of unity. We have to do here with an outward unity of mankind, symbolized in the new idea of an ecumene, and also with the invisible unity created by a *logos* penetrating the universe. The cosmos, then, was far more than a mere design (for the idea of order is inherent in the Greek word *kosmos* itself); it was a sentient and intelligent organism.

The most ordinary good sense dictated that an intelligent person thus could only accept the dynamic universe. He could not meaningfully reject it, for all such attempts betray a failure to realize one's own part in the *logos*. To acknowledge this great scheme of things is to "follow nature" (*naturam sequi*, for the original Greek *phusei hepesthai*) by acknowledging the leadership of the "guiding principle" (*to hêgemonikon*) within oneself.[2]

Such a man, having set his inward kingdom in order, has freed himself from the power of external circumstance. Though he is not an animal or a robot insensible to emotion, he refuses to permit fortune to destroy his serenity. Finally, the Stoic conceived of the divine in terms that tended strongly towards monotheism, but he found it difficult to posit the existence of a God who was not in every way identical with the universe. Problems of participation and transcendence had not disappeared with the passing of Plato.

The source cited earlier summarizes Epicurus' philosophy thus: "pleasure is the end of all morality and ... genuine pleasure is derived from a life of prudence, honor, and justice." To these three virtues frugality might well be added, as a corrective to distortions. Generally, however, the statement provides a reliable summary. Epicurus' followers revived the atomistic hypothesis and were thereby led to maintain that sense impressions as such do not err. To this thorough-going materialism was added a belief in gods who inhabited spaces between the several worlds and felt no concern whatever for man. Being divine, they were thought to possess in a perfect degree that freedom from inward disturbance, *ataraxia* or ataraxy, which was the Epicurean goal. For mortals death was dissolution. Traditional beliefs involving an afterlife and its rewards or punishments were accounted superstitions, to be attacked with the utmost fierceness rather than tolerated after the Stoic fashion.

It will be noted that these two systems, so markedly different in certain respects, are not antithetical. They display a larger measure of agreement, in fact, than has generally been recognized. They must both be understood in their proper terms if one is really to grasp their points of likeness or anything else about them. Such understanding too often has been lacking. As a result, the spacious and often joyfully serene Stoic creed is narrowed to a grim endurance purged of all feeling, and the scarcely less noble ethic of Epicurus reappears transformed into a rationale for self-indulgence. In the latter instance such an interpretation seems more understandable, for the voyage to Rome that gave Stoicism added strength had largely the opposite effect on Epicureanism.

So far as present evidence can show, Matthew Arnold had no meaningful encounter with either of these systems before his years at Oxford. As a schoolboy he spent much of his time in the enforced company of Vergil and Horace. We may take it as a near certainty that Vergil at least figured in the pre-school tutoring at Fox How and "Buckland's" or with Herbert Hill. The elements of

Stoicism in these authors nevertheless failed to make any visible impression on the boy. In later life he was to find Vergil "graceful" and "tender" and Horace "exquisite," but he could not term either poet "fortifying." Very probably his actual health was more important in the crucial early formation of character during these years, a character that has repeatedly been called stoical. The little boy growing up at Laleham suffered an appalling series of accidents, and when he was hardly more than a baby he wore iron leg braces for the greater part of two years.[3] These facts no doubt should not give rise to extreme interpretations, but it seems a little strange that recent scholarly studies should have ignored them.

This point illustrates the complexity of the issues involved. Where Arnold is concerned, little if anything can satisfactorily be explained on single and simple grounds; least of all will such an approach serve to explain his view of man as a social and ethical being. The common assumption that he wholly lacked a capacity for philosophical thinking is mistaken. It might be said rather that he could not be a dutiful schoolman, discovering the mind's happiness within the boundaries set upon thought by any single school or sect. Spiritual debtor of many, he gave lasting discipleship to none.

It is of some importance that we should understand the place of particular beliefs in his uncommitted attitude. Epicureanism underwent no important change (distortion is another matter) since the time of the founder himself. This static quality alone would have kept Arnold from becoming a wholehearted follower of the system. The changes in Stoicism, by contrast, were notable and long continued. To some considerable extent, moreover, they tempered absolute ethical ideals and placed the goal within the reach of average thoughtful men. The flexibility of Stoicism made it serve Matthew Arnold's needs uncommonly well. "Ondoyant et divers" as he was, he found it more congenial than a great part of the Christianity displayed by his contemporaries. Yet he rejected no wisdom that seemed capable of aiding him, nor did he greatly concern himself about the source. The catholicity of his spiritual desire as well as of his literary taste should keep critics from the academic pastime of imagining neat, separate compartments for itemizing "influences." The note-books themselves, through their striking neglect of documentation, warn vividly against such error.

What follows here is inevitably a partial portrait. While certain concepts may appear independent [thanks to the isolating tendency which is all too natural to critical argument], they had no such self-sufficient authority with Arnold. Again the note-books furnish evidence: ethical positions that a classicist naturally assigns to Stoicism may be found throughout their pages as the statements of Victorian thinkers. The Socratic moral posture or disposition of the mind which informed the Stoic tradition, and sometimes the Epicurean as well, has exercised a wide influence on modern thought, primarily through Cicero and the New Testa-ment; thus a specific Hellenistic or Roman source often cannot be assigned with certainty. Stoicism and its companion Epicureanism are still powerful when they move unacknowledged through the reflections of a Senancour, a Lacordaire, or a Sainte-Beuve.

The lesser of these two systems had little personal meaning for Arnold. During his probationary year at Oriel he was much taken with Béranger, the French balladist whose frank satirical verses had attained national popularity. The first enthusiasm cooled, and in September of 1848 he writes to Clough that he is well content to be done with Béranger: there is "something 'fade' " about his Epicureanism, which Arnold sees as the common ground between him and Horace. The two poets cannot properly be compared, a fact which has certain consequences for Arnold's estimate of them; yet there is no denying that Béranger does occasionally pretend to assume the literary personality of an Epicurean.[4] At other times, again, he does not refer to this school but affects the hedonism popularly associated with it, as in the famous *Roi d'Yvetot*. In any case, it is clear that he never was professing or implying anything more consequential than the misinterpreted or perverted version of Epicurus' doctrines that remains current even today.

Because he was born into the lower classes Béranger received no training in classical languages. This omission in his schooling may well have been his salvation as a *chansonnier*, but it left him without the poise and balanced taste that can be derived from an enlightened classical education.[5] He readily and uncritically ac-cepted a supposed Epicurean tradition of wine and mirth, the same background that he associated with Anacreon. In both cases the misinterpreted view was a widely accepted one, so that Béranger should not be blamed as an individual. The point is simply that he had no concern here with serious doctrine.[6]

It seems, then, that during a part at least of the Oxford years Matthew Arnold understood Epicureanism according to its later, distorted sense. The reason for this may be implicit in the known facts of his behavior at Balliol and Oriel, where he played the dandy almost to the exclusion of all other roles. In his prolonged celebration of independence from the brooding *manes* of a father who abhorred levity, this parading of a taste for Béranger would fit the larger pattern very convincingly.[7]

When Matthew dismisses his French poet with a damning French epithet, this too seems natural. The letters to Clough show with what seriousness he was seeking principles on which he could build—principles not to be derived, surely, from a Béranger. During these pivotal years he had sought the philosophers in surprising earnest, as close analysis of his reading-lists has shown, and among their company Spinoza and Epictetus figure importantly. Since some years passed before he acknowledged any acquaintance or concern with the first of these,[8] two points may suffice: Spinoza's pantheistic universe resembles the Stoic cosmos infilled with the divine *logos;* moreover, the requisite for individual happiness—realizing one's small place in the great pattern—is virtually the same in each system.[9] Arnold once or twice speaks of his indebtedness to Epictetus, but he says little until the mid-century is long past.

For the important period of the later 1840's and early 1850's evidence must be sought in the poems of his first two collections. During later years Arnold's poetry has only a limited and occasional relevance to this area of thought. It is the prose writings that require attention, and the many significant passages in the note-books which go back in one way or another to the great Hellenistic ethical systems. The altered attitudes marking this later period will be taken up in the next chapter.

The year 1847, in which Matthew Arnold's long stay at Oxford came to a close, brought one of the first poems of his maturity. "Horatian Echo," for all its respectable total of Horatian themes, is not much concerned with philosophic aspects. We have commented on Arnold's scorn of "the shouldering herd" and the bustling commercial world, on his disdain for the city and his preaching of simple pleasures—those "little threads" of which life is spun. Such attitudes could be thought Epicurean, and in some instances Stoic as well; so far as Horace would admit any allegiance, he revealed himself as a smiling, self-mocking follower of Epicurus. His deeper standards nevertheless were quite different. In his lesser poems he might laugh at the importunate street-corner evangelists of Stoicism; yet the *Odes* contain moving testimonials to the Stoic faith seen not from outside but as inward reality. A noted authority on Roman Stoicism has this to say of him:

In fact his works show a constantly increasing appreciation of the ethics of Stoicism. He recognises the high ideals and civic activity of its professors, and he draws a noble picture of the Stoic sage, confident in his convictions, and bidding defiance to the crowd and the tyrant alike. Of that practical wisdom and genial criticism which has made Horace the favourite poet of so many men eminent in public life, no small part consists of Stoic principles deftly freed from the paradoxical form in which they were conveyed to professed adherents.[10]

It is plain that if Arnold knew these facts he did not find them useful for his purposes. With no important exception, the Horace whom he considers meaningful is the poet of this world's ephemeral loveliness, so quickly destroyed by the death that claims all beautiful things.

The Yale MS. entry, "Eugenia—refusal of [limitation] by the sentiment of love," has been connected with "Horatian Echo," and the poem accordingly is described as "concerned with the limitations upon the human spirit by the love of woman and by the political world." [11] One may approach this problem by asking whether the entry just preceding, which reads "Empedocles—refusal of limitation by the religious sentiment," seems to state the actual theme of "Empedocles on Etna." If "Horatian Echo" could be shown to relate closely to the Eugenia entry of the Yale MS., we should have to deal with it as in some real sense a philosophical poem. This point may remain in dispute, but we can say with confidence that the philosophizing Horace did not interest Arnold, who had discovered even as early as 1847 the usefulness of the partial portrait.

During the summer of 1845 Arnold visited the Isle of Man. The lines "To a Gipsy Child by the Sea-shore," subtitled "Douglas, Isle of Man," may have been written at the time or not long afterwards, for the eighth stanza (29–32) reveals a less adequate understanding of Stoicism than the poet had achieved by 1849, when the poem was published:

> Is the calm thine of stoic souls, who weigh
> Life well, and find it wanting, nor deplore;
> But in disdainful silence turn away,
> Stand mute, self-centred, stern, and dream no more?

While the Stoic was by no means incapable of emotional response, his philosophy committed him to absolute belief in a master-plan:

the *logos* reconciled to a higher purpose all that seemed dissonant
or defective. Arnold's phrase "and dream no more" shows a strong
element of Romanticism. These lines would most naturally suit
the period before he began to read Epictetus, so that a date of
composition between 1845 and 1847 is a reasonable conjecture.

"Tristram and Iseult," roughly dated to the late 1840's, contains two long stanzas (3.112–50) which seem at first to constitute
a long digression. They turn away from this most romantic of all
tales of doomed love, to consider how it is "not sorrow, . . . Not
suffering" that takes away the power to feel or remember joy, but
either of two causes. "The gradual furnace of the world" is one:
it consumes our spirits or else tempers them steel-hard, leaving
only "the fierce necessity to feel." The other is the tyranny of
some single thought or passion, whether "ambition, or remorse,
or love"; here Arnold begins a Stoic sermon on restlessness that
fills an entire stanza. His examples are traditional ones, and in concluding with Alexander he takes the same illustration that Seneca
chose.[12]

All this is not so digressive as it may seem. The connection
can be found in a sentence of the *Commentary:* "The third part,
with its touching picture of uncomplaining suffering, has its own
characteristic charm." This section, "Iseult of Brittany," portrays
one who may justly be termed stoical, free from the restlessness
that Arnold criticizes so sharply.[13] Dead to joy, she follows the
quiet paths of duty and lives for her children; only through stories
of the enchanted past can she be "moved and soothed," forgetful of
all that has been. Nowhere, however, does the poet show any concern with Stoic beliefs. "Tristram and Iseult," like the verses to
the gipsy child, may have been written before Arnold had read
Epictetus. It offers a strange combination of classical and Romantic, endowed at times with a magical effectiveness.

Among the 1849 poems "To a Friend" offers the earliest
evidence of what "That halting slave" meant to Matthew Arnold.
The lines describing Epictetus occur in a letter written at the close
of the summer of 1848; they speak of the philosopher as "he,
whose friendship I not long since won" (5).[14] This gives 1848 or
perhaps 1847 as a trustworthy date for the beginning of Arnold's
serious concern with the Stoic doctrines which were taught by
Epictetus and transmitted by Arrian. It may be an indication of
the value he placed on them that Epictetus has been listed between
Homer and Sophocles. Aside from this possibility, "To a Friend"
is a reminder that Stoicism guided Arnold's thought for at least

forty years. In his early poems it is incomparably stronger than Christianity: it constitutes their central intellectual force.[15] Its doctrines are the foundations upon which he attempts to build an adequate idea of the world through poetry. With the successive failures to bring this Stoic universe into being, he turns more and more from the metaphysics and cosmology of the system to its ethics; even these will eventually be subordinated to a larger, composite scheme.

We have referred to a study of Arnold's reading-lists for the middle and later 1840's which shows that he gave great prominence to philosophy during these crucial years, searching for a respectable alternative to supernaturalism. That he quickly discovered "an ethical principle underlying the naturalism of his new world" would be difficult to deny, and it is reasonable to see this principle in a maxim he cites from Spinoza: *Non studemus, ut natura nobis, sed contra ut nos naturae pareamus*, "Our desire is not that nature should obey us but that we should be obedient to nature." [16] What one must remember is the omnipresence of Epictetus. Whether he speaks through an immediate pupil (as in the *Discourses* and *Manual*) or through a philosopher of much later times, he is a force to be reckoned with.

His voice, which will be heard throughout all the remaining years of Matthew Arnold's life, sounds in a number of the 1849 and 1852 poems. "Quiet Work" deals with Nature as man's teacher. Her lessons have been thought to suggest Goethe more strongly than Epictetus; but *Ohne Hast, ohne Rast* does not make a clearly plausible source, and Stoicism originated the idea in either case. If parallels are to be sought, lines 11 and 12 [Nature's ministers "move on, Their glorious tasks in silence perfecting"] bear a startling resemblance to a sentence of Seneca's.[17]

Central themes of Stoicism appear in two sonnets. "To George Cruikshank" holds that man can control "the bent of his own days"; "Religious Isolation" speaks of "Nature's great law, the law of all men's minds," with the further claim that each creature stirs "to its own impulse." In the latter instance Stoic coloring may not be apparent until one reads the entire sonnet, remembering Arnold's spiritual revaluations during the years around 1850. A similar coloring characterizes the title and theme of "In Utrumque Paratus"; here, however, the actual handling does not show it. Epictetus' and Marcus Aurelius' discussions of comparable alternatives stand in strong contrast to this treatment.

Stoicism provides a key to "The Second Best," with the distinction Arnold makes between two levels of morality. There is an ideal of moderation observed in suffering and pleasure alike, and there is also the quite different reality—a second best which must be accepted and which in the end proves profitable. Although the Stoic emphasis on moral progress does not tolerate such a division, Arnold's attempt to show what ordinary men may achieve in a confusing world resembles the successive efforts that made Stoicism a realistic way of life. He begins to part company with his Hellenistic and Roman teachers when he names hope, light, and persistence as man's inward goals. If the last of these is thoroughly Stoic, the second is pure Arnold and the first goes counter to all Stoic tenets.[18] Again, at the beginning of "Fragment of an 'Antigone' " the Chorus praise the man who, within the limits of justice, "Makes his own welfare his unswerved-from law"; such an attitude accords fully with Epicurus' hedonism. Yet they also praise him who declines the life Fortune offers and fashions his own instead, which suggests the rival school. Here the whole direction of thought has veered away from Sophocles.

For the teaching "Resolve to be thyself" which dominates "Self-Dependence," Stoicism is at any rate the sole source; citing the self-sufficient "mighty life" of the stars as a paradigm involves Epicurean doctrine as well. The need to be oneself recurs as a master theme in another and more celebrated of the 1852 poems whose title, "The Buried Life," owes something to Epicurus' command *lathe biôsas*. A meaningful literal translation of this phrase is hardly possible. It bids a man live a "hidden life," not as recluse or misanthrope but as one whose vital principles of conduct are contained within himself. The command was a meaningful one for Arnold; here he develops it with a poet's freedom, striking off into his private landscape of hill and river and sea.[19]

"Courage," a canceled poem which had been published in the 1852 edition, deals directly and rather curiously with Stoicism. It is true, the poet begins, that we must submit our wills to the law of Nature, "bear in silence" our evil fortune, and learn to "wait, renounce, withdraw." These first four lines amount almost to a précis of the Stoic creed, which is well summed up in Epictetus' famous counsel *anechou kai apechou*, "bear and forbear." By this, as our best authority has pointed out, he meant "Practise Courage and cast off Grief, practise Soberness and keep Hilarity far from you," the passive and defensive ideals of Stoicism in its later phase.[20] It is highly probable that Epictetus' words, taken in their full meaning, prompted both the initial stanza and the title of "Courage."

Having admitted the claims of orthodox resignation, Arnold counters (9–12) with a statement of his own impulse:

> Those sterner spirits let me prize,
> Who, though the tendence of the whole
> They less than us might recognize,
> Kept, more than us, their strength of soul.

He goes on at once to cite the courage with which "the second Cato" committed suicide. The example of Marcus Porcius Cato's death after the battle of Pharsalia had already become famous in antiquity, largely through the praise bestowed by the Stoic poet Lucan. Even here Arnold retains his orthodoxy, for the system condoned suicide under certain circumstances. But he also claims that the Stoics and other courageous souls of the past, such as Byron, recognized less fully than modern men "the tendence of the whole." This has a good deal of significance, coming as it does just when Arnold was abandoning the Stoic view as an adequate means of interpreting life through his poetry. It suggests that he now saw the validity of this system as real but partial; so he was later to describe Menander, the friend and admirer of Epicurus, as showing man with part of his life shorn away. His revaluation would enable him still to make use of Stoic thought in that later eclecticism, both public and private, which serves his own "tendence of the whole."

To theme and background of the early poems Hellenistic philosophy makes certain real contributions; it contributes very little indeed to poetic content. Perhaps it aided Arnold most by making available a noble ethic independent of Christianity. Wordsworth and Goethe rendered much the same service, and it is they and Epictetus who constitute, together with Emerson, the chief moral forces of this earlier poetry.[21] In the later poems Stoicism has become almost extinct—or rather, as will be seen, it has gone elsewhere, into private devotions and public prose. All but one of the long poems which we shall consider date from before 1850, and the lone exception is not an independent work. "Worldly Place," the uninspired sonnet of 1863 on Marcus Aurelius, may be left out of account. Its concluding line, " 'The aids to noble life are all within,' " shows how completely the subject had failed to move Arnold beyond versifying to poetic creation.

"Mycerinus" gives no impression of any single predominating philosophy. The gods who are "careless of our doom" if they exist at all can only be Epicurean. When Arnold describes them as fixed "in frozen apathy" he no doubt intends the ordinary sense of the term. Within its original context, however, *apatheia* was the highly praiseworthy Stoic quality of not being overborne by violent emotion. The second half of the poem contains the conjecture that Mycerinus, haunted by the sense of guilt and death, "took measure of his soul" and "by that silent knowledge" was given calm and comfort. The picture is that of a Stoic sage, a *vir sapiens;* Arnold, it would appear, is seeking an adequate personal view of life. Though he is aware of the answers given by ancient philosophy, his recognition is tentative, questioning. He has not yet decided what part they shall play in his spiritual progress.

"Resignation," hardly more unified than "Mycerinus," reveals broader concerns and certainly draws more heavily upon Stoic and Epicurean doctrines. For Epictetus, as later for Marcus Aurelius, resignation ranks among the highest ethical attainments. The pattern of behavior which it embodies is twofold, giving up attachments to persons and things and giving oneself up—assenting to the cosmic plan. Arnold's somber concluding lines obscure this point somewhat with their earth and sky that seem "to bear rather than rejoice"; the positive, fortifying quality appears earlier.[22]

The reader who seeks a total impression of "Resignation" may find that solitariness dominates it. This mood traces back in part to the vision of the Epicurean solitary, Lucretius. In Arnold's description of his imagined poet who "looks down" from "some high station" (164), those familiar with the chief passages of *De Rerum Natura* will recognize a deeper level of reference. It is remarkable that the Lucretian element went unnoticed until almost a century after the poem was written. "Resignation" embodies less harshness than the original, to be sure. The poet from his high and lonely prospect "Surveys each happy group" in the thronged city streets "And does not say: *I am alone*" (166, 169). On a pasture hilltop, as he gazes at the gracious country scene, "tears Are in his eyes" (186–87)—the tears that Lucretius scorns.

At times the Stoic strain cannot be distinguished from the Epicurean-Lucretian, but of the two it is undoubtedly the more important. The following passages (22–27, 189, 195–98, 241–48) display it:

> But milder natures, and more free—
> Whom an unblamed serenity
> Hath freed from passions, and the state

Of struggle these necessitate;
Whom schooling of the stubborn mind
Hath made, or birth hath found, resign'd . . .

Before him he sees life unroll,

    .   .   .

The life of plants, and stones, and rain,
The life he craves—if not in vain
Fate gave, what chance shall not control,
His sad lucidity of soul.

That heart, which burns in thee,
Ask, not to amuse, but to set free;
Be passionate hopes not ill resign'd
For quiet, and a fearless mind.
And though fate grudge to thee and me
The poet's rapt security,
Yet they, believe me, who await
No gifts from chance, have conquer'd fate.

These lines set forth a recognizably Stoic acceptance of the universe, an acceptance which arms the soul against any blow fate can deal by enabling us to look upon it simply as a part of the grand design. When we have attained this view fate cannot control us. We remain free, no matter how incessantly fate brings its power to bear, whether seemingly against us or, as in the "gifts from chance," furthering our aims. Unless a man has been born thus—free—he must abandon "passionate hopes . . . For quiet, and a fearless mind"; this may be from a celebrated line of Juvenal. With these "not ill resign'd" he will himself be "resign'd" (27). The double usage does not result from carelessness. It reflects the two aspects of ethical habituation, namely process and result, that are embodied in the title of the poem as well. Later this Stoic submission to the universal plan will reappear as the "sentiment of sublime acquiescence" which Arnold substitutes for Aristotle's katharsis.

Here too the Epicurean and Lucretian elements play a part. The "unblamed serenity" that liberates us from passion first suggests them; in the reference to the poet's "rapt security" they emerge unmistakably. Here is the *securitas* of Roman Stoicism, added to the slender philosophical vocabulary of Latin to render *ataraxia*, the key word of Epicureanism. Taken very literally the two mean "the state of freedom from worry or turmoil." In this sublime unconcern dwelt the Epicurean divinities, said philosophers; an early stanza of "Mycerinus" elaborates the idea, though without regard for accuracy of detail.[23]

The poet-figure of the 1849 volume is strikingly godlike, particularly in "Resignation" and "The Strayed Reveller." The first of these poems calls him more than man, and we recall that the historical Empedocles, as Arnold knew, had styled himself a god. In "The Strayed Reveller" (130–34, 207–9) the youthful votary of Dionysus says:

> The Gods are happy.
> They turn on all sides
> Their shining eyes,
> And see below them
> The earth and men.
>
> These things, Ulysses,
> The wise bards also
> Behold and sing.

There is a distinction, however: the poetic vision brings with it ineffable labor and pain (210–11). To poets is given understanding of the cares of men, but they must become what they sing: "care Must visit first them too, and make them pale" (245–46).

Underlying this view is a great classical heritage: Homer's blind or maimed bards who are termed godlike and who claim to be self-taught; Pindar's declaration that true knowledge comes by *phua*, that is, from one's inward nature. So Fausta (233–34) is bidden not to blame him "Whose natural insight can discern What through experience others learn." Still more relevant is Plato's suggestion that God takes away the poet's mind in order to make him his minister. This idea of the poet as possessed, one which is older than Plato, appears in Arnold's thought. Thus "Resignation" (246) speaks of "the poet's rapt security," which marks his separateness from ordinary men. Here "rapt" means possessed. Possibly the sense is not so strong as in the divine infilling that Greeks called *enthousiasmos*, the state of being *entheos* or "having the god within you"; nevertheless it is stronger than one may realize. Unfortunately its strength serves only to emphasize the paradox in the phrase "rapt security." Arnold has attempted to reconcile the intense involvement of Dionysiac possession with Stoic and Epicurean unconcern. This is not possible. The impossibility becomes evident through the poet's tears and his freedom from loneliness; he manifests sympathy, not apathy. "The Strayed Reveller" attempts no such paradox. In this respect as in others, it gives the impression of speaking with a single voice.

Among the poems of the first volume, "In Harmony with Nature" is an anomaly. It seems a direct attack on the central idea of Stoic ethics, the *vita secundum naturam* or life in accordance with nature. For the Stoics, *natura* embraces all existence. Man cannot be alien to it: he is inseparable from the cosmic whole, the *Weltall*. Throughout the poem, however, Arnold shows man differing from his natural environment. As Beach has said, he is using the word nature to designate the "world of things" as opposed to man's moral world. The authors of the *Commentary* find "the thought of Man as in strange spiritual isolation amid his 'natural' environment" conveyed here.[24] Their further point that Arnold is foreshadowing his later humanism receives some support from "On the Modern Element in Literature," which cites Cicero's description of man as the one creature that strives for moderation and propriety. Yet Cicero [a reserved adherent of the New Academy, so far as he can be categorized] assuredly intended no hostile division between man and the rest of animate creation. The puzzle remains: how are we to explain the anti-Stoicism of "In Harmony with Nature"?

If the question is legitimate it cannot be answered except by admitting a contradiction; but to suppose that Arnold intended a denial of Stoic views may be to misunderstand him. The language of the poem is anthropocentric: nature, so vast and majestic in "Quiet Work," has been narrowed to denote primarily man's natural instincts, which is to say his animal impulses. Whether there is a contrast between matter and spirit may be questioned. It does seem that Arnold utterly rejects any eighteenth-century belief in the "noble savage" and associates the natural man with brutishness. Unfortunately he extends this association to include the brute creation, and also whatever totality "nature" expresses here. This jars with "Quiet Work" and "Resignation," as with the later "Morality." The inconsistency, however, seems to come from a careless shift of attention, not from any falling out with Stoicism.[25]

The previous discussion of "Empedocles on Etna" referred

in passing to the borrowings from Hellenistic philosophy. Tinker and Lowry have summarized the elements that recall Lucretius and Epictetus:

> Most of the important themes of Empedocles' instruction to Pausanias are stressed at great length in *De Rerum Natura:* the vanity of luxuries and the contrast with the simple joys of outdoor life (2.20 ff.); the reiteration that the gods have not arranged the world for man's benefit (2.167 ff.; 5.155 ff.); the working of nature without respect even to the gods 2.1090 ff.); the conviction that lust and inordinate desire— not the gods—tear man to pieces (3.978 ff., 1053 ff.); the necessity for enjoying the simple pleasures of *this* life (3.931 ff.); the power of right reason to overcome our ills (3.319 ff.); and the conception of "mind as the master part of us" (3.396 ff.).... The stoical ethics, which forms so large a part of Empedocles as Arnold sees him, came . . . not from any one source. Much of it is in the spirit of Marcus Aurelius. Much is to be sought in many of Arnold's youthful favourites, and in none of these more clearly than in the Epictetus of his early sonnet. The central argument of Empedocles which issues in his final act gradually resolves itself into the main position of Epictetus:—the one way to be free is to despise the things which are not in man's power. And education is but learning to distinguish these things from the things that *are* in our power. "Make us not fly to dreams, but *moderate desire*," says Empedocles; this is the very theme of Epictetus, particularly of the *Enchiridion*, which commanded Arnold's special admiration. The final desire of Empedocles, for freedom in death, lest he succumb to error and darkness, reads like a paraphrase of the opening of the great chapter on freedom in Epictetus (*Discourses*, Bk. 4, ch. 1), which repeats an equally stirring earlier passage in Book ii, chapter I. Epictetus, even as Lucretius, attacks the desires of men and insists that the good lies not in material things and in estates, but in right reason.[26]

The Stoic and Epicurean systems show a great measure of agreement, or at least of compatibility. Their adherents disputed fiercely during antiquity, yet the two appear in Arnold's Empedocles so well combined that a reader without a special interest in these sources will hardly sense any lack of unity. The efficacy of this combined teaching is another matter: Arnold later said,

"The creed of Empedocles..., as exhibited in my poem, [was not] a satisfying one." [27] The cardinal doctrine of this creed, Stoic self-sufficiency, won Arnold's lasting admiration and strengthened him throughout his life; but he could not rest in it. To take account of its possibilities was an inevitable and fitting part of the long search for personal meaning in the face of the world's multitudinousness. That it constituted only a stage in the journey becomes apparent from the fact that Arnold eventually acknowledged a Divinity "not ourselves." Although this comes near to being a total rejection of Stoic pantheism, certain Stoics who grappled with the idea of a supreme Deity encountered much the same difficulties and contradictions, arising out of the corollary notion of transcendence.

Possibly the most important thing about the Stoics was the fact that their philosophy was a living, developing belief. For this reason Matthew Arnold could find Stoicism congenial, whereas the fixed nature of Epicureanism limited its usefulness to him. His note-book entries witness to the contrast: not one of them is taken from Epicurus. "Empedocles on Etna" constitutes earlier evidence, from the years of inner unrest. It makes good use of Lucretius, and yet the Epicurean elements have no central and essential place. At the heart of Empedocles' belief is the teaching of Epictetus.

Among the other poems of the 1852 edition, none shows a more striking and diverse relationship to the two great Hellenistic systems than "A Summer Night." It is spoken by one "*Never by passion quite possess'd And never quite benumb'd by the world's sway*" (32-33): the alternatives deliberately exclude any resolution of this inner disturbance through philosophy. The poet wonders whether any life is possible except that of a slave to routine or a mad adventurer. He finds his answer in the night sky (78-82):

> Ye heavens, whose pure dark regions have no sign
> Of languor, though so calm, and, though so great,
> Are yet untroubled and unpassionate;
> Who, though so noble, share in the world's toil,
> And, though so task'd, keep free from dust and soil!

He is tempted with the thought that the heavens are tinged with the silent pain of man's unrequited longings, but he concludes that they are "A world above man's head" (83-85, 87).

An understanding of the issues here involves the difference

between Stoic and Epicurean concepts of ataraxy. For both schools the meaning of the term was freedom from disquiet in the soul. The point on which they differed profoundly was the relation of the heavens to this calm. Epicureans actively opposed the newly developed celestial science of the later Academy: they saw in the firmament no paradigm of serenity. By contrast, Stoic thinkers adopted a cosmology similar to the Academic. Their writings, moreover, often reveal an awed delight in the majestic calm and regularity of the processions of the heavens.[28]

As in "Quiet Work," it is the Stoic approach that Arnold now follows. What complicates his poetic statement of faith is a belief, within the frame of the poem at least, that the heavens and stars are alive. Stoics held precisely this view, while Epicureans assumed a universe composed of matter; but Stoicism did not personalize the heavenly bodies. Arnold does deal with them as personalities, sentient beings almost capable of emotion, and the complications caused by this attitude are a mixed blessing to his manner of expression. Not merely "A Summer Night" but a great many of his other poems show him seeking an external world that will somehow feel sympathy for man's "silent pain," and realizing in the end that the heavens to which he has turned for solace are "calm, . . . untroubled and unpassionate." [29] The Christian and emphatically unclassical concept of infinity enables him to close his poem with an analogy that brings in the boundless horizons of the soul. This work, which several times recalls the Stoic-Epicurean figure of Arnold's Empedocles, is a valuable composite of the ideas and images that were most insistently present to the poet's thought during the period around 1850. It is also a reminder that among such concerns the differing beliefs of late classical philosophy hold a central place.

Halfway through "The Scholar-Gipsy" natural description gives way to extended commentary and conjecture; this at last yields in turn to the vividness of the "Tyrian trader" coda. The more prosaic intervening stanzas (141–230) are difficult to interpret at times, but they bear upon our subject. At their beginning the poet speaks of the numbing, exhausting shock of alternating between pleasure and pain and expending our thought on a host of schemes. Thus, he says (143–50), most of us wear ourselves out; then "To the just-pausing Genius we remit Our worn-out life, and are—what we have been." Nowhere else does so technical a reference to Stoic belief occur; perhaps it might better have been omitted. At all events, the *genius* is the guardian spirit, not merely a protector but an unsleeping judge [30] who can never be deceived. Every man is invisibly accompanied, from birth to death, by his individual *genius*. The surprising feature here is the fact that the *genius* seems detached from life rather than the companion and tutor (*comes, paedagogus*) described by Horace and Seneca. The Stoic reference is no longer furnished with its classical background.

The scholar-gipsy differed from the troubled mass of men, Arnold continues. He had "*one* aim, *one* business, *one* desire" instead of a multitude (152); he awaits eternally "the spark from heaven" (171), having never known the "strange disease of modern life, With its sick hurry, its divided aims" (203–4). The poet warns him repeatedly against any contact with modern man's sick restlessness (205–10, 221–23, 231). His undivided aim has never been satisfactorily explained, and probably we shall not come nearer to a final answer than the judicious statement of the *Commentary*:

> His search is philosophical—that of the sage living in retirement from the noisy and distracting world, and he may, therefore, fairly be associated in mind with Empedocles, with Obermann (that "*solitaire inconnu*"), and with the abbey-children at the close of the Chartreuse stanzas.[31]

Empedocles and Obermann are analogues to make one wonder if the Stoicism of this remarkable poem is confined to the single point discussed earlier. It has been evident that Stoic influence disappeared almost completely from Arnold's poetry even before the 1853 collection, but we have found no single work which signalizes the fact. "The Scholar-Gipsy" may be that work. Its strange hero, who must keep apart from men if he is to maintain his quest, may symbolize the Arnold who had come to realize that he could retain the values of Stoicism only by making it a private part of his life, a sacrament rather than an impulse to poetic creation. Of all his many attempts to formulate through poetry a conception of the world based on Stoic ideas, none had proved successful; the 1853 Preface shows that he had now adopted a new view of the poet's task.

Arnold had already begun to set down in his note-books passages from his reading. From the very first, as we shall see, his entries reflected Stoic doctrines, and in this private devotional world they continued to influence his thought. To the work of literary criticism, however—work which would dominate the next fifteen years—they could make only a limited contribution; for in theory at least the Stoic, like the Epicurean, regarded belles-lettres with a fine utilitarian contempt. For this and other reasons, late classical ethics operated unseen or rarely glimpsed in Arnold's writing until the period of *Culture and Anarchy*, just before the close of the central Victorian period.

These celebrated essays could draw upon the essential individualism of Stoic doctrine because the writer, like Plato in his *Republic*, had succeeded in establishing a vital connection between state and individual through culture. Thus, for example, Epictetus' aristocratic doctrine of inner excellence (*euphuia*) can play its part openly, although it must undergo a drastic adaptation. It will become evident, also, that in *Culture and Anarchy* the individualism which so often dominates Stoic thinking gives way of necessity to a larger view. We have noted that the central dualism of this work is suggested at the conclusion of "The Scholar-Gipsy," when the Semitic trader's seriousness rebukes the sensuous happiness and levity of the Greeks.

On this eclectic basis Arnold is to fashion his idea of culture. The new era that began in 1870 finds him turning often to the subject of religion, and liberal Christianity enters ever more strongly into his eclecticism. *St. Paul and Protestantism* and more especially *Literature and Dogma* and *God and the Bible* make extensive use of Stoic principles as concealed structural elements; as philosophy these principles continued to have a living force only in the quiet world of Matthew Arnold's devotional life. Such are the spheres of influence which will remain open to the forces of Hellenistic ethical thought.

Stoic and Epicurean: The World Accepted

With one exception, Matthew Arnold's poetry after 1853 shows no meaningful relation to either Stoicism or Epicureanism. That exception is "Obermann Once More" the sequel to "Obermann [Stanzas in Memory of the Author of]," a poem which dates from 1849. Before examining the later poem we shall note how Senancour's death is thought of in "Obermann" itself:

> For thou art gone away from earth,
> And place with those dost claim,
> The children of the second birth,
> Whom the world could not tame;
>
> And with that small transfigured band,
> Whom many a different way
> Conducted to their common land,
> Thou learn'st to think as they.
>
> Christian and Pagan, king and slave,
> Soldier and anchorite,
> Distinctions we esteem so grave,
> Are nothing in their sight.
>
> They do not ask, who pined unseen,
> Who was on action hurled,
> Whose one bond is, that all have been
> Unspotted by the world.

The "king and slave" may be Marcus Aurelius and Epictetus. Both, as we know, were important to the thought of Matthew

Arnold; but what must count far more heavily here is their importance for Senancour.[1] He adapted their teachings to his own purposes, intensifying or altering the tone by his fragile melancholy. It is with them that Arnold places Senancour, as one of a saintly company who come from every age and every walk of life. All possess one characteristic in common: they have been "Unspotted by the world." From the sonnet "To a Friend," written perhaps a year before "Obermann," we know that Epictetus at least had a positive, bracing effect, and that during this difficult period of his life, Arnold paid almost unique tribute to Epictetus' guidance. The view presented in "Obermann" counters this one; negative and alien from ordinary reality, it has a startling narrowness by comparison.

Arnold has now reached mid-century, a crucial time for him. To gain some preliminary idea of his later concern with Stoic and Epicurean doctrine, certain portions of "Obermann Once More" are worth considering. This sequel, which might more accurately be termed a palinode, dates from the first months of 1866. It arraigns the "hard Pagan world" whose "heart was stone, And so it could not thrive" (91–93). This pagan world, whose power the preceding lines emphasize, must be that of Rome. Arnold at once illustrates its satiety and disgust through Lucretius' portrait of the restless noble. The great age of Athens is not under indictment, for what Matthew Arnold thought censurable in antiquity he regularly attributed to a period later than the Hellenic, as his father had done at Rugby. Here he blamed Rome; in the essay on "Pagan and Mediaeval Religious Sentiment" it was Greek Sicily of the third century.

The visionary figure of Obermann goes on (276–80, 323–24) to address Arnold as " 'thou, who . . . Didst find the solitary man, And love his cheerless truth,' " telling him that in this new and brighter age he must use his remaining strength to further the great end: " '*One common wave of thought and joy Lifting mankind again!*' " His vision ended, the sleeper wakes to see dawn breaking over the mountains.

As the authors of the *Commentary* point out in their discussion of "Obermann Once More," the exhortation to Arnold is the "message of hope" contained in the so-called "Manual of Pseusophanes," Senancour's treatise within a treatise. Senancour presents it as a fragment of moral philosophy by Aristippus, who founded the Cyrenaic school of hedonistic ethics. But we must not be misled by this grave display of scholarship. No such work was ever seriously attributed by anyone to Aristippus, nor did the learned Varro ever mention it. The name Pseusophanes gives the whole thing away: it is impossible as a Greek formation. Altering one letter produces *pseudophanês*, "shining with false, *i.e.* borrowed light," a rare epithet used of the moon.[2]

The mild scholarly deception practiced by Senancour here— and there is at least one other elsewhere in his work—should now be plain. The "Manual" is his own creation, patterned on Arrian's handbook summary of the chief doctrines of Epictetus. We must not assume an unreal antithesis and distinguish the negation embodied in the Stoic and Epicurean teachings adopted by Senancour himself from the bracing, positive message attributed to Aristippus that he seems merely to transcribe. Such an antithesis would suit very well the obvious contrast that Arnold wished to establish through "Obermann Once More," but it is not valid. Joy and resoluteness and transcendence of self are integral aspects of the great Hellenistic systems along with solitary melancholy and renunciation; and they too have a place, though a much less prominent one, in Senancour's work.[3]

" 'Men have such need of joy' " the spirit of Obermann cries, " 'But joy whose grounds are true. . . .' " The alternative has just been named: "old-world cures men half-believe" (235–38). Although he speaks of all mankind and of the world's new order, his chief concern clearly lies with England: Anglo-Catholic ritual is "old-world." So, in "Stanzas from the Grande Chartreuse," its rites are "externe." The faint note of provinciality has of course nothing in common with Stoicism, and yet other phrases from "Obermann Once More" seem related to it if not actually derivative. Thus men need "joy whose grounds are true"; nor can this be a private happiness, for "who can be *alone* elate, While the world lies forlorn?" (247–48). Again, Obermann's spirit looks forward to a "common wave of thought and joy" lifting mankind, and the conjunction of these two terms is not without importance. If we turn to the standard Roman authorities for the Stoic definition of joy—*gaudium* as opposed to the agitation that is *hilaritas* —we find Cicero saying that joy is experienced "when the mind is stirred by reason in a calm and steady manner," while Seneca's definition is "elation of the mind trusting in its good and true possessions (*elatio animi suis bonis verisque fidentis*)."[4]

The precise nature and degree of the connection cannot be established, and this fluidity is typical of the place that Stoicism and Epicureanism held in Arnold's later thought. The reader may sense a meaningful relationship or uncover a parallel passage, but with remarkably few exceptions the connection is not made explicit. Furthermore, as these systems of philosophy move into the background of Arnold's thought their power turns sharply away from poetry. They need almost never be taken into account in any poem written after 1852. This reverses the earlier tendency, which persists only as a fashioning of attenuated likenesses such as those in "Obermann Once More." From mid-century onwards Stoic and Epicurean ethics served Matthew Arnold in two ways: as a prominent part of his devotional life reflected in the note-books, and again as an impulse behind his prose writings, usually a concealed force but a powerful and surprisingly pervasive one. The philosophy of the Porch greatly overshadows that of Epicurus in Arnold's works, whatever their period. We shall not find it necessary to stress the distinction, especially since there is valuable common ground held by both.

This very distinction never greatly mattered to Arnold. No analysis based on it, therefore, could suggest his later use of Hellenistic doctrine so characteristically as the summary of that doctrine, taken from both systems, which Senancour presents as the "Manual of Pseusophanes." [5] The following excerpts appear to be relevant:

> All that man experiences is in his heart, all that he knows is in his thought. . . .
> Is anything extrinsic to yourself which belongs to you? What matters that which can perish? . . . . All is vanity for man if he [does] not advance with equable and tranquil pace in harmony with the laws of his intelligence . . . . Whatsoever comes must also pass away, and for ever. . . . What evils afflict you? Imaginary apprehensions, fanciful needs, the crosses of a single day. . . . Abandon that which is illusory, vain and perishable to the deluded throng. Consider only the understanding which is the principle of the world's order, and man who is the instrument thereof; the understanding which must be conformed to, and man who needs our succour.
> When you have served the order of the world, what more would you have? You have acted in conformity with your nature, and what is better for any being who feels and knows than to abide in such harmony?
> Reborn each day into a new life, put to heart afresh your determination that you will not pass through this world to no purpose. . . .

Live in yourself and seek that only which does not perish.... Only in itself does understanding find the food of its life: be just and strong.... You will find no peace in things which are external, seek after it in your heart within. Force is the law of nature; power is will; energy amidst sufferings is better than apathy amidst pleasures. He who obeys and endures is often greater than he who enjoys or commands. That which you fear is vain, and vain also is that which you desire. Your welfare follows only in conformity to the will of Nature. You are at once intelligence and matter. The world itself is not otherwise. Bodies are modified by harmony, and all tends to perfection by the continuous amelioration of all its parts. This law of the universe is also that of individuals.

All is good when it is ruled by understanding, and all is bad when understanding forsakes it.... A pleasure that is possessed in harmony with universal Nature is better than a privation which she does not enjoin, and the most mediocre action of our life is less mischievous than the strain of those purposeless virtues which impede wisdom.

There is no other ethic for us than that of the heart of man, no other science or wisdom than the knowledge of its requirements, and the just estimation of the means of happiness. Leave useless knowledge, supernatural systems and mysterious doctrines....

Console, enlighten and sustain your kind; the place which you fill in the immensity of life sets forth your mission. Know and follow after the laws of man, and you will assist others to know and to follow them. Contemplate and show forth to them the centre and end of things; let them recognise the reason of all that excites their wonder, the instability of all that troubles them, the nothingness of the things which allure them.

Do not isolate yourself from the whole of the world, ever keep your eyes on the universe, and remember justice. You will then have fulfilled your life, you will have performed the part of a man.[6]

The Obermann stanzas of 1849 name two desires contending within the poet: one drives him to the world, the other to solitude. Well before 1866 and "Obermann Once More" the struggle has been decided, at the cost of poetry. The "Manual," similarly, displays egoism and altruism exerting their counter-forces; but in the end an altruistic note, at first tentative, sounds with compelling power. Senancour himself moved beyond the world-weariness of *Obermann;* fifteen years later his *Méditations* illustrate the change. At about the time of Senancour's death in 1846 a young and deeply troubled Matthew Arnold set out on much the same path, and he recorded his journey in two similarly spaced and equally contrasting works. In the second of these the "Manual" is his ethical charter for the future.

Arnold also referred to a signally important aspect of his experience at some point as early as 1852 and not later than the first months of 1855, when "Stanzas from the Grande Chartreuse" reached publication. The passage (67–78) is well known.

> For rigorous teachers seized my youth,
> And purged its faith, and trimmed its fire,
> Showed me the high, white star of Truth,
> There bade me gaze, and there aspire.
> Even now their whispers pierce the gloom:
> *What dost thou in this living tomb?*
>
> Forgive me, masters of the mind!
> At whose behest I long ago
> So much unlearned, so much resigned:
> I come not here to be your foe!
> I seek these anchorites, not in ruth,
> To curse and to deny your truth. . . .

The "rigorous teachers" have never been satisfactorily identified. The irreverent Béranger, an anti-Papist and anti-Jesuit, may conceivably be meant; a more likely candidate is Senancour, who so brutally attacked the Catholicism that he saw around him; yet neither the good-hearted *chansonnier* nor the disorganized author of *Obermann* would normally be described as rigorous. The "Manual of Pseusophanes," however, may be another matter. No doubt Goethe and certain of the modern philosophers whom Arnold had begun to read by 1845 make reasonable choices for the reference here.[7] To their number one might add the great voices who speak through Senancour and so many others, the voices of Epictetus and of that rival school which originates with Epicurus and gains new life through Lucretius' advocacy.

For a dozen years after 1850 the voices remain silent in Arnold's published prose. The Oxford lecture of 1857, "On the Modern Element in Literature," recalls several passages from *De*

Rerum Natura; one of these appears again after some years as part
of "Obermann Once More." [8] The poetic second thoughts on
Senancour, however, actually achieved publication before the
lecture finally came out, and the rest is silence—understandably
enough, when we recall the attitude of Stoics and Epicureans towards literature. The world of English letters could not know
that during these first hectic years of itinerant school-inspecting a
mature personality and literary talent were forming. Evidence is
now available, fortunately, for Matthew Arnold's development
towards the firmly defined ethical, social, and religious views that
mark the prose works. One finds it in the letters and the note-
books, and a good deal of it proves to derive from Stoic or Epicurean positions.

Early in 1848 Arnold criticizes England's indecision to
Clough. "Yet," he adds tentatively, "it is something for a nation
to feel that the only true line is its natural one?" And a few days
later, to another correspondent, "I cannot help thinking of Lucan's
famous line, *Victrix causa Deis placuit, sed victa Catoni.*" ("The
gods esteemed the winning cause; Cato, the defeated one.") [9] The
temper of mind remains essentially the same, and Lucan's Stoic
ethics, typified by the hard-bitten Cato, appear to be supplemented
by the concern with what is "according to nature." Already Arnold is revealing his bent for utilizing Stoic ideas in discussions of
the national interest, an approach that sets him apart from Epictetus and Seneca, and even from the administrator Marcus
Aurelius.

September of the same year finds him abroad. "I have with
me only Béranger and Epictetus," he points out, adding that
Epictetus is familiar to him; for at least a year he had known the
chansons as well. Now he finds the philosophy hard going at
times, but he frankly tires of Béranger.[10] The two works he has
chosen to take with him symbolize the two attitudes he is weighing, a Stoic doctrine of duty and a light-hearted hedonism that
passes itself off as Epicurean. Clearly he cannot serve both masters,
and here we see him coming to a choice.

By 1852 the results of that choice have begun to appear. "I
submit myself to the order of events," he writes quizzically to
Clough, "and revolve with the solar system in general." Despite
his tongue-in-cheek solemnity, the context is as unmistakable as
in an earlier reference to "the law of nature." "A great career,"
he tells Clough some months later, ". . . can hardly be purchased
now even by the sacrifice of repose dignity and inward clearness

—so I call no man unfortunate." One hears the authentic tones of
a Stoic who finds himself living in unpropitious times. This very
letter contains Arnold's comparison of himself and his similarly
minded contemporaries to "a gifted Roman falling on the uninvigorating atmosphere of the decline of the Empire." "Still," he
adds, "nothing can absolve us from the duty of doing all we can
to keep alive our courage and activity." Here one meets the Stoic
"cheerfulness—a sort of Tüchtigkeit, or natural soundness and
valiancy," as a letter of the following year describes it; this is
precisely the *gaudium* of reasoned contentment as against the
hilaritas that represents mere undue elation.[11]

So far as materials now available indicate, the year 1852 also
marked the beginning of Arnold's custom of livening his diary
note-books with excerpts from reading, a practice which he continued throughout the rest of his life. The excerpts come from
many periods and from a half-dozen literatures; but a great many
of them, whatever their source, embody ideas that either derive
from Stoicism or are in striking accord with its doctrines. Three
of the four entries for 1852 illustrate this accord: men's happiness
lies in devoting themselves to the things they were born to do;
domination by the passions is deplorable; human life, pointless as
an end, makes sense as a means. The French writers from whom
Arnold quotes are obscure. His interest lies not in them but in the
moral truths they have expressed, and the one context which
forms a suitable background for their ethics is that of Hellenistic
philosophy. It was perhaps partly this philosophy, with its belief
in cyclic recurrence, that Arnold had in mind when he wrote
early in 1851, "I . . . retire more and more from the modern world
and modern literature, which is all only what has been before and
what will be again." [12]

We may now have the key to an entry made in 1856. Taken
from George Sand's autobiography, it speaks of prayer as a communion of thought with the divine. So Epictetus, in a counsel
that Arnold knew, had bidden men to "Look up to God, and say:
—deal with me for the future as thou wilt: I am of the same mind
as thou art." At the close of this same year he writes:

> "Hide thy life," said Epicurus, and the exquisite zest
> there is in doing so can only be appreciated by those who,
> desiring to introduce some method into their lives, have suf-
> fered from the malicious pleasure the world takes in trying
> to distract them till they are as shatter-brained and empty-
> hearted as the world itself.[13]

With these words Arnold touches upon one of the two central ideas for which he felt indebted to Epicureanism. The other was the folly of religious superstition, understood essentially as Lucretius argues it rather than from primary sources. This second idea was not only less directly conveyed but had less personal significance. *Lathe biôsas*, Epicurus' exhortation to the secret life, stirred Arnold to a deeply personal response. Besides making this plain, the present passage marks the secret life as one of order. Thus it is the means, so long and earnestly sought, of prevailing over the world's multitudinousness by "the seeing of one's own way." Paraphrased in the language of Stoicism, this is the fact of recognizing and obeying the "guiding principle" within oneself, *to hêgemonikon*.

Six years pass with only an occasional indication that such ideas continue to have importance in Arnold's thought. For the 1857 note-book he takes from Horace an aphorism on self-reliance, that cardinal virtue which unites the Stoa with the school of Epicurus. In 1858 he reads, or plans to read, a dozen books as background for his long-planned tragedy on Lucretius. The entries for 1862 contain Sainte-Beuve's reference to the idea of a long, difficult task that might keep one in *l'équilibre moral et la sérénité*, the Stoic *aequanimitas* and *tranquillitas*. Arnold has also included Maurice de Guérin's praise of the "hidden life" of thought and study, *une vie studieuse et cachée*, as a continual joyous celebration.

The essay on de Guérin dates from this same year. His remarkable prose poem, *Le Centaure*, is there represented by several passages; one of them sets forth a wholly and distinctively Stoic concept, "the elements of the universal fire." From the French priest and educator Lacordaire come passages, copied in 1863, on the joys of solitude and of withdrawing into oneself. The ultimate source of these reflections, and also of Maurice de Guérin's remark just noted, appears in the essay on Joubert completed towards the end of that year: " 'He has chosen,' Chateaubriand (adopting Epicurus's famous words) said of him, *'to hide his life'* "; the italics are Arnold's. But the most significant entry in the note-books for 1863 is the maxim that "A man can even live well in a palace." It is taken from the *Meditations* of Marcus Aurelius, to whom Arnold now devotes a celebrated essay.

His characterization of the emperor has become so widely known that Marcus tends to be thought the leading spirit of Stoicism as interpreted by Matthew Arnold, and a powerful influence upon the latter's ethical position. This assumption is largely incorrect. The note-books cite very few non-Biblical sources as frequently as Epictetus; [14] from the *Meditations* we find just two excerpts. Notations of private reading offer little to alter the impression that this makes.

It would almost appear, in fact, that Arnold's serious concern with the imperial Stoic began and ended in 1863. Throughout the whole of his mature life the only fundamental ancient sources to which he turns for Stoicism are those to which Marcus himself turned: the *Discourses* and *Manual* of Epictetus, strongly supported at times by Cicero's treatises on the late Greek ethical systems. The essay points out that while the sentences of Seneca stimulate the intellect and those of Epictetus fortify the character, Marcus Aurelius' reflections "find their way to the soul" with their almost Christian quality; but the fact remains that of these three famous Stoics only Epictetus had lasting importance for Arnold. Strength of character, the quality singled out in "Courage" as Stoicism's great contribution, was precisely what he sought.

The fidelity of Arnold's portrait may be judged from the remarks of a highly accomplished scholar writing fifty years later:

> We do not go to Aurelius to learn what Stoic doctrine was; this is taken for granted throughout the book; but we can see here [in the *Meditations*] how it affected a man in whom the intellectual outlook was after all foreshortened by sympathies and yearnings which had grown up in his nature. The traditional criticism of the school as being harsh, unsympathetic, unfeeling, breaks to pieces as we read these "thoughts"; rather we find an excess of emotion, a surrender to human weakness.[15]

With regard to the last statement, we may gain some idea of the place that Marcus Aurelius holds in the history of Stoic ethics by examining successive attitudes towards the four *perturbationes* or disturbances of judgment. Cicero records and defines these Stoic equivalents of sinful error as fear (Greek *phobos*, Latin *metus*), greed (*epithumia*, *libido*), grief (or worry or vexation; *lupê*, *aegritudo*), and hilarity (or exaltation or excitement; *hêdonê*, *laetitia*).[16] They all consist in mistaking things that are indifferent —mere advantages or disadvantages—for actual good or evil: that is, they arise out of ignorance.

Zeno, the founder of Stoicism, came to manhood in the still vigorous times of the later fourth century B.C. With him it is the active errors of fear and greed, looking to the future, that receive a special emphasis. In the constricting conditions of the Empire Epictetus shifts the stress to grief and hilarity, passive errors concerned solely with the present. During this later period, when Stoicism had so to speak taken out Roman citizenship, its followers turned more and more towards a passive scheme of ethics in which the supreme virtues had become resignation and forbearance. This was the outlook which Marcus Aurelius, in the second century of our era, made his own by coloring it with a personal melancholy. After reading the *Meditations* one wonders whether Arnold and certain modern critics have not attributed to this element a great prominence than it actually possesses; yet it is certainly present at times, and it can attain a disturbing intensity.

Perhaps the only notable shortcoming in Arnold's lucid and winning study is his failure to realize how much common ground Stoicism and Christianity shared. Epictetus, for example, used the same nonliterary Greek as did his near contemporaries among the Christian writers who have given us the books of the New Testament. During an earlier part of the first century Paul and the author of John's Gospel (one instance that Arnold does note) both adapt Stoic concepts to their individual purposes.[17] Marcus' own time saw many young men trained in Stoicism turn from the senseless rituals of state-supported Roman religion, which the emperor championed with more vehemence than intellectual respectability—a point ignored by Arnold. Deserting paganism, they sought the persecuted Christian faith and brought into the early Church Stoic habits of thought and behavior which have never ceased to strengthen Christianity.

All this places in a somewhat altered light the essay's concluding description of an agitated figure stretching out his arms "for something beyond—*tendentemque manus ripae ulterioris amore.*" Arnold has beautifully fitted to his context Vergil's line describing the souls who cannot cross the Styx and find rest. But the barrier between Stoic and Christian did not prove to be impassable; and in fact the imperial sage was far from feeling the yearnings imputed to him. A writer who has carefully compared the beliefs of Marcus Aurelius with those of second-century Christians finds Arnold's analysis unsubtle:

> When a popular moralist like Dean Farrar or Matthew Arnold endeavours to draw from the Stoic writers arguments and illustrations for moral lessons which he is desirous of

enunciating for the benefit of a particular public, everything in Marcus Aurelius, Epictetus or Seneca which is neither precisely Christian nor precisely opposed to Christian doctrine makes apparently no impression on him, and is therefore passed by.[18]

Even if these criticisms are entirely valid, Arnold's essay furnishes the ordinary reader with an introduction to the *Meditations* and their author that has not yet been surpassed. Here, recognized and made recognizable to us, is a moralist who retains value because he so often urges right action and assigns the valid motive behind the act, and who therefore remains "the especial friend and comforter" of every rational and morally sensitive person. Years later Arnold was to describe Emerson by pointing out his essential kinship with the great Roman: neither had attained the first rank as writer or philosopher, but each was "the friend and aider of those who would live in the spirit." [19] Though New England audiences contained their enthusiasm, it was a handsome tribute. Why, then, did Marcus Aurelius have so little perceptible influence on Arnold's thought?

A part of the answer has already been suggested; the chief factor is one of temperament. In certain respects Arnold's nature resembled that of his great exemplar to a degree that becomes strikingly evident when one turns again to the *Meditations*. There is the same distaste for systematic philosophy, the same low estimate of the common man, the same magisterial self-will in dealing with received doctrine. Both writers show a deep sadness; for both, accomplishment is always set in a sobering private perspective by the thought that "the night cometh." Despite the perfectly real differences, similarities were sufficiently numerous and meaningful to justify Arnold's feeling that he had found a kindred spirit.[20] Epictetus, like Homer or Sophocles or Goethe, was his revered guide; Marcus Aurelius, a "second self," was his friend and good companion.

The following year, 1864, saw the completion of "The Function of Criticism at the Present Time." At one point Arnold admits the relativity of law and conscience but affirms that "the prescriptions of reason are absolute, unchanging, of universal validity." His thesis, which does not suggest any specific Stoic source, parallels and perhaps derives from the doctrine of the *koinos logos* or universal reason. During the late spring and summer he was reading a good deal in Cicero, and his essay "On the

Literary Influence of Academies" cites the characteristics of virtue listed in *De Officiis*, a strongly Stoic treatise "On Moral Duties." [21] Cicero had avowedly based his work on an earlier one written by the great Stoic leader Panaetius; this he supplemented with material from Posidonius, Panaetius' successor and the teacher of Cicero himself. Arnold thus was dealing with doctrine that goes back to the very beginnings of established Stoic influence at Rome. Neither here nor anywhere else, however, does he cite philosophy for its own sake: his interest centers rather in the analogy that it affords with critical procedure.

During the early months of 1866 Arnold was rereading the work that had been so much a part of himself, Senancour's *Obermann*. From this second view came not only the palinode but two entries for the diaries, one of them suggesting that a tendency towards order may be instinctive in the individual and essential to him. Arnold was to note down this thought repeatedly in his diaries. The essay "Theodore Parker," written by August of 1867, cites it in an expanded form as "the idea of a *tendance à l'ordre* present in the universe 'groaning and travailing in pain together.' " [22] Taken with its context, this borrowing proves to be Senancour's suggestion of a motive for well-doing other than the Christian hope of immortality. So in ancient times the challenge to choose good actions without an ulterior motive presented virtue as its own reward, the most celebrated of the "Stoic paradoxes."

The note-books for 1867 show a sudden outpouring of primary or clearly derivative passages relating to Stoicism; no comparable interest will be seen until the final period of 1882–87. Quotations in Greek come from Epictetus' *Enchiridion*, the summary of his essential teachings compiled by Arrian. Almost all of these are entered again for several years afterwards. Translated and provided with context where necessary, they read as follows:

> (How long will you wait to think yourself worthy of the highest and) to transgress in nothing the clear pronouncement of reason? ... Let all that seems best to you be a law that you cannot transgress.... (Take care that you do not harm your governing principle.) And (if) we guard this in everything we do, (we shall set to work more securely.) ....
> Whatever principles you put before you, hold fast to them as laws which it will be impious for you to transgress.... (As in walking you take care not to tread on a nail or to twist your foot, so) take care that you do not harm your governing

principle.... This was how Socrates attained perfection, paying heed to nothing but reason in all that he encountered. ... What is my object? To understand Nature and follow her.

The last of these, which embodies the central ideal of Stoic ethics, will recur in the note-books more frequently than any of the rest. Now the second and final quotation from Marcus Aurelius appears, and a number of the excerpts from French writers reflect the great doctrines of Stoicism so markedly that the reason for their choice cannot be in doubt.

During 1868 Arnold wrote all but one of the essays collected and published under the title *Culture and Anarchy*. Passing by Marcus Aurelius with a hasty tribute, he finds Epictetus more useful for his special purposes; from the *Discourses* he takes the terms *euphuia* and *aphuia*. These express the presence or absence, respectively, of inner excellence as a natural endowment, and their use by Epictetus has been thought to reflect an aristocratic bias inherited from such earlier sources as Plato.[23] Hereditary excellence is of course the last thing on which Arnold would wish to base his doctrine here. With typical dexterity he shifts the emphasis to Epictetus' lively concern with moral progress, illustrated in the claim that we must occupy ourselves with forming the spirit and character. Yet these are no more than preliminaries. The real function of Stoicism in *Culture and Anarchy* may be seen from two passages which make the same point, one of them near the beginning of the work and the other near its conclusion:

> Culture places human perfection in an *internal* condition, in the growth and predominance of our humanity proper, as distinguished from our animality.... Men are all members of one great whole, and the sympathy which is in human nature will not allow one member to be indifferent to the rest.... The individual is required ... to carry others along with him in his march towards perfection....
>
> Culture, or the study of perfection, leads us to conceive of no perfection as being real which is not a *general* perfection, embracing all our fellow-men with whom we have to do. Such is the sympathy which binds our humanity together, that we are indeed, as our religion says, members of one body.... Individual perfection is impossible so long as the rest of mankind are not perfected along with us.[24]

From a Christian point of view, one of Stoicism's greatest weaknesses is an essentially self-centered notion of moral perfectibility. This attitude Arnold here transcends through his emphasis on altruism, which he seems to consider a Christian addition: his examples come from the *Imitatio Christi* and Bishop Wilson's inexhaustible store of maxims. The entire basis for this part of his argument nevertheless is Stoic so far as ultimate origins are concerned (one has only to recall Senancour's "Manual"), and other passages may be called in evidence. "Trying to do violence to nature instead of working along with it," "the intelligible law of things," "right reason," [25] "a paramount best self" can have no other main source than Stoic and perhaps Platonic doctrine. Arnold, however, takes them beyond their proper range for his own purposes. Thus "the habit of fixing our mind upon the intelligible law of things" actually proves to be his closing definition of Hellenism, and in the section on *euphuia* and *aphuia* he discusses Epictetus as if this contemporary of Pliny and Tacitus were a representative of the Hellenic period. The relativism which he habitually displayed in dealing with social and political problems is paralleled here by an eclectic approach employed to gain the syncretism of his goal.[26]

Arnold's first prose account of Senancour, whom he had already celebrated in two major poems, appeared during the autumn of 1869. The essay "Obermann" reveals no change of attitude from the palinode composed three years earlier. Like "Obermann Once More," it allows us to see its subject as one who could not be happy if other men around him were in misfortune. Once again Arnold recognizes and esteems a fellow-feeling that he did not perceive in the morality of Epictetus or Marcus Aurelius. The present instance, nevertheless, makes it particularly clear that this altruism represents an extension of their views; for Senancour has rejected all systems that place hope in immortality, especially Christianity.

When Arnold published *St. Paul and Protestantism* in 1870 he seldom found occasion to introduce Stoic arguments. After 1873, when *Literature and Dogma* appeared, they have no obvious importance in his writing, although the reader may come upon an occasional reference to Epictetus or a reinforcing quotation. Even in *Literature and Dogma* they are, at most, noticeable rather than essential.[27] The note-books, on the other hand, excerpt a striking number of Stoic or Stoically derived maxims for a decade after 1876: for 1882 alone more than twenty items in Greek or Latin have been entered. Arnold continues to draw upon Epictetus, but in the period 1882–84 passages from Cicero and especially from the *Tusculan Disputations* occur with notable frequency. The entire range of relevant quotations is so extremely wide that it cannot be adequately suggested here.

Concerning the place of Epicureanism in Arnold's prose works we have said little, and indeed there is not a great deal to say. It does not appear to have held any deep importance for him as a mode of argument after "Empedocles on Etna." Whenever the term "epicureanism" appears in his lectures and essays—and the occasions are by no means frequent—its meaning and reference are loose, as if it carried little personal significance; there appears to be no awareness of a serious ethical system.[28] Epicurus himself figures in only one or two references, but his *lathe biôsas* enjoining the "hidden life" moves through a large part of the poetry and prose alike. A further possible connection has gone unrecognized: though the matter remains unsettled, some scholars believe that Menander, the friend and warm admirer of Epicurus, embodied the master's ethical teachings in his plays. It is conceivable that in this sense Arnold was a follower of Epicurus when he copied down or cited Menander's moral reflections.[29]

If there was a connection, apparently it was not realized. Broadly speaking, for Matthew Arnold Hellenistic and Roman philosophy meant Stoicism. Its metaphysical problems and inconsistencies gave him no concern. Usually he was aware of its ethical shortcomings, but he knew also that it could take him far on the road he wished to travel—and without supernatural baggage. During the earlier years of his maturity he voiced in poetry his preoccupation with the teachings of Stoicism, and occasionally with Epicurean thought as well. As time passed and prose became Arnold's chief medium, these teachings were no longer debated before the public. He employed them now as moral-intellectual stiffening, and they came to play an ever less prominent part. Whenever there was immediate need he would unhesitatingly ignore their original context and even their meaning.[30]

It is to his note-books that we must turn if we wish to see what Stoicism meant to Arnold throughout the major part of his life. The entries from Epictetus and countless other sources do not necessarily reappear in the prose works; yet if one reads these works with the entries in mind it becomes evident that, far from being mere souvenirs of reading, the Stoic excerpts act as quickening forces. One example is the statement of Epictetus that we have a natural fellowship with one another and must preserve it by every possible means: this sense of man as a social being adds strength to many of the prose writings.[31]

Above all else it is strength for his private needs that Arnold seeks when he copies down the exhortations of the Stoics. These needs do not appear to have changed significantly with the passing years. His entries begin in 1852 and keep the same general tone until they cease, only shortly before his death. The last one is a fragment of Epictetus' teachings, now entered for the third time: "You must know that it is not easy for a man to arrive at a judgment, unless he should state and hear the same principles every day and apply them all the time to his life." [32] More clearly perhaps than any other type of entry, those which derive from Stoicism suggest the consistent nature of Arnold's moral concerns. The actual range of quotations that can legitimately be traced to Stoic teachings is startlingly wide. Indeed, one cannot read any passage bearing on morality and feel entirely certain that the influence of these teachings is absent.

Edwardian critics, like certain of their successors, called Arnold a Stoic and were little concerned with proving their claim. Had they been able to see the full extent of reading and thought now so admirably displayed in *The Note-Books of Matthew Arnold*, they might have taken a different position. The man who made these entries, however courageous despite frustration and bereavement, was spiritually a descendant of Cicero, committed not to Stoicism but to eclecticism. Unconcerned with systems (there was no Eclectic school), Arnold devoted a lasting concern to ideals, syntheses, tendencies. What he required, he took; the source of a statement mattered much less to him than its effectiveness. It does seem fair to say that the convictions or instincts which guided his eclectic procedure very often led him to adopt moral positions directly or indirectly attributable to Stoicism.[33] These Stoic views, fusing with Christian thought as in the early history of Christianity itself, became an essential part of the mind of Matthew Arnold.

X

The Greeks and Their Achievement

The life of fifth-century Athens was for Matthew Arnold "one of the highly developed, one of the marking, one of the modern periods in the life of the whole human race." This does not necessarily imply a time scheme of an exact century from 500 to 400 B.C., and if we ask what period he did usually have in mind the answer is not to be had easily. According to one of the earlier *Essays in Criticism*, it was at Athens between 530 and 430 that poetry made "the noblest, the most successful effort she has ever made as the priestess of the imaginative reason." Taking 430 as a terminus excludes much of Sophocles' and Euripides' surviving work and the whole of Aristophanic comedy; it is likely that these are merely round numbers.

Elsewhere Arnold praises, as the most enlightening and stimulating part of the study of antiquity, Greek literary and artistic achievements from the birth of Simonides in 556 to Plato's death in 347. In "A Speech at Eton" he deals with a broad range of Hellenic morality and literature. Here he agrees with Curtius that after 406, the year of Sophocles' death, the same influences which destroyed the foundations of national life undermined poetry. He maintains also that the Peloponnesian War, which lasted from 431 to 404, ended in the swift demoralization of Greece.[1] The terminus thus would seem to be fixed no earlier than the final decade of the fifth century.

On a realistic estimate, however, all that these passages prove is the futility of seeking historical precision in a writer who was not concerned with it. Only pragmatic evidence has any meaning here. One must be able to say what period it is that Matthew Arnold actually talks about when he refers to the Greeks in other than generalizing terms. The answer cannot be in doubt: it is the

Periclean age. Broadly speaking, this means the middle third of the fifth century. Pericles was already important in Athenian politics by 469; from 444 until his death in 429 he decided state policy. During the years of peace after 444 he had Phidias direct a great building program, with the Parthenon as its master work. The relationship between the two men was one of personal friendship, and Sophocles and the radical philosopher Anaxagoras likewise were Pericles' intimates. Spartan invasions of Attica brought to an end the golden period that had seen the production of Sophocles' *Antigone* and the Parthenon dedication.

We may surmise, accordingly, that if Arnold speaks of a hundred years' period ending at 430 B.C. his attention is not on chronologies but on the Periclean age and what preceded it. For him it symbolized all that has proved enduring in Hellenic achievement. As an actual span of years it is too brief to contain the whole sum of memorable conditions and events, but to Arnold this was not an important consideration. He was guided by an unfaltering belief that, just as noble writing presupposes nobility of soul, a truly great literature is the image of a great age. The writers of such an age, therefore, are its true and adequate spokesmen. This view may justly be called Hellenic, and only fifth-century Hellas can meet its terms with something approaching completeness. Here it would be better to say fifth-century Athens: the essay "Equality" aptly recalls Isocrates' claim that Athens was "the school of Hellas." [2]

That it was a remarkable period none will question. Arnold's tributes never appear extravagant; their fault, when they have one, is not *hubris* but *hamartia*—they do not go to excess, but sometimes they miss the mark. One must ask whether it is really true that the middle and lower classes achieved at Athens "the highest development of their humanity that these classes have yet reached"; or that Thucydides represents "the general intelligence of his age and nation"; or again that Sophocles is an instance of "grace and light" idealizing and glorifying the same vigor, freedom, and intelligence as in the body of the Athenians. [3] Such claims are more likely to express preconceptions than careful reflection. Arnold also affirms that every Athenian of Pericles' day knew how to read, though his own familiarity with Greek literature should have warned him against accepting uncritically the word of a German philologist. Again, it will be recalled that he spoke of shopkeepers and tradesmen taking part in Plato's dialogues, which he had confused with the reminiscences compiled by Xenophon. These positions, like the preceding ones, evidently were taken up because he was determined to portray the great age of Athens as a period of universal culture, "the culture of a *people*" and that people "a nation with a genius for society." [4]

When the lines are not accidentally out of drawing, the portrait is a tolerable likeness. In its broad grouping Pericles himself is hardly visible.[5] He emerges only momentarily as the most perfect of all orators, matchless in his ability to combine thought and wisdom with feeling and eloquence. The portrait in fact has little interest in any single individual: what it attempts to capture is an entire age. Here was a period which in "maturity of reason" reminded Arnold of the nineteenth century, yet seemed unique for its view of art and literature as necessities vital to the nation. While he never could make anything of Greek art, the written word was another matter; fifth-century poetry delighted him with its adequacy as a reflection of the age. Modernity is not in question—he ascribes modernity of thought to the historian Thucydides, and he credits Lucretius with modernity of feeling. The Periclean poets are related in his thinking not to the Victorian present but to the Goethean past and to the future: "Goethe's task," he says, "was,—the inevitable task for the modern poet henceforth is,—as it was for the Greek poet in the days of Pericles, ... to interpret human life afresh, and to supply a new spiritual basis to it." [6]

Arnold's view of literature made him conceive of this task as a moral and religious obligation consciously undertaken. Such an interpretation can be highly tendentious, but it has some relevance to Athens in the central portion of the fifth century. Philosophy had not yet taken notice of man's problems; drama alone dealt with the human condition. Too much, perhaps, has been made of the didactic and paideutic elements in the tragedians and Aristophanes; nevertheless, they come to grips with ideas in a manner not easily described by keeping to other terms. Arnold's subjective interest here came into happy conjunction with a measure of objective fact. Because the foundations are enduring, what he says has not altogether lost its value.

For Arnold Hellenic tradition meant above all the age of Pericles, but he set its limits far wider than this. The great majority of his references to the Greeks are generalized; they show him ranging without hesitation from the pre-Hellenic era of Homer to the Roman Empire under Diocletian and Marcus Aurelius. As a result, his view at times appears to be a superficial one. There are also times, however, when it is genuinely synoptic and resembles in breadth if not in depth the Platonic ideal that he admired. Arnold is not merely the first English literary figure equipped with a truly European field of reference: he is also the first to grasp and use the classical past as a continuum. Samplings from its literature had embellished countless pages throughout preceding centuries, lending substance to the anatomizings of Burton and the nameless charm of the Sirens' song to *Hydriotaphia*. Arnold takes another path. His Greek and Latin tags are thrown off lightheartedly for the most part; the lines that really moved him were not for casual show. What held his interest was the play of ideas making character manifest through style, and this he found in the Greeks.

His essay on Byron suggests the ideal nature for a creative artist: it is "that of the finely touched and finely gifted man, the *euphuês* of the Greeks." *Culture and Anarchy*, which in every sense stands at the midpoint of Arnold's long career as a prose writer, had already shown that he considered the ideal of the *euphuês* a universal human goal of the highest importance. Starting from a comment of Epictetus on *aphuia*, the nature "not finely tempered," he goes on to say in the Byron essay that the Greek terms *aphuia* and *euphuia*

> give exactly the notion of perfection as culture brings us to conceive of it: a perfection in which the characters of beauty and intelligence are both present, which unites "the two noblest of things,"—as Swift most happily calls them,— "*sweetness and light*." The *euphuês* is the man who tends towards sweetness and light; the *aphuês* is precisely our Philistine. The immense spiritual significance of the Greeks is due to their having been inspired with this central and happy idea of the essential character of human perfection.[7]

Thus an unimportant ethical antithesis from Stoicism combines with a symbolic use of honey and beeswax from *The Battle of the Books* to produce a phrase destined for fame. Its parentage is in a sense doubly classical, since Swift's bee claimed to speak for "the ancients." Testimony from Pindar and Aristotle has not been cited, although the former is much concerned with *phua*, innate excellence, and the latter recognizes *euphuia* as a predisposition towards ethical virtues which is found in the children of civilized peoples.

Arnold may not have known this point in Aristotle; Pindar he knew well. Nevertheless, he could hardly have used either writer to establish his own claim. Unlike them he speaks not of an inward gift, a heritable tendency, but of an acquired state to which men must consciously aspire: his *euphuês* "tends towards" perfection. Epictetus, the writer who serves Arnold's purpose, lived more than five centuries after Aristotle. His Stoic thought has roots in the late Hellenic teachings, Aristotelian and also Platonic. Arnold, however, was either ignorant of the connection or unconcerned with it. He stresses the idea of moral progress, a basic principle of Hellenistic ethics; this he reinforces at times with excerpts from the two earlier philosophers which recognize the intellectual and aesthetic aspects of culture scorned by the Stoics. From these diverse materials he builds his composite conception of the true nature of culture. The fact that the completed structure is far from purely Hellenic troubles him not at all.

At one point Arnold mentions Leonardo's sense of lacking *symmetria prisca*, the "antique symmetry" of the Greeks. He goes on to define this as "fit details strictly combined, in view of a large general result nobly conceived." The Greek striving after harmonious proportion, not clearly acknowledged here, gains recognition in a fine passage from *Culture and Anarchy*: "The true grace and serenity is that of which Greece and Greek art suggest the admirable ideas of perfection,—a serenity which comes from having made order among ideas and harmonised them." As Arnold saw, the ideal of harmonious and complete human perfection regulated all Greek pursuits, whether of mind or of body. Thus, he says, Curtius rightly holds that "the idea of a culture comprehending body *and soul* in equal measure" chiefly distinguishes the Greeks from barbarians ancient and modern.[8]

In these references the approach varies from aesthetic and intellectual to cultural and broadly educative. Arnold felt ill at ease in dealing with any of the fine arts. On the other hand, he realized that one can never adequately assess the Greek experience in terms of literature alone, and there are brave attempts to give the ceramics and architecture of Athens their due praise. These references to Greek art may also reflect an awareness of what his classicism owed to Goethe's view of Greek harmoniousness, and so ultimately to the thought of Winckelmann.[9] The great majority of his judgments, however, bear either upon morals or upon literature; he seldom isolates and weighs aesthetic factors. His whole posture of criticism sets him apart from Ruskin in this regard, even as Plato's attitude contrasts with that of Aristotle.

It is all the more rewarding, accordingly, to find Arnold describing the Greeks as "the great exponents of humanity's bent for sweetness and light united, of its perception that the truth of things must be at the same time beauty." The first point brings *euphuia* once more to mind, and the mention of a "bent" suggests that perhaps he did know Aristotle's point about natural receptiveness to the moral virtues.[10] The Keatsian equation of truth with beauty reappears on several occasions, but it nowhere functions as a cardinal principle for interpreting classical thought. Probably its chief service is to mirror certain lasting fondnesses and aversions.

What qualities did the Greeks actually possess? "The flower of Hellenism," Arnold replies, "is a kind of amiable grace and artless winning good-nature, born out of the perfection of lucidity, simplicity, and natural truth." The Greeks who emerge are remarkably complaisant; they come from the pages of *St. Paul and Protestantism*, written during the period when Arnold would sometimes trim his estimate of Hellenism to suit his current homily. In an article of 188. "An Eton Boy," the same ideas recur. There Arnold calls the young Etonian, Arthur C. B. Mynors, "Greek in his simplicity and truth of feeling." [11] Bland, amiable, uncomplicated: such, apparently, was the race who originated so much of the modern world.

On the Study of Celtic Literature, an earlier work, suggests a different estimate. It ascribes to the Greek "the same perceptive, emotional temperament as the Celt" but also a sense of measure. Where such a sense prevails the zealot finds little company; and *Culture and Anarchy*, another work which precedes the theological period, says that to an unusual degree the Greeks escaped "the fanaticism which we moderns, whether we Hellenise or whether we Hebraise, are so apt to show." [12]

All these assessments seem to be describing an abstract individual: "the Greek," as it were *in vacuo*. Plato had related man to the *polis* or city-state as microcosm to macrocosm, so that the State was the individual writ large. By calling man a *politikon zôon*, an essentially social being, Aristotle indicates a comparable relationship. Arnold never took this peculiarly Greek view for his own, despite his intense interest in education and religion on a national scale. When he does show any concern it is for individualism, and he is careful to point out that State control does not inhibit this:

> In ancient Greece, where State-action was omnipresent, ... we see the individual at his very highest pitch of free and

fair activity. This is because, in Greece, the individual was strong enough to fashion the State into an instrument of his own perfection. . . . He was not enslaved by it, he did not annihilate it, but he used it.[13]

Whether or not this is a tenable position, one thing seems certain: Arnold is not speaking from the assumptions that a Hellene would have found natural.[14]

A point that he does not wish his readers to forget is the difficulty, and yet the absolute necessity, of balancing intellect and morality. The Greeks furnish an excellent historical example, and it is chiefly on this score that he turns his attention to them. "The power of intellect and science, . . . of beauty, . . . of social life and manners,—these are what Greece so felt, and fixed, and may stand for." And again, "Greece was the lifter-up to the nations of the banner of art and science." Even so unlikely a source as "The French Play in London" brings Arnold to a realization of "how eminently this intellectual power counts in the actor's art as in all art, how just is the instinct which led the Greeks to mark with a high and severe stamp the Muses." What they failed to do, he points out repeatedly, was to "give adequate practical satisfaction to the claims of man's moral side." They sought to reconcile fully the two sides of human nature, but they lacked sufficient flexibility to give the claim of moral ideas due recognition. If the "imperious ideal of art and science" prevented the triumph of *l'homme sensuel moyen*, it proved injurious because the Greeks were (as he thought) excessively faithful to it, and it proved intrinsically unsound because Western man had not yet attained its absolute prerequisite, "the indispensable basis of conduct and self-control." [15]

In the best creative achievements of Greece religion and poetry are one, Arnold believes: "The idea of beauty and of a human nature perfect on all sides adds to itself a religious and devout energy." In the same way, only the Greeks and Goethe have achieved any appreciable success in "the grand business of modern poetry,—a moral interpretation, from an independent view, of man and the world." Perhaps Arnold specifies critical independence with some thought of his own lack of orthodoxy in religious matters. The major Athenian poets showed this quality to a striking degree: not one of them reproduced uncritically the conventional beliefs of the day. The dominantly civic character of worship in antiquity and the freedom from dogma and bigotry in henotheism help to make their attitude understandable. The divided sects of Victoria's England were quite another matter. When Arnold told Clough that poetry must become "a complete *magister vitae*" as it had been for the ancients, the issue at which he was striking was precisely that of religion. His failure to strike accurately therefore laid him open to particularly strong criticism both in his own age and in ours.[16]

Compared with faith and morals the intellectual element appears to have a modest role, but on one occasion it becomes all-important. "On the Modern Element in Literature" was written, says Arnold, to show that Greek literature "is, even for modern times, a mighty agent of intellectual deliverance." This deliverance consists in understanding our complex present and past by grasping "the general ideas which are the law of this vast multitude of facts." Its perfect attainment is marked by "that harmonious acquiescence of mind which we feel in contemplating a grand spectacle that is intelligible to us." [17] To conduct he assigned three-fourths of life, but the controlling element was the remaining fourth that represented thought.

Concerning general matters of a purely literary nature one remaining question should be noted: it concerns the relative importance of style. When he is summarizing various methods of natural description Arnold speaks of the Greek way. This he defines partly through a contrast with mere fidelity: "In the faithful way of handling nature, the eye is on the object, and that is all you can say; in the Greek, the eye is on the object, but lightness and brightness are added." According to the Oxford lectures on Homer, moreover, Wordsworth had held that "wherever Vergil seems to have composed 'with his eye on the object,' Dryden fails to render him." Here the context shows that the opposite of classical directness is a preoccupation with style, a literary self-consciousness.[18]

At this point discussion becomes more difficult. On the one hand we find such a derogation of style as in the passage just cited; on the other, a tendency to exalt the doctrine of *le style, c'est l'homme même*. The difficulty can best be explained by examining a striking instance of this doctrine, contained in a letter that Arnold wrote early in 1849:

> In Sophocles what is valuable is not so much his contributions to psychology and the anatomy of sentiment, as the grand moral effects produced by *style*. For the style is the

expression of the nobility of the poet's character, as the matter is the expression of the richness of his mind: but on men character produces as great an effect as mind.[19]

The lectures on Homer twelve years later retain this conviction, applying it to translators rather than poets, yet they also condemn those who make stylistic excellence a chief concern. The one important prose work of the intervening years, the 1853 Preface, has almost no mention of the whole topic.

A key to the puzzle can be found in this letter to Clough. We note that for Arnold the grand effects of stylistic power—he has just referred to the "grand style" [20] in this letter—are moral effects, reflecting the moral excellence of their creator. They constitute the poet's interpretation, being precisely that criticism of life which Arnold has given as the essential definition of poetry. It seemed to him that Pope's translations of Homer, like the great mass of eighteenth-century conventional verse, mistook the means for the end and glorified manner at the expense of matter. This kind of poetry, he declared, was conceived in the wits rather than the soul. Several modern critics have shown how limited his position was here.[21] For present purposes, however, the one thing needful is to acknowledge the position for what it was.

The eighteenth century as Matthew Arnold saw it dissociated style from true expression, which is the embodiment and not the mere statement of true nobility. This detached variety we might call false style, though he does not actually use the phrase; it may serve here as resembling the *simplesse* which he contrasts with *simplicité*. He believed that its presence witnesses to a want of "high seriousness," and he condemns or approves according to the moral standard, which he applies universally. His verdicts often prove to be invalid, since more complex criteria are needed. What, for example, are the "lightness and brightness" of Greek dealings with nature if not aesthetic or intellectual factors? On several occasions Arnold tries to solve difficulties of this kind by insisting that a very broad meaning must be given to the term "moral." Whether it can possibly acquire sufficient breadth to include the intellectual and the aesthetic as well is a difficult question.

The fourth and fifth chapters of *Culture and Anarchy* have achieved a separate existence under the title "Hebraism and Hellenism." Arnold owes the antithesis to Heinrich Heine and ultimately to Heine's source, Ludwig Börne. It originated in the last years of the eighteenth century as a distinctively Jewish problem, formulated and worried over by the intellectuals of a minority group who were seeking their place in a non-Jewish society. Out of this same setting comes Heine's *Hellenismus*, presumably the source of Arnold's term. The Greek original of "Hellenist" (*Hellênistês*, like *Hellênismos* a nonclassical word of the late Graeco-Roman period) described a Jew who had adopted the Greek way of life.[22]

Arnold accomplishes a transformation of Heine's conception that may justly be called remarkable. He shifts the scene from the Continent to England, advancing the time by three-quarters of a century. A Jewish minority yields its role to an Anglo-Saxon majority; the complacent Victorian bourgeois replaces the introspective man of thought. Finally, a problem of cultural penetration and adjustment emerges, quite unrecognizably, as a statement of the need to revise established attitudes and alter radically the accepted perspective. The view Arnold recommends is that very philhellenism advocated among Jewish intellectuals two generations earlier, but he finds the balance quite reversed in the case of his English contemporaries. Whereas Heine and other writers had introduced Hebraism "just as a foil and contrast to Hellenism," Hellenism in England has now been "reduced to minister to the triumph of Hebraism."[23]

The essay contrasts Hellenic spontaneity of consciousness with Hebraic strictness of conscience. Arnold italicizes the phrases, which he takes to embody the governing ideas in either case. He has already made a secondary distinction: "The uppermost idea with Hellenism is to see things as they really are;... with Hebraism ... conduct and obedience." Aware that some would be quick to charge him with oversimplifying, he qualifies the contrast slightly and acknowledges a certain surface agreement. The gesture is insufficient, the presentation remains too neatly antithetical. To the ordinary reader Old Testament morality does not seem noticeably misrepresented, although there is no recognition of the strangely Hellenic nature of Job, who would not cease from demanding of God a *logos* to explain fate's apparently meaningless blows. The unfairness lies in claiming that the Hellenic consciousness was devoted to intellectual clarity rather than right conduct. To show the fundamental difference that he sees beneath the superficial agreement, Arnold cites the views of Plato and Aristotle. For the former it is the man who prizes intellectual

things, and that man only, who may possibly attain to a vision of
the divine; the Aristotelian hierarchy ranks the moral virtues
below those of the intelligence.[24]

These two points are correctly taken. Their fault lies in the
fact that they contain partial truths which cannot give the larger
view. After all, what the *Republic* seeks to understand is the moral
quality of justness. In the end it proves to be not a separable virtue
but a relationship—harmonious proportion among the rational,
"spirited," and sensual parts of the soul. On such a view the moral
and the intellectual are inseparable. The central text of Literae
Humaniores in Arnold's day, the *Nicomachean Ethics*, heavily
stresses *êthikai aretai*, literally "excellences which come through
habituation" (for *êthos*, "character," is what results from habit).
Finally, Arnold says that the Greek is happy when he thinks
aright, when his thought "hits the mark." Underlying this last
phrase must be the term *hamartia*, "error." [25] This derives from
hamartanô, literally "to miss the mark" as an archer might do,
figuratively "to err." *Hamartia* in the *Poetics* has often been translated as the "tragic flaw" that brings disaster. The question of
whether this so-called flaw constitutes a moral or an intellectual
failing is still being debated. Those who have raised the issue may
err in taking the alternatives for granted; it has been claimed that
fourth-century Attic usage did not precisely distinguish the two
meanings. In any case, the importance of the moral element is
clear.

What Arnold needs to present in "Hebraism and Hellenism"
are the real grounds of difference. Israel was a nation, though its
people might be homeless wanderers; no comparable unity existed
among Greek-speaking peoples. The worship of Jahweh was a
nationally established monotheism; the Greeks practiced an aggregate of more or less henotheistic rites which varied widely from
one locale to another, and in them Zeus was not always the real
center of interest. Most important, Greek religion was not controlled by a powerful priesthood who made known a cosmogony
and a code of behavior towards God and man. These are truisms,
but their truth might have been acknowledged. There is no question of conduct being exalted by one people and made clearly
secondary by the other. The question concerns the place of intellect, of the curiosity that seeks to be shown a reason for the
scheme of things and man's place in it. The issues that Athenian
tragic poets and philosophers discussed were ignored among Old
Testament peoples save by the outlander from the far country of

Uz; and it was not dialectic that silenced him, but a whirlwind. Here the antithesis that we have been considering stands up well to examination. Where it makes play with conscience and conduct the shakiness becomes evident.

"By the law of its nature," says Arnold, Hellenism "opposes itself to the notion of cutting our being in two." Possibly the finest service rendered by his essay is this emphasis on the need for wholeness, for the completely realized man. The distinctive contribution of Hellenism, it seems, is to the intellect; yet one of the two main divisions of the Greek schoolboy's curriculum was physical training, which Arnold found overemphasized among his contemporaries. He therefore took Englishmen to task for pursuing muscular Christianity mechanically and as an end in itself, without that "constant reference to some ideal of complete human perfection and happiness" which he saw in the Greeks. He seems to pattern his approach somewhat on Plato's: according to the *Republic*, a disproportionate concern with physical culture makes us brutish.[26] Presumably he did not know the actual balancing of physical and intellectual in education was already a thing of the past when Plato wrote. Gymnastics had in fact been reduced to the insignificant role which it has played ever since in the Continental tradition of education.

The balance that Arnold advocated was quite a different one. Heine had already made plain the necessity for it, but the Englishman who could read German easily was still a great rarity. The insularity against which Arnold fought so determinedly was to some considerable extent a matter of language barriers. He gladly acknowledged the benefit Carlyle's translations had brought to the previous generation; his own role he saw as that of interpreter, a kind of Victorian Cicero. So it was that he indicted England's Puritanical, unreflective Christianity by means of the contrast that German Jews had drawn between Hellas and Israel. His manner is eclectic, as always. The Greek experience is called upon when it seems able to further a distinctively English wholeness in which Hellenic intelligence will balance Hebraic strength of conscience.[27] Whatever the cost in accuracy, the result is the single most striking use of classical thought in the entire range of Arnold's prose works.

The Heritage of Rome; Religion, Philology, and the Classical

To come from Arnold's Greece to his Italy involves a drastic change of scene. The landscape becomes strangely flat and conventional: there are pretty views, but the grand perspectives are lacking. Moreover, the country through which the Hellenizing Arnold passes often provides a background that enables him to be seen with great vividness. In the Italian landscape he is seldom even visible as an individual.

The case of Vergil forms a partial exception, and almost the only one. Arnold agrees with Joubert that his poetry possesses supreme elegance. This elegance, he adds, exercises a fascination that "makes us return to his poems again and again, long after one thinks one has done with them." So also, when Francis Newman called Homer elegant, Arnold pointed out that the epithet properly describes Vergil. "This suffering, this graceful-minded, this finely-gifted man is the most beautiful, the most attractive figure in literary history," though he does not adequately interpret his age: thus the 1857 lecture "On the Modern Element in Literature." According to the same source an "ineffable melancholy" shadows the entire *Aeneid;* and many years later in an address to the Wordsworth Society, after quoting and beautifully translating several lines from the *Georgics,* Arnold speaks of "the ineffable, the dissolving melancholy" displayed in them.[1] No doubt he had referred to the files, but this is something more than a phrase-maker's careful husbanding of reserves. It is a repeated acknowledgment of the element to which his own nature never failed to respond. If his attempts to be Homeric come out more often than not as Vergilian, we need seek no further for the reason.

In "On the Modern Element in Literature" Arnold claims to feel "a profound, an almost affectionate veneration" for Vergil; yet he finds in the very form of the *Aeneid* a proof of its author's failure to achieve real adequacy. Arguments are brought forward to support his contention:

> The epic form, as a form for representing contemporary or nearly contemporary events, has attained, in the poems of Homer, an unmatched, an immortal success. . . . But for [Vergil's] purpose, for the poetic treatment of the events of a *past* age, the epic form is a less vital form than the dramatic form. . . . The dramatic form exhibits, above all, *the actions of man as strictly determined by his thoughts and feelings,* . . . what may be always accessible, always intelligible, always interesting. But the epic form takes a wider range; . . . the thought and passion of man, that which is universal and eternal, but also the forms of outward life, the fashion of manners, the aspects of nature, that which is local or transient.

These, Arnold concludes, can only be portrayed adequately by a contemporary; antiquarian "reconstruction" is not capable of proving really interesting.[2]

The debatable statements here make an imposing total. Arnold was himself at least as contemporary with Chaucer as Homer had been with the siege of Troy, and the dramatic form of which he speaks is certainly one outside the experience of Aeschylus and Sophocles. His assurance that the minds and hearts of dramatic characters from the past are always accessible to our understanding shows a critic undeterred by historical context; it ignores differences that would make many slow to use such absolutes as "universal" and "eternal." We must consider, finally, whether custom and nature are really "local or transient." If the outward world changes yet much recurs, and most of all in nature, from which the great majority of epic similes derive. It has usually been thought a cardinal feature of Homer's similes that, with one or two exceptions, they are not local or transient.

The reason for these strange arguments is probably that Arnold wished to align theory with practice. A belief in dramatic action governed solely by thought and feeling underlies the 1853 Preface, and five years later *Merope* exemplifies it with the greatest clearness. Arnold attempted no epics or even epyllia; yet "Sohrab and Rustum" fairly groans beneath the weight of its similes, and of these the greater number show a failure to understand the ends for which Homer used comparison.

In 1854 Sainte-Beuve writes to Arnold, clearly with the Preface of the previous year in mind:

L'Éneide a vécu et vit par l'appropriation d'un sujet antique à un temps présent et par l'infusion d'un souffle et d'un esprit tout romain refluant jusqu'aux origines.... Apollonius, au contraire,... n'a fait dans l'ensemble qu'un poème savant et mort.[3]

Not antiquarian "reconstruction" but a filling of the past with the spirit of the present: this is the point about the *Aeneid* that Sainte-Beuve rightly makes clear. Apparently Arnold failed to discern it. We can guess the reason: except for *Merope*, that *poème savant et mort*, his own poetry showed the same quality. Many critics have remarked on its Vergilian strain, and indeed Arnold himself showed a certain awareness of this. The awareness did not, however, go deep enough to let him see that Vergil actually appealed to him because of *un souffle et un esprit tout arnoldien*.

"We come to Horace," he continues:

and if Lucretius, if Virgil want cheerfulness, Horace wants seriousness.... Men of the world are enchanted with him; he has not a prejudice, not an illusion, not a blunder. True! yet the best men in the best ages have never been thoroughly satisfied with Horace.

He is inadequate, says Arnold, for the same reason that Menander is inadequate: faith, enthusiasm, energy do not enter into his view of life. He sees its variety, its movement, but ignores its depth and significance.

Horace warms himself before the transient fire of human animation and human pleasure while he can, and is only serious when he reflects that the fire must soon go out:—

"Damna tamen celeres reparant caelestia lunae:
Nos, ubi decidimus—"

"For nature there is renovation, but for man there is none!"— it is exquisite, but it is not interpretative and fortifying.

Years earlier he had written to Clough that Horace, like Béranger, "had to write only for a circle of highly cultivated desillusionés roués, in a sceptical age." The present age was likewise one of doubt, he noted, but a far different and wider audience had arisen.[4]

Not often in Arnold's dealings with the poetry of an earlier age will one meet such willingness to consider the historical factor, however erratically. Moreover, the picture of Horace musing on death is beautifully drawn, whether it convinces or not. Less than a year before his own death Arnold wrote in the *Fortnightly Review*, "I should say that no passages have moved and pleased me more than, in poetry, the lines describing the pity of Zeus for the horses of Achilles..., and the famous stanza of Horace, 'Linquenda tellus,'...." If seriousness is not involved here, then words have no meaning. There were cynical rakes among Horace's audience, but he wrote for Augustus as well, champion of the ancient morality; and as it turned out he wrote also for Matthew Arnold, who responded not to the "Roman Odes" that counsel *virtus* and *disciplina* but to pale Death, and Charon's wherry, and the mourning cypress—the eternal note of sadness.[5]

Arnold discusses only one other Latin poet, the Epicurean Lucretius,[6] and does so at some length in "On the Modern Element in Literature." Stamped upon Lucretius' work, as well as consciously pictured in it, he finds depression and ennui. This he considers a proof of its remarkable modernity of feeling. And yet, "how can a man adequately interpret the activity of his age when he is not in sympathy with it?" Surrounded by the rich and varied life of an extremely busy world, Lucretius keeps himself and his disciples apart from its activity. His message is that one must learn the nature of things, *naturam cognoscere rerum;*

> but there is no peace, no cheerfulness for him either in the world from which he comes, or in the solitude to which he goes. With stern effort, with gloomy despair, he seems to rivet his eyes on the elementary reality, the naked framework of the world, because the world in its fulness and movement is too exciting a spectacle for his discomposed brain. He seems to feel the spectacle of it at once terrifying and alluring; and to deliver himself from it he has to keep perpetually repeating his formula of disenchantment and annihilation.... Lucretius is... overstrained, gloom-weighted, morbid; and he who is morbid is no adequate interpreter of his age.[7]

The passage, like so many others in Arnold's prose, does not close on a sustained strong note. Its cadences nevertheless move with the power of an incantation, and only by a conscious effort can one get back of them and assess the actual content of what has been said. To begin with, Arnold ignores the ancient tradition that love-potions had driven the poet to intermittent madness. He was bent on portraying a mind overburdened and depressed, "discomposed" but not wrenched from its hold on reality. This same passage indicates that he saw in Lucretius the typical oversensitive individual who pays the price for "the predominance of thought, of reflection, in modern epochs." Theories of aphrodisiacs could only falsify the portrait of one for whom the time itself was out of joint.

Arnold's intention can be surmised more fully from "Empedocles on Etna," where there can be little doubt that the figure of Empedocles to some extent represents the author himself. If we accept a measure of identity among the group Lucretius-Empedocles-Arnold, there may be a special significance in the sentences that most directly indict Lucretius: "How can a man adequately interpret the activity of his age when he is not in sympathy with it? . . . He who is morbid is no adequate interpreter of his age." Arnold himself succeeded in avoiding morbidity. Unlike Swinburne he was never more than half in love with death, nor was his grip on life allowed to become flaccid. The charge of being unsympathetic towards one's age, however, is a self-indictment. He also claimed that his poems represented "the main movement of mind" in the mid-nineteenth century. These are polar: he cannot be right on both counts. In an age of deep internal stresses the discordant view may well be the most revealing, but Arnold could not have recognized this without abandoning his theory of significant literature as the adequate interpretation of significant epochs. The 1853 Preface begins by speaking of Empedocles as

> one of the last of the Greek religious philosophers, one of the family of Orpheus and Musaeus, having survived his fellows, living on into a time when the habits of Greek thought and feeling had begun fast to change, character to dwindle, the influence of the Sophists to prevail.

Empedocles, Arnold, and undoubtedly Lucretius as well merge into a single figure—that of the sensitive, highly gifted man born too late, thwarted by an ignoble and fevered age.[8] "We hear . . . the doubts, we witness the discouragement, of Hamlet and of Faust."

Ovid, Lucan, Juvenal: each appears once or twice in Arnold's prose, usually to furnish him with a verse tag. The impassioned, forthright Catullus does not appear at all. Propertius, with his strange mixture of the *raffiné* and the macabre, receives a single passing mention, though the diary reading-lists include his name with remarkable frequency.[9] Even the supreme figures of Latin poetry are given relatively little attention: Vergil and Horace appear most often in single lines, and their use sometimes has neither wit nor relevance. Like any other schoolboy of his time, Arnold had learned extensive portions of the work of both poets; his criticism nevertheless makes no special use of either.

Latin prose writers of the classical period seem to have made almost no impression: Cicero himself figures importantly only once. This one occasion, however, is worth noticing. "The Literary Influence of Academies" cites his thesis that man alone strives to learn "*quid sit* ordo, *quid sit quod* deceat, *in factis dictisque qui* modus—the discovery of an *order*, a law of *good taste*, a *measure* for his words and actions." This, says Arnold, holds good in intellectual as well as moral matters; thus Sainte-Beuve can make the point that " 'what we French seek above all to learn is, whether *we were right* in being amused . . . or moved' " by a work of art or literature that happened to make an impression. To hold such principles is to possess what may be called "a conscience in intellectual matters." [10]

While Cicero has not been misused here, it is not clear that he ought to have been brought in at all. Plato's *Laws* defines this very kind of "rightness" (*orthotês*) in a group of passages that could hardly be more relevant. We should not hold Arnold accountable for a work neglected even by classicists, but the missed opportunity is particularly to be regretted because his attitude differs so little from Plato's proposals for judging rightness in poetry, music, and art. Both are moralists first and last; neither can bring himself to regard aesthetics as a separate province. Others about them find this possible: Aristotle holds that perception as such does not err, that every art or skill should be judged on its own terms according to the *oikeia hêdonê* or characteristic pleasure it affords; Ruskin ultimately defends artistic morality as self-contained, separable from the personal ethics of a Wagner or a Turner.[11]

For Plato, on the other hand, perception must always be fallacious and pleasure is a meaningless criterion. Arnold on his part will not give up the belief, inherited largely from Plato through Longinus, that noble expression can only be the manifestation of nobility in character. This position will not immediately accord with his view of the poet as rapt, and like Plato he was compelled to resolve such difficulties through various expedients. Here he has recourse to Cicero's treatise on moral duties, *De Officiis*, and from it he skillfully derives a concept of intellectual duty with the help of Sainte-Beuve's remarks.[12] Properly speaking, the feat shows sleight-of-hand rather than dexterity. On one view aesthetics is the handmaid of morality; according to another it may have an independent existence. Assuming the first alternative, Arnold argues as if the second did not exist.

The Romans did not occupy Arnold's thought in a general way, and here the contrast with the Greeks appears most vividly. The lack of a controlling concept may have put him off, since *Romanitas* never acquired associations comparable with those which have gathered about *Hellênismos, Hellenismus,* and "Hellenism" successively. What proved decisive was the lack of any literature commensurable with Rome's historical significance. The hundred years before Christ's birth were in his opinion possibly the greatest, fullest, most significant period the world had ever known, a time historically superior to the Periclean age.[13] Since he found the poets of that mighty time inadequate to represent it, he could not make use of it as he did of the fifth century and Athens. At times it held his thought, if we may judge from scattered references, but it lacked the power to move him.

At only one point does Arnold seem to have sensed the full power of *Romanitas,* the Roman way: not in matters of language, for his few tributes to Latin are conventional, but (oddly enough) in architecture. From Nîmes he writes:

> I like to trace a certain affinity in the spirit of these [Gallo-Roman] buildings between the Romans and the English. . . . Ludicrously as we fail in the practice of Architecture there is a gravity composure and strength about the Roman buildings which reminds me of the English character more than of anything else in the world.[14]

Gravity, composure, strength: it is the voice of Cicero himself. But these very virtues consorted with Hebraic stolidness in the collective personality of the Victorian middle class, and the message of "Hebraism and Hellenism" is that character, though it comprise three-fourths of life, must yet be balanced by intellect.

Most of the references to Greek and Roman religion are confined to two works, *Culture and Anarchy* and *God and the Bible;* there is no widely diffused or thoroughgoing interest. As a matter of fact, there is almost no interest at all in classical religion for its own sake. Here Arnold once again ignored Rome and built up a Hellenic setting for his favorite themes, morality and poetry.

As early as 1852 he had written that classical poetry included religion and was a complete *magister vitae.* In *Culture and Anarchy* he maintains that the best Greek art and poetry combine the religious and the poetic: "The idea of beauty and of a human nature perfect on all sides adds to itself a religious and devout energy, and works in the strength of that." It seems clear that this describes a system of conscious compounding, not something effective simply by virtue of being what it is. The essay on "Numbers" takes a distinctly different line. There Arnold calls the highest art that "which by its height, depth, and gravity possesses religiousness," such as the art of Pindar and Phidias.[15] According to the one account, religious and devout energy is superadded; the other supposes that religiousness is inherently present as the combined effect of various qualities. He cannot have it both ways.

The contradiction, trivial in itself, illustrates Arnold's failure to deal with religion as reality. His attitude towards Christianity has been described as willingness to do anything except believe in its truth;[16] the same must be said of his attitude towards Greek religion. It would have embarrassed him signally to admit that Pindar and Aeschylus and Sophocles held, or sought to hold, emphatic beliefs about Zeus.

Arnold actually deals with the whole problem in the way one would expect. Believing religion to be essentially morality, he interprets its development among the Greeks by the presence or absence of righteousness. Their history and religion thus arose out of "ideas of the moral order gathering strength and making themselves felt." Apollo was "the law of intellectual beauty" for Hellas but also "the author of every higher moral effort" and the prophet of his father Zeus "in the highest view of Zeus, as the source of the ideas of moral order and of right." These ideas constituted the main elements of the early religion, the worship of the Delphic Apollo. They gave "character and steadiness" to the Athenian people; moreover, even though the living influence of Delphi had ceased by the time of the Persian War, they continued to penetrate the fifth century in a certain measure by inspiring the poets. "Greek poetry was now more religious than Greek religion, and partly supplied its place. Finally, they ceased even to inspire poetry, and took refuge with philosophic thinkers." After the early decades of the fifth century "the Attic nation gave its heart to . . . expansion, intellect, beauty, social life and manners," forgetting the importance of conduct. The old Greek religion needed to be transformed, and this need was felt by "the greatest and best Hellenic souls, Anaxagoras, Pericles, Phidias, Sophocles, Socrates, Plato"; but the current had set too strongly in the opposite direction.[17]

Like so much of what Arnold says about the classical world,

the portrait that he gives us misleads more than it misinforms. Morality has been placed in a central position and kept there. Greek religion, we are told, arose out of moral ideas and lost vitality through ceasing to have regard for them. With the supernatural he has no patience. Speaking in the authentic manner of Lucretius, he proclaims that "Satan and Tisiphone are alike not real persons, but shadows thrown by man's guilt and terror." [18]

All this has vividness and charm, but it cannot seem adequate to the average cultured reader today, let alone the specialist. Our knowledge of primitive and ancient religions has come largely during the last seventy-five years, and it is only by a major effort that we can realize how inadequately the field had been studied a century ago. Enough had been done, nevertheless, to make possible a more realistic picture. Arnold might have noted the predominantly ceremonial nature of Greek and Roman worship, for one thing, and the importance of the magical element. In point of fact, he cared nothing for such matters. What he sought to present was a kind of Old Testament faith complete with great single figures like Amos or Jeremiah, men who saw the shortcomings of their people and spoke out in a conscious attempt to restore righteousness. Subjectively it can still fascinate; objectively it shows no very strong connection with historical reality.

We take philology to mean the systematic study of languages and their literatures. Though distinguishing adjectives have long been necessary, men of Arnold's day understood the noun as referring in itself to classical studies, and it will be so used here. For Arnold personally philology did not cease to be a vexing problem. He had undertaken to make available to a broad, nonspecialist reading public the fruits of classical scholarship, yet he profoundly disagreed with its procedures. To him the term philology meant excessive concentration upon grammar and composition. The thought of hundreds upon hundreds of students detained in this "philological vestibule," never getting beyond it, caused him a feeling of concern that becomes evident in many passages.[19]

"Higher Schools and Universities in Germany" deals with this matter extensively, placing it within a larger context. The great aim of instruction, we are told, is to enable a man to know himself and the world; and in order to gain self-knowledge

> a man must know the capabilities and performances of the human spirit; and the value of the humanities, of *Alterthums-wissenschaft*, the science of antiquity, is, that it affords for

this purpose an unsurpassed source of light and stimulus. . . . [But] to combine the philological discipline with the matter to which it is ancillary,—with *Alterthumswissenschaft* itself, —a student must be of the force of Wolf. . . . Such students are rare; and nine out of ten, especially in England, where so much time is given to Greek and Latin composition, never arrive at *Alterthumswissenschaft,* which is a knowledge of the spirit and works. . . . Such a person has not any sense at all of Greek and Latin literature as *literature,* and ends his studies without getting any. . . .

I am convinced that of the hundreds whom our present system tries without distinction to bring into contact with *Alterthumswissenschaft* through composition and philology almost alone, an immense majority would have a far better chance of being brought into vital contact with it through literature by treating the study of Greek and Latin as we teach our French, or Italian, or German studies.

Classical teaching in Germany is another matter. There, even at school level, the ancient authors are treated as literature, and an attempt is made to grasp "the place and significance of an author in his country's literature, and in that of the world." A more "vital and lasting" concern for Greek and Latin results from this approach.[20]

When he dealt with English education Arnold was on solid ground. The dangers that so wrought upon him were real dangers. They remain even today, when American students entering a university with any previous training in Latin know much less of it, in all probability, than the boys of Arnold's time already knew when they entered one of the great public schools. The remedy that he suggests would seem to be to teach a reading knowledge of Greek and Latin, as distinguished from a scholar's precise command.[21] The past thirty years have seen this adopted in some measure, but not widely enough to make a real difference. Classicists have not yet solved the problem of being realistic without becoming at the same time unscholarly.

Arnold himself recognized this dilemma and was no little troubled by it. "I was . . . brought up in the straitest school of Latin and Greek composition," he points out; and this is true. On the other hand, it is also true that at Winchester he had been required to memorize countless pages of rules for Greek grammar which never were put to any use. Moreover, even Rugby's extensive training in composition failed to produce a pure classical style; and the exercise was quite meaningless to the vast majority of the boys who practiced it. These facts he does not point out, though it is unlikely that he had forgotten them. Indeed, he is reluctant to speak of composition with anything but respect, for close study of the originals as models "may beget . . . an intimate sense of those models, which makes us sharers of their spirit and power." This, as he has already observed, "is of the essence of true *Alterthumswissenschaft.*" It was not without reason, he believes, that this training had been concentrated chiefly upon Latin. "The power of the Latin classic is in *character*," which can be learned, while the great mark of Greek literature is beauty, which cannot. Yet such benefits are only a part of what the knowledge of antiquity can give us. "The love of the things of the mind, the flexibility, the spiritual moderation . . . is for our time and needs still more precious." [22]

Having reached this conclusion, Arnold undertakes to solve the whole problem by detaching the philological vestibule from the temple of antiquity itself, the *pronaos* from the *naos*. What remains he calls *Alterthumswissenschaft.* This is irresponsible: *Wissenschaft* always refers to systematic knowledge, whatever its field. The person who acquires enough Latin and Greek to read the masterworks of ancient literature cannot be praised highly enough, and if he claims to have grasped their spirit and power we must hear him out; but he may not pretend to a systematic knowledge of antiquity. A solution which would throw out the baby with the bathwater hardly promises well.

One aspect of British public school education in the earlier nineteenth century particularly surprises us: the memorization of classical poetry in prodigious quantities. Winchester seems to have made more of this than any other school, not excluding Rugby, but the public school system as a whole stressed memorization to a startling degree. In Arnold's case the consequences of this emphasis proved to be considerable. *Friendship's Garland* mentions "the grand, old, fortifying classical curriculum" and states, as a known and obvious fact, that its value lies "rather in training and bracing the mind for future acquisition,—a course in mental gymnastics . . . ,—than in teaching any set thing." The context shows that these remarks are seriously meant, and we find the Headmaster of Rugby employing very much the same argument twenty years earlier; it is certainly orthodox enough. Yet Arnold's tone is not that of a man altogether happy in his convictions, nor does he recur to this point as one might expect. What he really found fortifying in the classical curriculum was evidently its strong element of memorization. This becomes clear from the *Reports on Elementary Schools 1852–1882,* which had more practical effect on English culture than all the rest of his writings combined. "The merit of the old classical education," he writes,

> was that it kept the pupil in continual contact with a few first-rate models. . . . The learning of thousands of lines of Homer and Virgil has insensibly created a good literary taste in . . . many persons, who would never have got this by studying the rules of taste.[23]

He saw that the old order must change, that it was passing away even in his own time. To our great good fortune, he also saw a way to make use of it in the new age when Latin and Greek were becoming increasingly endangered. The cardinal principle of memorization—cardinal because it represented the habituation without which character cannot form—could be applied seriously to the study of English literature in the elementary schools. Its work was not done, but only beginning. There is a great advantage in learning poetry by heart, the *Reports* continue: it supplies that "formative character" which is required of education, and which the elementary schools were largely failing to supply through their secular instruction.

> Good poetry is formative; it has, too, the precious power of acting by itself and in a way managed by nature. . . . I believe that even the rhythm and diction of good poetry are capable of exercising some formative effect, even though the sense be imperfectly understood.
>
> [The reading lessons] should be treated as in connexion with the good and sterling poetry learned for recitation, and should be made to contribute to the opening of the soul and imagination, for which the central *purchase* should be found in that poetry.
>
> The acquisition of good poetry is a discipline which works deeper than any other. . . . Good poetry does undoubtedly tend to form the soul and character; it tends to beget a love of beauty and of truth in alliance together, it suggests, however indirectly, high and noble principles of action, and it inspires the emotion so helpful in making principles operative.

> People talk contemptuously of "learning lines by heart"; but if a child is brought, as he can easily be brought, to *throw himself into* a piece of poetry, an exercise of creative activity has been set up in him.

Arnold comes back to one of these points in "A Speech at Westminster," addressed to a group of teacher trainees:

> The science of teaching is still in its infancy, the right programme of studies has yet to be discovered. Give your pupil a whole of some important kind for his thoughts to crystallize around; that is the best advice I can give you. The reason why I have taken such interest, as you know, in introducing the exercise, so novel to our schools, of learning passages of standard poetry by heart, is this: that to give a child the possession of two or three hundred lines of sterling poetry is to give something to nature to work upon, something that we cannot manipulate by our codes and schedules, but are obliged to permit nature to work upon freely.[24]

Until the middle of the nineteenth century English public schools retained a mediaeval way of life; the academic regimen still resembled that of their actual prototypes, the *ludi* of the Roman Empire. Matthew Arnold's achievement was to preserve in some measure, through memorization, the classical and mediaeval training of the mind and still more of the character. He greatly reduces the amount to be learned and emphasizes expressive recitation, but the original aim of a richly furnished mind has not been abandoned. His successful advocacy of learning and saying aloud the best English poetry in elementary classes has had an incalculable influence both in England and in America. Here is an unlooked-for result, but a signally happy one, to issue from the attacks on excessive philologizing and from the arbitrary redefinition of classical learning.

Arnold's various defenses of traditional method in teaching classical literature indicate that he saw its great strength in the fact of dealing with the original texts. At twenty-five he writes to Clough: "Those who cannot read Greek sh[oul]d read nothing but Milton and parts of Wordsworth: the state should see to it." Forty years later the essay on Milton shows the Platonic rigor smoothed away, but the literary sentiment remains unchanged:

> The verse of the poets of Greece and Rome no translation can adequately reproduce. Prose cannot have the power

of verse; verse-translation may give whatever of charm is in the soul and talent of the translator himself, but never the specific charm of the verse and poet translated. In our race are thousands of readers, presently there will be millions, who know not a word of Greek and Latin, and will never learn those languages. If this host of readers are ever to gain any sense of the power and charm of the great poets of antiquity, their way to gain it is not through translations of the ancients, but through the original poetry of Milton, who has the like power and charm, because he has the like great style.

In 1868, however, he writes thus to M. E. Grant Duff:

> I have long promised Macmillan a sort of sketch of the developments of Greek poetry, illustrated by extracts in a plain translation into harmonious prose. What is the good of forever talking about the Greeks and Hellenism if nine people out of ten can have no notion at all, from practical experience, what they are like and wherein is their power? While for Hebraism they have the Bible. . . . To give something of a like currency to the best of Greek poetry has long been a notion of mine.

Twenty years later he was still affirming his intention of completing this anthology.[25]

The passages just cited reflect above all an unwillingness to recognize the ever greater need for translations of classical literature. Even when he has *Culture and Anarchy* in hand and is troubled by the thought of Hellenism struggling against odds to counterbalance Hebraic morality, Arnold has nothing more solid to propose than a collection of extracts pieced together with commentary. This hardly seems an adventurous challenge to the Old and New Testaments. It accords perfectly, however, with a firm belief in the sovereign power of style to express a writer's character and to mold the character of his readers. It is not possible to hold this belief and accept translation as valuable. The fact that the proposed anthology never came to completion is regrettable, but we cannot think it a matter of chance. Had Arnold really wished to complete the task, he would have managed to do so during the two decades or more that it remained on his literary agenda.[26]

Arnold's works never discuss at length the nature of the classical as a literary concept; they do provide brief comments. "The

Study of Poetry" takes "the true and right meaning of the word *classic, classical*" to be "[of] the class of the very best," and in *Last Essays on Church* and *Religion* Arnold suggests a criterion when he singles out experience as the only thing which "assures us that . . . the poetry and artistic form of certain epochs has not, in fact, been improved on, and is, therefore, classical." The essay "On the Literary Influence of Academies" notes the need for getting rid of provinciality if one is to reach the level where "the best and highest intellectual work," which is classical, can be accomplished. It goes on to describe classical prose, for example that of Bossuet, as "prose of the centre." This somewhat cryptic reference becomes clear when Burke's prose is called too remote from "the centre of good taste; prose, in short, with a note of provinciality." [27]

These scattered approaches to the problem do not wholly satisfy. Etymologizing is a sound opening move but no more, and defining by means of negatives or superlatives tends to have a limited value. The contrast between provinciality and a central position of good taste is suggestive—the reader thinks, perhaps, of Catullus' emphasis on *urbanitas*—yet Arnold was speaking only of prose. What we need from him is some more direct and detailed attack; and this comes just once, in the lectures *On Translating Homer*.[28] The balladist translator Maginn had said, "The *truly* classical and the *truly* romantic are one; the moss-trooping Nestor reappears in the moss-trooping heroes of Percy's *Reliques*."

This, Arnold replies, may mean that "human nature under like circumstances is probably in all ages much the same." If such is the meaning intended, we shall agree; but that is of little use, because

> we know the human nature of other ages only through the representations of them which have come down to us, (and the classical and romantic remain eternally distinct modes of representation,) and have created for us a separation between the two worlds which they respectively represent.

Nestor, he continues, may in fact have been like a moss-trooper, but his mode of portrayal has made him exist in our imagination as utterly unlike, and as belonging to another world. The Greeks in *Troilus and Cressida*, on the other hand, are un-Homeric, because Shakespeare has shown them to us "through a mode of representation of the romantic world."

Arnold's retort is weakened slightly by his failure to realize one fact: the portion of the *Iliad* which Maginn had in mind sketches a time earlier than the one normally portrayed by Homer, a berserker's age of raiding and pillage. An Achaean adventurer of the twelfth century B.C. probably behaved in very much this way; a Homeric hero did not. Nevertheless, the contrast between Homer and Shakespeare effectively suggests the opposition between classical and Romantic, a distinction not always observed in Arnold's own works.[29] In "What Is a Classic?" T. S. Eliot proposes canons which exclude Homer; his rigid selectiveness is at the other extreme from the catholicity of Sainte-Beuve's "Qu'est-ce qu'un classique?" We have seen, moreover, that the fact of Homer's appearance in an unremarkable age somewhat embarrassed Arnold himself. Sainte-Beuve cheerfully imagines a crowded Parnassus; Arnold, rather like Eliot in this respect, thinks only a few deserving of the highest immortality.

Representativeness, however, mattered less than greatness, and the stature of a Homer or a Sophocles seemed as incontestable as that of a Dante or Milton. The criteria that underlay these judgments of the classical show the mind of the critic who chose them. For Arnold the essayist no less than for Arnold the poet, it is the inward man that predetermines outward patterns. His own use of the classical cannot be gathered adequately from his comments on its nature. It must be sought in the working reality of his prose and poetry, where we have attempted to recognize its many forms. The task which remains is to try to see it in a final perspective.

XII

Essence and Value

Victorian reviewers tirelessly declared that Matthew Arnold was of the Hellenes Hellenic. They did indeed recognize *Merope* as a failure, and many of them had previously dismissed the two attempts at epic verse. With no important exception they had felt reservations on various counts ever since the publication of "The Strayed Reveller" and its companion poems. Yet these objections amounted to maintaining the right thing for the wrong reason. A perceptiveness drastically narrowed by the assumptions and denials of the age, an unconscious subjectivity, made such a reaction inevitable; by the same token, they prevented any serious examination of Hellenism. This was the age of Newman and Carlyle, of Pater and Swinburne, and merely to name these men in the present context brings to mind the incommensurable quality of their approaches to Greek civilization. No doubt much can be claimed for the individualistic nature of Victorian thought, but such diversity will not yield judgments made according to any accepted basis or exemplar.

If we are less sure than the Victorian critics that Arnold was so eminently Hellenic, our skepticism comes partly from a lack of sympathy for their concern with externals and explicit morality. From our point of view these standards will not bring anyone to the heart of the matter, for it is the half-hidden impulses behind them that now seem important. Arnold's powerful, continuing involvement with matters of form and style is as well known as his moral concern; the difficulty lies not in discerning them but in explaining them. Earlier chapters have sought to interpret his attitude towards the classical in individual poems and in the prose discussions of classical authors or topics. At this point we shall attempt a brief examination of English classicism as a developing concept and of Matthew Arnold's place in that development. The eighteenth century may fittingly be the starting-point.

Johnson's England presents a scene almost unimaginably different from the England Victoria ruled. It could still deal in traditional values accepted with little question, patterns of life that gave their blessing to the past and seemed to promise a future without change. Educated men subscribed to the aristocratic values of the Greek and Latin literature that had dominated their schooling. Homer, Vergil, Horace were a part of the mind's landscape, like the miniature "classical" temples raised among the groves and lawns of the great country houses. But such authors provided a good deal more than decoration. They were the exemplars, the sources of justification and strength as well as delight. They held the field, and no challenger seriously threatened their sovereignty; Shakespeare had not yet been truly claimed by his people.

Throughout this age the tradition of public service was markedly Roman, and it was Rome far more than Athens that set the classical tone generally. Though her poets were city men, they wrote again and again of country life as a joyful deliverance from crowded streets and a thousand tiresome duties. *Beatus ille qui procul negotiis* . . . , "Happy the man far from business cares": this was the keynote. If its sincerity does not have quite a perfect ring to our ears, it sounded well enough in the still unspoiled country setting of eighteenth-century England. The combination of pastoral felicity and moral precept, recalling Horace's counsel to offer pleasure joined with profit in literary creation, did much to accredit antiquity as an immediate presence rather than a distant unreality. In this immediacy there existed no thought of any fundamental separation. The ghosts of Greece and Rome were ancestral spirits, potent counselors with unquestioned authority.

These habits of thought were forever shattered by the Industrial Revolution. England began to change into a great complex of cities overshadowing the countryside; inevitably, an aristocracy of wealth rose to power in place of the landed nobility. As the old social and economic order gave way before new pressures, traditional religious beliefs came increasingly under attack, an attack that the Established Church was ill prepared to meet. Whitefield and Wesley had already done their work; now the voices of Dissent sounded ever louder from a thousand Little Bethels. It was not ceremonial alone that the chapel folk abhorred: they had set their faces against the whole tradition of Anglican practice, with its classical ambiance that presupposed an education from which they were excluded.[1] Their obscurantism, as old in Christianity as the ministry of St. Paul, does not appear to have been an attitude consciously taken up. It was real, nevertheless, just as it is real among Fundamentalists today. All in all, a classicist can hardly look back at the second quarter of the nineteenth century in England without feeling that this was an oddly changed and troubled time.

Such were the decades during which Matthew Arnold came to manhood. They set their tone upon his personality and upon the greater number of his significant poems, completed when the second half of the century had barely begun. More than thirty-five years of active literary life lay ahead for him; the difference was to be that the central and later Victorian periods would find him active almost entirely in the field of prose. His critics have perhaps tended to make too much of the division: certainly one belief never left him—his belief in classical literature as a living, creating force.

An educated Englishman of the nineteenth century looked at antiquity with interests far different from those of his predecessors. The classical world no longer constituted a dimension of accepted reality and a source of uncritical precedent: the sight of a Johnson *en famille* with Juvenal was not to be seen again. In a word, there had ceased to be an accepted tradition. Men who sought an understanding of Greece and Rome had to use their own resources.

Classicism, the present's estimate of the past, thus became almost an individual matter. The situation was never actually in danger of turning into chaos, for individual attitudes tended to reflect the dominant interests of a given period. Swinburne and Pater, with their aestheticism that was sensuous and passionate if not simple, were out of the main stream: this had begun its course earlier, and it ran more powerfully.[2] It was the current of thought of those who brought a deliberate perspective to bear upon antiquity. The common name for such a perspective is the historical sense, and it is taken so much for granted that one forgets at times how recent a phenomenon it is. In nineteenth-century England it marked an essentially new development, breaking with venerable traditions. When men pondered the record of Greece or Rome, their thoughts now ran on such lines as these: "Here is a striking civilization with problems like our own problems, with a literature as great as ours. It will profit us to consider what these ancients said and did." In historical and literary inquiry a strong comparative sense began slowly to develop. Objectivity, however, did not necessarily accompany it. Moreover, the inquiry was likely to reflect a special interest in some one author or school or period —Aristotle, the pre-Socratics, the age of Pericles.[3]

As these instances would suggest, the civilization of Greece received much more attention than Roman culture. Dr. Arnold's *History of Rome* must be counted a considerable work for its time, but it lacks the representative quality and the scholarly stature of his edition of Thucydides. No previous English editor had offered a commentary that took account of what Continental scholars had done in Thucydidean studies. Thomas Arnold's achievement fairly suggests the general advances of Greek scholarship, and this increased knowledge brought an increase of interest on the part of those who were not themselves specialists. There was a marked shift of emphasis from Latin to Greek in the leading public schools; [4] here a small group of educators, notably Butler, Kennedy, and Arnold himself, used their influence to good effect.

Another point to be taken into account is that of the similarities between nineteenth-century England and fifth-century Athens. Professor J. E. Baker has compared the two civilizations:

> Both were leading commercial states whose coin was standard throughout the civilized world; but both succeeded in keeping the trader "in his place" because they preserved the older tradition of the cultivated gentleman of leisure. Their maritime empires, held by powerful navies, were subordinated to the preservation of a rich civilization at the capital city, but this culture was not subordinated to commercialism. The keenest intellectual activity did not serve, but rather fed upon, material prosperity. Athenians too were familiar with the conflict between aristocratic tradition and middle-class libertarian "democracy," between "science and religion," between convention and instinct. Religion, art, and morality underwent much the same changes in Athens and England. Both had their breakdown of age-old traditions, the "radical" assaults of sophistic relativists, the philosophic reconstruction on a basis not of convention or of instinct but of reason. The Victorians naturally found themselves at home with Greek minds, and made fruitful use of the work of their predecessors.[5]

These parallels cannot all be accepted without question. Matthew Arnold himself illustrates the growing divorce in England's polite society between an individual's leisure and his degree of cultivation. Whether we consider him as drudging school inspector or as anti-Barbarian, the point becomes abundantly clear. As for the trader being kept in his place, neither civilization could manage this with more than relative success; the developing pressures of an imperialist economy were not to be denied.[6] In such circumstances the strident voice of a Cleon will always make itself heard, and if England was less vulnerable to demagogues this may be ascribed largely to the more indirect nature of her parliamentary democracy.

In other respects Professor Baker's comparison is a helpful one. A further point may be mentioned: Victorian England shared with Periclean Athens a remarkable degree of communication between men of letters and men of great wealth or political power. Such communication is not always necessary for the creation of a major literature, but the troubles that follow upon its breakdown can be seen in the intellectual history of Tsarist Russia or of the great Western nations today. The society Matthew Arnold entered was one which took it as natural and proper that the writer should speak with a public voice.

Certainly Arnold was so much a part of his times that he cannot justifiably be dissociated from them; in some measure they were what they were because of him. The fact is that his relationship to the Victorian milieu was not a simple one. It combined conformity with individualism, the latter far more consciously maintained.

On the side of conformism his championing of classical virtues displays the *Zeitgeist* to a greater degree than he realized, or at any rate a greater one than he ever admitted. This becomes most immediately evident in his marked habit of preferring the Greek achievement to the Roman. The attitude is so inveterate that critics who speak of his "classical" bent could usually substitute "Hellenizing" with greater accuracy. What may not always be remembered is that the same attitude was found among other educated men during Victoria's reign. Again, his selective, comparative approach is to some preliminary degree that of a child of his age; and the quest for moral utility seems deeply Victorian, more representative than the enthusiasms of the Oxford aesthetes.

As Arnold's involvement with his own times became more intense, his writing took on increasingly the tones of public speech. The distinctive point to be set against this is that the corollary of his involvement is a disengaging action. He carried out a planned withdrawal from the risks of intimate contact with the disturbing, unpredictable, many-faceted classical experience. His attitude towards the classical underwent a change accordingly, becoming an inner detachment. Objectivity is a doubtful term here, for Arnold lacked the powers of systematic thought which constitute the very life of an objective mind. He himself knew this lack and admitted it, not without a certain defiance. The change in attitude enabled him to stand just far enough from the generative complex of the classics' power so that he could use it without being drawn into its field of force. The use he made of it was subjective, as our many instances have shown; to attempt any other course would have been impossible for him. This combining of sincere public dedication with a personal tendency towards aloofness is a fundamental pattern in his life.[7]

Preceding chapters have suggested that several early poems show Arnold tending towards involvement with deep classical feeling of the kind often called Dionysiac. In "The Strayed Reveller" that tendency became pronounced. It reached a crisis with the writing of "Empedocles on Etna," where he chose the serenity of Apollo in preference to the raptures of Dionysus. The reveller had already forsaken the established, public Dionysiac rites but not the god himself: in the later poem Arnold seems to decide against the god as well. If the essence of the classical is passion made significant through order, then he chose the ordered over the passionate.

This explanation endeavors to account for the change which clearly occurred in Arnold's work. It is less evident, and somewhat less generally accepted, that any profound change occurred in his nature. We have chosen to study the more limited problem of whether his classicism shifted essentially at any time. If the arguments presented here are sound, it did shift. What remains to be considered is how this fact affects an estimate of his role as lifelong mediator between the classical and modern worlds.

Here one faces the task of distinguishing between subjective and objective validity. A writer achieves the first of these when he is true to himself; Arnold was never anything else, except perhaps in the decisions he made around 1850. As for objectivity, it is at best a relative term. We do expect it, nevertheless, in an interpreter of cultures past or present; at least we look for a broad awareness of the main factors and proportions. This expectation

Arnold was unable to satisfy. Whenever he deals with classical material at length, the stresses and omissions give evidence of his inability. Bad faith is not in question: the instances of one-sided or even misleading argument in his presentation are hardly the manipulations of a conscious imposture. They should be viewed as the loci of a highly individual personality; they place in a commonsense perspective the protestations about "seeing the thing as in itself it really is."

Misgivings about subjective bias or scholarly inadequacy cannot alter the fact that Arnold's classicism rendered a notable service to Victorian thought. He came to an age which had no clear attitude towards the cultural achievement of Greece and Rome; and he came bringing forthright doctrines, memorable phrases, catchwords that lodged stubbornly in the memory, all of them phrased with a virtuosity capable of charming and irritating the reader almost in the same moment. Homer had been a remote figure, a school text memorized by countless boys and comprehended as great writing by scarcely one in a hundred. Arnold revealed Homer's true place, no longer in the customary narrow classical setting but in the whole sweep of Western literature. His Oxford lectures opened a new age of English criticism, and the new comparative approach which they embodied was to be the foundation of his literary method. Precisely because he lacked that type of objectivity known as the historical sense, he was able to travel in an instant between Victorian London and the Athens of Pericles without any real consciousness of being on a journey at all. No doubt this makes for shocking scholarship and deserves to be condemned on many grounds, but it does have the quality of its defects: it is undeniably lively. No such Athens as he described ever existed; yet this may after all be less important than the fact that, for a considerable part of literate England, Matthew Arnold's brilliance compelled it to exist.

There will be little to add concerning the poems until the modern scene is discussed. During the author's lifetime their classical elements passed for conventional decoration, if one may judge from the reviewers. These men, whose number included Swinburne and Clough, had all been trained in ancient poetry with a thoroughness beyond our imagining; the relatively superficial nature of their insights into Arnold's poetry therefore seems all the more surprising. Yet it may be that this superficiality was the natural, even inevitable result of the limitations of a public-school education. We have noted that when the reviewers did turn their attention to assessing Arnold's Hellenism, the majority declared him at least as Greek as the Greeks. Much Edwardian criticism echoes this strange verdict, which was to be silenced only in the years after the first World War. It is not likely to be heard again.

In what tones, and with what effect, does Arnold the classicist speak to our own time? So far as the audience of student or non-specialized readers is concerned he speaks through a very limited number of works. The most highly regarded are probably *Culture and Anarchy*, the two famous elegies, and "Dover Beach." Any one of these would assure its author a secure place in the lesser ranks of English letters. But Arnold was not a Dowson or a Henley: his place is among the major Victorians. The fact that his talent remains viable within so restricted a compass speaks for its timelessness and strength.

Although *Culture and Anarchy* may still exercise more influence in England than in America, it has an impressive ability to command readers on either side of the Atlantic. The task Arnold set himself was the dramatizing of a crucial alternative: culture or anarchy, the one inevitable if the other should fail.[8] This device of equating the cultural with the political typifies his public thought; it also shows how strongly the achievements of Periclean Athens had fired his imagination.

The heart of this work is the famous "Hebraism and Hellenism." It remains the best known of all comparisons between the two modes of inner life. In our time, however, it is read for reasons that Matthew Arnold could not easily have foreseen. He intended a counterbalance against excessive Hebraizing, a specific measure to meet the needs of his countrymen during a specific phase of their national development. Such are not the needs or preconceptions that readers bring to "Hebraism and Hellenism" today. This example of Victorian polemic has come to be regarded as an exercise in comparative cultural analysis, almost a reference source. Its virtues remain, to be sure; so do its shortcomings, too seldom made clear even now. In Arnold's portrait of a typical Hellene the lines are somewhat out of drawing—more so, oddly enough, than when he sketches for us the child of Israel. Uninstructed readers will conclude that the Greeks were morally obtuse; discerning ones will be led to question the writer's claims and credentials. It seems a pity that until recently the significant inaugural lecture "On the Modern Element in Literature" and the delightful "A Speech at Eton" have not been widely available; they could have placed the whole matter in a more balanced setting.

Somewhat better known are the Oxford lectures *On Translating Homer* and their literary coda, *Last Words*. Arnold's famous list of cardinal Homeric qualities still commands respect, unlike his advocacy of an English hexameter. Our critic-translators, particularly those who deal with the *Iliad*, show his continuing influence. The situation holds a certain irony, since his declared purpose of counseling future translators was not the real force behind the Oxford lectures. But what he actually sought—the presentation of Homer's timeless poetry in its true wider perspective—was achieved for his own time, as he had meant it to be. Since none of the other prose works except for *Culture and Anarchy* has continued to reach a wide audience, there will be no need to discuss the effect of their classical content. This element nevertheless has shaped critical thinking, especially the doctrines of T. S. Eliot, in ways that have still to be studied adequately.

"Thyrsis" has quietly taken a place with "Lycidas" and "Adonaïs" as one of the major pastoral elegies. "The Scholar-Gipsy" joins it in honoring a great tradition, one which is well served by both poems. In them we see what Arnold's mature, deliberate classicism could accomplish: magic of language, near-perfection of form, and a transfer of the spirit (not the letter) of Sicilian pastoral to the English countryside. Neither poem, however, has spoken to the modern reader with the eloquence of "Dover Beach." According to our conjectures the last nine lines of this work probably date from the period of the early poems. Their special tone and power would thus reflect a classical orientation very different from that of the Oxford pastorals, indicating the course that might have been taken.

In several ways it seems peculiarly fitting that so much of Matthew Arnold's fame should rest upon "Dover Beach." The imagery of sea-strife, of Channel tides that mingle with the tide of dubious battle, fills many of his finest poems; his metrical finesse and his skill in employing the colors of language are nowhere more delicately displayed; and if it is correct to date the "clash by night" considerably earlier than the preceding lines, the use of classical materials epitomizes Arnold's change in attitude. Far beyond textual or metrical factors, however, the essential wonder of the poem is that it moves us with a sense of meeting our own troubled image. Victorian reviewers were not so moved, though a few noted their admiration; for "Dover Beach" is in some degree a work written before its time, prefiguring the twentieth century's wasteland. Yet the author's thoughts were on himself and his place in the scheme of things. These two themes are to be found at the heart of all his most serious work. The object of his deepest search was the relation between them, whether it be called an idea of the world or a seeing of one's own way. Within this area of concern, accordingly, we may expect to find Arnold's closest ties with the classical.

The poems of the 1849 edition display two evident characteristics. They seek an individual relationship with classical experience; they also attempt to construct an "idea of the Universe" in main accordance with Stoicism. These two interests, the one literary and the other philosophical in essence, attain a varied success both in their own right and as a combination brought into being by the poet's creative nature. Whether separately or in combination, they worked to turn Arnold away from any serious identification with those wilder, stronger elements of the Greek past to which decorum and pattern and balance did not readily apply. By the same token, they turned his thought towards a natural use of the logical, discursive pattern that regularly identifies prose. It is also a pattern that can be discerned not infrequently in certain types or periods of poetry, and among Victorian poets it was almost universal.[9] Matthew Arnold proved to be no exception. "The Strayed Reveller," as we have maintained, shows his one close approach through the classical to a different and more direct experience, while "Empedocles on Etna" may be said to mark the beginning of his classicism.

During the writing of "Empedocles" Stoicism was still a new element in Arnold's thought, yet it had a strikingly broad influence on his early poetry. The 1852 edition indicates that this influence has already begun to lessen, and after the collection of the following year it all but disappears. Gone with it is the long-continued effort to construct a scheme of things through poetry. What remains is the newly established relationship with the conventionally classical. This had its contribution to make, and not merely by bringing the conventional virtues of dignity, balance, and lucidity. Yet Arnold had chosen to accept the world in all its multitudinousness, a decision that led him to approach his varied audience with combinations of varied concepts and arguments. Many of these which had classical origins were undeniably important, but they were not parts of a systematic controlling idea.

System did not interest Matthew Arnold; he never made any reference to classicism as a doctrine, nor is there any evidence that he ever sought to follow it.[10] If his attitude towards the classical possessed any unity, that unity was subjective. Whenever his presentation of the ancient world rose above the merely perfunctory, he was filling in the light and shadow of a self-portrait; to criticize him without taking this into account is to misunderstand him radically.

The matter involves a dualism which characterized Arnold's work from the beginning, namely the tendency just noted that led to the subjective expression of self and the opposing or counterbalancing impulse to express the objective world beyond the self. Unlike the transcendentalists, he did not trust the mind's power to see the pattern of the cosmos in every leaf. Neither was he able to take as an idea of the world that other use of the mind, the Romantic faith in imagination as the magic casement.[11]

In this latter instance his attitude was one of reluctance to commit himself rather than rejection. Romanticism had a strong hold on Arnold, though the efforts of critics to assess its power have not yet met with any clear success. What concerns us here is the other side of the equation, for a creative mind so constituted must seek and accept an attitude which fixes upon the finite as its central principle. Within our literary tradition this principle is classicism, with its constant striving for proportion. Yet the literature and history of Greece and Rome sometimes are very far from exemplifying such balance. "Do nothing in excess," "Follow the golden mean," "Realize that you are mortal and not a god" were the self-exhortations of men well aware of passion and unreason.[12] Classicism is not necessarily identical with the classical, and the allegiance of a writer who concerns himself with antiquity may consequently be a divided one.

This was manifestly true in Matthew Arnold's case. His own classicism can be described as a varying combination of four elements: the subjective-objective relationship is linked with the division of interests between conventional and irregular manifestations of the classical. Opposing terms of the division have often been set forth as rational and irrational, serene and ecstatic, Apolline and Dionysiac. However it is conceived, we have seen the emphasis shift between its extremes even before the 1852 edition. The other divided relationship maintained a steady tension of subjective-objective opposites, as the prose works illustrate with particular clearness. On many occasions this inquiry has sought to point out the subjective element in Arnold's dealings with antiquity. It would be less than just to close without paying tribute to the positive value, even the necessity, of his self-involvement.

Necessity is not an exaggerated term. The creative writer can use only what his own nature has encompassed through an intimate union. Here, as in the physical relation, knowing is the precondition of bringing to life. This can less easily be defined or called to account than the scholar's objective knowledge. Whenever Matthew Arnold pretends to scholarship or attempts the kind of judgment which is inadequate without it, we must apply the standards to which he has exposed himself. When he speaks as artist, with his true voice, we must use the standards of art. The classical world that he brings before us is the only one that could have had truth for him, because it is created in his image.

Appendix

CLASSICAL SOURCES IN ARNOLD'S POETRY
The order of the poems and line numbering are those of *The Poetical Works of Matthew Arnold*, ed. C. B. Tinker and H. F. Lowry (London and New York, 1957). Abbreviations used in referring to classical authors and works follow the practice of the lexicons of Liddell-Scott-Jones, ninth edition, and Lewis and Short. Multiple sources are listed in chronological order. These identifications have been collected in the hope that they may prove a working aid to the student of Matthew Arnold's poetry; it is not supposed that they are either beyond dispute or definitive in their extent. *See also* p. 280.

"In Utrumque Paratus" (Title): Verg. *Aen.* 2.61.
14: cf. Sen. *Ep.* 90.42.

"Horatian Echo"
1–9: Hor. *C.* 2.16, 3.1, 3.16, 3.29.11 and 25–28; *Ep.* 1.6, 2.2.
32: Hor. *C.* 4.7.16.
33–36: Hor. *C.* 1.25, 2.11, 4.10, 4.13.

"Consolation"
71–75: S. *Tr.* 124–35.

"Resignation"
93: Hor. *C.* 3.29.12.

"Sohrab and Rustum"
4–7: *Il.* 10.1–4, 24.2–5.
26–27: *Il.* 10.73–75.
55–57: *Il.* 3.68–70, 7.49–51.
65: *Il.* 3.60.
67: *Il.* 13.358 and 635, 18.242.
96–99: *Il.* 10.21–24.
111–16: *Il.* 2.459–65.

154–59: *Il.* 2.147–49, 23.597–600.
178–79, 182: *Od.* 11.543–44 and 554–55.
187–91, 195–96, 199–206: *Il.* 9.182–98?
206: *Od.* 3.69–70.
232–37: *Il.* 24.486–89; *Od.* 11.494–503.
241: *Il.* 24.478–79, cf. 18.317, 23.18, 24.724.
293–98: *Il.* 11.67–71.
314: *Od.* 6.163?
337: *Od.* 11.556?
341–42: *Il.* 1.500–1.
345 eyed askance: *Il.* 1.148?
353–54: *Il.* 6.218–21.
369 Rash: *Il.* 3.414; *Od.* 9.494, 12.21?
376–78: *Od.* 1.161–62.
390–91: Verg. *Aen.* 1.106.
398–99, 402–11, 415–19: *Il.* 7.258–69, 16.139–44 and 610, 17.525–
    26, 22.139–42 and 273–76.
439: *Il.* 6.213. (Hor. C. 1.3.40 *iracunda ... fulmina?*)
443–46: *Il.* 6.226–29.
451–53: *Il.* 22.26–32, 317–20.
454 glittering arms: *Il.* 18.617?
457: Verg. *Aen.* 11.390?
458 dancer: *Il.* 16.617. (Verg. *Aen.* 9.615?)
462–63 the dance Of battle: *Il.* 7.241.
465: *Il.* 22.261 and 265–66.
472–74: *Il.* 16.428–29, 22.308–10.
480–88: *Il.* 17.366–73.
497–98: *Il.* 16.794–97.
501–2: *Il.* 17.426–27.
511–13: *Il.* 3.362–63.
514–15 his dreadful eyes Glared: *Il.* 1.200.
528–29: *Il.* 22.331–32?
538–39: *Il.* 11.162.
541–47: *Il.* 16.844–50?
556–73: A. *Ag.* 49–59.
579: *Il.* 15.246, 16.843, 22.337.
589–95: *Il.* 6.450–55 and 479–81.
634–38: Catull. 11.22–24; Verg. *Aen.* 11.68–69.
651–52: *Il.* 16.503–4.
669–76: *Il.* 4.141–45.
692–93: *Il.* 22.466–67.
699–702: *Il.* 18.22–27.

706 saw his thought: *Od.* 6.67?
730–32, 736: *Il.* 17.437–38, 23.15–16, 24.9.
757 lofty house: *Il.* 5.213, 19.333; *Od.* 4.757, 13.5?
767: *Il.* 1.364.
768–70: *Il.* 6.345–48.
787–91: *Od.* 11.74–76, 12.14–15.
787 lovely earth: *Il.* 3 239; *Od.* 7.79?
796–97: *Il.* 24.669.
854–56: *Il.* 16.856–57, repeated verbatim 22.361–63.
871: *Il.* 24.801–2?
891 new-bathed: *Il.* 18.489; *Od.* 5.275; *h.Merc.* 241?

"The Sick King in Bokhara"
185–88: Hor. *C.* 3.1.5–6?

"Balder Dead"
    1. *Sending*
15–16: *Il.* 23.154–55, 24.713–15.
23–25: *Il.* 19.9?
32: A. *Pr.* 1005?
40–42: *Il.* 23.49–51.
45: *Il.* 16.675.
51–60: *Il.* 13.1–9. (Verg. *Aen.* 1.223–26?)
68: *Il.* 1.470; *Od.* 1.148.
71: *Il.* 11.194, 17.455.
74–75: *Od.* 6.262–65?
77–78: *Il.* 1.34, 23.59–61.
95: *Il.* 1.352.
114: *Il.* 22.179.
155–58: *Il.* 18.487–89; *Od.* 5.273–75.
174: *Od.* 10.521 and 536, 11.29 and 49.
177 flit (cf. 174 shadowy): *Od.* 10.495; Verg. *Aen.* 6.293 and 329.
177 like . . . leaves: Verg. *Aen.* 6.309–10.
202: *Il.* 1.475.
210–13: A. *Pr.* 469–71.
219: *Il.* 1.606; *Od.* 1.424, 2.397, 18.428.
238: *Od.* 4.826–27.
246 fleet-footed: *Il.* 1.58.
248: see on 219.
271–74: *Il.* 24. 720–23.
276: *Il.* 23.10; *Od.* 19.213.
277–79: *Od.* 1.362–64.

282–87: *Il.* 23.65–68.

290–91: *Il.* 16.7–11?

302: *Od.* 11.173 and 199.

332–34: *Il.* 23.99–101; *Od.* 11.206–8; Verg. *Aen.* 2.790–92; *Georg.* 4.500–502.

335–37: Verg. *Georg.* 4.499–500.

339–40: see on 302; Verg. *Aen.* 4.695.

2. *Journey to the Dead*

41–43: *Il.* 23.50–51.

47–64: *Il.* 23.114–23.

69: see on 1.219.

113 high-roof'd: *Il.* 5.213, 19.333; *Od.* 4.757, 13.5.

125–26: *Od.* 11.12–15.

139–40: *Od.* 11.15–19.

152–54: *Od.* 10.513–15.

157–59: Verg. *Aen.* 6.309–12?

163 twittering: *Od.* 24.9.

164–68: *Od.* 24.38–41; Verg. *Aen.* 6.306–8.

172–73: Tac. *Germ.* 12.

179, 201 solemn queen: *Od.* 11.213, 226, 635.

180–81, 184: *Od.* 11.155–56.

189–91: *Od.* 11.79–80 and 97.

250: *Il.* 23.19 and 179.

257–61: *Od.* 11.482–86.

265–67: *Od.* 11.488–91.

3. *Funeral*

29: *Od.* 1.35; Verg. *Aen.* 4.696–97.

50–52: *Il.* 23.8–9.

53–56: *Il.* 23.50–54.

60–64: *Il.* 23.13–16; Verg. *Aen.* 11.189–91.

65–66: *Il.* 18.316–17, 23.17–18.

89–90: *Il.* 19.301 and 338, 24.746–47.

96 Names...many: A. *Pr.* 212.

96 Vanadis–97: *Il.* 14.290–91, 20.74.

112–13: *Il.* 24.771–72.

121 and Balder–122: *Il.* 24.724–25.

123: see on 89.

154–57: *Il.* 24.713–17?

160–72: *Il.* 23.161–74; cf. Verg. *Aen.* 6.212–35.

176: *Il.* 13.333.

186: *Il.* 23.216.

208–9: *Il.* 24.802–3.
212 sacred morn: *Il.* 8.66.
307–16: cf. Hor. *C.* 1.4.1, 1.9.2–3.
357–63: cf. *Od.* 1.58–59.
424–25: A. *Pr.* 619.
487–88: *Il.* 4.164–65, 6.448–49.

"The Neckan"
51–52: *Il.* 1.234–36.

"Switzerland.
4.   Isolation. To Marguerite"
19–24: cf. Theoc. 20.37–39.
37–39: cf. Hor. *C.* 4.1.30.
5.   "To Marguerite"
22: Hor. *Epod.* 14.6.
24: Hor. *C.* 1.3.22.

"The Strayed Reveller"
162–65: A. *Pr.* 709–10; Pind. *Fr.* 105; Hor. *C.* 3.24.9–10.
223–32: cf. Hor. *C.* 1.18.8–9, 2.12.5–7; also Ov. *Met.* 12 *passim*,
    esp. 210–306.
227 biting spears: Hor. *C.* 4.6.9.
238 unkind spring: cf. Hor. *C.* 3.1.32.
287 much enduring: *Il.* 8.97, 9.676; *Od.* 5.171, 7.133; *et freq.*
288 Wave-toss'd: A. *Pr.* 467?

"Fragment of an 'Antigone' "
67: *Od.* 5.123–24.
82 Argive seer: Hor. *C.* 3.16.11–12?

"Fragment of Chorus of a 'Dejaneira' "
28: cf. S. *Ant.* 876.
29 the gates–30 of death: Thgn. 427, cf. 709.

"Philomela"
2: Ar. *Av.* 214.
31–32: Hor. *C.* 4.12.7?

"Faded Leaves.
2.   Too Late"
4: cf. Pl. *Symp.* 189d5–191d5, Hor. *C.* 1.3.8.

"Dover Beach"

15–18: cf. S. *Ant.* 583–92, *Tr.* 112–19 and 129–30, *Ph.* 686–95,
    OC 1239–48.
35–37: Th. 7.43–44.

"Bacchanalia; or, The New Age"

20–27: cf. E. *Ba.* 862–65.

"Epilogue to Lessing's Laocoön"

43–48: cf. Theoc. 11; (Mosch.) *Epitaphium Bionis* 61–62.

"Palladium"

7: Hor. *C.* 2.7.15–16.
13–16: cf. Verg. *Ecl.* 4.34–36.

"A Summer Night"

56–58: cf. Hor. *C.* 1.3.15–16, 1.5.11–12.

"A Wish"

39: A. *Pr.* 1091–92?

"The Scholar-Gipsy"

193–94: cf. Hor. *C.* 1.24.19–20.
208–9: Verg. *Aen.* 6.469–74.

"Thyrsis"

72–77: cf. (Mosch.) *Epitaphium Bionis* 106–11.
82–90: cf. (Mosch.) *Epitaphium Bionis* 121–33.
90: cf. Hor. *C.* 1.24.13–14.
169: (Mosch.) *Epitaphium Bionis* 111.
184–85: cf. Theoc. 10.41; Verg. *Ecl.* 5.20, 8.68.

"Memorial Verses"

29–33: Verg. *Geor.* 2.490–92; cf. Lucr. 2.1–13.
35–39: Verg. *Geor.* 4.454–56.

"Haworth Churchyard"

125–28: Hor. *C.* 4.15.1–2.

"Stanzas in Memory of the Author of 'Obermann' "

89–92: *Il.* 21.106–7.

"Obermann Once More"
97–100: Lucr. 3.1056–67; Hor. *Epod.* 4.14; cf. Juv. 1.60–61, 8.146–48.
101–2: Lucr. 3.912–13.

Merope
1–28: cf. S. *El.* 1–22.
51–55: cf. A. *Ch.* 10–15.
71: S. *El.* 448–51; cf. A. *Ch.* 6.
152: *Il.* 22.60.
307–8: S. *Ant.* 473–76, 710–17.
341: Men. *Mon.* 85?
385–544: cf. A. *Ch.* 306–478; S. *El.* 121–250.
425–33: Paus. 1.32.
448 all-wept: S. *El.* 1085.
463–68: Paus. 3.1.
477–86: A. *Ch.* 345–53.
477: S. *Ant.* 857–58.
492–94: cf. S. *El.* 198–99.
505–6: S. *El.* 153–54, cf. Cic. *Tusc.* 3.33.3.
516: cf. A. *Ch.* 449.
523, 526 Zeus–527: S. *El.* 173–75.
541: A. *Ch.* 459–60?
543 Gods of the dead: A. *Ch.* 405?
571–78: S. *Aj.* 845–49.
585: cf. A. *Ch.* 1.
589 wise–590: S. *Aj.* 550–51.
622–23: cf. A. *Ag.* 958.
652: Bias *ap.* D.L. 1.5.88.
713–14: S. *El.* 673.
721: S. *El.* 680.
735–38: Paus. 8.11, 8.8.
741–43: Paus. 8.9, 8.13.
775–77: Paus. 8.5.
822–34: Paus. 8.22.
857: S. *Ant.* 599–600.
869–71: A. *Ch.* 668–69, 712–15.
890–913: E. *Cresphontes* (398 Nauck).
911–13: S. *Ant.* 586–89.
988: Plaut. *Poen.* 443–44?
1032–53: cf. S. *OT* 1337–39, 1371–77, *Ant.* 897–99.
1056–59: cf. S. *Aj.* 831–44.

1100 all-common: A. *Th.* 608; S. *El.* 138.

1139–41: cf. A. *Ch.* 319–20.

1147–52: cf. A. *Ch.* 877–79.

1191–92: E. *Cresphontes* (397 Nauck).

1209: S. *El.* 59–60.

1251–52: cf. A. *Ag.* 758–60.

1382: cf. A. *Ch.* 299–301.

1445: S. *El.* 22?

1610–12: Paus. 8.21.2.

1734–35: S. *El.* 491, 489.

1870–81, esp. 1876–81: A. *Ag.* 1005–6, *Eum.* 561–65.

2021–23: S. *El.* 1508–10.

2024: cf. S. *Tr.* 1278.

"Empedocles on Etna"

Act 1, Scene 1

25: D.L. 8.60.

31 Peisianax: D.L. 8.67, 71.

59–63: Diels 31B112; D.L. 8.73.

108–19: D.L. 8.59–61, 68–70; cf. D. 31B111.

147–48: D.L. 8.58–59.

Act 1, Scene 2

30–31: D. 31B2.

57–76: cf. Pi. *N.* 3.53, 57–58, *P.* 6.21–27.

80: cf. D. 31B109a.

87–88: Hor. *C.* 3.29.31–32.

89–90: cf. D. 31B110, 132.

111 thou . . . Anchitus: D. 31B1.

128: cf. Lucr. 3.1053–59.

247–55: cf. Lucr. 6.387–95.

287–90: cf. D. 31B35.

347–48: D. 31B11.

369–71: cf. Lucr. 3.1003–10.

414: Hor. *Epod.* 2.41–42.

427–60: cf. Ov. *Met.* 4.563–69, 603.

435–60: E. *Ba.* 1352–62?

449–51: Pi. *P.* 3.88–93.

Act 2

41–88: Hes. *Th.* 820–80; A. *Pr.* 353–74; Pi. *P.* 1.5–30; Ov. *Met.* 5.352–58.

112–17: D. 31B112.

125–90: Ov. *Met.* 6.383–400.
227–34: D. 31B115.
238–39: D. 28B1.
293–94: D. 28B10.
313 Liparëan: cf. Hor. *C.* 3.12.6.
345–46: cf. Lucr. 3.396–97.
355–58: cf. Lucr. 3.1053–59.
358–63: D. 31B115.
365–66: D. 31B121.
371: cf. Lucr. 3.273–75.
406: Hor. *C.* 3.30.6?
441–44: cf. A. *Pr.* 115.
444–68: Hes. *Th.* 1–21, 36–52, 60–71, 104–10.

"Westminster Abbey"
83–110: *h.Cer.* 231–81.

"Geist's Grave"
21–26: cf. Hor. *C.* 3.30.3–5.

"Poor Matthias"
77–78: cf. M. Aur. 3.1; Max. Tyr. 61.3.
132–35: cf. Ar. *Av.* 465–85.
134 Before the gods: Ar. *Av.* 700–703?
139–40: Ar. *Av.* 710–11.
141. Ar. *Av.* 504–6?
142–43: Ar. *Av.* 714–15?
145: Ar. *Av.* 709.

"Kaiser Dead"
65–66: Hor. *C.* 4.7.14–15.

See also p. 281.

Notes

1. On Thomas Arnold's elder brother Matthew (1786–1820) see Arnold Whitridge, *Dr. Arnold of Rugby* (London, 1928), p. 5, and Norman Wymer, *Dr. Arnold of Rugby* (London, 1953), pp. 37, 40. He preceded Thomas at Corpus Christi College, Oxford, and became Classical Professor at the Royal Military College at Marlow.

2. On the unfinished *History of Rome* (1838–43) see Oliver Elton in *A Survey of English Literature 1830–1880*, 2 vols. (London, 1932), 1:153–54. He gives examples of Dr. Arnold's special way of interpreting Roman history: Julius and Augustus are "hostile to the divine purposes." A. P. Stanley, *Life of Thomas Arnold, D.D., Head-Master of Rugby* (London, 1904), p. 132, recalls the Doctor's "casual allusions" to "the providential government of the world" in the ancient history classes; in the lectures prepared for delivery at Oxford, just such an allusion characterizes the change effected by Philip of Macedon (*Introductory Lectures on Modern History* (Oxford, 1842), pp. 247–48). This view of history is itself post-classical.

3. Understanding past and present: *Introductory Lectures*, p. 109; see also p. 236. Ancient history as really modern: Stanley, *Life*, p. 180. Reading Herodotus: *ib.*, p. 211.

4. For details see Wymer, p. 138. This period is wrongly dated by W. S. Knickerbocker, "Matthew Arnold at Oxford: The Natural History of a Father and Son," *Sewanee Review*, 35 (1927) 401; it ended in December, 1832.

5. E. H. Coleridge, *Life and Correspondence of John Duke Coleridge, Lord Chief Justice of England*, 2 vols. (London, 1904), 1:25–26, 29.

6. Clough's Rugby friend John Philip Gell had made progress in Latin, Greek, and Hebrew by the time he was eleven, at the end of his first year of schooling at Gainsborough (Frances J. Woodward, *The Doctor's Disciples* (London and New York, 1954), p. 74).

7. Stanley, *Life*, pp. 320–21; Letter of Oct. 23, 1833. Dr. Arnold's son Thomas calls Hill "a good, but rather a severe tutor" under whom he and Matthew made fair progress in Greek and Latin (Thomas Arnold, *Passages in a Wandering Life* (London, 1900), p. 10).

8. See Kenneth Allott, "A Birthday Exercise by Matthew Arnold," *Notes and Queries*, 5 (1958) 225; also Gerhard Müller-Schwefe, *Das persönliche Menschenbild Matthew Arnolds in der dichterischen Gestaltung* (Tübingen, 1955), p. 18 and n. 23. The metre is the Third Asclepiadean, used nine times by Horace in the *Odes*. One of these, 4.10, may have been especially in young Arnold's mind when he composed the first stanza of his birthday tribute: compare his *effugere dies, brumaque frigida* (2) with 4.10.1 *diffugere nives* and 12 *bruma . . . iners.*

9. Iris E. Sells, *Matthew Arnold and France* (Cambridge, 1935), Appendix A: "Lines Written on the Seashore at Eaglehurst, July 12, 1836."

10. Dr. Arnold felt that they had "taken a very good place in the school" (Stanley, *Life*, pp. 416–17; Letter of Sept. 14, 1836).

11. W. A. Fearon, *The Passing of Old Winchester* (Winchester, 1924), p. 2; Fearon entered Winchester in the early 1850's. M. L. Clarke, *Classical Education in Britain, 1500–1900* (Cambridge, 1959), pp. 3–4. For an account of J. A. Froude's appalling experiences at Westminster School around 1830, see Waldo H. Dunn, *James Anthony Froude: A Biography*, 2 vols., vol. I (Oxford, 1961), pp. 31–38 (Ch. 3, "Ordeal at Westminster").

12. Wymer, p. 140. On the Victorian conception of life as warfare see W. E. Houghton, *The Victorian Frame of Mind 1830–1870* (New Haven, 1957), p. 233. Thomas Arnold had called the Christian life "a soldier's battle" (*ib.*, p. 250); see below, n. 27.

13. Mr. J. C. Harvey, Archivist of Winchester College, kindly made available the contents of this list and of the schedule mentioned above. Thomas Arnold (in Whitridge, p. 9) lists Demosthenes, Sophocles, Cicero, Vergil, and Homer as "regular School Business" in a letter of September, 1810, when he was a sixth-former at Winchester.

14. Until late in the nineteenth century, boys invariably translated orally. Composition and memorization were "the surest means of rising in the School," according to R. B. Mansfield, *School-Life at Winchester College* (London, 1866; 'by R. B. M.'), p. 107; he entered Winchester shortly after Matthew Arnold. He goes on to mention that prefects and Senior Part boys were occasionally required to write Latin criticisms of Greek plays. Arnold's apprenticeship in literary criticism, accordingly, may have begun in the school year 1836–37.

15. Furneaux: Tuckwell, *The Ancient Ways. Winchester Fifty Years Ago* (London, 1893), p. 97. Thomas Arnold: (E. G. Selwyn), "Dr. Arnold as a Winchester Boy," *Theology*, 24 (1932) 311. A. K. Cook, *About Winchester College* (London, 1917), p. 308 and n. 2. Exemptions: H. C. Adams, *Wykehamica. A History of Winchester College and Commoners*, etc. (Oxford and London,

1878), p. 356. In the eighteenth century one boy repeated the entire *Iliad*, according to H. A. L. Fisher, "Winchester in the Eighteenth Century," in *Winchester College, 1393–1893. By Old Wykehamists* (London, 1893), p. 84. On the ordinary lessons see in this same volume E. C. Wickham's "Life in the College About 1850," pp. 96–111.

16. On admission procedures see Fearon, p. 7; also Woodward, p. 20, for Dr. Arnold's cursory examination of Arthur Stanley, and Wymer, p. 27, for the ease of entering Winchester at the beginning of the century. The incident with Dr. Moberly: T. H. Warren, *Essays of Poets and Poetry Ancient and Modern* (New York, 1909), p. 49.

17. Wymer, p. 178, reports Matthew's reserve and constraint but does not take account of his mischievous behavior at Rugby: on this see Margaret Woods, "Matthew Arnold," *Essays and Studies*, 15 (1929) 9. Choice of schools: Thomas Arnold, *Passages*, p. 13; Knickerbocker, p. 402, draws an incorrect inference. Thomas also says that during the year at Winchester Matthew was regarded almost as a rebel, and that his crude way of speaking actually made his father contemplate keeping the boy apart from the other Arnold children during school holidays; see Louis Bonnerot, "La jeunesse de Matthew Arnold," *Revue Anglo-Américaine*, 7 (1929–30) 522. Bonnerot's claim that Matthew was ostracized at Winchester is based on *Passages in a Wandering Life*, but the same statement was made before its publication: see Louise M. Hodgkins, *Matthew Arnold's Sohrab and Rustum* (Boston and New York, 1890), p. 3. These may have been darker years for young Arnold than has yet been realized.

18. Clarke, p. 80.

19. Parsing and Winchester: Clarke, pp. 40, 54. Stanley, *Life*, pp. 128–30. See also below, n. 22.

20. Stanley, *Life*, p. 323; Letter of Nov. 8, 1833. See p. 463 for Dr. Arnold's rejection of "common English" as absurd for rendering Homer and Herodotus.

21. "On the Method of Translation Employed at Rugby School," *The Rugby Magazine*, vol. I, no. 1 (July, 1835), pp. 30, 34. The author, listed only as 'O.,' is identified as one Highton in a penciled list added by a contemporary on the flyleaf of the copy now at Rugby School. Clough, writing in November of 1835, names Highton as a contributor (*The Correspondence of Arthur Hugh Clough*, ed. F. L. Mulhauser, 2 vols. (Oxford, 1957), 1:28, Letter 19).

22. In the first weeks of the previous school year Dr. Arnold speaks of his efforts to provide the Sixth form with "rules or formulae for them to work with, *e.g.* rules to be observed in translation, principles of taste as to the choice of English words" (Stanley,

Life, p. 230; Letter of Oct. 23, 1833). He distinguished mere word-by-word "construing" and true translation: the latter he terms "the exact expression of the mind of the original" in feelings, images, and arrangement of words (*Introductory Lectures*, pp. 214–15.)

23. Sir Joshua Fitch, *Thomas and Matthew Arnold and Their Influence on English Education* (London, 1899), p. 6, says that Dr. Arnold was always fascinated by ballad poetry. The Doctor himself speaks as follows: "In translating Homer, hardly any words should be employed except Saxon, and the oldest and simplest of those which are of French origin"; the language should consist of simple propositions simply connected ("Rugby School—Use of the Classics," in *Arnold of Rugby*, ed. J. J. Findlay (Cambridge, 1897), p. 217). Matthew Arnold sharply rejected F. W. Newman's extreme advocacy of Saxon words for rendering Homer, but "Sohrab and Rustum" and "Balder Dead" adopt the principle of simplicity.

24. Stanley, *Life*, p. 120. C. H. Newmarch, author of the anonymous *Recollections of Rugby* (London, 1848), says Dr. Arnold told the boys that "what had been hitherto considered of paramount importance was not so in reality, but that he looked for—'1st, religious and moral principles; 2ndly, gentlemanly conduct; and 3rdly, intellectual ability'" (p. 97). Religion he defined as "a system directing and influencing our conduct, principles, and feelings" (cited in J. D. Jump, *Matthew Arnold* (London, 1955), p. 8), and true education was to him moral knowledge (Stanley, *Life*, p. 450; Letter of Apr. 30, 1837). To the end of his life he maintained this belief in morality as the supreme concern of education (*Introductory Lectures*, p. 49).

25. Stanley, *Life*, p. 119; quoted from Dr. Arnold's *Sermons*, Vol. III, Preface, pp. x-xi.

26. Thuc. 1.22.4; Stanley, *Life*, p. 169; Arist., *E.N.* 1.1–3, 1094a–95a. The quotation, not precisely placed by Dean Stanley, is from *THOUKUDIDÊS* [Greek letters]. *The History of the Peloponnesian War, by Thucydides: . . . with Notes by Thomas Arnold, D.D.*, 3 vols. (2d ed., Oxford, 1842), 3:xxiv.

27. Stanley, *Life*, pp. 418 (Letter of Sept. 23, 1836), 129. The italics are mine. Thomas Hughes' *Tom Brown's Schooldays* (Part 1, ch. 7) shows that Dr. Arnold's Rugby sermons presented life as "a battlefield ordained from of old, where there are no spectators, but the youngest must take his side" (in Whitridge, p. 93). See above, n. 12.

28. Arnold nevertheless won several prizes, including the Fifth Form Prize for Latin Verse (R. H. Super, "Matthew Arnold's Rugby Prizes," *Notes and Queries*, n.s. 2 (1955) 357). See also Bonnerot, *art. cit.*, p. 522 (above, n. 17).

29. *Prose Remains of Arthur Hugh Clough: with a Selection from His Letters and a Memoir,* edited by his wife (Blanche Smith Clough) (London and New York, 1888), p. 399. Whitridge gives in detail, following p. 122, the Rugby curriculum of 1834: while Plato is not mentioned, apparently Rugbeians of the time read a half-dozen Greek tragedies even before reaching the Sixth form.

30. Stanley, *Life,* pp. 615 (Letter of Oct. 15, 1841), 604 (Letter of Sept. 22, 1841), 598 (Letter of June 26, 1841). On Thomas Arnold's remarkable knowledge of Aristotle and esteem for his thought, see the tribute by John Duke Coleridge quoted in Stanley, pp. 15–16.

31. J. G. Watson says in "Arnold and Oxford"(*Quarterly Review,* 294 (1956) 44), "The form, though not the reality, of the university was still mediaeval." The choice of college may be connected with the fact that Matthew and his brother Thomas were for a time pupils of W. C. Lake, then a tutor at Balliol. Lake (quoted in Bonnerot, p. 28) remembers Matthew as "equally brilliant, desultory, and idle," but the young idler went up to Oxford with the Balliol Scholarship, a very high honor indeed; see Jowett's letter of sympathy to Mrs. Clough (Mulhauser, 2:605, Letter 569), which makes clear what "the Balliol" meant.

32. In the late eighteenth century a degree could actually be gained "without any reading at all," Dr. Arnold noted with some asperity (*Introductory Lectures,* p. 337). C. A. Fyffe ("The Universities," in *The Reign of Queen Victoria,* ed. T. H. Ward, 2 vols. (London, 1887), 2:290; cf. 290) speaks of reform as beginning with the new century: "The first step in reform was the establishment of an examination for the B.A. degree, accompanied by the publication of the names of the twelve men who had most distinguished themselves. This . . . soon afterwards developed into the Honour Lists in Classics and Mathematics." In 1795, as J. G. Watson notes (p. 45), Oriel began a new method of electing Fellows which attracted brilliant men, the future reformers of the University; the year 1800 saw the introduction of Pass and Honours degrees; and in 1809 examination in the Greek text of Aristotle was made compulsory in the Final Schools (*i.e.* examinations). The quotation regarding the subject matter of Literae Humaniores is from Ward and Heywood's *Oxford University Statutes,* 2:166; Clarke, p. 99. The account of "set books" given below is based on material in Clarke, p. 100.

33. This grouping of subjects, taken together with the required or optional "books" given below in the text, represents in modern terms a combination of "Mods" with "Greats." The two levels are now distinct, and each level has its own set of examinations. In Matthew Arnold's time no such distinction existed: Honour Moderations, the intermediate examinations, were not instituted

until 1850. See Sir Charles Mallet, *A History of the University of Oxford*, 3 vols. (London, 1927), 3:297 and n. 2.

34. These were made available through the kindness of Dr. Howard F. Lowry. Arnold's name appears several times in brief lists of names and dates, written on the fly-leaves.

35. Stopford Brooke, *Life and Letters of Frederick W. Robertson*, 2 vols. (London, 1865), 2:208; in Clarke, p. 100.

36. Knickerbocker's statement (p. 413) that during Arnold's first year at Balliol Jowett "was . . . deep in his reading of Hegel and was beginning the famous lectures on Plato" is wrong on both counts. On the Plato lectures see n. 35 to Ch. VII. Jowett did not begin his study of Hegel until the summer of 1844, when he and Arthur Stanley visited Germany. See Geoffrey Faber, *Jowett: A Portrait with Background* (Cambridge, Mass., 1958), pp. 24, 178–83. As a portrait of Balliol and of Oxford generally in Arnold's time this book possesses great value.

37. Stanley's experience: Clarke, p. 102. Clough: *Prose Remains*, pp. 400–401. Thomas Hughes, *Tom Brown at Oxford* (London, 1889), p. 6. The Temple Reading Room at Rugby School possesses two small notebooks which contain Stanley's notes of Dr. Arnold's lectures. These indicate a thoroughness in dealing with Thucydides such as could seldom be matched even today except at a postgraduate level. Arnold's Thucydides at Rugby and Winchester: see Fearon, p. 13.

38. H. W. Carless Davies (*Balliol College* (London, 1899), pp. 196, 209–10, 222) has described the intellectual milieu. He claims that for several years after 1841 Ward's influence seemed to paralyze the best minds of the College, and he includes Matthew Arnold as well as Clough among the sufferers. (As regards Arnold, I cannot agree.) In *Loss and Gain: The Story of a Convert* (London, 1881), p. 93, J. H. Newman speaks of "the whirl of opinions and perplexities" at Oxford in these years. Matthew Arnold's closest friends in the Decade were Clough and Theodore Walrond of Balliol and his own brother Thomas, who entered University College in 1842. Faber, p. 154, speaks of Arnold as a member of the Decade in 1841. The quoted material is taken from E. H. Coleridge, 1:77.

39. In 1843, Clarke notes (pp. 109–10), the famous Latinist John Conington declared that at Cambridge the "intellectual exercise," with its "verbal criticism and philological research," is too often viewed "as sufficient in itself, instead of as a preparation for higher things. Oxford men, without any such preparation, which they affect to despise, proceed to speculate on great moral questions before they have practised themselves with lower and less dangerous studies." Sixty years later Sir Leslie Stephen drew much the same distinction (*Studies of a Biographer*, 4 vols. (New York and London, 1907), 2:74, 118).

40. W. P. Ker, *The Art of Poetry: Seven Lectures 1920–1922* (Oxford, 1922), p. 141, cites the remark as reportedly made by Arnold himself, who looked back on this period as "the critical moment of opening life." Sir Arthur Quiller-Couch believes the years at Fox How and Oxford were indeed critical for the formation of Arnold's genius (*Studies in Literature, First Series* (Cambridge, 1924), p. 220), and J. Churton Collins gives an exaggerated estimate of the importance of Oxford for his character and writings (*The Posthumous Essays of John Churton Collins*, ed. L. C. Collins (London and New York, 1912), pp. 173–74). In his lectures (p. 89) Thomas Arnold had strongly urged the Oxford undergraduates to "seize this golden time for your own reading. . . . To this hour I look back with the greatest gratitude to the libraries and the comparative leisure of this place."

41. The details are given by Alan Harris, "Matthew Arnold, the 'Unknown Years,'" *Nineteenth Century*, 113 (1933) 502; see also E. K. Chambers, *Matthew Arnold* (Oxford, 1947), p. 8. Clough's later remark that Wordsworth had "taken Matt under his special protection as a 2nd classman," referring of course to the outcome in the Schools, has been misinterpreted by Bonnerot (*Matthew Arnold: poète* (Paris, 1947), pp. 15–16), who relied on a shortened version in the *Prose Remains*, pp. 98–99, and by Leon Gottfried (*Matthew Arnold and the Romantics* (London, 1963), pp. 7–8). For the full text see *Clough Letters* (n. 7 to Ch. II), p. 29.

42. In early February of 1845 Clough writes, "Matt Arnold . . . is probably going to act as Master at Rugby for four months in the place of Grenfell, who is ill" (Mulhauser, 1:145, Letter 110). Arnold's election let him get away from Rugby after only two months. J. D. Jump, p. 16, says he taught the Lower Fifth form; so also C. H. Harvey, *Matthew Arnold: A Critic of the Victorian Period* (London, 1931), p. 20. Harvey and Chambers (p. 9) give the chronology incorrectly. Since Arnold was a temporary replacement, the list of Assistant Masters in the *Rugby School Register* (Rugby and London, 1867) does not include his name.

43. Oriel's tendency to ignore the Class Lists in choosing its Fellows was well known; see Mallet, 3:185, and Faber, p. 101. Arnold was elected March 28, 1845; his Fellowship was of course vacated (April 6, 1852) when he married.

CHAPTER II

1. E. H. Coleridge, 1:125; see also Bonnerot, p. 343 and n. 3.

2. So Bonnerot, pp. 62–63. Müller-Schwefe, p. 172, rightly says that the poem shows Arnold still without a style of his own, but the claim that he nowhere else deals with love *als menschlicher Situation* is a strange one.

3. As Bonnerot observes (p. 419), Arnold never finished making order in his soul; his need of introspection governs the course of the poem. Arnold nowhere else pays any attention to Sappho; both

she and Alcaeus were active around 600 B.C., a period of Greek history too early to interest him. Müller-Schwefe's explanation (p. 164) of "Horatian Echo" as nature's calm contrasted with the unrest within Sappho seems to apply to the first two lines only.

4. Müller-Schwefe (p. 89, n. 14) says in this connection that for Arnold the center of emphasis (*Schwerpunkt*) is the ego rather than what happens in the extra-personal sphere; thus he did not follow Herodotus and demonstrate a law of existence transcending individual circumstance.

5. U. C. Knoepflmacher ("Dover Revisited: The Wordsworthian Matrix in the Poetry of Matthew Arnold," *Victorian Poetry*, 1 (1963) 19, n. 4) has pointed out, however, that Arnold's justification of the gipsies directly rebuts the view taken by Wordsworth in the 1807 poem "Gipsies," and that he sees in them a kind of stoicism.

6. In C. B. Tinker and H. F. Lowry, *The Poetry of Matthew Arnold: A Commentary* (London and New York, 1940), p. 46. Future references will be to *Commentary* alone.

7. The précis will be found in *The Letters of Matthew Arnold to Arthur Hugh Clough,* ed. H. F. Lowry (London and New York, 1932), pp. 105–7; Letter 30, (?)March, 1849; also *Commentary,* pp. 47–49. Future references will be to *Clough Letters.*

8. See Clyde de L. Ryals, "The Nineteenth-Century Cult of Inaction," *Tennessee Studies in Literature,* 4 (1959) 51; on Arnold see pp. 57–58. "The Romantic overemphasis on the individual and the individual imagination" surely is involved here, as Ryals maintains; Senancour's *Obermann* surely is not, despite Mrs. Sells (pp. 60–61).

9. See A. H. Roper, "The Moral Landscape of Arnold's Poetry," *PMLA,* 77 (1962) 289–96; also see below, n. 19 to Ch. VIII.

10. It is these (1–56) and not the first six stanzas which make up the opening section of the poem, despite Arnold's strategy of asterisks after line 48. The text and line numbering of Arnold's poems given in the present work are those found in *The Poetical Works of Matthew Arnold,* ed. C. B. Tinker and H. F. Lowry (London and New York, 1957).

11. Greek beliefs concerning the ethical qualities which were imputed to different modal patterns stressed above all the strong contrast between the weak, mournful Phrygian and the manly, Hellenic Dorian.

12. Professor Walther Vetter, the Berlin musicologist, has said of the Sirens' song that it contained *etwas Sehrendes*—that is, something *intellectually* "injurious," an entrancing marvel; he points out also the irrelevance of all ethical or aesthetic considerations (*Real-Enzyklopädie der klassischen Altertumswissenschaft,* ed. A. Pauly, G. Wissowa, and W. Kroll (Stuttgart, 1935), art. "Musik,"

16:857). "Homer's Sirens," says Stanford, "did not try to entice Odysseus with erotic pleasures. They offered him knowledge of 'whatsoever happens upon all the all-nourishing earth,' together with the charms of music, most intellectual of the arts" ("No Rest for Ulysses: From Homer to Kazantzakis," *Encounter*, 13 (1959) 45–46).

13. Kenneth Allott, "Matthew Arnold's 'The New Sirens' and George Sand," *Victorian Poetry*, 1 (1963) 158. On *Lélia* generally see Wladimir Karénine (pseud.), *George Sand: Sa vie et ses oeuvres*, 4 vols., 2d ed., Paris, 1899, 1:421–45.

14. *Commentary*, p. 161.

15. George Saintsbury, *Matthew Arnold* (Edinburgh and London, 1902), p. 13, can find no justification for any such mild effect of "the dread Wine of Circe." But an explanation is not far to seek: the draught that Homer tells of was too strong for Matthew Arnold. Clough ("Recent English Poetry," *North American Review*, 77 (1853) 20) was the first to point out that the youth drinks not for "gross pleasure" but for the sake of "the glorious and superhuman vision and knowledge it imparts." Its lure is much like that of the Sirens' song in Homer: see above, n. 12.

16. Augustine Birrell (*Res Judicatae. Papers and Essays* (London, 1892), p. 198) quite rightly observes that Arnold would have been as ill at ease at a Greek festival as Newman at a Spanish *auto da fé*.

17. Euripides' play demonstrates the power of the irrational, a force Arnold distrusted profoundly.

18. No classical poet would have presented her thus, as the bringer of poetic inspiration. Theocritus (9.35–36) declares that "those whom (the Muses) look upon with joy Circe cannot harm with her draught."

19. R. A. Donovan ("Philomela: A Major Theme in Arnold's Poetry," *Victorian Newsletter*, No. 12 (Autumn, 1957), p. 1) suggests that the poet's vision is presented as attainable by divine help, symbolized in Circe or her cup, or alternatively by long and bitter experience, the way that Ulysses represents and the only normal and practicable way for the poet. Any such explanation surely would make Arnold's Ulysses much like Tennyson's, whereas the two conceptions are at opposite poles. See below, n. 24 to Ch. III.

20. Bonnerot, p. 366, explains that when the youth is deprived of the magic potion he has only fragmentary, fleeting glimpses; but the reveller does not speak of his visions of Dionysus in terms of deprivation. He has moments of painless vision even without Circe's wine because he is still young, according to Lionel Trilling (*Matthew Arnold* (New York, 1955), p. 97); more convincing, because more cogently related to the main themes of the poem, is Gottfried's suggestion (p. 122) that pain will come "when the Dionysiac reveller . . . begins to bring some Apollonian

order into his ecstatic visions and seeks to mould meaning out of the chaos of experience." To make play here with meaning and chaos, however, is risky: the Dionysiac may be terrifying or even horrible, as it is in the *Bacchae*, but it must not be thought to lack its own levels of order. Gottfried views "The Strayed Reveller" as a representation and also an implied critique of various Romantic attitudes (see pp. 126–27); this is too intricate to be plausible. Moreover, Arnold attacked allegory as a technique; see below, n. 56 to Ch. IV. The different levels in the poem have been perceived by H. C. Duffin (*Arnold the Poet* (London, 1962), p. 84, cf. p. 30): life as seen first "in its ideal form as designed by the gods, then from a worm's-eye view," and finally through the eyes of the reveller himself, who in moments of happiness had glimpsed the "visionary beauty" beyond actuality.

21. *Unpublished Letters of Matthew Arnold*, ed. Arnold Whitridge (New Haven, 1923), p. 18; Letter of (?)1853. "A person who has any inward completeness," he continues, "can at best only like parts of them." W. S. Johnson, *The Voices of Matthew Arnold* (New Haven, 1961), p. 11, quotes the entire passage and goes on to consider the lack of steadiness and wholeness in Arnold's poetry.

22. When Arnold deals with poetical stage settings that involve architecture the result is contrived and Palladian; when he simply describes a natural scene, as in "Empedocles on Etna" or "Tristram and Iseult," the result is natural and charming.

23. John Heath-Stubbs gives a uniquely perceptive appreciation of "The Strayed Reveller" in *The Darkling Plain* (London, 1950), pp. 106–7, terming it the one poem in which Arnold attained to "an intensity of imaginative creation which transcends the limitations imposed upon him by his time and the inner conflict of his personality."

24. Sir Herbert Read, *The True Voice of Feeling* (London, 1953), p. 88, remarks upon the freshness of imagery, noting also the "exotic *items* (rather than images)" jewelling the descriptive passages. It is preferable, he believes, to "the Tennysonian equivalent—the smooth Parnassian of 'The Hesperides' or 'The Lotus-Eaters'." For Heath-Stubbs, p. 106, the vividness of the images has "a quality of strange and fresh beauty like nothing else in English poetry." T. G. Tucker, *The Foreign Debt of English Literature* (London, 1907), pp. 67–68, argues that when Arnold speaks of the "echoing" oars and the "unknown" sea he is using "exactly the two epithets which a Greek might put." But "startled," with its personifying force, is exactly what a Greek would not have put. See below, p. 53, on personification in Vergil.

25. Professor Trilling, pp. 98–100, finds in the song of the poet reveller a characteristically Romantic attitude, the assumption of roles whereby man puts himself in the place of others. This leaves no

explanation for the youth's closing lines, nor is it clear why the assumption of roles should be assigned exclusively to Romanticism.

26. Apollo is mentioned by name ten times in Arnold's poetry, Dionysus never. Under the name Iacchus Dionysus does appear four times, but only in "The Strayed Reveller" (38, 79, 281) and "Bacchanalia" (30). See S. M. Parrish, ed., *A Concordance to the Poems of Matthew Arnold* (Ithaca, 1959), *s.v.*

27. On Arnold's fear of the "demonic" element—a term covering a multitude of experiences that he did not wish to face—see W. A. Madden, "The Victorian Sensibility," *Victorian Studies*, 7 (1963) 69; see also below, n. 22 to Ch. III.

28. The power of this poem was for a time painfully real to Clough ("It had a great effect on me . . . , it and its writer"): see Mulhauser, 1:301, Letter 262, written January, 1852.

29. Terminology and approach here reflect F. W. Bateson's *English Poetry and the English Language* (New York, 1961; first published 1934).

30. Bonnerot, p. 368. He also names the companion piece "Fragment of Chorus of a 'Dejaneira,' " "Philomela," and "Dover Beach."

31. Such piling up of noun upon noun, adjective upon adjective may often be found in Hebrew or in Greek written by those of Hebrew background; except for comic effect the Hellene uses it very sparingly. P. F. Baum, however, thinks that this first chorus uniquely reproduces the effect of "compression, complexity, and weightiness" of a chorus of Sophocles (*Ten Studies in the Poetry of Matthew Arnold* (Durham, N.C., 1958), p. xii).

32. See the summary of this argument given by F. L. Lucas in *Tragedy* (London, 1935), pp. 40–42. It is, as he says, a travesty of the *Antigone*.

33. The first of the choruses from the *Antigone* contains a masterly example of Sophoclean irony: lines that seem to apply to the unrevealed violator of Creon's decree prove true of the king himself. Arnold, an adherent of the view that the tragic chorus is an "ideal spectator," evidently took the lines at face value and missed the irony. His emphasis on the omnipotence of death—for "fate" means principally death in the poem—can be matched from this chorus. An ode from *Oedipus at Colonus* which echoes Theognis' pessimism ("Never to have been born at all is best") seems to have suggested the tone of Arnold's opening stanzas; see Soph. O.C. 1225–29, Theogn. 425–28. The latter fragment refers to the "gates of Hades"; "Fragment of Chorus of a 'Dejaneira,' " 29–30 "the gates of the city of death," may reflect this, as Bonnerot supposes (p. 376 and n. 3). The fundamental source, however, is Sophoclean lyric.

34. Haemon's account of Antigone in lines 76–79 could hardly be more opposed to Sophocles' portrait of her.

35. At the very beginning of the tragedy Dejaneira says that, although

we have been bidden to call no man's life well or ill lived until it has ended, she knows even now with certainty that her life is marked by misfortune (lines 1–5). Here, of course, one sees the main source for Arnold's last two stanzas. Later (162–74) she recounts the prophecy that if Heracles remains alive past a certain time he will have "a life free from pain." The chorus comment on the hidden sense of this phrase (821–30), revealed as the play progresses.

36. The authors of the *Commentary* note (p. 163) the obvious connection between this poem and "Early Death and Fame," first published in May of 1855.

37. The poem has two unusual features, an intelligent and beneficent Nature and the doctrine of katharsis, which Arnold normally avoids.

38. *Rep.* 617e4–5.

39. In "Matthew Arnold's Diaries, the Unpublished Items: A Transcription and Commentary," 4 vols. typescript (Charlottesville, 1957) W. B. Guthrie reads "Wordsworth; pindaric" (1:13; see also 2:3, where the passage is transcribed). The reference might then be to the last seven lines of "The Youth of Man"; see pp. 34–35 and next note. It has been suggested to me by Professor Geoffrey Tillotson that "Wordsworth's pindaric" (accepting the usual reading) refers to the "Ode on Intimations of Immortality." This would mean that Arnold, who had known Wordsworth for years as a neighbor in the Lake Country, was reading the poem for the first time when he was almost thirty. The only other possibility is that for some reason he made a special record of a rereading.

40. Read, p. 87, speaks of "The Youth of Nature" and "The Youth of Man" as "presumably inspired by the Pindaric ode," but no evidence supports his assumption. We shall see that in "Westminster Abbey" Arnold came closer to Pindar's style.

CHAPTER III

1. "Glimpses of Poetry," *North British Review*, 19 (1853) 212. George Saintsbury, *Matthew Arnold*, p. 23. T. S. Eliot, *The Use of Poetry and the Use of Criticism* (London, 1945), p. 105. Baum, p. 122, considers it Arnold's masterpiece. W. E. Houghton's article, "Arnold's 'Empedocles on Etna,'" *Victorian Studies*, 1 (1958) 311–36, has much to offer both as defense and as analysis. References to this author cited without title involve his book *The Victorian Frame of Mind 1830–1870*.

2. No one has produced a comparative study setting Arnold's poem alongside the *Empedokles auf Aetna* (1798) and *Empedokles Tod* (second version, 1799–) of Hölderlin. There are a few such comments in *Poems of Hölderlin*, translated by Michael Hamburger

(London, 1943), pp. 46–47. The intensity of his involvement with the classical past is conveyed in M. B. Benn's *Hölderlin und Pindar* (The Hague, 1962).

3. Kenneth Allott, "Arnold's *Empedocles on Etna* and Byron's *Manfred*," *Notes and Queries*, n.s. 9 (1962) 300. The statement that Empedocles is not Titanic may be correct; he does nevertheless identify himself with one of the Titans, as we shall note. Arnold's *On the Study of Celtic Literature* contains a description of Byron's Titanic heroes: see *The Works of Matthew Arnold*, ed. G. W. E. Russell, 15 vols. (London, 1903), V, 129–30. This edition will be referred to only by volume and page number, *e.g.* V.129–30.

4. In *Romantic Image* (London, 1957), p. 13, Frank Kermode rightly speaks of the poem as "designed with extraordinary care, a professional job of architectonics," and notes the tensions that it embodies.

5. III.229.

6. Baum, p. 123, rightly terms Callicles a good analyst. Bonnerot (*Empédocle sur l'Etna, Traduction et Étude Critique* (Paris, 1947), p. 65) holds that Callicles disbelieves the myths which he invokes. No evidence supports this interpretation, and it would leave him scarcely distinguishable from the philosopher who cries, "He fables, yet speaks truth!" (2.89).

7. Prose outline and summary in the Yale Papers; *Commentary*, pp. 291–92.

8. Kermode, p. 13, calls Empedocles the Romantic poet who knows enough and Callicles the Romantic poet who does not know enough. In the few pages which he devotes to the poem only Romanticism comes under consideration; this is understandable, but the result is a one-sided account of Arnold's intentions.

9. E. D. H. Johnson, *The Alien Vision of Victorian Poetry* (Princeton, 1952), p. 175, believes that Callicles' lyrics call up a myth which is relevant to Empedocles' mood but also objectifies his introspective struggle and raises it to a higher sphere; also that each suggests a "philosophic solution" to this struggle. The present analysis takes a different approach in several respects. See Houghton, "Arnold's 'Empedocles,'" p. 334. D. J. Gray ("Arthur, Roland, Empedocles, Sigurd, and the Despair of Heroes in Victorian Poetry," *Boston University Studies in English*, 5 (1961) 11) has suggested that in Act 1 Callicles follows Empedocles' denial "with a song contrasting 'the hot noon, without a shade' . . . of Empedocles' present rationalism to the cool shadows of the grove and the simple natural knowledge of myth."

10. At this point Pausanias quotes Empedocles' own words against him, so that the historical figure is for a moment identified with the poet's creation: "'The wit and counsel of man was never

clear, Troubles confound the little wit he has' " (1.2.30–31) is a
compressed paraphrase of the first part of the fragment now referred to as Diels 31B2. Empedocles says of men, "For limited are
the means of grasping (*i.e.* the organs of sense-perception) which
are scattered throughout their limbs, and many are the miseries
that press in and blunt the thoughts. And having looked at [only]
a small part of existence during their lives, doomed to perish
swiftly like smoke they are carried aloft and wafted away" (tr.
Kathleen Freeman).

11. Many instances of indebtedness to the *De Rerum Natura* are suggested in the *Commentary*, pp. 295–96 and nn. 10–20; quoted
below, p. 146.

12. *Clough Letters*, p. 123; Letter 39, written June 7, 1852.

13. Houghton, "Arnold's 'Empedocles,' " p. 333, strongly maintains
that Empedocles' long speech in Act 1 is neither dated nor superficial, but in fact a view widely held today.

14. The phrase "and all that Theban woe" may be meant to recall
Milton's "all that pain" (*P.L.* 4.271; cf. 9.505–6 on the transformation of "Hermione" and Cadmus). S. G. Owen ("Ovid and
Romance," in *English Literature and the Classics,* ed. G. S. Gor-
don (Oxford, 1912), p. 194 and n. 1) wrongly calls this lyric a
"resetting" of Ovid, *Met.* 4.572 ff. and mentions 4.706 ff. as an
additional source. There is very little possible relevance in the
former passage and none at all in the latter. Arnold's manner here
is anything but Ovidian. Although only lines 449–51 come wholly
from Pindar (*P.* 3.88 ff.) the prevailing tone is Pindaric, with an
admixture of the elegiac serenity that illumines the fragments of
this poet's *thrênoi,* the so-called "dirges." Arnold knew these: one
of them, *Fr.* 137, is twice quoted in the note-books (pp. 84, 219).
Page references are to *The Note-Books of Matthew Arnold,* ed.
H. F. Lowry, Karl Young, and W. H. Dunn (London and New
York, 1952). This work will hereafter be referred to by short title
alone.

15. Nietzsche saw a similar opposition between the pre-Socratics,
especially Heraclitus, and the rationalist Socrates (F. A. Lea, *The
Tragic Philosopher: A Study of Friedrich Nietzsche* (New York,
1957), p. 44). Arnold is not reviving the Romantic theory, rejected by Nietzsche, of the Greeks as "a race of 'naïve' children,
propagating art out of sheer delight in their unbroken unity with
nature" (Lea, p. 34); Callicles is no simple child of nature. J.
Hillis Miller, "The Theme of the Disappearance of God in Victorian Poetry," *Victorian Studies,* 6 (1963) 213, has in mind the
Calliclean element when he says that there was a time when man
"had joy, and having joy possessed himself, the deep buried self
making him one with the whole world." He goes on to speak of
"the happy unselfconscious acceptance of a narrow, limited life."

The question of whether Callicles' world-view is indeed narrow and limited constitutes perhaps the chief crux of the poem.

16. The view of J. D. Jump, p. 109, that Callicles' finest lyrics express "an essentially personal impulse of escape" dismisses too easily a complex inner struggle; see below, p. 44. Müller-Schwefe, p. 97, interprets the Cadmus and Harmonia passage on this same escapist basis. Professor Houghton, "Arnold's 'Empedocles,'" p. 314, n. 9, has pointed out that the real function of Callicles' lyrics is quite different.

17. Houghton has well said that if one reads "Empedocles" as a psychological and not a philosophical poem, there is no problem ("Arnold's 'Empedocles,'" p. 318). Kermode will have it that the Cadmus and Harmonia lyric contains precise structural ironies: the "happy immortality of the tormented soul" is "the lie hidden in the joy" (p. 16). With sure insight Trilling has said of the poem, "Its drama lies not so much in the internal struggle of its hero or in its resolution as in its juxtaposition of two kinds of poetry" (pp. 82–83).

18. Empedocles identifies himself unconsciously as well as consciously with the overthrown Titan (see above, n. 3): "self-helping" (2.103) recalls his first word of counsel to Pausanias (1.2.28–29).

19. As the myth proper begins (2.129), Arnold shifts his measure to a pattern already hinted at (note lines 2.121, 125), trochaic dimeters with occasional initial anapaests. The trochee, especially in combination metres, was set aside by the Greek poets for the expression of agitated feeling.

20. In early Italic religion the native *Fauni* were equated, not wholly satisfactorily, with the Greek *saturoi*.

21. "Philomela" (1853) and "Dover Beach" (1867), which contradict this, could both have been written considerably earlier than the dates of publication, and "Philomela" may be interpreted in the light of Arnold's later classicism. See below, pp. 55–56.

22. He perfectly expresses this attitude in a letter of 1865: "No one has a stronger or more abiding sense than I have of the 'daemonic' element—as Goethe called it—which underlies and encompasses our life; but I think, as Goethe thought, the right thing is, while conscious of this element, and of all that there is inexplicable round one, to keep pushing on one's posts into the darkness, and to establish no post that is not perfectly in light and firm." See *Letters of Matthew Arnold 1848–1888*, ed. G. W. E. Russell, 2 vols. (London, 1904), 1:249; Letter of Mar. 3, 1865. This collection will be referred to as *Letters*. See above, n. 27 to Ch. II.

23. S. Nagarajan ("Arnold and the *Bhagavad Gita*: A Re-interpretation of *Empedocles on Etna*," *Comparative Literature*, 12 (1961) 336), says that Arnold read Wilhelm von Humboldt's essay on the *Bhagavad Gita*, published in 1826. Humboldt uses words like

Vertiefung and *Insichgekehrtlichkeit* to express the meaning of "yoga," and he refers in his essay to the fragments of Empedocles. For a comparison of the doctrines of the *Gita* with those of Epictetus, see John Hicks ("The Stoicism of Matthew Arnold," in *Critical Studies in Arnold, Emerson, and Newman* (Iowa City, 1942), pp. 21–22); the two systems, he says, "mark out for man much the same path toward ethical completion." Arnold was reading in both around 1848, as well as in Senancour; this explains Clough's well-known gibe at his friend's "rehabilitated Hindoo-Greek philosophy" (*Prose Remains*, p. 373).

24. When Empedocles cries to the stars, "ye are alive . . . ," this is not the pathetic fallacy but a part of various Greek systems, notably the hylozoism (the conception of the entire universe as an organism) of the Stoics. Again, when he suddenly sees himself as a "devouring flame of thought" we recognize the spiritual form of Ulysses appearing to Dante in the *Inferno*. Arnold was to conclude a later prose work by quoting from this same passage of the *Commedia*, and "S.S. 'Lusitania,'" published in 1879, alludes to it. These instances confirm what we might have suspected from "The Strayed Reveller," namely that he chose to follow the interpretation of Ulysses as a restless seeker after experience, the Faustian figure inherited from Dante by Tennyson. This wandering Romantic never attained a place of importance in Arnold's work, whether prose or poetry; the weather-beaten guest in Circe's palace contributes nothing much more than picturesqueness. Here Ulysses, the eternal wanderer, symbolizes knowledge-as-experience. Arnold, for whom the widest vision of life is always the poetic vision, rejects the validity of such knowledge and stands by what he first said of the poet in "Resignation": "Action and suffering though he know—He hath not lived, if he lives so" (152–53).

25. "Resignation," 191, 195. W. E. Houghton, *The Poetry of Clough* (New Haven and London, 1963), pp. 160–61, speaks of Arnold's Empedocles and Clough's Dipsychus as representing "the modern, highly educated intellectual" who seeks "to preserve a kind of high integrity from contamination." He correctly describes the new creed of Empedocles as largely Stoic and partly Epicurean; see also above, n. 13. R. A. Foakes, *The Romantic Assertion* (London, 1960), p. 165, apparently has Stoic and Epicurean self-sufficiency in mind when he says that in Arnold's poetry "the vision of the one life within us and abroad is replaced by the ideal of the self-dependent single life, calm and free from passion"; but this he terms the disintegration of the Romantic vision, an interpretation which limits unduly the idea of the one life pervading all things. Donovan, pp. 3–5, finds the relevance of Callicles' songs often obscure: he like Kermode thinks that it is

Empedocles and not Callicles who possesses wholeness of vision, as the complete poet. His contention that such powers always entail pain or misfortune surely is refuted by Arnold's repeated statements concerning Sophocles. In any case, the Empedocles of Act 2 speaks as philosopher rather than poet. Houghton, in his noteworthy article on the poem, has well characterized Callicles as "the young poet with an alert sensibility, dedicated to the broad contemplation of life, and writing—singing with joy—a poetry of elemental experience: the beauty of nature and the cycle of human existence from birth to death" (p. 334). R. A. Greenberg ("Matthew Arnold's Refuge of Art: 'Tristram and Iseult,'" *Victorian Newsletter*, No. 25 (Spring, 1964), p. 4) has contrasted the role of Callicles with that of the impersonal narrator of "Tristram," noting that the young singer "must fail in his primary role just because he is committed to the action." But we must recognize also that Arnold could not possibly have dissociated himself from the areas of experience to which the figure of Callicles has reference. Even the impersonality ultimately achieved in "Empedocles" is not a formal device, as in the other poem, but the outcome of an unseen struggle.

26. The metre of the split couplets reproduces, in slightly modified form, the anapaestic dimeters particularly associated with the entrance-song (*parodos*) of the chorus in Greek drama.

27. This was actually the title Arnold gave to the lyrics when they were published separately.

28. Callicles' outburst on first witnessing the epiphany has been called the passage of English poetry that most nearly recalls the cry of Prometheus (in line 115 of Aeschylus' play) when he becomes aware of the divine fragrance of the Oceanids and the rustle of pinions from their winged steeds: "What echo, what fragrance, steals faint on my senses?"

29. "The conclusion is what you make of it when you have read the song of Empedocles and the songs of Callicles together: the philosophic argument of the vanity of gods and men; the poetry of the Greek legend" (Ker, p. 157).

30. Allan Brick, "Equilibrium in the Poetry of Matthew Arnold," *University of Toronto Quarterly*, 30 (1960) 54–55, sees the conclusion of "Empedocles" as the only one possible: we are left with the absolute question of whether the suicide is a transcendentalist assertion, as Empedocles hopes, or is instead futile nihilism. See above, p. 46.

31. In *Matthew Arnold: A Study in Conflict* (Chicago, 1948), p. 44, E. K. Brown says, "Apollo and the Muses, representing thought as well as beauty, as they have done throughout the poem, offer an interpretation of the universe in which there is no fever or distortion. . . . The serene and contemplative wisdom of the harp-

player is a mark of the disinterested disposition; he thinks as he perceives and feels, without bias or heat, and he sees life steadily and sees it whole." This well describes the concluding lyrics, but not the earlier ones. W. S. Johnson, *Voices*, pp. 111–15, establishes valuable distinctions between the philosophical and the poetic modes of thought which the two protagonists represent, particularly in relation to nature. One might question whether the proper alternatives are involved in speaking of "the poet, deluded or more than humanly perceptive in his celebration of a mythical harmony" (p. 112). There is no doubt, however, that Arnold refers to the gift of poetry as divine. The first possibility, that of delusion, is the controlling idea in Kermode's interpretation of Callicles.

32. In 1858 Arnold wrote, "People do not understand what a temptation there is, if you cannot bear anything not *very good*, to transfer your operations to a region where form is everything" (*Letters*, 1:62; Sept. 6, 1858). Hugh Kingsmill (pseud.), *Matthew Arnold* (London, 1928), p. 160, takes this statement to be a direct contradiction of the 1853 Preface; he has misinterpreted both. What must be noted in Arnold's words is, in fact, the assumption that there is any region in which "form is everything."

33. Bonnerot, *Empédocle sur l'Etna*, p. 13. Professor Douglas Bush (*Mythology and the Romantic Tradition in English Poetry* (New York, 1957), p. 255) says of the poem, "Arnold cannot . . . surrender wholly to the one part of himself; the dilemma remains a dilemma."

34. Charles Williams (*The English Poetic Mind* (Oxford, 1932), p. 212) says of Callicles' final lyric, "The voice of the young Greek singer is heard floating up the mountain, in a prophecy of poetry upon its way to its Olympian conclusion." But it is really Matthew Arnold, on his way to the lower slopes of Parnassus. The image of Excellence enthroned among the rocks (VI.103) is taken from Simonides, *Fr.* 37 Diehl, who echoes Hesiod's *Works and Days*, 289–92. See Sir Maurice Bowra, *Greek Lyric Poetry* (Oxford, 1936), pp. 396–97. E. D. H. Johnson, p. 179, at the beginning of a section entitled "Poetry as Magister Vitae," declares that a "*volte-face* in aesthetic intent" took place "between the publication of the *Empedocles* volume and the collected *Poems* of 1853"; this places the *terminus post quem* too late, ignoring the shift within Empedocles. Baum, p. 78, speaks of the "youthful crisis" that confronted Arnold around the year 1850.

CHAPTER IV

1. Whitridge, p. 58, n. 1, comments that a hundred years ago a schoolboy's leisure was his own—provided he could escape fagmasters; and Matthew Arnold entered Winchester at a level high enough

to exempt him from fagging (see Whitridge, p. 140). The number of hours devoted to actual classes was not nearly so great as in modern schools, even at Rugby after Thomas Arnold had stiffened the curriculum. See also Lytton Strachey, *Eminent Victorians* (London, 1934), p. 206. C. H. K. Marten (*On the Teaching of History and Other Addresses* (Oxford, 1938), pp. 31–32, 99, 130–31) says that Swinburne was always in the Library at Eton and gained a remarkably full knowledge and appreciation of English literature; Thomas Arnold had read Gibbon and Mitford twice over before he left Winchester.

2. XI.27; Super, 1.1.20–27. References are to the volume, page, and line numbers of material in the first four volumes of *The Complete Prose Works of Matthew Arnold*, ed. R. H. Super (Ann Arbor, 1960–64).

3. Super, 1.2.35–3.6.

4. *Poet.* 6.9, 12–13, 1450a.

5. Greek literary techniques: XI.287–88; Super, 1.12.6–7, 11.26. Adaptability of subject, poetic structure: XI.280; Super, 1.7.16–18. The three prefaces and Arnold's dislike of the capricious: Super, 1.15.19, 17.30, 64.30. In Ward's *The Reign of Queen Victoria*, 2:462, Richard Garnett asserts that the 1853 Preface checked the tendency towards faultiness of construction which was "the besetting sin of the poetry of that day." S. M. B. Coulling's extensive study, "Matthew Arnold's 1853 Preface: Its Origin and Aftermath" (*Victorian Studies*, 7 (1964) 233–63) appeared too late to be given the recognition here that it eminently deserves. Many of its statements provide a valuable perspective for the alteration in Arnold's relationship to the classical.

6. XI.271; Super,1.12.31–37. In his Preface to *Merope* (pp. xlii–iii; Super, 1.60.27–61.4) Arnold says that for the Greeks "the aim of tragedy was *profound moral impression:* and the ideal spectator, as Schlegel and Müller have called the chorus, was designed to enable the actual spectator to feel his own impressions more distinctly and more deeply. The Chorus was, . . . at the end of the tragedy, . . . to strike the final balance." "We are often divinely fuddled," says Trilling, p. 376, "by the implications of the tragic curtain. This *sense* of reconciliation, however, is exactly what Arnold wants."

7. XI.272; Super, 1.2.14–23. Here is the secondary source, after Aristotle's *Poetics*, of Arnold's "high seriousness."

8. II.272; Super, 1.2.28–33. Arnold translates line 35 of Hesiod's *Theogony* (Super, 1.2.17–18). His following analysis of tragic "enjoyment" seems to have been prompted by *Poet.* 14.5, 1453b, which states that the specific pleasure afforded by tragedy comes from feeling pity and fear. Arnold pays no direct attention to this thesis.

9. Whitridge, pp. 38, 41. In the second of these letters Arnold translates *Poetics* 6.2, 1449b26–31, omitting lines 28–29.

10. It is essentially the structure of the Preface, not its broad content, that is Aristotelian. A. H. Warren, Jr., *English Poetic Theory, 1825–1865* (Princeton, 1950), pp. 161–62, lists the particulars of Arnold's debt to Aristotle. Concerning emphasis on the "action" the third paragraph of the Preface (XI.271; Super, 1.1.29–2.4) states: "We all naturally take pleasure, says Aristotle, in any imitation or representation whatever: this is the basis of our love of poetry: and we take pleasure in them, he adds, because all knowledge is naturally agreeable to us; not to the philosopher only, but to mankind at large." This summarizes *Poet.* 4.1–4, 1448b4–16. *God and the Bible* (IX.168) mentions "that buoyant and immortal sentence with which Aristotle begins his *Metaphysics, All mankind naturally desire knowledge*" (*Met.* 1.1, 980a21).

11. In "Literature as Knowledge: Comment and Comparison," *Southern Review*, 6 (1941) 630–33, Allen Tate has indicted Arnold's poetic theory for treating language as a mere vehicle. He makes the important point that for Arnold the subject is what we commonly call the prose subject. Trilling, p. 153, charges that in using the Aristotelian poetic Arnold betrays Aristotle's method by arguing *a priori*. D. G. James (*Matthew Arnold and the Decline of English Romanticism* (Oxford, 1961)) dismisses Arnold's 1853 classicism as the useless escape of a Romanticist *manqué*, but he is demolishing a lay figure.

12. The *locus classicus* for this technical use of "Parnassian" is Gerard Manley Hopkins' letter of Sept. 10, 1864 to A. W. M. Baillie (*Further Letters of Gerard Manley Hopkins*, ed. C. C. Abbott (2d ed., London, 1956), pp. 216–18). He postulates three categories of poetry: first and highest is "poetry proper, the language of inspiration"; second is what he calls "*Parnassian*," which is not in the highest sense poetry and is spoken (not sung) "*on and from the level* of a poet's mind."

13. "Sohrab and Rustum" has the length of an average single book of the *Iliad*.

14. Of the 58 passages which derive from Homer, only 13 express simile. Moreover, 18 of the 31 similes show no Homeric origins. Only a very few of these, however, bring to mind any other classical author: Vergil, in 390–93, 634–38; Aeschylus, in 556–72. The latter borrowing is of some importance. T. R. Henn (*Longinus and English Criticism* (Cambridge, 1934), p. 29) calls it Homeric; the same mistake is made by J. B. Broadbent, "Milton and Arnold," *Essays in Criticism*, 6 (1956) 406.

15. In a Homeric simile "the significance of the image is the main thing," says W. H. D. Rouse, "and there is no thought of its

dignity if it be suitable" (Introduction to his edition of *On Translating Homer* (London, 1905), p. 6). See *Il.* 17. 389–95, 570–73.

16. See Broadbent, p. 408, for a theory of moral meaning in the Miltonic simile and the contrast with Arnold's use of simile for decoration.

17. See Bernard Groom, *The Diction of Poetry from Spenser to Bridges* (Toronto, 1955), p. 246. Arnold's awareness of his debt to Milton: Letter of Nov. 22, 1853; in E. H. Coleridge, p. 210. The relevant passage is cited in the *Commentary*, p. 83, n. 12 to p. 82.

18. *Letters*, 1:32; Nov. 26, 1853; see *Commentary*, p. 77. E. K. Brown, pp. 3–4, summarizes critical responses to the problems of organization and relevance posed by Arnold's extended similes. W. S. Johnson, *Voices*, pp. 129–31, who treats them with unusual respect, discusses their correspondence to the action.

19. Undated letter to Longfellow; cited in W. E. Houghton, *The Poetry of Clough*, p. 99, n. 1.

20. M. A. Potter's *Sohrab and Rustem. The Epic Theme of a Combat Between Father and Son* . . . (London, 1902), is an exhaustive study of the father-son combat. Its hundreds of examples include very few from classical tradition, and of these the famous encounter between Oedipus and Laius is the only one worthy of mention.

21. H. W. Garrod ("Matthew Arnold's 1853 Preface," *Review of English Studies*, 17 (1941) 318) quotes a comment from the *North British Review* for 1854 (vol. 21, p. 496): "Such a close is not Homeric, not Greek, but modern, and none the worse for that." Alone among contemporary critics Heath-Stubbs, p. 105, has realized the unclassical nature of the Oxus "coda."

22. W. S. Johnson, *Voices*, pp. 131–33, shows how the water imagery of the poem embodies the sense of death as consummation; he compares the Oxus passage with the close of "Dover Beach." I have not seen the special study by W. Oxenius, "Das Meer als Gleichnis bei Matthew Arnold" (Diss. Tübingen, 1951).

23. "Here," says Müller-Schwefe (p. 92), "the heart of man is shown to us as an instrument (*Werkzeug*) of fate, but no longer as its helper, rejoicing in activity." In Firdausi's story the agent is the traitor Afraziyab.

24. In "Milton and Arnold," (a reply to Broadbent) *Essays in Criticism*, 7 (1957) 227, John Holloway makes the point that "Sohrab and Rustum" is unsuccessful because it lacks a "great action" and bears no firm relation to the larger fabric of existence. The failure to relate to Homer and Hellenic tradition has been made clear by Professor Douglas Bush, pp. 263–64. The subject, he declares,

is "a particular pathetic accident which is not brought about by qualities of character . . . nor, in any philosophic sense, by fate"; it is not universal and inevitable, like so many of Homer's episodes, nor is it tragic. H. W. Garrod's defense of Arnold's conception in *Poetry and the Criticism of Life* (London, 1931), pp. 47–48, rests upon a singular view of Greek tragedy.

25. "Dover Beach," 15–16; "Empedocles on Etna," 1.2.442.

26. "The Strayed Reveller," 207–10.

27. See G. H. Ford, *Keats and the Victorians* (New Haven, 1944), pp. 81–85, on Keatsian elements in "The Scholar-Gipsy" and "Thyrsis"; also pp. 78–80, on Arnold's deliberate "anti-Keatsian" style in many of the lesser poems.

28. Henn, p. 29, calls the image Homeric; nothing could be further from the case. W. S. Johnson, *Voices*, p. 60, finds in the trader a "dim Romantic figure." C. W. Stanley, *Matthew Arnold* (Toronto, 1938), pp. 65–67, has grasped in a general way the historical meaning of this passage; his moralizing interpretation, however, is not easily accepted. In "*The Scholar Gipsy*: An Interpretation," *Review of English Studies*, 6 (1955) 53–62, G. Wilson Knight acknowledges the broad historical basis. Thucydides' statement (1.8.1) that the Carians and Phoenicians colonized most of the Greek islands may conceivably have been in Arnold's mind; its extreme brevity and lack of supporting material do not commend it as the main source for the "Tyrian trader." Professor Super ("Arnold's 'Tyrian Trader' in Thucydides," *Notes and Queries*, 3 (1956) 397) proposes Thuc. 6.2.6. In a recent note ("Arnold's 'Tyrian Trader,'" *Victorian Newsletter*, No. 24 (Fall, 1963), pp. 24–26) E. E. Stevens refers several times to "the Homeric simile" of the final stanzas.

29. Writing as a reviewer many years after "The Scholar-Gipsy" appeared, Arnold gave a prose summary of the same historical pattern that underlies his coda. See "Curtius's 'History of Greece,'" pp. 9–10; p. 127, *Essays, Letters, and Reviews by Matthew Arnold*, ed. Fraser Neiman (Cambridge, Mass., 1960). This collection will be designated by the name of the editor.

30. *Commentary*, pp. 104–5.

31. Müller-Schwefe, p. 232, holds that the function of the simile in Arnold's poetry is not to heighten pictorial vividness but to intensify the rational and emotional element.

32. "Balder" is the only work which draws upon the *Odyssey* to any considerable extent.

33. Oliver Elton, 1:258, well says of "Sohrab" and "Balder" that "Virgil, and scenery, and pathos are always breaking in." On the passage from "Balder," see the *Commentary*, p. 103, n. 31.

34. *Commentary*, p. 184.

35. Bonnerot, p. 367.

36. *Letters*, 1:324; Apr. 7, 1866. R. T. Kerlin, *Theocritus in English Literature* (Lynchburg, Va., 1910), p. 120; also in Bonnerot, p. 488, n. 3.

37. *Commentary*, p. 218. In *The Pastoral Elegy: An Anthology* (Austin, Texas, 1939), p. 23, T. P. Harrison, Jr., suggests that Arnold had in mind Shelley's description of *Adonais* as "a highly wrought *piece of art*."

38. R. J. Cholmeley, *Theocritus* (London, 1911), pp. 58–60.

39. *Letters*, 1:327; Apr. 12, 1866. See *Commentary*, p. 230. J. P. Curgenven ("'Thyrsis' IV. Models, Sources, Influences. The Landscape Hellenised," *Litera*, 5 (Istanbul, 1958) 7–16) is correct in claiming that pastoral elegy is too simple a medium for the portrayal of so complex a nature as Clough's; but Clough is not the real subject. J. L. Mazzaro ("Corydon in Matthew Arnold's 'Thyrsis,'" *Victorian Poetry*, 1 (1963) 304–6) very plausibly suggests that "the Corydon reference is a direct reference to the Thyrsis-Corydon pastoral battle in Vergil's Seventh Eclogue." His arguments against the Corydon-Arnold identification, however, are open to question. Line 81 need not imply that Corydon is still singing, and making this name symbolize "all poetic competition for Thyrsis (Clough)" leaves out of account the fact that in this early Eclogue Vergil was taking pains to imitate Theocritus, who used his Sicilian shepherds as masks for poet friends. From the late classical period onwards, Vergil's own *formosum pastor Corydon ardebat Alexim* (*Ecl.* 2.1, quoted in 5.86) has been interpreted by various commentators as a personal reference. Some such liaison or dangerous strong attachment is possible, in his case as in Arnold's, but it is neither likely nor demonstrable. *Korudôn* means "lark"; the term is a rare variant of *korudos*, which Aristophanes uses in his *Birds*. Thyrsis, on the other hand, seems to take his name from the Dionysiac ceremonial wand (*thursos*), the "fir-staff" mentioned in "The Strayed Reveller" (33).

40. Stopford Brooke, p. 125, sees the modern and classical elements happily combined here. R. E. C. Houghton (*The Influence of the Classics on the Poetry of Matthew Arnold* (Oxford, 1923), p. 24) strangely contends that Arnold's affection for the Oxford country is Latin rather than Greek in tone. See W. P. Ker, p. 18.

41. Bush, p. 259.

42. W. E. Houghton, *The Poetry of Clough*, p. 174. William Robbins, *The Ethical Idealism of Matthew Arnold* (Toronto, 1959), pp. 164–65, concludes that Arnold preferred to express the buried or hidden self not by logical description but instead by "a poetic if variable statement of what he felt to be a profound truth about the self." In the present poem the central thought is perhaps of

individuality: the authors of the *Commentary* (p. 190) have noted that the source of the poem may be a phrase of Edmond Scherer's, "ce palladium de l'humanité, de la vérité, de la vie, l'individualité" and its context (*Alexandre Vinet* (Paris, 1853), p. 161). Arnold underlined the words in his copy and wrote at the side: "Yes—l'individualité is all this. . . ."

43. Bonnerot, p. 377.

44. See *Commentary*, p. 173.

45. "A Question. To Fausta" (1849), 1–2; "Sohrab and Rustum" (1853), 616–18; "Isolation. To Marguerite" (1857), 11; "East London" (1867), 11; "Obermann Once More" (1867), 189–90; "Palladium" (1867), 7, 16. On life as a flux see "Westminster Abbey," 152. In "The New Sirens," 195, "this flux of guesses" merely describes Romanticism.

46. Professor Tillotson's point was made in a letter to me. In his Oxford sermon "Faith and Reason" J. H. Newman said, "Controversy, at least in this age, does not lie between the hosts of heaven, Michael and his Angels on the one side, and the powers of evil on the other; but it is a sort of night battle, where each fights for himself, and friend and foe stand together." Again, in 1848, five years after the publication of Newman's sermons, J. C. Shairp speaks of Christianity in a letter to Clough (Mulhauser, 1:218, Letter 182): "We like the men in Thucyd[ides'] night battle know not friend from foe." Professor Kathleen Tillotson ("Matthew Arnold and Carlyle," *Proceedings of the British Academy*, 42 (1956) 137) has noted the close of Carlyle's "Characteristics": "Here on earth we are as Soldiers, fighting in a foreign land; that understand not the plan of campaign." The clear derivation not from Thucydides' history but from *Hamlet* is noteworthy here. Arnold's indebtedness to the account of the fighting at Epipolae may well (as suggested in the *Commentary*, p. 176) relate chiefly to the historian's sudden rhetorical question, 7.44.1: "In a night battle . . . how could anyone know anything with certainty?"

47. Brooke, pp. 113–14, compares lines 1–14 with Tennyson's "The scream of a maddened beach dragged down by the wave," in which nature is personalized and thus cannot represent human life. Arnold's scene, being pure nature and not humanized, can become an image of man's spiritual existence. We may add that Tennyson follows the practice of Vergil here, while Arnold is perceptibly nearer to Homer. In *Last Words* (V.313; Super, 1.205.15–17) he contrasts Homer's supposed naturalness with the Tennysonian "distilled thoughts in distilled words."

48. See John Press, *The Fire and the Fountain. An Essay on Poetry* (London, 1955), pp. 185–86.

49. Compare "Poor Matthias," 62–64; also *Note-Books*, p. 527. The titles of two of these late elegies seem to parody earlier and more serious works, "Heine's Grave" and "Balder Dead."

50. Lines 131–46 and 153–54 are quoted. Arnold's note directs the reader to lines 465–85 of Aristophanes' play, but only the very beginning of his stanza (132–35) derives from this particular passage. Lines 143–44, which introduce the un-Hellenic starling, were not added until 1885.

51. The late Gilbert Norwood, a noted though controversial scholar and interpreter of Pindar, praised "Westminster Abbey" as the only modern poem known to him which exhibited the genuine Pindaric technique. "The spiritual light," he explains, "becomes a symbol dictating the language and—here comes the most finely Pindaric quality—the choice of myths" (*Pindar* (Berkeley and Los Angeles, 1945), p. 159; cited by E. K. Brown, p. 204, n. 35 to p. 97). On the choice of myths see the next note.

52. Bonnerot, pp. 269–70, mentions elements of English legend concerning the Abbey that Arnold did not use. Among these was a tradition that a pagan temple had once stood on the site.

53. Less than half of the total (184–98) cited in Arnold's note is actually relevant.

54. His rearrangement and expansion of the Demeter story indicates nothing more significant than a typically Victorian fastidiousness, together with a pardonable desire to accommodate the myth to his theme.

55. E. K. Brown, pp. 87–88, gives examples of Arnold's concern with light elsewhere. In "Matthew Arnold's Poetic Imagery," *Dissertation Abstracts*, 17 (1957) 3016–17, W. S. Johnson maintains that the later poems usually show imagery of light expressing ethical or religious overtones.

56. It is important to note, says Müller-Schwefe (p. 99), that Arnold did not grasp the role of the figures of Greek mythology as life forces: "For him they remain foreground manifestations of specific spiritual tendencies," given meaning by a secularized rationalism. "That he should have a feeling for the original duality (*Doppelsphärigkeit*) of the ancient gods is not to be expected." Müller-Schwefe gives the example of Apollo, the god of radiant youthful beauty and also the god of death; yet Arnold in his own way—that is, with his concern for "specific spiritual tendencies" —does credit Apollo with a dual nature, as a force embodying and promoting intellectual beauty "but . . . also the author of every higher moral effort" (VIII.114). On Arnold's use of mythology see Müller-Schwefe, pp. 95–104 generally; the central thesis is that it reveals Arnold himself. As Heath-Stubbs, p. xiii, points out, Shelley and Keats incarnated the forces of the subconscious world in the gods and spirits of classical mythology; but towards such symbolism Arnold had a professed hostility. See *Clough Letters*, p. 60 (No. 3, (?)late 1847), X.293, and in a religious context XI.305. The absence of this kind of symbolism from his poetry is the best witness of all.

CHAPTER V

1. Arnold was only one of many voices, says Saintsbury (*Matthew Arnold*, p. 72), "but he was the earliest . . . , the clearest, most original, most potent; and a great deal of what followed was directly due to him." In our own time H. A. Mason ("Arnold and the Classical Tradition," *Arion*, 1 (1962) 88) praises *On Translating Homer* as "the first and only book to put into the hands of the beginner who would make something of Homer as a poet."

2. *Letters*, 1:11, 175; July 29, 1849, and Nov. 19, 1862.

3. *Letters*, 1:126; Oct. 29, 1860.

4. "Dr. Stanley's Lectures on the Jewish Church," *Macmillan's Magazine*, 7 (1863) 334; Super, 3.77.1–6. Arnold probably knew of Goethe's claim before he prepared the Homer lectures. Apparently he did not know that Goethe, both as separatist and as unitarian, was governed by his own subjective state of mind. The theory of a collective Homer was, as he himself wrote to Schiller, convenient for his proposed *Achilleis;* later he abandoned the theory along with the project. See the review of J. F. J. Arnoldt, *Friedrich August Wolf in seinem Verhältnisse zum Schulwesen und zur Pädagogik dargestellt*, 2 vols. (Braunschweig, 1861–62), in the *North British Review*, 42 (1865) 279. Arnold was influenced by this review in dealing with Wolf and *Alterthumswissenschaft;* see below, n. 20 to Ch. XI.

5. That he did have views on the historical Homer has now become clear from the Gladstone Papers. See W. H. G. Armytage, "Matthew Arnold and W. E. Gladstone: Some New Letters," *University of Toronto Quarterly*, 18 (1949) 219; Letter of Feb. 21, 1861.

6. Whitridge, p. 52; Letter of Feb. 8, 1861. Professor Geoffrey Tillotson, normally a severe critic of Arnold, has said that in the Homer lectures his power of perception "is pinned down by an elaborate pattern of hard thinking. In these four lectures Arnold's powers of co-ordination, of *architectonicé*, is probably more complicated than anything he demanded of the architectonic powers of the poet"; this combination constitutes "the power of all good critics" ("Matthew Arnold: The Critic and the Advocate," in *Essays by Divers Hands*, Vol. XX (London, 1943), p. 30).

7. Rapidity as direct and flowing: V.164; Super, 1.104.27. Distinction between rapid and flowing: *Clough Letters*, p. 146; No. 51, Nov. 30, (1853). In this chapter "lectures" refers to *Last Words* as well as the three Oxford lectures.

8. V.168; Super, 1.107.1–9. The Greek is transliterated here. Arnold translates these lines as follows: "Neither would I myself go forth to fight with the foremost, Nor would I urge thee on to enter the

glorious battle, But—for a thousand fates of death stand close to us always—"

9. Of the eleven feet cited for the first two lines, only three variable feet are spondees (the sixth foot is always a spondee). The difference between these lines and 326 is like that between two melodies in 4/4 time, one made up predominantly of measures containing a half note followed by two quarter notes (2-1-1, in beats) and the other of measures with two half notes (2-2).

10. The scholar's explanation is offered by Rouse, pp. 4–5: "The first quality (rapidity) depends . . . on the strict observance of quantity, and the recurrence of long words with light body or terminations."

11. Duration, stress, and pitch, the three necessary dimensions of spoken language, sometimes become confused when we deal with Greek. Thus Arnold, who took more than a passing interest in Greek accents (see *Letters*, 1:128), apparently never realized that they were tonic—*i.e.* quasi-musical—but instead confused pitch with stress. The effect upon his already shaky prosody was not helpful: in the Homer lectures (V.248, n. 1; Super, 1.194, n. 1) he misinterprets the dactylic hexameter at length. Rouse, p. 196, has corrected this particular error. T. S. Omond, "Arnold and Homer," *Essays and Studies*, 3 (1912) 84–85, correctly notes that the opposition between Homeric quantitative accent and English stress accent involves an essential difference of movement—4/4 as against 3/4 time. Scholars have not realized this till recently, he continues, because they "habitually read Homer and Virgil to our own English measure." The true basis of the Homeric hexameter was very clearly stated by F. W. Newman in his outraged reply to Arnold (*Homeric Translation in Theory and Practice*; in *Essays by Matthew Arnold*, Oxford Edition (Oxford, 1914), pp. 313–76; see p. 320 on the "duplicate time" of Homer's metre).

12. On the metrical qualities of Homer translations which appeared between 1861 and 1888, see Richard Garnett's "On Translating Homer," in *Essays of an Ex-Librarian* (London, 1901), pp. 3–27.

13. Unfortunately one example (V.226; Super, 1.146.29–32) cited to show Homer's directness reveals a misunderstanding of the Greek text. He takes *Od.* 4.563–64 to refer to "going down to the grave"; but "the immortals will escort you to the Elysian plain" refers to translation, not to death. Lines 561–62 say explicitly that Menelaus is fated not to die and meet his doom. See J. A. Scott, "Matthew Arnold's Interpretation of *Odyssey* iv.563," *Classical Journal*, 16 (1920) 115–16. Arnold himself had described such a fate in "Empedocles on Etna," 1.2.435–60, derived partly from the *Bacchae* of Euripides (1354–62) but with an altered interpretation.

14. Gilbert Highet, *The Classical Tradition* (New York and London, 1949), pp. 481–82.

15. Jowett remained silent; E. C. Hawtrey, Provost of Eton, publicly dissociated himself from several of Arnold's contentions. W. H. Thompson, Regius Professor of Greek at Cambridge, did send Arnold an approving letter; see Super, 1.241, n. on 99.18-19.

16. Trilling, p. 123. Müller-Schwefe, p. 96, notes that Arnold never presents the traditional view of Achilles as the greatest and most glorious of heroes; but this traditional view has overlooked a good deal.

17. In his *Literary Essays* (London, 1896), pp. 350-51, R. H. Hutton makes the point that Arnold's criticisms are too much concentrated on the superficial moral nature of their subjects, with "little comparative interest in the deeper individuality beneath. . . . Read his fine lectures on translating Homer, and observe how exclusively the critic's mind is occupied with the form, as distinguished from the substance, of the Homeric poetry." One might further note Arnold's obliviousness to the emphasis in Longinus on grandeur of content, not of style; see below, n. 20 to Ch. X.

18. V.256-57; Super, 1.168.8-16. Arnold gave a special effectiveness to his cutting edge here: the words occur at the close of the third and final lecture. Rouse (p. 195, n. to p. 83) defends the translation of epithet animal-names against Arnold's objections (V.207-8; Super, 1.134.17-22); this is of course a defense of his own practice.

19. V.285-86; Super, 1.186.20-27.

20. V.189-90, 287, 291-92 have particular relevance; Super, 1.121-22, 187, 189-90.

21. V.154; Super, 1.97.18-22.

22. "As a poet," says Arnold (V.321; Super, 1.211.24-30), Homer "belongs to an incomparably more developed spiritual and intellectual order than the balladists, or than Scott and Macaulay. . . . He is, indeed, rather to be classed with Milton." See below, n. 25.

23. "For the first time," says Saintsbury (*Matthew Arnold*, pp. 67-68), "we find the two great ancient and the three or four great modern literatures of Europe taken synoptically, used to illustrate and explain each other, to point out each other's defects and throw up each other's merits. Almost for the first time, too, we have ancient literature treated more or less like modern—neither from the merely philological point of view, nor with reference to the stock platitudes and traditions about it." The effect on the violent unitarian-separatist controversy is noted by C. W. Stanley, p. 118: "Arnold's purely literary criticism of Homer did much to make men feel that most of the German account of the origin of Homer was fantastic, and that, however wide and diverse the origins of epic were, *one* great poetic mind had shaped the *Iliad*." For aspects of the background of critical thought since the seventeenth century see M. T. Herrick, *The Poetics of Aristotle*

in England (New Haven, 1930), pp. 119, 161, and on Arnold himself, pp. 166–71.

24. *Letters*, 2:291; Nov. 14, 1885. "To a Friend," 2. V.173–74, 232; Super, 1.111.8–10, 151.7–9. "With his eye on the object" is Wordsworth's phrase describing Vergil's method of composition; it comes from the armory of Romanticism.

25. V.321; Super, 1.211.31–212.1. See above, n. 22 to p. 157; these words follow immediately upon the tribute to Homer's maturity.

26. *Il.* 24.505–6, 543, 525–26. "Kiss the hand" is an intentional mistranslation. A. E. Housman, otherwise an admirer of the Homer lectures, took Arnold to task for this same rendering. Arnold greatly admired Chateaubriand's selection of this line as an example of the true pathetic (III.303–4).

27. *Il.* 12.322–28. This passage and the next are given in the verse translation of Richmond Lattimore.

28. *The Fortnightly Review*, 42 (1887) 299.

29. Rouse, p. 193, n. to p. 50, noted this. What is left unsaid in the Oxford lectures suggests that Arnold was not quite prepared to attribute the *Odyssey* to the same person whom he so confidently recognized as the single author of the *Iliad*. Even F. A. Wolf had acknowledged what he called the *unus color* of the two poems; not so Arnold, it would appear.

30. The tone of sadness: Jump, p. 166; E. D. H. Johnson, p. 212; J. S. Eells, Jr., *The Touchstones of Matthew Arnold* (New York, 1955). In his own Oxford lectures Thomas Arnold said, "It is vain to judge of any writer from isolated quotations. . . ." (*Introductory Lectures*, p. 101).

31. On these see III.120; IV.103–4.

32. Houghton, p. 308 and n. 13, declares that "the criticism of Arnold and Ruskin embodied the heroic tradition as it came down to the Victorians from both the art schools of Europe and the literary revival of Homer and the ballad." This is true of Ruskin (see his chapter on the grand style in *Modern Painters*), but such neoclassic exaltation was not the spirit in which Matthew Arnold approached Homer.

33. V.161; Super, 1.101.28–102.–26. Aspects of Ruskin's interpretation are defended by Gilbert Murray, "What English Poetry May Still Learn from Greek," *Essays and Studies*, 3 (1912) 9; Bernard Groom, "Some Kinds of Poetic Diction," *Essays and Studies*, 15 (1929) 143, criticizes it as a very doubtful explanation which shows Ruskin's failure to recognize the impersonal quality of much epic language.

34. *Letters*, 1:55; May 2, 1857. The German text is copied in Arnold's note-book for 1860: "Wir aber, wie ich nun immer deutlicher von Polygnot und Homer lerne, die Hölle eigentlich hier oben vorzustellen haben" (*Note-Books*, p. 10). Concerning Arnold's

use of this comment Müller-Schwefe says that this is the response of a man utterly worn out by the press of everyday existence; that it is not a mere commonplace, but rather the expression of a deep experience which goes to the very nerve of life (p. 167). Goethe's principal concern with the celebrated Greek muralist Polygnotus involved the writing of an article on the three wall-paintings in the Lesche at Delphi, as originally described by Pausanias. Polygnotus is supposed to have been an innovator, bringing contemporary meaning into his work through symbolism. The third of his Delphi panels showed Odysseus' visit to the underworld as told by Homer; Goethe was quick to point out its *hoher poetischer Sinn* and its various connections with the world of the living, including frustration as a punishment. What Arnold took to be a reference to Homer was in fact a reference to Polygnotus. See Ernst Grumach, *Goethe und die Antike: Eine Sammlung* (Berlin, 1949), 2:636 (the full text of the letter to Schiller), 642–63; see also index entries *s.v.* Polygnot.

35. V.170 (Super, 1.108.28–32); *Clough Letters*, p. 146 (No. 51; Nov. 30, 1853); VIII.216.

36. The other side of the coin is seen in H. A. Mason's reference to Arnold's "failure to expose himself to Homer and discover himself" (p. 97; cf. pp. 90–93).

CHAPTER VI

1. Arnold's statement may reflect his dislike of the bustle—not commercial merely, but intellectual and literary—of Victorian England at mid-century.

2. So Professor Trilling, p. 32. In *The Poetry of Experience* (New York, 1957), p. 137, Robert Langbaum explains the reference as seeing life "with its moral and emotional meaning inside it."

3. In *Homer and the Aether* (London, 1959), pp. 19–20, J. C. Powys meets Arnold's statement with the contention that the tragedian, in contrast to Homer's naturalness, "has an intellectual vision of things that may turn out to be . . . no reality at all"; but every work which is reflective as well as creative takes such a risk.

4. In *Last Words* (V.289; Super, 1.181.31–33) Arnold answered the criticism that he had equated nobility and the grand style without properly defining either: "I think it will be found that the grand style arises in poetry, *when a noble nature, poetically gifted, treats with simplicity or with severity a serious subject.*" Gottfried, p. 130, unwarrantably calls this statement "typically Romantic and expressionistic." J. Churton Collins, *Studies in Poetry and Criticism* (London, 1905), p. 274, notes that the poet as good man first appears in Strabo (1.2.5, p. 17 Meineke); but a case might be made for Plato's *Laws*. It is difficult to see why A. H. Warren, Jr., p. 22, hesitates to ascribe this doctrine to Arnold.

Later, however, Arnold said, "Goethe, like Sophocles, was in his own life what the world calls by no means a purist" (X.312).

5. "On the Modern Element in Literature," *Macmillan's Magazine*, 19 (1869) 309–10, 313; Super, 1.28.10–30, 35.20–31.

6. Arnold would have been amused by T. E. Lawrence's claim that his own adventurous life was a qualification for translating Homer's tale of the adventures of Odysseus.

7. III.320. Arnold is quoting Joubert.

8. The author (probably J. S. Blackie or J. M. Ludlow) of "Glimpses of Poetry," *North British Review*, 19 (1853) 209–18, speaks for his age: "It is not merely as an artist that men love to regard a favourite poet. He must not only himself obey the dominion of moral and religious ideas, he must do more—he must teach others to go and do likewise." See R. L. Brooks, "Matthew Arnold's Poetry 1849–1855: An Account of the Contemporary Criticism and Its Influence," *Dissertation Abstracts*, 20 (1960) 4107; Brooks has shown that Arnold suppressed and revised his poetry according to the criticism from reviewers and individual readers.

9. "Empedocles on Etna," 2.242–43; cf. 240 "Then we could still enjoy," and 249 "dead to every natural joy."

10. VIII.154.

11. "On the Modern Element," p. 309 (Super, 1.28.14–30); XI.212. This seems to derive from a passage (p. 86, marked "Good" in Arnold's copy) in Gustav Dronke's *Die religiösen und sittlichen Vorstellungen des Aeschylos und Sophokles* (Leipzig, 1861) which states that Sophocles anticipated Plato's theory of ethical awareness *in der eignen Brust* as a "full counterweight against the pressure of the bitterest sorrows."

12. *Clough Letters*, p. 124; No. 40, Oct. 28, 1852.

13. See C. H. Whitman, *Sophocles: A Study of Heroic Humanism* (Cambridge, Mass., 1951). He also contends that other men may acknowledge the ascendancy of the absolutist heroic ethic. In such a case, as notably with Philoctetes, there is no tragic disaster.

14. On this concept see Bonnerot, p. 371, n. 3.

15. As Knoepflmacher says (p. 24), the "thought" is derivative and intellectualized, not a sudden inspiration.

16. Quoted material from *The Oxford Companion to Classical Literature*, ed. Sir Paul Harvey (Oxford, 1940), "Sophocles," p. 401. Sixty years ago the great scholar Wilamowitz believed in a Sophocles of staggeringly simple piety: for his remarks see T. H. Warren, pp. 13, 327–28. On the dilemmas of Antigone and Orestes, Professor Trilling (p. 344) points out that "the agreement of moral teachers which Arnold offers as the core of morality does not solve problems of allegiance and of the clash of cultural ideals."

17. For the total portrait of Sophocles the main source is "On the

Modern Element," pp. 309, 313; Super, 1.28, 35. In 1868 Arnold
copies two extracts from Saint-René Tallandier's review of a
work dealing with the antiquities of the Lateran Museum: these
speak of Sophocles as the ideal man, combining vigor and
serenity (*Note-Books*, p. 75).

18. Arnold may have been led to think that the religious side of
Sophocles could be ignored. In 1868 (*Note-Books*, p. 87) he
copied from p. 25 of Dronke's work the claim that the highest
task of the struggling human spirit is to demonstrate the harmony
(*Einklang*) of the divine world-order with mortal understanding.

19. With some justice G. E. Woodberry (*Literary Essays* (New
York, 1920), p. 81) calls Arnold "as little Sophoclean as he is
Homeric, as little Lucretian as he is Virgilian."

20. III.44, 242; IV.247; V.86. "On the Modern Element," pp. 310, 313;
Super, 1.29, 34.

21. III.120–21. Prometheus: XI.275–76.

22. "On the Modern Element," p. 306; Super, 1.21.37–22.3.

23. *Ib.*, 313; Super, 1.35.22–26.

24. Arnold's comment is reproduced in Mary A. (Mrs. Humphry)
Ward's *A Writer's Recollections* (London, 1918), p. 43, and cited
by Bonnerot, p. 386.

25. See the prefaces to Murray's translation and Jebb's edition.

26. Among other sources Homer appears once, as does Bias of Priene,
one of the Seven Sages of early Greek tradition. Such echoes from
pre-Periclean times seem perfectly fitting; suggestions of Plautus
and Seneca are another matter.

27. Bonnerot, pp. 390–91, correctly describes Arnold's tragedy as *un
drame psychologique,* in which the gods actually play no part; see
below, p. 110, and n. 29. Müller-Schwefe, p. 90, notes this characteristic and explains that for Arnold the goal of tragedy was not
the specifically dramatic but the "sentiment of sublime acquiescence in the course of fate"; a central Stoic concept is made to
serve as an aesthetic principle. Perhaps the explanation confuses
the nature of tragedy with its effect, though the same confusion
may have figured unconsciously in Arnold's thinking. I would
maintain, against Müller-Schwefe (*ib.*), that Arnold had no intention of setting up a counter-theory in place of Aristotle's
katharsis. A letter of 1858 (Whitridge, p. 41) speaks of *Merope* as
based squarely on Aristotle's "celebrated definition."

28. On the Euripidean qualities of *Merope* see J. Churton Collins,
Matthew Arnold's Merope (Oxford, 1917), p. 23, and W. R. Rutland, *Swinburne: A Nineteenth Century Hellene* (Oxford, 1931),
pp. 46–47. Rutland (p. 45) compares it with Swinburne's *Erech-
theus*, Sir Maurice Bowra (*The Romantic Imagination* (London,
1950), pp. 224–25, 237) with "Atalanta in Calydon"; for Arnold's
own feelings about its relationship to the latter work, see *Letters*,
1:264.

29. E. K. Brown (p. 51) justly remarks, "Arnold is inviting the reader to refrain from taking sides in the drama, . . . to conclude that each character acted for the best as he conceived the best. . . . To see an action or a character from a multitude of points of view, each presented as neither more nor less valid than the rest, is . . . fatal to that intensity of emotion which great tragedy must stimulate." There is a derivative and uncritical encomium of *Merope* in Johanna F. C. Gutteling's "Hellenic Influence on the English Poetry of the Nineteenth Century" (Diss. Amsterdam, *ca.* 1925), pp. 96–102. John Bailey's erratic but penetrating "Ancient Tragedy and Modern Imitations" in *Poets and Poetry* (Oxford, 1911), pp. 170–80, is effectively counterbalanced at times by the discussion in Ruth I. Goldmark, *Studies in the Influence of the Classics on English Literature* (New York, 1918), pp. 84–90. Saintsbury (*Matthew Arnold*, p. 61) calls *Merope* much more Romantic than classical, and W. S. Johnson (*Voices*, p. 106) criticizes the absence of a proper resolution.

30. A. Koszul ("Comment noter les vers anglais . . . ," *Revue Germanique*, 3 (1907) 313–25) effectively criticizes Collins' scansion.

31. A comparison of the initial *kommos* or lament, 385–544, with that of the *Electra* shows that Arnold shortened the Greek rhythms: thus the dactylic tetrapody of *El.* 121 *ô pai, / pais dus- / tanota- / tas* is paralleled by a more or less dactylic tripody in *Merope* 385 "Draw, draw near to the tomb!"; and for the more obviously dactylic 124 we have in 388 "Deck it with garlands of flowers." These two patterns are at the base of Arnold's metrical usage in *Merope*. One hardly knows how to take Arnold when he says of his choric songs, "It must not be supposed that these last are the reproduction of any Greek choric measures" and claims to have followed rhythms which seemed to him comparable in their effect to the Greek originals (*Merope*, pp. xlv-xlvi; Super, 1.62.32–63.1).

32. Latinate syntax or diction: 384, 534, 1317, 1453. Archaisms: 131, 290, 297, 330, 342, 682, 738, 964.

33. Compare "Obermann Once More," 1–2.

34. H. C. Duffin's remark (p. 93) typifies much of his approach to Arnold. "Merope," he says, "is a fine Greek matron."

35. Just after the publication of *Merope*, Clough (Mulhauser, 2:546, Letter 495) wrote, "The fault I found with it was that on its own hypothesis it was defective, from the want of unity of interest." It actually was brought on the stage, though hardly in the West End: see C. H. Harvey, p. 55. T. Sturge Moore ("Matthew Arnold," *Essays and Studies*, 24 (1938) 25) was a spectator: "*Merope* is effective too," he maintains. "My ears retain another mother's shriek which cleft the intense silence, when [Merope] raised her axe over her sleeping son in the performance given by Gwendoline Bishop and her People's Free Theatre Company at Hoxton."

36. The final word on Arnold and the tragic sense has been said by Gottfried, p. 207: classical art showed that man could achieve dignity in an alien world, and the Greek dramatists rose to tragic grandeur in accepting this situation with total clarity of vision; Arnold's feeling does not advance beyond disillusionment—an attitude which seems Romantic when contrasted with the stern realism of antiquity.

CHAPTER VII

1. *Letters*, 1:37–38; Oct. 17, 1854. *Theogony* 515, 519–25.
2. XI.272 (Hesiod, *Theogony* 55); Super, 1.2.17–18. Houghton, p. 332, suggests that when the modern poet is counseled in the Preface to delight himself and others with "the contemplation of some noble action of a heroic time," the delight lies as much in being forgetful as in feeling inspirited.
3. VII.240.
4. Arnold's inference (XI.178) from Gubernatis' remark about Hesiod and Plato's *Republic* has been corrected by J. M. Robertson, *Modern Humanists* (London, 1895), pp. 152–53.
5. III.242; V.112. VIII.115, 123; "On the Modern Element," p. 310 (Super, 1.29.1–3). Arnold cites Pindar's line "My words have a sound only for the wise" (*O.* 2.93, adapted; cf. 91–92) to support his theory of the enlightened few, in "The Bishop and the Philosopher," *Macmillan's Magazine*, 7 (1863) 243 (Neiman, 49).
6. The adjective *eutrapelos* and noun *eutrapelia* refer to attitudes varying between the extremes of an accommodating social manner and moral irresponsibility. E. M. Goulburn (ed., *The Book of Rugby School* (Rugby, 1856), pp. 227–28), who succeeded Tait as Head-Master of Rugby in 1849, wrote of etymology as "a key to processes of thought" and "the tracing of stepping-stones." "In exacting from the pupil such a derivation," he continues, "we are really causing him to pursue the study of mind, and not of empty words." "A Speech at Eton" may owe an unacknowledged debt to Matthew Arnold's training at Rugby.
7. XI.187–88. In "Le Christianisme et ses origines (troisième partie)," *Revue Moderne*, 41 (1867) 478, Ernest Havet claims that for Sophocles the Delphic injunction "Connais-toi" meant "Gouverne-toi." This article appears in Arnold's list of reading for 1867 (*Note-Books*, pp. 581, cf. 633).
8. IV.306; V.116 (Super, 3.364.2–5).
9. V.112, 114, 120; Super, 3.361.28–30, 362.34–36, 66.15–19.
10. Arnold nowhere develops the theme of Villemain's remark concerning Pindar: "Le grand lyrique de l'antiquité était le *modérateur des âmes par l'harmonie*." This is copied in the notebook for 1867 (*Note-Books*, p. 52).
11. Page 310; Super, 1.29.6–18.

12. Stanley, *Life*, p. 130. The Temple Reading Room at Rugby School has a note-book of Dr. Arnold's which deals with the period from March to June, 1842; "Aristophanes, Pax" figures in a syllabus list headed "Exhibition Work." Such assignments were of course special ones, and the complete play would not have been read.

13. "On the Modern Element," pp. 310–11, 314; Super, 1.30. 6–7 and 26–29, 36.13–16. Menander the critic of life: X.50, cf. 93. The prose-like simplicity of his style: V.114; Super, 3.362.30–34.

14. Arnold's statement about the "instinct of humanity" consigning Menander to oblivion has been explained by N. N. Feltes ("Matthew Arnold and the Modern Spirit: A Reassessment," *University of Toronto Quarterly*, 32 (1962) 32, cf. 30–31) as part of an earlier concern with developmental concepts; see IX.9 and XII.16, 43, 76.

15. IV.104.

16. *Clough Letters*, p. 90; No. 21, August or early September, 1848. VIII.44–45, 134.

17. Thucydides and the rule of reason: XI.190–91. As a representative figure: "On the Modern Element," p. 308; Super, 1.26.21–26.

18. Almost sixty passages mention Plato. Plato as a great Hellenic soul: XI.194–95. As a spokesman for mankind: "Sainte-Beuve," in *Five Uncollected Essays of Matthew Arnold*, ed. Kenneth Allott (Liverpool, 1953), p. 78. Schleiermacher's view: *Letters*, 1:381; Christmas Day, 1867.

19. III.322.

20. Form, treatment, and style: IV.363, VII.353, X.193. Lack of solidity and seriousness: in *The Hundred Greatest Men*, etc., 8 vols. (London, 1879), 1:iii; Neiman, 239. Arnold wrote an Introduction for the first volume.

21. The Platonic and Xenophontic Socrates: VI.128, VII.171. In *God and the Bible* (VIII.272) Arnold calls Plato "an idealising inventor" in his treatment of Socrates. Shopkeepers and tradesmen: X.37.

22. XI.195, 49–50; XII.138; *Letters*, 1:392 (June 13, 1868); IX.73. With XII.138 compare *Note-Books*, p. 183 (*Gorgias* 521d6–8; entry of 1872). Arnold has Plato in mind still more strongly than Socrates when he declares (VI.220–21) that "public life and direct political action" mark the believer in culture "as would-be usurpers, not as disinterested apostles of the good." This apparently comes from *Rep.* 487b1–497b5; note 495c3.

23. In 1871 Arnold copied out, under the heading "Plato's object," the words of Victor Cousin (*Oeuvres de Platon*, 4:179; *Note-Books*, p. 150): "Élever le caractère athénien à son véritable idéal, qu'il grave . . . dans l'imagination populaire, pour le faire passer de l'imagination dans la conscience, et de la conscience dans les mœurs et dans la vie." They describe his own mission.

24. IV.287–89 (*Rep.* 496d6–e2); XI.75–76 (*ib.* 493a5–c8, esp. a9–b5); VI.88. J. Dover Wilson tentatively suggests *Charmides* 170 ff. as the source for this last quotation, but it seems to come in fact from the *Apology* (36c5–6), somewhat vaguely recalled. Abraham Flexner's comment is relevant: Arnold tried to make the equipment of a superb literary critic answer the needs of a social philosopher; it proved "altogether inadequate" ("Matthew Arnold's Poetry from an Ethical Stand-point," *International Journal of Ethics*, 5 (1895) 213).

25. IV.314; VI.34–36, 89. At the end of his life, in the article "Schools" for T. H. Ward's *The Reign of Queen Victoria* (2:279), Arnold again identifies terms as he had done in *Culture and Anarchy:* of the English middle class he says, "Unformed itself, it exercises on the great democratic class, rising up beneath or rather around it, no formative influence." Arnold also warned in 1887 that if the Conservatives should fail on the Irish Question, "then inevitably must come the turn of Cleon and his democracy"; at the close one can almost hear Arnold's tone. ("The Zenith of Conservatism," *The Nineteenth Century*, 21 (1887) 155; Neiman, 319.) Sir Harold Nicolson ("On Re-Reading Matthew Arnold," *Essays by Divers Hands*, 24 (1948) 131–32) argues that Arnold had in mind a totalitarian state ruled by a cultivated minority but ultimately dismissed this Platonic or Hegelian ideal as unrealistic. For a larger view, see the various discussions in Trilling's study. In *Notes Towards the Definition of Culture* (London, 1954), p. 23, T. S. Eliot points out more moderately that while Arnold's triple classification does indeed represent "a critique of classes, his criticism fails to get beyond a negative indictment": it "does not proceed to consider what should be the proper function or 'perfection' of each class." Here Eliot employs the Platonic criterion that Arnold ignored. In *Matthew Arnold and the Three Classes* (New York and London, 1964) P. J. McCarthy makes no comparison with Plato; pp. 73–74, however, deal with Arnold's Tory attitude towards the Periclean democracy of Athens.

26. Plato's influence on education: IV.318–19. Plato on the aim of education: "A Word More About America," *Five Uncollected Essays*, p. 44. The reference is apparently to *Laws* 965c1–3; relevant is *Rep.* 537c7 (*Note-Books*, p. 276). IV.320 (Greek text in *Note-Books*, p. 339), on the same theme, is essentially a translation of *Rep.* 591c1–3; Arnold interpolates the virtues from 591b5.

27. VI.127 (*Rep.* 490a8–b7, cf. 475–80; on 490b6, see below, n. 33). The severe training that formed a prerequisite to this philosophical contemplation is regularly ignored by Arnold.

28. IX.197. *The Dialogues of Plato*, tr. Benjamin Jowett, 5 vols. (Oxford, 1924; first published 1871), 1:127. Jowett is commenting on the Socratic thesis that virtue is knowledge. In 1871 Arnold noted

down the Greek text of Plato's dictum (*Menexenus* 246e7–247a2)
that knowledge without justness is in every case wickedness
(*Note-Books*, p. 151; *kaleitai* wrongly for *phainetai*).

29. X.33–34; VIII.115 (*Rep.* 401b8–d3).
30. Conduct and righteousness: VII.16 (*Prot.* 325c6–d5 is translated
by Arnold); VI.xlvi; VIII.115 and n. 1 (*Amatores* 138a9–10; *Note-
Books*, p. 81). See also *Charmides* 164d3–165b4, where Charmides
defines the injunction as simply a greeting, *sôphronei* ('be moderate'); Arnold does not seem to have used this passage. Dissoluteness: XI.306; IV.310 (*Rep.* 588e3–589a1, cf. 588c7–8). On Plato
and the higher morality of the soul see R. C. Cross, "Virtue and
Nature," *Proceedings of the Aristotelian Society*, 50 (1949–50)
137.
31. IV.333 (*Symp.* 206a–b, 207a). Arnold paraphrases and compresses,
adding something of his own in the following sentence. The first
sentence comes from Shelley's translation of the *Symposium*; see
Note-Books, p. 76, entry for 1868. In 1872 Arnold copies out
Plato's statement, *Gorgias* 499e8–500a1, that the good is the goal
of every activity (*ib.*, p. 184).
32. On the dialectical method employed by Arnold himself see W. S.
Knickerbocker, "Thunder in the Index," *Sewanee Review*, 47
(1939) 438–39 (Arnold accepted his oscillating nature as the law
of his being and thereby discovered a principle of intellectual
action), and H. J. Muller, "Matthew Arnold: A Parable for
Partisans" *Southern Review*, 5 (1940) 553, 557 (Arnold, like Marx
and Engels, believed the world to be a complex of processes, with
nothing absolutely good or bad in itself). On Arnold's conviction
that one must "try and approach truth on one side after another"
(III.v; Super, 3.286.9–17), see Houghton, pp. 177–78. On Hipple,
see below, n. 34.
33. VI.134; VIII.378; XI.x, 143; "A Word More About America,"
Five Uncollected Essays, p. 48. Apparently XI.143 is based on
Rep. 352d5–6 (*Note-Books*, p. 258, under the heading "Plato's
dialectics"); see also *Gorgias* 500c1–8. The quotation from "A
Word More About America" may refer to *Rep.* 490b6, which
describes the philosopher's attainment of knowledge and true life
—the two processes are closely linked in the Greek text.
34. W. J. Hipple, Jr. ("Matthew Arnold, Dialectician," *University of
Toronto Quarterly*, 32 (1962) 1–26), believes that Arnold was
"born a Platonist" and treats him as a philosophical writer with a
coherent system and a fundamentally Platonic dialectic. Though
often rewarding, this article claims too much for Platonic influence and too little for other factors such as Stoicism.
35. As noted below, Plato was not formally required in Greats. For
a strangely equivocal reference by Arnold to Plato's "absolute
ideas," see IV.317; this argues a considerable naïveté. Between

1842 and 1845 Jowett's lectures "made no specifically remembered mark," according to Faber (p. 160); in 1845 or thereabouts he began to lecture on the early Greek philosophers, and his originality gained recognition; only later—in 1847, according to Clarke (p. 102)—did he deal systematically and at length with Plato. Professor Kathleen Tillotson, "Matthew Arnold and Carlyle," p. 137, states that in 1840 William Sewell was lecturing on Plato at Oxford.

36. Nonconforming individuals: X.56–57, a summary of *Phaedrus* 273e8–274a2. (The whole Greek passage is given in the *Note-Books*, p. 284.) Arnold renders the last line with no regard for fidelity, inserting "the heavenly Gods" from 273e7. Arnold's notions read back into Plato: VI.144, 135, cf. 127. The references are elusive: *Phaedrus* 247c–e, especially c7 and e1–2, may have been in Arnold's mind.

37. On the vigor and excellence of the study of Aristotle at Oxford from 1800 to 1850, see Herrick, p. 172, with the comment of Mark Pattison there quoted; see also n. 32 to Ch. I. Arnold's comments below: IX.259–60.

38. VI.62–63. E. K. Brown, pp. 126–32, has shown how Arnold in this essay applied Aristotelian methodology to the social problems of his day, with mixed results.

39. *Clough Letters*, pp. 111–12 (No. 32, Sept. 23, 1849; *E.N.* 2.6.15, 1107a1–2, as inaccurately recalled by Arnold); X.280. It occurs also in the Homer lectures, V.157; Super, 1.99.24.

40. Moral and intellectual virtues in Aristotle: VI.126. Aristotle on ethical habituation: *E.N.* 2.4.3, 1105a26–b5 (summarized).

41. VII.205 (*Pol.* 1.2.9–10, 1254a28–b3), 208. See *Note-Books*, p. 186. For a minor quotation from the *Metaphysics* see above, n. 10 to Ch. IV. It is surprising that Arnold passed over the celebrated remark earlier in the *Politics* (1.1.8, 1252b30–31) that the *polis* "comes into existence for the sake of life, but exists for the good life." See Otto Elias, *Matthew Arnolds politische Grundanschauungen* (Leipzig, 1932), p. 135.

42. Among those who see a strong Aristotelian element in Arnold are Robbins, p. ix, and especially Gottfried, p. 171.

43. The *Poetics* (9.3, 1451b5–6) illustrates this from quite another direction. In 1880 Arnold seconded its claim that poetry is *philosophôteron kai spoudaioteron* than history, and rendered the two adjectives as "possessing a higher truth and a higher seriousness" (IV.16), imparting moral and transcendental overtones. Context reveals that Aristotle terms poetry "more philosophical" because it is universal, while history particularizes; the second adjective refers to what must be taken seriously, what cannot be dismissed from consideration. On Arnold's error Henn, p. 5, and John Bailey, *The Continuity of Letters* (Oxford, 1923), p. 23. A few

pages later (IV.24) he speaks of the *spoudaiotês,* "the high *and excellent* seriousness, which Aristotle assigns as one of the grand virtues of poetry" (italics mine); the moral element has gained strength. Eight years earlier, in "Matthew Arnold on M. Renan," *Academy,* 3 (1872) 63 (Neiman, p. 191), Arnold had spoken of "seriousness in the *highest* sense (italics mine), . . . what the Greeks called *to spoudaion,* and Virgil calls *virtus verusque labor.*" Here he has connected the idea not only with morality but with a concept from Stoic ethics: see *Aen.* 12.435.

44. *Rhet.* 2.15.3, 1390b30–31. The review is "Curtius's History of Greece (I)," p. 135 Neiman; on p. 150 Arnold speaks of the faultier side of a nation prevailing. "Brilliant" renders *euphuês,* with which he had made considerable play two years earlier in *Culture and Anarchy;* there the usage was that of Epictetus. See the following note. On Arnold's bias in dealing with Curtius see McCarthy, p. 73.

45. VI.219. The passage is based on the *Nicomachean Ethics,* 1179b7–16, with line 16 translated. Aristotle's mention in 15–16 of a lack of concern with *to kalon kai hôs alêthôs hêdu* ("excellence and true pleasure"; the basic meaning of *hêdu* is "sweet") does give a reasonable basis to Arnold's "sweetness and light," a phrase deriving from Swift and Epictetus rather than from Aristotle. In line 16 *tis (an) logos* is "what argument"; Arnold may have carelessly taken *tis* as "who."

46. Professor Trilling, pp. 258–59, sees *Culture and Anarchy* as reflecting Aristotle in many ways, chiefly in that it undertakes above all to make that distinction between "results" and "activities" which Aristotle notes at the beginning of the *Nicomachean Ethics;* but the connection seems a minor one.

47. XII.387; Super, 4.291.11–17.

CHAPTER VIII

1. F. W. H. Myers ("Matthew Arnold," *Fortnightly Review,* 43 (1888) 724) applied this point to Arnold: "By no arts, no flexibility, could he pour Christian wine into Stoic bottles; by no unction, no optimist temper, could he identify the religion of renunciation with the religion of hope."

2. Gilbert Murray has remarked of the phrase "living according to *phusis*" that it "does not mean 'living simply,' or 'living like the natural man.' It means living according to the spirit which makes the world grow and progress" (*The Stoic Philosophy* (London, 1915), p. 34).

3. Wymer, pp. 73–74, 138. I find that McCarthy has noted this aspect of Matthew's childhood. His book (see n. 25 to Ch. VII) did not come into my hands until my own work was in the press.

4. In his diary for February 6, 1847, Arnold wrote "bought Béranger";

see Kenneth Allott, "Matthew Arnold's Reading-Lists in Three Early Diaries," *Victorian Studies*, 2 (1959) 264. *Clough Letters*, p. 92, No. 22 (Sept. 29, 1848); *fade* is "insipid." For a refutation of the idea that Béranger is truly comparable with Horace, see the unsigned preface to *Chansons de Béranger* (Paris, 1875), p. xxxi. The comparison had been made, however, and by no less a critic than Sainte-Beuve. In the *Causeries* he places Béranger with such poets as Burns, Horace, and La Fontaine; he also gives the definitive classification of Béranger's poems, making *la chanson épicurienne* one of the main categories. (*Causeries du Lundi*, 4th ed., 16 vols. (Paris, n.d.), 2:286–308: "Chansons de Béranger," July 15, 1850. See also J. E. Mansion, *Chansons Choisies de Béranger* (Oxford, 1908), p. xxxix.)

5. Latin was actually banned in the school at Péronne that he attended; see P. J. de Béranger, *Ma Biographie* (Paris, 1875), p. 22. His inability even (as he put it) to decline *Musa* at the age of twenty brought him endless grief, according to the letter quoted in *Chansons de Béranger*, pp. xxx–xxxi; but by a diligent reading of translations he made himself a surprisingly good judge of their literatures (Charles Causeret, *Béranger* (Paris, 1895), p. 182). J. O. Fischer (*Pierre-Jean de Béranger*, tr. from the Czech by Richard Messer (Berlin, 1960), p. 23) says, "Das Lied blieb unbeschwert von der klassizistischen Tradition"; but see Mansion, p. xlv, on the defects, first pointed out by Sainte-Beuve.

6. Béranger and Anacreon: René Canat (*La Renaissance de la Grèce Antique (1820–1850)* (Paris, 1911), pp. 105–7) remarks that in France of the early nineteenth century the Greek lyric poets were little known, and that the leading figure among them was Anacreon—the un-Hellenic, precious Anacreon of Ronsard and Chénier. Thus, says Canat, "Anacréon inspire, et bien mal, l'épicurisme de cette génération, les chansons du Caveau, les romances de Béranger." Nevertheless, Clough (Mulhauser, 1:287, Letter 246; Dec. 18, 1850) thought Rousseau and Voltaire had met "in Goethe and in Beranger." J. C. Shairp's Balliol poem "Glen Desseray" (in Bonnerot, p. 33) shows that Arnold too associated the two poets, however casually. During Goethe's last years Béranger was his favorite among the French poets of the time.

7. Clough's remark (Mulhauser, 1:178, Letter 144; Feb. 22, 1847) is well known: "Matt is full of Parisianism . . . : he enters the room with a chanson of Beranger's [*sic*] on his lips."

8. See Kenneth Allott, "Matthew Arnold's Reading-Lists." In "Comments and Queries," *Victorian Studies*, 3 (1960) 320, he has shown that Arnold almost certainly knew Spinoza by late 1847.

9. Mrs. Sells, p. 236, quotes A. W. Benn's *History of Modern Philosophy* on Spinoza: "In interpreting pantheism as an ethical enthusi-

asm of the universe, he returns to the creed of Stoicism." Arnold himself, commenting on Spinoza, singles out for special mention 'his stoicism, a stoicism not passive, but active," and calls it "cheerful and self-sufficing" (III.364–65; Super, 3.176.2–177.28). A detailed study of Spinoza's training in Stoic doctrine has been provided by S. von Dunin Borkowski, S.J., *Spinoza*, 4 vols. (Münster, 1933), 1:492–504.

10. Stoic evangelists in Horace's *Satires* and *Epistles:* E. V. Arnold, *Roman Stoicism* (London, 1958; first published 1911), p. 111. The altered attitude in the *Odes: ib.*, p. 389.

11. *Commentary*, p. 14.

12. The reference to those who "spend their lives in posting here and there" (140) recalls the lines of the devout Epicurean Lucretius (3.1056–67) which are evidently a main source for "Obermann Once More," 99–100. Stoic sources, however, can be cited for any allusion to the restless Greek or Roman, used by both schools to exemplify the lack of inward repose. Alexander as an example in Seneca: *Quaest. Nat.* 5.18.10.

13. *Commentary*, p. 120. Brick, p. 51, sees the longings of Sappho and Iseult of Brittany as representing "an inward pull toward stoical control."

14. *Clough Letters*, p. 90; see *Commentary*, p. 24 and n. 1.

15. See Robbins, pp. 120–21. As he says, the very titles of many of these early poems indicate "the bleakly stoical basis from which Arnold started." The major role of Stoicism here has been stressed by Evelyn A. Hanley, *Stoicism in Major English Poets of the Nineteenth Century* (New York, 1949) (actually an abridged chapter, "Arnold: Stoic Influences and Early Poetry," from a doctoral dissertation). See also the introductory essay on Arnold in *Victorian Poetry and Poetics* (Boston, 1959), ed. W. E. Houghton and G. R. Stange, especially pp. 391–92.

16. Allott, "Matthew Arnold's Reading-Lists," pp. 257, 265.

17. *Ep.* 90.42 *mundus in praeceps agebatur silentio tantum opus ducens.* Translation and context are provided by E. V. Arnold, p. 176: "In the golden age which preceded our iron civilisation 'men lay at nights in the open fields, and watched the glorious spectacle of the heavens. It was their delight to note the stars that sank in one quarter and rose in another. The universe swept round them, performing its magnificent task in silence.' "

18. So, in the 1863 essay "Marcus Aurelius," he will introduce imagery of light with no precedent in the *Meditations;* rather than looking backward it looks ahead, to *Culture and Anarchy.* On this link with the treatise of 1869 see the brief reference by Henry Ebel, "Matthew Arnold and Marcus Aurelius," *Studies in English Literature*, 3 (1963) 564. In pre-Christian ethical thought, hope is a distinctively Epicurean idea.

19. On Arnold's poetic landscape see J. M. Wallace, "Landscape and 'The General Law': The Poetry of Matthew Arnold," *Boston University Studies in English*, 5 (1961) 96–104. See also above, n. 9 to Ch. II; cf. Wordsworth, *The Prelude*, 13.171–81.

20. E. V. Arnold, p. 350. Goethe's "'Entbehren sollst du! sollst entbehren!'" (see *Note-Books*, p. 187) appealed to Arnold as being in this tradition.

21. On Emerson's role see R. H. Super, "Emerson and Arnold's Poetry," *Philological Quarterly*, 33 (1954) 396–403. This study deals with Stoicism only in passing (p. 398 and n. 8). As Professor Super suggests, however, Emerson's 1841 and 1844 collections of essays are likely to have made an impression upon Matthew Arnold in this respect as in others. From the poetry of Emerson I can see only faint influences on Arnold's first volumes; but the reader who turns back to the essays with a possible relationship in mind may be surprised at how much will seem relevant, especially in "Character," "Nature," and of course "Self-Reliance." In his essay "Matthew Arnold" in *The Poets and the Poetry of the Century: Charles Kingsley to James Thomson* (London, n.d.), p. 88, Samuel Waddington says, " 'There were voices in the air when I was at Oxford!' With these words I remember hearing Mr. Arnold commence a lecture...; and the voices to which he referred were those of Goethe, Emerson, and Carlyle."

22. Epictetus on resignation: *Disc.* 3.24 (a long chapter). With regard to "Resignation" Bonnerot, p. 152, argues that the stoicism of nature is perfect and therefore implies an utter detachment from circumstances; this view results from a common misunderstanding of Stoic doctrine. For a correct account, see E. V. Arnold, p. 324, on the "good affections" and "eupathy" rather than apathy.

23. Thus the gods do not dwell in *intermundia*, the supposed spaces between the worlds, but are chariot-borne.

24. J. W. Beach, *The Concept of Nature in Nineteenth-Century English Poetry* (New York, 1936); cited in *Commentary*, p. 31. Man's spiritual isolation: *ib.*, p. 30.

25. See Professor Trilling's discussion, pp. 89–94, of what he terms the cosmological, aesthetic, and metaphysical senses of the term nature. As he says, Arnold "has not yet come to his mature sense of 'what pitfalls there are in that word Nature!' "

26. *Commentary*, pp. 295, 297.

27. Yale Papers; in *Commentary*, p. 288.

28. The paradigm of serenity: see the close of Plato's *Republic* (500e). When Socrates says that the ideal city is perhaps not to be found anywhere upon earth, but that a *paradeigma* of it may be set in the heavens, his reference may be to the patterns discerned by celestial science (*astronomia*). On Stoic writings dealing with the wonders of the heavens, see E. V. Arnold, p. 176. A. J. Festugière

(*Epicurus and His Gods*, tr. C. W. Chilton (Oxford, 1955), pp. 86–87) treats the distinctions regarding ataraxy discussed in the text.

29. The suggestions of Epicurean *ataraxia* and Stoic *apatheia* are strong in Arnold's choice of terms here.

30. "Just-pausing" suggests a mode of being and pattern of activity distinct from that of the human individual; "remit" hints at the genius as superior, perhaps a force to which we are accountable.

31. *Commentary*, p. 208. Professor Houghton, p. 297, takes the view that "the scholar-gipsy, in point of fact, has no aim." I would question his accompanying statement that Arnold's only remedy for the Victorian malaise is to turn to sensuous experience, and also the supposed parallel with Tennyson's Ulysses.

CHAPTER IX

1. Van Wyck Brooks differentiates Arnold's Stoicism and the Stoicism of Senancour in *The Malady of the Ideal* (Philadelphia, 1947; first published 1913), pp. 39–43, 47. He can see nothing positive in *Obermann*. The analysis, particularly of Arnold, seems superficial. In two out of three instances, the ideas that Arnold himself underlined in his copy of *Obermann* (Paris, 1840) are positive ones: the real life of man is inward, and what he receives from without is merely fortuitous and of a lesser order; also, at every moment what matters most is to be what one ought (both from Lettre I).

2. *Commentary*, p. 266. *Manuale* is the Latin equivalent of Greek *engcheiridion* or *enchiridion*, "handbook." The deception has been pointed out in detail by André Monglond, *Le journal intime d'Oberman* ⌊*sic*⌋, 3 vols. (Grenoble and Paris, 1947), 1:170.

3. For a number of years the "Manual of Pseusophanes" became Senancour's rule of life, according to Monglond (1:169). Apparently it dates from 1792, when his Stoic fervor was at its height. Looking back on this period he said, "I knew the enthusiasm of demanding virtues . . . , my Stoic firmness braved unhappiness no less than it braved the passions." This side of Senancour's Stoicism is usually ignored. A typical remark is that of H. N. Fairchild (*Religious Trends in English Poetry*, 5 vols. (New York, 1957–), 4:485) to "the weakly agitated *ennui* of Senancour"—characteristic, he believes, of Arnold's Stoicism.

4. Cic. *Tusc.* 4.6.13; Sen. *Ep.* 59.2. See E. V. Arnold, p. 324 and notes.

5. Mrs. Sells (p. 43 and n. 1) does not seem to have a clear idea of the nature of the "Manual." Monglond (1:170) offers a precise description: "This *Manual* . . . draws its teaching much less from Epicurus than from the Stoics, and from Marcus Aurelius very directly. . . . Certainly Obermann's *Manual* owes the essentials of its teaching to Marcus Aurelius: contempt for learning, the primacy of morality, the dualism of intelligence and matter, the

necessity of submitting oneself to the world-order, and the duty of consoling and sustaining one's fellows. He is still more indebted to it for the tone, which is that of self-exhortation."

6. Étienne Pivert de Senancour, *Obermann*, tr. A. E. Waite (New York, 1903), pp. 96–99.

7. Again Emerson's *Essays* may be cited, most of all "Self-Reliance" with such statements as "Accept the place the divine providence has found for you, . . . the connection of events," or "The only right is what is after my constitution, the only wrong is against it." A. J. Lubell ("Matthew Arnold: Between Two Worlds," *Modern Language Quarterly*, 22 (1961) 250) conjectures that Arnold's teachers "were, in the first instance, the authors of classical antiquity," who first taught him naturalism; he singles out Lucretius in particular. Lucretius' handling of Epicurean theory was of no concern to Arnold, who seems to have ignored the primary sources. Professor Kathleen Tillotson, p. 150, maintains that "the 'rigorous teachers' . . . must be Dr. Arnold, Carlyle, and perhaps Emerson"; the first of these choices appears unlikely.

8. Lucr. 3.1060–68 (echoed in "Obermann Once More," 97–104), 1034–52, 944–45.

9. *Clough Letters*, p. 73; No. 10, Mar. 6, 1848 (but Wordsworth may be the source here). *Letters*, 1:7. Lucan, *Pharsalia*, 1, 128.

10. *Clough Letters*, pp. 92–93; No. 22, Sept. 29, 1848.

11. *Ib.*, pp. 120, 122–23, 146; Nos. 37, 39, 51.

12. *Note-Books*, p. 1. *Letters*, 1:18.

13. Epict. *Disc.* 2.16.42. *Letters*, 1:62.

14. There are 32 different entries and 29 repetitions; these range throughout the entire extent of the note-books. The only authors or works appearing with noticeably greater frequency, except for the Bible, are Goethe and the *Imitatio Christi*. Renan, George Sand, and Bishop Wilson (an interesting trio) rank only slightly ahead of Epictetus.

15. E. V. Arnold, p. 127. In his definitive edition of the *Meditations* A. S. L. Farquharson (*The Meditations of the Emperor Marcus Antoninus*, 2 vols. (Oxford, 1944), 2:465) notes that in citing at the outset those persons who have aided and inspired him "Marcus seems . . . to desire to emphasize those human traits which correct the coldness and apathy usually ascribed to the Stoic creed." Elsewhere (2:848) he says, "Marcus endeavours in a variety of ways to express the joy which ensues from right action." This attempt to emphasize joy is worth noting, since we tend to credit Marcus Aurelius with a noble melancholy and little else. Yet the element of strength was wanting, as we have seen. The 1858 volume of Sainte-Beuve's *Causeries du lundi* (15 vols., Paris, 1851–62), 13:309, quotes Maine de Biran: "Il faut que la volonté préside à tout ce que nous sommes: voilà le Stoïcisme. Aucun autre système

n'est aussi conforme à notre nature." Arnold underlined these words; they were of the greatest importance to him as doctrine, but their vigor is not a trait of Marcus Aurelius. As Arnold came nearer the period of his preoccupation with the *Meditations* and their author, he may have passed through a period of doubt concerning the lasting worth of Stoic thought. At any rate, his copy of the 1862 volume of the *Causeries* (15:100) shows underlinings in a passage dismissing Stoicism as idealizing and ineffective, a system remote from the true and continuing moral-political philosophy that takes man as he actually is.

16. Cic. *Fin.* 3.10.35; *Tusc.* 4.7.14.

17. The failure to realize this has made Bonnerot, p. 379, impute Christian rather than Stoic attitudes to Arnold's Empedocles. On Epictetus' use of Koine see D. S. Sharp, *Epictetus and the New Testament* (London, 1914).

18. Leonard Alston, *Stoic and Christian in the Second Century* (London and New York, 1906), pp. 26–27.

19. IV.368. In VI.ix he mentions the "peculiarly sincere and first-hand quality" of the *Meditations*.

20. They were, as Bonnerot (p. 244) has phrased it, "deux espirits de la même famille." Ebel (p. 566) concludes that "Arnold's sense of affinity with Marcus Aurelius is at the heart of the ambiguous and revealing essay"; his proofs of this are questionable at times. Hermann Hille (*Die Kulturgedanken Matthew Arnolds und ihre Verwirklichung in der Pädagogik* (Halle, 1928), p. 18) greatly overestimates the fortifying influence of the *Meditations* on Arnold.

21. The prescriptions of reason: III.11; Super, 3.264.31–32. Arnold's reading in Cicero: Guthrie, 2:443–56. The characteristics of virtue: III.51; Super, 3.235.34–236.5.

22. Neiman, p. 122.

23. In Epictetus the corresponding adjective *euphuês* also means "natural" or "suitable": see Adolph Bonnhöffer, *Die Ethik des Stoikers Epictet* (Stuttgart, 1894), p. 256. Arnold speaks of *euphuês* and *aphuês* but has nothing on this other meaning, which would seem better suited to his purpose.

24. Marcus Aurelius: V.ix. *Euphuia, aphuia:* V.19, 20. Altruism stressed: V.11–12, 204.

25. See Houghton, p. 151 and n. 60; he mentions Senancour and Hooker as later sources. On the doctrine of the higher self as Stoic see John Hicks, "The Stoicism of Matthew Arnold," p. 42. His remarks provide a needed corrective to speculation concerning supposed Stoic dualism in Arnold. Here a direct and clear classical influence is, as a matter of record, that of Aristotle: his *Politics* predicates the existence of ruling and ruled elements in every composite whole and gives as an example the relation of

soul to body. Arnold copies the Greek text in his diary for 1872 (*Note-Books*, p. 186, two entries); in *Literature and Dogma*, published 1873, he translates and discusses it (VII.205). See above, pp. 127-28 and n. 41. Arnold's diary comment shows that dualism as dichotomy or antinomy was not in his mind: his word of summary is "harmony." Underlying the Stoic use of dualistic arguments in particular instances was always an ultimate monism: see E. V. Arnold, pp. 156-57, 172, and cf. p. 33, n. 22. Finally, with regard to Platonic doctrine the key term *hêgemonikon* of the Stoics (above, p. 132) seems to derive from Plato and Aristotle; see Farquharson, 2:497, and the references there cited.

26. Houghton, p. 16, makes the point (frequently ignored or denied) that Arnold "threw his whole weight against relativism" where the liberal dogmas of individualism and private judgment were concerned, though not in the areas of historical or scientific thought. His approach was emphatically not relativism in Pater's sense. The opening chapter of *Culture and Anarchy* and the 1864 essay "On the Literary Influence of Academies" show his affirmation of absolutes. See J. O. Waller, "The Arnolds and Particular Truth," *Notes and Queries*, 6 (1959) 163-64. For the various phrases from *Culture and Anarchy* see V.62, 166, 210, 215.

27. *Literature and Dogma* (1873): VII.40, "No man . . . who simply follows his own consciousness, is aware of any *claims*, any rights, whatever" (cf. *Culture and Anarchy*, VI.181); 43-44, St. Paul in Philippians 3:3 and Thessalonians 1:9 and Epictetus in his wish to learn " 'the true order of things, and comply with it,' " both mean we should "obey a tendency, which is *not ourselves*, but which appears in our consciousness, by which things fulfil the real law of their being"—a remarkable warping of Stoic monism into the validation of an absolute. "Ecce, Convertimur ad Gentes" (1879): XI.111-12, "Indifference to the real natural and rational rule of things . . . renders us very liable to be found fighting against nature, and that is always calamitous." "A 'Friend of God,' " Neiman, pp. 334-35 (1887): Bishop Butler horrified at the thought of "leaving the course marked out for us by nature"; "To follow [Christ] and his life is really to follow nature, to be happy." "Disestablishment in Wales," Neiman, pp. 372-73 (1888): see below, n. 32.

28. References to "epicureanism": VI.346, VII.69, VIII.xxii. Hille, p. 26, notes that Arnold took a separate way from that of the majority of ethical thinkers in England, who grounded their thought in Epicurus' teachings and prized utilitarianism. It is possible that a specialized study of Arnold's works would reveal more individual instances of Epicurean influence than have yet been noticed. References to faith and hope (see also above, n. 18 to Ch. VIII) constitute an example: considered within the framework of

Hellenistic philosophy, both of these are distinctly and exclusively Epicurean concepts. Again, it is difficult to determine the antecedents of *epieikeia*, the "sweet reasonableness" of Jesus which becomes important in *Literature and Dogma* (see especially VII.87). The term is thoroughly classical—a Euripidean usage is copied in the *Note-Books*, p. 173—but it also developed into one of the most distinctive ethical ideas associated with Epicureanism.

29. The 1878 essay on "Equality," which draws briefly upon Stoic sources, begins and ends with a quotation from Menander (X.46–47, 93). The question of Epicurean thought in Menander is a vexed one. Professor T. B. L. Webster, who has gone into this matter with great care, finds no passage in which either Stoic or Epicurean influence can be shown; he points out that since Menander produced his first play in 321 B.C., traces of either system would appear only in the latest plays, if at all (*Studies in Menander* (Manchester, 1950), pp. 198, 217). Festugière, p. 11, similarly believes that in his references to the gods Menander reflects the disenchanted mood of his time rather than Epicurean doctrine. In *Epicurus and His Philosophy* (Minneapolis, 1954), pp. 52–53, Professor N. W. DeWitt argues that the plays do contain certain teachings of Epicurus, deliberately concealed and exploited for dramatic possibilities. Where Arnold is concerned, the whole matter is further complicated by the possibility that a number of the aphorisms he accepted as Menander's are merely attributed to him by tradition.

30. *Note-Books*, p. 60; IV.378.

31. Epictetus on natural fellowship: *Disc.* 2.20.8. For some readers in the period around 1870–80, the strength imparted by this and other comparable Stoic doctrines was a real force: Janet E. Courtney (*Freethinkers of the Nineteenth Century* (New York, 1920), p. 74) says with some feeling that "it is the stoic quality of Arnold's thought, the lessons learnt from his close study of Epictetus and Marcus Aurelius, that seemed to bring to that generation just the stiffening it needed."

32. *Note-Books*, p. 434. As a heading Arnold wrote, in capital letters, "Again and again!" In the spring of 1888 he made his last reference to the doctrine that had steadied him for forty years: "The Stoics, with whom the great matter was adherence to the moral will and purpose, the living, as we commonly express it, *by principle*, used to tell their pupils to say to themselves, whenever they found themselves desiring a thing: 'This I desire; *and also to keep my principle.*'" ("Disestablishment in Wales," pp. 372–73 Neiman; see above, n. 27. The quotation is an altered version of Epict. *Manual* 4, " 'I want to bathe, and I want to keep my will in harmony with nature'" (tr. Long).)

33. Arnold regularly drew his entries from the Cicero who had

championed Stoic ethics in the *Tusculan Disputations* and *De Officiis* rather than from the Cicero who had followed Antiochus, skeptic and opponent of the Stoics, in the treatise *De Finibus*. On Cicero's eclecticism see R. D. Hicks, *Stoic and Epicurean* (New York, 1910), pp. 356, 359. As for the fusing of the two systems in Arnold's thought, Houghton and Stange, p. 392, justly observe that his concept of God and the worship of God—the tendency towards righteousness, and following a law found in our conscience—is more Stoic than Christian.

CHAPTER X

1. "On the Modern Element," p. 306 (Super, 1.23.9–13); III.241; XII. 386 (Super, 4.290.14–23); XI.195–96. As an Eton boy A. C. Benson heard Arnold's speech. "The whole discourse," he recalls, "had the charm of a mysterious secret. . . . There was something harmonious and seductive about what he was telling us, a sense of living men and living ideas" (*The Leaves of the Tree: Studies in Biography* (New York and London, 1911), pp. 389–90). Arnold drew many of his ideas about Greek history and religion from Ernst Curtius' five-volume study, translated by A. W. Ward under the title *The History of Greece* (London, 1868–73). Arnold reviewed the English volumes for the *Pall Mall Gazette* (Neiman, 124–55). See also above, n. 44 to Ch. VII.

2. X.62–63. Arnold refers to the famous statement that to be Greek is primarily to share in Athenian culture (*Panegyricus* 51). He may have been reminded of this by Havet's reference, p. 504; see above, n. 7 to Ch. VII. It was of course Pericles (Thuc. 2.41.1), not Isocrates, who called Athens the school of Hellas. On the Periclean and Elizabethan ages as great "modern" epochs see "On the Modern Element," pp. 306–7; Super, 1.23.9–28.7.

3. X.37; "On the Modern Element," pp. 308–9 (Super, 1.26.25–26, 28.21–26). For this idea Arnold is probably indebted to Goethe, who believed that the great qualities of Periclean literature were characteristic of the nation and the entire period (*Gespräche mit Eckermann*, 1:327; May 3, 1827). Ten years after his inaugural lecture, Arnold read—doubtless with no little pleasure—Havet's remark, "La sagesse de Socrate était en général celle de son temps"; see above, n. 7 to Ch. VII.

4. VII.1 (also *Note-Books*, p. 133); X.37, 66. In his moving article "On the Modern Element in Modern Literature," *Partisan Review*, 28 (1961) 24, Professor Trilling suggests that Nietzsche's *Birth of Tragedy* has utterly destroyed for us "that rational and ordered Greece, that modern, that eighteenth-century, Athens that Arnold so entirely relied on as the standard for judging all civilizations." This raises Nietzsche too high at Arnold's expense, but its criticism cannot be wholly dismissed.

5. Arnold deals specifically with Pericles only in his five-part review of Curtius' *History of Greece*, where he is quoting or paraphrasing rather than setting down his own thoughts. The involvement is a general one throughout, based on the parallel Arnold saw between Periclean Athens and his own time (so Neiman, 124).

6. VI.224; "On the Modern Element," pp. 309, 311 (Super, 1.28, 31.22–23); IX.350; V.142–43. In 1872 Arnold (*Note-Books*, p. 187) copied out Curtius' statement that "the art of the age of Pericles had received a very definite religious mission—to satisfy, in its religious representations, the progress of human consciousness, and to reconcile the traditions of the past with the reason of the present." This is undoubtedly the sort of thing a Victorian liberal would have found congenial to his thinking. As for Goethe's supplying "a new spiritual basis" to life, he went to Greek art and literature "for an escape from the 'moral interpretation' which Arnold sees in him and in the Greeks alike" (J. B. Orrick, "Matthew Arnold and Goethe," *Publications of the Goethe Society* (London, 1928), 4:49).

7. IV.131; VI.19–20. The idea of human perfection of which Arnold speaks here is derived from Goethe as well as from classical sources. See Houghton, p. 288. Though Swift professes to be championing the cause of the ancients, he shows the absurdity of reckoning the worth of a book by its age at the same time that he attacks the extreme subjective and destructive methods of modern critics. See Anne E. Burlingame, *The Battle of the Books in Its Historical Setting* (New York, 1920), pp. 143–50; cf. pp. 129, 131.

8. IV.346 (*Note-Books*, p. 446); V.85; VI.xiv, 60, 163–64; VII.1. Arnold very possibly had in mind also a statement made by F. A. Wolf: "The Greek ideal is this; a purely human education, and elevation of all the powers of mind and soul to a beautiful harmony of the inner and outer man . . ." (*Note-Books*, p. 40). Still more likely is the concluding portion of a passage of Dronke's on "Greek perfection" (Arnold's heading) (*ib.*, pp. 143–44). Elias, p. 24, claims that Arnold's conception of the humane ideal is of Greek origin, transmitted particularly through the New Humanist thinkers of Germany; see the following note.

9. Greek art: VII.56, IV.346. On Greek sculpture see *e.g.* VII.53, 326. Hille, p. 22, notes that for Arnold Greek antiquity and its ideal of perfection (*kalokagathia*, the combination of inward and outward beauty) was not an end but a means to full humane development; in this respect, says Hille, he is close to the thought of the New Humanism represented in Germany by Goethe and Humboldt.

10. VI.146; *E.N.* 2.1.3, 1103a23–25.

11. IX.xxxvi; *Fortnightly Review*, 31 (1882) 695. In the *Causeries* (vol.

V (3rd ed., 1852), p. 378) Arnold found the following quotation from Gourville: "Au commencement de chacune (he is speaking of recent years), je souhaite pouvoir manger des fraises; quand elles sont passées, j'aspire aux pêches; et cela durera autant qu'il plaira à Dieu." He underlined the words in his copy and wrote a descriptive phrase: "Greek view of life."

12. V.9, 85; VI.146.

13. XII.69. In 1870 Arnold writes, "The Greek ideal for each man to strive after—'die reichste Blüthe menschlicher Vollendung durch die volle Entfaltung der Individualität'" (*Note-Books*, p. 132; the quotation is from Dronke, p. 114). E. L. Hunt ("Matthew Arnold and His Critics," *Sewanee Review*, 44 (1936) 453) states that "Abraham Flexner in 1895 attacked Arnold's Greek notion that the state is the individual writ large"; but only a single phrase in Flexner's article (see above, n. 24 to Ch. VII) even hints at this view. Arnold himself pointedly avoided Plato's approach and in the end could solve his problem only through a Christian interpretation of the "best self."

14. On this point see J. V. Cheney (*The Golden Guess: Essays on Poetry and Poets* (Boston, 1892), p. 99), who warns against pressing Arnold's Hellenism too far by arguing from the assumption that his view of the individual is Hellenic. The shortcomings of Arnold's work, says Professor Geoffrey Tillotson (*Criticism and the Nineteenth Century* (London, 1951), pp. 61–62), "are particularly noticeable when Arnold is dealing with the past, when he is employed in glancing back at older civilisations. . . . On those occasions we cannot help wishing that he had studied closely enough to strike the proper balance between interpretation and facts, between intelligence and its material."

15. X.63; VII.355; XI.204; VI.146; XI.198; VII.356, 359; VI.130.

16. VI.21; V.141; *Clough Letters*, p. 124 (No. 40, Oct. 28, 1852).

17. "On the Modern Element," pp. 304–5; Super, 1.19–20. In considering Greek literature as an "agent of intellectual deliverance," Arnold believed he had Goethe as his chief mentor. The 1856 note-book quotes Goethe's tribute to the educative power of Greek antiquity (*Note-Books*, p. 2; *Werke*, 60 vols. (Stuttgart and Tübingen, 1827–42), 46:50).

18. XI.287–88 (Super, 1.12.6–7, 11.26); V.136, 173 (Super, 1.111.6–8).

19. *Clough Letters*, p. 101; No. 26, *ca.* Mar. 1, 1849.

20. On the "grand style" see Henn, p. 10; J. Churton Collins, *Studies*, p. 253; R. A. Scott-James, *The Making of Literature* (London, 1928), p. 107; and for the background of this whole problem Bateson's Chapter 3, "Poetic Diction and the Sublime."

21. V.173–74; Super, 1.111.8–15. See Cleanth Brooks, *Modern Poetry and the Tradition* (London, 1948), pp. 28–29, 35, 45–46. T. S. Eliot's attack in *The Use of Poetry*, pp. 117–18, does not interpret Arnold's language altogether fairly. In *Selected Essays* (London,

1951), p. 309, he conjectures that Arnold here "may have been stirred to a defence of his own poetry."

22. See Heine, *Über Ludwig Börne* (Hamburg, 1840), especially pp. 27–28. An English translation of this material and also of the statement by Moses Hess in *Rom und Jerusalem* (Arnold does not seem to have known about this work, published 1862) is provided by F. E. Faverty, *Matthew Arnold the Ethnologist* (Evanston, 1951), p. 229, n. 38 to p. 174. Heine's poem *An die Mouche* refers to "Die Gegensätze . . . Des Griechen Lustsinn und der Gottgedanke Judäas." Hille, p. 36, n. 55, points out that "Hellenismus" in German designates not the Hellenic but the Hellenistic period of Greek history, and A. P. Kelso (*Matthew Arnold on Continental Life and Literature* (Oxford, 1914), p. 2) says, "The thoroughly un-Hellenic passion with which Matthew Arnold proclaimed his gospel of culture is exactly what we would have expected in a Jew who had deserted the disquisitions of the Synagogue for those of the Porch and the Academy."

23. VI.122. *Hellênismos*, from *hellênizô* ("to speak Greek"), originally meant the correct use of the Greek language, as Werner Jaeger notes in *Early Christianity and Greek Paideia* (Cambridge, Mass., 1961), n. 6 to p. 6. On the change of this term under Julian the Apostate to designate a cultural and political classicism, see Jaeger's discussion on p. 72.

24. The secondary distinction: VI.123–24. Not until 1871 does Arnold note, with the accompanying comment "Judea . . . Greece," the division laid down by Goethe on the basis of formlessness *versus* beauty of form in the conception of divinity (*Note-Books*, p. 147; for a generalizing comment of Heine's, see p. 479). Emphasis on the intellectual in Plato and Aristotle: VI.126–27. A Victorian classicist, Ernest Myers (*The Extant Odes of Pindar Translated Into English* (London and New York, 1892), pp. 16–17) attacked Arnold's description of Hellenism, maintaining that morality is always given its due. "But," he adds, "it is not thrust forward unseasonably or in exaggeration, nor is it placed in a false opposition to the interests of the aesthetic instincts." See also Lane Cooper, *The Greek Genius and Its Influence* (New Haven, 1917), p. 8, and J. M. Robertson, p. 157. Bonnerot, p. 362, states that by classicism Arnold meant a combination of moral and intellectual qualities derived from Hebraism as well as Hellenism. This claim seems to me completely unfounded; see below, n. 27.

25. VI.122. The preceding sentence concerning habituation is stated from Aristotle's point of view; he wrongly supposed a semantic link between *êthos*, "character," and *ethos*, "habit" (*E.N.* 2.1.1, 1103a17–18). Arnold's note-book for 1867 contains the dictum of Frederick the Great, as quoted by Sainte–Beuve: "C'est le bonheur des hommes quand ils pensent juste" (*Note-Books*, p. 48).

26. VI.182, 168, 194. *Rep.* 410d1–4, 411c4–e2.

27. Arnold's Platonizing condemnation of either extreme (which might almost equally well be termed Aristotelian) follows Heine, *Über Ludwig Börne*, who speaks of the harmonious blending of the two elements as the duty of European civilization. Cheney, p. 97, states that by culture Arnold means (broadly speaking), not pure Hellenism, but Hebraism plus Hellenism. This is the correct application, I believe, of the combination that Bonnerot (see above, n. 24) wrongly supposes to constitute Arnold's classicism.

CHAPTER XI

1. III.324; V.268 (Super, 1.175.20–31); "On the Modern Element," pp. 313–14 (Super, 1.36.3–5, 35.27–28); "Address to the Wordsworth Society, May 2nd, 1883," *Macmillan's Magazine*, 48 (1883) 155. The reference is to *Georg.* 3.66–68.

2. "On the Modern Element," *loc. cit.*; Super, 1.34.20–35.9.

3. Whitridge, pp. 68–69; Sept. 6, 1854. Sainte-Beuve's *Étude sur Virgile* appeared during 1855–56, as eight articles.

4. "On the Modern Element," p. 314; Super, 1.36.7–33. *Clough Letters*, p. 92; No. 22, Sept. 29, 1848.

5. See above, p. 89 and n. 28. The ode is 2.14 (*Eheu fugaces, Postume, Postume . . .*). At about this same time, in "From Easter to August" (*The Nineteenth Century*, 22 (1887) 324; Neiman, p. 69), he wrote, "There is always profit in being, as Horace says the poets are, a counter-influence to asperity, envy, and anger— *Asperitatis et invidiae corrector et irae*'; the reference is to *Ep.* 2.1.129. Such didactic use of Horace is exceptional. The 1887 essay on Shelley (IV.175) speaks of Leigh Hunt in relation to the Shelley circle as "the Horace of this precious world."

6. A letter of 1866 reveals that for twenty years he had been planning a tragedy with the poet as chief figure; elsewhere he acknowledges the adequacy of the Lucretian hexameter and the skill of Lucretius himself. See *Letters*, 1:322 (Mar. 17, 1866); III.92; VI.110.

7. "On the Modern Element," pp. 311–12; Super, 1.32–34.

8. *Letters*, 2:9 (June 5, 1869); XI.270–71 (Super, 1.1.13–16).

9. V.137; Super, 3.377.24–25.

10. III.51–52. The reference is from Cicero's *De Officiis*, 1.4.14.

11. For a countering view see C. T. Dougherty, "Ruskin's Moral Argument," *Victorian Newsletter*, No. 9 (Spring, 1956), p. 4.

12. Elsewhere (IV.104) the need led him to a remarkable broadening of the term "moral."

13. "On the Modern Element," p. 311; Super, 1.32.3–6.

14. Whitridge, pp. 44–45; Letter of May 22, 1859.

15. *Clough Letters*, p. 124 (No. 40, Oct. 28, 1852); VI.21; IV.306.

16. "That Christianity is true: that is, after all, the one thing that Arnold cannot really say" (Trilling, p. 332).

17. VIII.129, 89, 114–16 (Arnold's conceptions here are based on

Curtius' *History of Greece,* as they are when he deals with Pindar and Delphi); XI.194–95.

18. VIII.xxii.

19. The same concern is evident in an unpublished letter (Bodleian MS Eng. misc. c. 107) of February, 1871, written on Athenaeum stationery to (Frederic William) Farrar. Speaking of Farrar's Grammar Arnold says, "It is just the book to do what is wanted for philology—to make it interesting not only to a *rara avis* with a passion for [*illegible; perhaps* "verbal"] scholarship, but to every youth of intelligence who has a sense for history and human development. I am convinced a yet simpler book might be made on the same principles for the lower forms, so as to banish mere grind and absolutely dry lifeless rule even from these." Farrar (1831–1903), who became widely known as Dean of Canterbury and as a writer, had made philology and grammar his first serious studies. In 1867 he published *A Brief Greek Syntax;* this evidently is the work to which Arnold refers. For a criticism of Farrar's *Seekers After God* (London and New York, 1906) see above, pp. 161–62. For a brief reference to Farrar in Arnold's published writings see Super, 4.298.36–39.

20. XII.386, 391, 394–96, 357; Super, 4.290.11–18, 294.13–15, 22–28, 296.23–25, 297.34–298.4, 242.1–6. "A Speech at Eton" contains a clear criticism directed against Eton and Rugby (XI.179). Dr. Arnold's enlightened approach met with a disappointing response from his subordinates (Trilling, pp. 66–67). His keen sense of frustration, especially marked between 1838 and 1841, probably was related to this; see Stanley, *Life,* pp. 491–92, 533, 704. Underlying Arnold's remarks on *Alterthumswissenschaft* is the definition given by F. A. Wolf: "The characteristic of university instruction may be denoted by the word *Wissenschaft.* I call all teaching scientific which is *systematically laid out and followed up to its original source. E.g.,* A knowledge of classical antiquity is scientific when the remains of classical antiquity are connectedly studied in the original languages." These words, copied in the *Note-Books* (p. 494) and quoted in *Literature and Science* (IV. 324–25), come from p. 262 of an 1865 review of J. F. J. Arnoldt's book on Wolf; see above, n. 4 to Ch. V.

21. Hille, p. 73, claims that Arnold was willing to settle for the reading of "a characteristic selection," but I do not believe this is well grounded. His fourth chapter (pp. 60–75) deals with Arnold as educational reformer. For a brief survey of Matthew Arnold's influence as a writer on popular education, see W. S. Knickerbocker's essay "The Idea of Culture," in *The Reinterpretation of Victorian Literature,* ed. J. E. Baker (Princeton, 1950), pp. 102–3. A. C. Benson, pp. 399–401, argues that Arnold overrated the power of classical culture.

22. XII.394–95; Super, 4.296.30–31, 35–297.6, 23–25. In *Reports on Elementary Schools 1852–1882* (London, 1910), p. 228, Arnold says he believes that the effort required for Greek and Latin composition, is more healthy than that required for "receiving and storing a number of 'knowledges.'" Latin grammar, on the other hand, seemed to him profitable only for "the mainly moral discipline of learning something much more exactly than one is made to learn anything else"; it was badly taught, he believed, and needed to be delimited (*Letters*, 1:314; January, 1866). "We bar a learner's approach to Homer and Virgil," he declares elsewhere (XI.425–26), "by our *chevaux de frise* of elaborate grammar."

23. VI.289; Goulburn, pp. 221–31; *Reports*, pp. 168, 163, 88–89 (cf. 230: "'Of education,' says Butler, '*information itself is really the least part*'"). The same position has been defended with considerable power by Faber, pp. 79–81. On the wide public interest in Arnold's *Reports* and their significance, see Thomas Healing (his assistant in the Westminster schools) in Fitch, pp. 178–79.

24. *Reports*, pp. 186–87, 191–92, 200–201, 228–29. "A Speech at Westminster," *Macmillan's Magazine*, 19 (1874) 366. G. W. E. Russell (*Matthew Arnold* (London, 1904), pp. 91–92) says, "In 1872 he wrote to an enquirer: 'A single line of poetry, working in the mind, may produce more thought and lead to more light, which is what man wants, than the fullest acquaintance (to take your own instance) with the processes of digestion.'" He did not, however, favor learning fragments of poetry. This, as Sir Joshua Fitch tells us (p. 184), was a practice he detested; he insisted that the context must always be known as well.

25. *Clough Letters*, p. 95 (No. 24, late 1848 or early 1849); IV.49; *Letters*, 1:396 (Sept. 6, 1868). Arnold's letters to George Smith (Feb. 6, 1869) and Alexander Macmillan (Apr. 27, 1872; June 1, 1877) are now published in W. E. Buckler's *Matthew Arnold's Books: Toward a Publishing Diary* (Geneva and Paris, 1958), pp. 154, 157. They show that Arnold worked on the proposed anthology but could never get to the point of completing it.

26. Professor Buckler ("Studies in Three Arnold Problems," *PMLA*, 73 (1958) 268) says, "Implicit in the failure of the *Guide to Greek Poetry* to materialize is a subtle, perhaps even unconscious, questioning of the Hellenic ideal which Arnold had earlier espoused." There is nothing to support this claim, so far as I know.

27. IV.8; IX.260; III.65–66, 68–69. In his article "Sainte-Beuve" for the *Encyclopaedia Britannica*, 11th ed. (1911), 23:1024, Arnold says that by late 1849 "he had become a perfect critic—a critic of measure, not exuberant; of the centre, not provincial." (The 1961 edition gives Arnold's article in an abridged form, 19:827–28.) When he discusses prose styles Arnold generally follows Sainte-

Beuve's use of the terms Attic, Asiatic, provincial, and urbane. He differs, however, in always associating urbanity with the Attic style. See J. C. Major, "Matthew Arnold and Attic Prose Style," *PMLA*, 59 (1944) 1086–1103; this article is not concerned with classical topics. Arnold read Sainte-Beuve's "Qu'est-ce qu'un classique?" in vol. III, pp. 39–55 (3rd ed., 1851) of the *Causeries;* his copy is heavily marked. One sentence (p. 40) is clearly reflected in his thinking after 1850, although he himself never offered a comparable definition: "L'idée de *classique* implique en soi quelque chose qui a suite et consistance, qui fait ensemble et tradition, qui se compose, se transmet et qui dure." On the essay see below, p. 195. Arnold ignored Sainte-Beuve's clear warning (pp. 44, 49) against supposing that one can imitate the chaste elegance of the classical without knowledge of its inwardness and fire.

28. V.208–9; Super, 1.135.2–27.
29. See J. D. Jump, "Matthew Arnold and 'Enoch Arden,'" *Notes and Queries*, 1 (1954) 82–83. The incident which he relates may indicate that by 1864 Arnold's attitude towards classical and Romantic had changed.

CHAPTER XII

1. "The pietistic core of the Wesleyan movement soon came to the front," says Professor Houghton, p. 125. He quotes Mark Pattison's reference to "the professed contempt for all learned inquiry, which was a principle with the Evangelical school."
2. T. S. Eliot's charge that the view of art held by Pater derives from Arnold's conception of culture is refuted by Leonard Brown, "Arnold's Succession: 1850–1914," *Sewanee Review*, 42 (1934) 158. On the critical inheritance from Arnold see W. A. Madden, "The Divided Tradition of English Criticism," *PMLA*, 73 (1958) 69–80.
3. The "historical method" and its attendant relativism (see Houghton, pp. 14–15) were separate and later phenomena that began to appear about 1870, when the central Victorian period was ending.
4. There were individual instances of this as early as the close of the eighteenth century: at Christ's Hospital Coleridge was taught by a Hellenophile master to prefer Demosthenes to Cicero and Homer and Theocritus to Vergil (Herrick, p. 141). A decade later Thomas Arnold, as a schoolboy at Winchester, asked that English and Greek composition be included in the curriculum; the other boys thought he had gone mad (Wymer, p. 31).
5. J. E. Baker, "Our New Hellenic Renaissance," *The Reinterpretation of Victorian Literature*, pp. 219–20.
6. Athens began to build an empire only a few years after she had led her sister city-states in turning back the Persian invader.

7. On Arnold's concern for society see R. D. Spector, "Eliot, Pound, and the Conservative Tradition," *History of Ideas News Letter*, 3 (1957) 2–5.

8. It cannot be disproved that Arnold had intellectual anarchy in mind, but at the close of the 1860's civil anarchy seemed a real possibility to thoughtful Victorians. It is very difficult, moreover, to believe that Arnold, who repeatedly shows his sense of shock and outrage at mob action, was unaware of the way in which the term would normally be taken.

9. Bateson (pp. 124, 126) analyzes the structure of the average Victorian poem as a poetic superficies on a narrative or dramatic framework of prose.

10. The term "classicism" itself is no older in English than Carlyle's *French Revolution* (1837). Arnold pointedly avoids it.

11. "Matthew Arnold," says Brick (p. 47), "rejects the assertion that the 'outer world' (both as physical and as conceptual phenomena) exists only in relation to a transcendental power which focuses through a perceiving ego"; hence his difference not only from Shelley and Coleridge but from Tennyson and Browning as well.

12. This is well illustrated in Professor Trilling's comment on the larger significance of *Merope*. "Now," he says (p. 156), "Arnold sees only the advantages of order, not the volcanic disruptive forces in life to which order refers."

Bibliography

The list of works below is a supplementary bibliography, consisting of items not included in the notes. The latter cite books and articles in full when they first appear. All references to every author cited may be found by means of the index.

I. PRIMARY SOURCES

A. Poetry

Matthew Arnold's Poems. London and New York, 1955. (Everyman's Library.)

Poems by Matthew Arnold, ed. G. C. Macaulay. London, 1928.

Sohrab and Rustum, ed. G. E. Hollingworth. London, 1928.

Sohrab and Rustum . . ., ed. W. J. Cunningham Pike. Oxford, 1916.

B. Prose

Culture and Anarchy, ed. J. Dover Wilson. Cambridge, 1955.

"Curtius's 'History of Greece,'" *Pall Mall Gazette,* issues of October 12, 1868, pp. 9–10; April 28, 1871, pp. 10–11; June 4, 1872, pp. 11–12; July 22, 1872, pp. 11–12; March 25, 1876, p. 12.

"Italian Literature Before Giotto and Dante," *Macmillan's Magazine,* 33 (1876) 228.

"The Nadir of Liberalism," *Nineteenth Century,* 19 (1886) 645–63.

"Sainte-Beuve," *Academy,* 1 (1869) 31–32.

II. SECONDARY SOURCES

A. Reviews of Arnold's Works, Chiefly Poetry

"Belles Lettres," *Westminster Review,* 32 (1867) 593–608.

"Homeric Translators and Critics," *Saturday Review,* 12 (1861) 95–96.

"Merope," *Saturday Review,* 5 (1858) 19–20.

Review of *Essays in Criticism, North British Review,* 42 (1865) 158–82.

Swinburne, Algernon Charles, "Mr. Arnold's New Poems," *Fortnightly Review*, 2 (1867) 414–45.

B. General

Allott, Kenneth, *Matthew Arnold*. London and New York, 1955. (Writers and Their Work, No. 60.)

Armstrong, Isobel, *Arthur Hugh Clough*. London, 1962.

Bailey, Cyril, *Epicurus: The Extant Remains*. Oxford, 1926.

Batho, E. C. and Bonamy Dobrée, *The Victorians and After, 1830–1914*. London, 1950.

Bronowski, Jacob, *The Poet's Defence*. Cambridge, 1939.

Brooke, Stopford A., (*Four Poets*.) *A Study of Clough, Arnold, Rossetti and Morris*. London, 1908.

Buckley, Vincent, *Poetry and Morality*. London, 1959.

Butler, A. G., *The Three Friends: A Story of Rugby in the Forties*. London, 1900.

The Cambridge History of English Literature, ed. A. W. Ward and A. R. Waller, vol. XIII. Cambridge, 1932.

Carlyle, Thomas, *Critical and Miscellaneous Essays*, 6 vols. London, 1869.

Carré, J. M., *Goethe en Angleterre*. Paris, 1920.

Cecil, Lord David, *Poets and Story-Tellers: A Book of Critical Essays*. London, 1949.

Chorley, Lady Katherine, *Arthur Hugh Clough, The Uncommitted Mind*. Oxford, 1962.

Collins, J. Churton, *Greek Influence on English Poetry*. London, 1910.

Connell, W. F., *The Educational Thought and Influence of Matthew Arnold*. London, 1950.

Corbett, J. A., "Matthew Arnold and Germany," unpublished thesis. London, 1937.

Derham, M. G., "Borrowings and Adaptations from the Iliad and Odyssey in Matthew Arnold's 'Sohrab and Rustum,'" *University of Colorado Studies*, 7 (1909) 73–89.

Dyment, Clifford, *Matthew Arnold*. London, 1948.

Dyson, A. E., "The Last Enchantments," *Review of English Studies*, 8 (1957) 257–65.

Faverty, F. E., *The Victorian Poets: A Guide to Research*. Cambridge, Mass., 1956.

Furrer, Paul, *Die Einfluss Sainte-Beuve auf die Kritik Matthew Arnolds*. Diss. Zurich, 1920.

Gottfried, Leon, "Matthew Arnold's 'The Strayed Reveller,'" *Review of English Studies*, 11 (1960) 403–9.

Groom, Bernard, *On the Diction of Tennyson, Browning and Arnold.* Oxford, 1939. (Society for Pure English Tract No. 53.)

Grube, G. M. A., "Notes on the *PERI HUPSOUS* [Greek letters]," *American Journal of Philology,* 78 (1957) 355–74.

(Hölderlin, Friedrich,) *Poems of Hölderlin,* tr. Michael Hamburger. London, 1943.

Jamison, W. A., *Arnold and the Romantics.* Copenhagen, 1958. (Anglistica, vol. X.)

Johnson, W. S., "Victorian Self-Consciousness," *Victorian Newsletter,* no. 21 (Spring, 1962), pp. 4–7.

Knickerbocker, W. S., "Semaphore: Arnold and Clough," *Sewanee Review,* 41 (1933) 152–74.

Kranz, Walther, *Empedokles: Antike Gestalt und Romantische Neuschöpfung.* Zurich, 1949.

Maas, Ernst, *Goethe und die Antike.* Leipzig, 1912.

Maison, Margaret M., "Tom Brown and Company: Scholastic Novels of the 1850's," *English,* 12 (1958) 100–103.

Maitland, F. W., *The Life and Letters of Leslie Stephen.* London, 1910.

Oates, W. J., ed., *The Stoic and Epicurean Philosophers.* New York, 1940.

Pattison, Mark, *Memoirs.* London, 1885.

Paul, H. W., *Matthew Arnold.* London, 1907.

Powys, J. C., *Visions and Revisions.* London, 1915.

Prothero, R. Ernle, *The Life and Correspondence of A. P. Stanley,* 2 vols. London, 1893.

Rouse, W. H. D., *A History of Rugby School.* London, 1898.

Saintsbury, George E. B., *A History of Criticism,* 3 vols. London and Edinburgh, 1917.

———, *A History of English Prosody.* Oxford, 1906.

———, *A History of Nineteenth Century Literature (1780–1900).* London, 1916.

Schärer, Irene, *Oberman* [sic]: *Lettres publiées par E. P. de Senancour. Versuch einer Analyse.* Diss. Zurich, 1955.

Seturaman, V. S., "*The Scholar Gipsy* and Oriental Wisdom," *Review of English Studies,* 9 (1958) 411–13.

Shumaker, Wayne, "Matthew Arnold's Humanism: Literature as a Criticism of Life," *Studies in English Literature,* 2 (1962) 387–402.

Stanford, W. B., *The Ulysses Theme: A Study in the Adaptability of a Traditional Hero.* Oxford, 1954.

Steinmetz, Martha S., *Die ideengeschichtliche Bedeutung Matthew Arnolds*. Diss. Tübingen, 1932.

Studies in Honor of Basil L. Gildersleeve. Baltimore, 1902.

Swinburne, Algernon Charles, *Essays and Studies*. London, 1875.

Thomson, J. A. K., *Classical Influences on English Poetry*. London, 1951.

Tillotson, Geoffrey, *Essays in Criticism and Research*. London, 1942.

Tillotson, Kathleen, "Arnold and Carlyle," *Notes and Queries*, n.s. 2 (1955) 126.

———, "Rugby 1850: Arnold, Clough, Walrond, and *In Memoriam*," *Review of English Studies*, 4 (1953) 122–40.

Trawick, B. B., "The Sea of Faith and the Battle by Night in *Dover Beach*," *PMLA*, 65 (1950) 1282–83.

Trevelyan, Humphry, *Goethe and the Greeks*. Cambridge, 1941.

Turner, Paul, "*Dover Beach* and the *Bothie of Tober-na-Vuolich*," *English Studies*, 28 (Amsterdam, 1947) 173–78.

Vines, Sherard, *A Hundred Years of English Literature*. London, 1950.

Willey, Sir Basil, *Nineteenth Century Studies: Coleridge to Matthew Arnold*. London, 1949.

Winchester College, 1836–1906: A Register. Winchester, 1907.

Additional
Bibliography and Classical Sources
Prepared for This Edition

Relevant Bibliography since 1965:

The poetry: Kenneth Allott, ed., *The Poems of Matthew Arnold* (London and New York, 1965). The prose: R. H. Super, ed., *The Complete Prose Works of Matthew Arnold,* 11 vols. (Ann Arbor, 1960–77). General studies: Kenneth Allott, *Matthew Arnold: His Intellectual and Poetic Background* (London, 1973); Kenneth Allott, ed., *Matthew Arnold,* Writers and Their Background (London, 1976); Douglas Bush, *Matthew Arnold* (New York, 1971); William E. Buckler, *Matthew Arnold's Prose: Three Essays in Literary Enlargement* (New York, 1983); William E. Buckler, *On the Poetry of Matthew Arnold: Essays in Critical Reconstruction* (New York and London, 1982); A. Dwight Culler, *Imaginative Reason: The Poetry of Matthew Arnold* (New Haven and London, 1966); Carl Dawson, ed., *Matthew Arnold, the Poetry: The Critical Heritage,* Critical Heritage Series (London and Boston, 1973); Carl Dawson and John Pfordresher, eds., *Matthew Arnold, Prose Writings: The Critical Heritage,* Critical Heritage Series (London and Boston, 1979); David J. DeLaura, *Hebrew and Hellene in Victorian England: Newman, Arnold, and Pater* (Austin, 1969); David J. DeLaura, ed., *Matthew Arnold: A Collection of Critical Essays,* Twentieth Century Views (Englewood Cliffs, N.J., 1973); Howard W. Fulweiler, *Letters from the Darkling Plain: Language and the Grounds of Knowledge in the Poetry of Arnold and Hopkins,* University of Missouri Studies, 58 (Columbia, Mo., 1972); Park Honan, *Matthew Arnold: A Life* (New York, 1981); Richard Jenkyns, *The Victorians and Ancient Greece* (Cambridge, Mass., 1980); William A. Madden, *Matthew Arnold: A Study of the Aesthetic Temperament in Victorian England* (Bloomington and London, 1967); Fraser Neiman, *Matthew Arnold* (New York, 1968); Alan Roper, *Arnold's Poetic Landscapes* (Baltimore, 1969); James Simpson, *Matthew Arnold and Goethe* (London, 1979); G. Robert Stange, *Matthew Arnold: The Poet as Humanist* (Princeton, 1967); R. H. Super, *The Time-Spirit of Matthew Arnold* (Ann Arbor, 1970); Michael Thorpe, *Matthew Arnold* (London, 1969). Articles and short studies: Kenneth Allott, "A Background for *Empedocles on Etna,*" in *Essays and Studies,* 21 (1968) 80–100; Kenneth Allott, "Pater and Arnold," *Essays in Criticism,* 2

(1952) 219–21; Kenneth Allott, "the 'Scythian' in 'The Strayed Reveller,' " *Victorian Poetry*, 11 (1973) 163–66; Warren Anderson, "Arnold and the Classics," in *Matthew Arnold*, edited by Kenneth Allott (London, 1976), 259–85; Warren Anderson, "Arnold's Undergraduate Syllabus," *Arnoldian*, 6 (1979) 2–6; Warren Anderson, "Matthew Arnold and the Grounds of Comparatism," *Comparative Literature Studies*, 8 (1971) 287–302; Warren Anderson, "Types of the Classical in Arnold, Tennyson, and Browning," in *Victorian Essays: A Symposium*, edited by Warren Anderson and Thomas D. Clareson (Kent, Ohio, 1967), 60–70; Josephine M. Barry, "Goethe and Arnold's 1853 Preface," *Comparative Literature*, 32 (1980) 151–67; James A. Berlin, "Matthew Arnold's Rhetoric: The Method of an Elegant Jeremiah," *Rhetoric Society Quarterly*, 13 (1983) 29–40; Charles Berryman, "Matthew Arnold's *Empedocles on Etna*," *Victorian Newsletter*, 29 (1966) 5–9; R. R. Bolgar, "Classical Elements in the Social, Political, and Educational Thought of Thomas and Matthew Arnold," in *Classical Influences on Western Thought, A.D. 1650–1870*, edited by R. R. Bolgar (Cambridge, 1979), 327–38; Eugene N. Borza, "Sentimental Philhellenism and the Image of Greece," in *Classics and the Classical Tradition*, edited by Eugene N. Borza and Robert W. Carrubba (University Park, Pa., 1973), 5–25; Michael Bright, "*Merope* and the Poetics of Literary Revivalism," *Arnoldian*, 15 (1988) 49–58; William E. Buckler, "The Humanities Tradition of Matthew Arnold," *Victorian Newsletter*, 73 (1988) 20–23; William E. Buckler, "Matthew Arnold and the Crisis of Classicism: An Introduction," *British Institute Studies*, 10 (1982) 27–39; R. Peter Burnham, " 'Empedocles on Etna' and Matthew Arnold's Argument with History," *Arnoldian*, 12 (1985) 1–21; David R. Carroll, "Arnold's Tyrian Trader and Grecian Coaster," *Modern Language Review*, 64 (1969) 27–33; John Coates, "Two Versions of the Problem of the Modern Intellectual: *Empedocles on Etna* and 'Cleon,' " *Modern Language Review*, 79 (1984) 769–82; Sidney Coulling, "The Grave Tyrian and the Merry Grecian Once More," *Victorian Poetry*, 26 (1988) 11–24; David H. Covington, "Aristotelian Rhetorical Appeals in the Poetry of Matthew Arnold," *Victorian Poetry*, 24 (1986) 149–61; Robert A. Donovan, "The Browning Version: A Case Study in Victorian Hellenism," *Greyfriar: Siena Studies in Literature*, 25 (1984) 62–76; Dennis Douglas, "Matthew Arnold's Historic Sense: The Conflict of Greek and Tyrian in 'The Scholar-Gipsy,' " *Review of English Studies*, 25 (1974) 422–36; Richard Dowgun, "Some Victorian Perceptions of Greek Tragedy," *Browning Institute Studies*, 10 (1982) 71–90; Henry Ebel, "Arnold, H. A. Mason, and the Classical Tradition," *Arion*, 2 (1963) 108–13 (a reply to Mason; see p. 244 n. 1); Henry Ebel, "A Discreet Vote for Apollo," *Arion*, 5

(1966) 254–62 (an extended review of the present work); Henry Ebel, "Matthew Arnold and Classical Culture," *Arion*, 4 (1965) 188–220; Henry Ebel, "Matthew Arnold and Marcus Aurelius," *Studies in English Literature*, 3 (1963) 555–56; Sidney Feschbach, "Empedocles at Dover Beach," *Victorian Poetry*, 4 (1966) 271–75; L. M. Findlay, "From Helikon to Aetna: The Precinct of Poetry in Hesiod, Empedokles, Hölderlin, and Arnold," in *The Existential Coordinates of the Human Condition: Poetic—Epic—Tragic: The Literary Genre*, Analecta Husserliana, 18 (Dordrecht, 1985), 119–40; Norman Friedman, "The Young Matthew Arnold 1847–1849: 'The Strayed Reveller' and 'The Forsaken Merman,'" *Victorian Poetry*, 9 (1971) 405–28; Eric Glasgow, "The Greek Factors in the Poetry of Matthew Arnold," in *Romantic Reassessment*, 11 (Salzburg, 1973), 45–56; Ellen S. Grahtan, "'Nor Help for Pain': Matthew Arnold and Sophocles' *Philoctetes*," *Victorian Newsletter*, 48 (1975) 21–26; Alan Grob, "Arnold's 'Mycerinus': The Fate of Pleasure," *Victorian Poetry*, 20 (1982) 1–20; Gerhard Joseph, "The *Antigone* as Cultural Touchstone: Matthew Arnold, Hegel, George Eliot, Virginia Woolf, and Margaret Drabble," *PMLA*, 96 (1981) 22–35; Jane A. McCusker, "Browning's *Aristophanes' Apology* and Matthew Arnold," *Modern Language Review*, 79 (1984) 783–96; Dorothy M. Mermin, "The Two Worlds in Arnold's 'The Strayed Reveller,'" *Studies in English Literature*, 12 (1972) 735–43; Kevin O'Brien, "Matthew Arnold and the Hellenists of the 1890's," *Antigonish Review*, 35 (1978) 79–93; Gabriel Pearson, "The Importance of Arnold's *Merope*," in *The Major Victorian Poets: Reconsiderations*, edited by Isobel Armstrong (Lincoln, Nebr., 1969), 225–52; Linda R. Pratt, "Empedocles, Suicide and the Order of Things," *Victorian Poetry*, 26 (1988) 61–74; Linda L. Ray, "Callicles on Etna: The Other Mask," *Victorian Poetry*, 7 (1969) 309–20; Meredith B. Raymond, "Apollo and Arnold's 'Empedocles on Etna,'" *Review of English Literature*, 8 (1967) 22–32; C. A. Runcie, "Matthew Arnold and Myth: A Reading of the Preface of *Poems* (1853)," *Journal of the Australasian Universities Language and Literature Association*, 35 (1972) 5–17; Clyde de L. Ryals, "Arnold's *Balder Dead*," *Victorian Poetry*, 4 (1966) 67–81; Mary W. Schneider, "Arnold's 'Flaying of Marsyas,'" *Notes and Queries*, 24 (1977) 127–29; Mary W. Schneider, "Arnold's Two Regions of Form," *Victorian Newsletter*, 49 (1976) 22–24; Mary W. Schneider, "The Lucretian Background of 'Dover Beach,'" *Victorian Poetry*, 19 (1981) 190–95; Mary W. Schneider, "Orpheus in Three Poems by Matthew Arnold," *Victorian Poetry*, 10 (1972) 29–44; Mary W. Schneider, "Plutarch's Night-Battle in Arnold, Clough, and Tennyson," *Arnoldian*, 9 (1982) 32–38 (see above, 214); Ronald A. Sharp, "A Note on Allusion in 'Dover Beach,'" *English Language Notes*, 21 (1983)

52 – 55; M. G. Sundell, "Story and Context in 'The Strayed Reveller,'"
Victorian Poetry, 3 (1965) 161 – 70; Martin J. Svaglic, "Classical
Rhetoric and Victorian Prose," in *The Art of Victorian Prose*, edited
by George Levine and William Madden (New York, 1968), 268 – 88;
Michael Timko, "Arnold, Tennyson, and the English Idyl: Ancient
Criticism and Modern Poetry," *Texas Studies in Language and Lit-
erature*, 16 (1974) 135 – 46; Frank M. Turner, "Antiquity in Victorian
Contexts," *Browning Institute Studies*, 10 (1982) 1 – 14; Edward A.
Watson, "Wilde's Iconoclastic Classicism: 'The Critic as Artist,'"
English Literature in Transition (1880 – 1920), 27 (1984) 225 – 35;
René Wellek, *History of Modern Criticism, 1750 – 1950: The Later
Nineteenth Century* (New Haven and London, 1965), 4:155 – 80;
Paul Zietlow, "Failure and Integrity in Matthew Arnold's *Merope*,"
Modern Language Quarterly, 43 (1982) 67 – 86; Paul Zietlow, "Heard
but Unheeded: The Songs of Callicles of [sic] Matthew Arnold's *Em-
pedocles on Etna*," *Victorian Poetry*, 21 (1983) 241 – 56; Joyce Zo-
nana, "Matthew Arnold and the Muse: The Limits of the Olympian
Ideal," *Victorian Poetry*, 23 (1985) 59 – 74. Summaries of unpublished dissertations in *Dissertation Abstracts International:* Aburawan
El-Majdoub, "The Development of Arnold's Humanistic Thinking,"
45 (1985) 2883 – 84A (Oklahoma State); Lydia C. Giglio, "The Progress of Homer in Victorian England," 29 (1969) 2211A (North Car-
olina); Washington I. Hunt, "The Influence of Homer on the Poetry
of Matthew Arnold," 31 (1971) 6575A (Yale); John U. Peters, "Matthew Arnold: The Heroes of His Poetry," 35 (1974) 412A (Wisconsin); Mary W. Schneider, "The Classical Poetry of Matthew Arnold,"
29 (1966) 6052 – 53; Charles D. Svitavsky, "The Place of the Greeks
in Matthew Arnold's Conception of Poetry," 27 (1967) 1795A – 96A
(Wisconsin).

*Complete forms of the abbreviations used in the list on p. 209 and in the
supplementary list are as follows:*
A. Aeschylus: *Ag., Agamemnon; Cho., Choephoroe (Libation Bearers);
Eum., Eumenides; Pr., Prometheus Vinctus; Th., Septem contra The-
bas.* Ar., Aristophanes: *Av., Aves* (Birds). Catull., Catullus. Cic., Ci-
cero: *Tusc., Tusculanae Disputationes.* D., Diels *(Fragmente der
Vorsokratiker).* D. L., Diogenes Laertius. Epict., Epictetus: *Ench.,
Enchiridion (Manual, Handbook).* E., Euripides: *Ba., Bacchae.* Hdt.,
Herodotus. Hes., Hesiod: *Op., Opera et Dies (Works and Days); Th.,
Theogonia.* (Homer:) *Il., Iliad; Od., Odyssey.* Hor., Horace: *C., Car-
mina (Odes); Ep., Epistles; Epod., Epodes. h. Cer., hymnus (Homer-
icus) ad Cererem (Homeric Hymn to Demeter). h. Merc., . . . ad*

Mercurium (. . . to Hermes). Juv., Juvenal. Lucr., Lucretius. M. Aur.,
Marcus Aurelius Antoninus. Max. Tyr., Maximus Tyrius (of Tyre).
Men., Menander: *Mon., Monostichoi (Single Verses)*. Ov., Ovid: *Fast.,
Fasti; Met., Metamorphoses*. Paus., Pausanias. Pind., Pindar: *N., P.,
Nemean, Pythian Odes; Fr., Fragmenta*. Pl., Plato: *Phaedr., Phaedrus;
Rep., Republic; Symp., Symposium*. Plaut., Plautus: *Poen., Poenulus*.
Plot., Plotinus *(Enneads)*. Plut., Plutarch: *Mor., Moralia*. Sen., Seneca:
Ep., Epistles. S., Sophocles: *Aj., Ajax; Ant., Antigone; El., Electra;
OC, Oedipus Coloneus; OT, Oedipus Tyrannus; Ph., Philoctetes;
Tr., Trachiniae*. Suet., Suetonius: *Caes., Vita Caesaris*. Tac., Tacitus:
Germ., Germania. Ter., Terence: *Heaut., Heauton Timoroumenos (Self-
Tormentor)*. Theoc., Theocritus. Thgn., Theognis. Th., Thucydides.
Verg., Vergil: *Aen., Aeneid; Ecl., Eclogues; Georg., Georgics*.

*The following is an incomplete supplement to the list of classical
sources, limited by restrictions of space. Poems with the largest number
of additional source attributions are listed first.*

"The Strayed Reveller"
43 – 48: cf. *Od*. 10.210 – 13.
78 – 79: Ov. *Fast*. 3.409 – 10?
130 – 34: cf. Lucr. 2.646 – 51,
   3.18 – 22.
164: Hdt. 4.46.3.
206: Hes. *Op*. 171, P. O. 2.71,
   cf. P. 4.251.
258 – 60: cf. Ov. *Met*. 6.720 –
   21.
286 golden-haired: *Od*. 10.220?
See Liddell-Scott-Jones on
chrusokomês, chrusoplokamos.

"Empedocles on Etna"
   Act 1, Scene 2
82 – 86: cf. D. 31B2.
129 – 30: M. Aur. 7.59?
136: M Aur. 2.5?
147 – 50: cf. Epict. *Ench*. 8.
175 – 76: cf. Lucr. 5.156 – 57,
   164 – 65.
445 – 47: S. *Tr*. 112 – 18?
457 – 60: Ov. *Met*. 4.600 – 3.

"Sohrab and Rustum"
400 – 2: *Il*. 22.139 – 40.
402 – 4. *Il*. 16.610 – 13.
474 – 79: *Il*. 16.633 – 37.
537 – 39: *Il*. 22.333, 335 – 36?

"Balder Dead"
   1. Sending
127: Verg. *Aen*. 4.440, 6.438.
288: cf. *Il*. 23.69.
   2. Journey to the Dead
101 – 10: cf. Verg. *Aen*. 6.388 –
   91.
   3. Funeral
71: cf. *Od*. 14.55, 15.325,
   16.60, 17.311; *et freq*.
98: *Il*. 24.724.
225 – 29, 246 – 53: *Il*. 22.174 –
   80?
548: Verg. *Aen*. 6.466?

Merope
487 – 90: S. *El*. 193 – 96?
1054: cf. S. *El*. 947.
1219 – 22: cf. S. *El*. 1222 – 26.

"Resignation"
164 – 68: cf. Lucr. 2.7 – 10;
   M. Aur. 7.48, 9.30.
237: cf. Lucr. 2.15 – 16.
243 – 44: Juv. 10.357, cf. 356.

"Quiet Work"
(Title): cf. Plot. 3.8.4.

"Mycerinus"
47 – 48: cf. Lucr. 2.646 – 51,
   3.18 – 22.

"Cromwell"
39 – 40: Hdt. 6.105.1 – 2.
41 – 44: Hdt. 8.65.1.

"In Utrumque Paratus"
1 One all-pure: cf. Pl. *Symp.*
   211c1, cited in Plot. 1.6.7.
11 – 14: cf. Pl. *Phaedr.* 245c9,
   cited in Plot. 1.6.8 – 9.

"To a Gipsy Child by the Sea-
shore"
22 – 23: cf. Lucr. 2.5 – 6.

"The New Sirens"
44: cf. Od. 12.39 – 54, 151 –
   200.

"Tristram and Iseult"
   3. *Iseult of Brittany*
143 – 45: cf. Suet. *Caes.* 7.

"Thyrsis"
88 – 89, cf. 95: Ov. *Met.* 5.391 –
   92, 395?

"Epilogue to Lessing's Laocoön"
43 – 48: cf. Theocr. 11.7 – 16,
   (Mosch.) *Epitaphium Bionis*
   58 – 64.

"Bacchanalia; or, The New Age"
67 – 68: cf. Ter. *Heaut.* 77, Juv.
   1.85.

"The World and the Quietist"
25 – 28: Hdt. 5.105.2.

"Self-Deception"
5 – 12; Pl. *Rep.* 614b3 – 621b7.

"The Scholar-Gipsy"
246 – 50: Hdt. 4.196.1 – 2.

"Obermann Once More"
293: Verg. *Ecl.* 4.5.

"S.S. 'Lusitania' "
10: cf. *Il.* 1.485; *Od.* 1.430; *et
freq.*

"Geist's Grave"
15 – 16: Verg. *Aen.* 1.462.

"Westminster Abbey"
134 – 40: Plut. *Consolatio ad
   Apollonium*, ch. 14 (*Mor.*
   109A).

"Poor Matthias"
6: cf. Catull. 3.6 – 7.
209: cf. Catull. 3.11, Lucr.
   6.1225.

"Fragments from 'Lucretius' "
(Allott No. 145, p. 585; not in
   Tinker and Lowry)
Fr. i: Epicurus, *Epistula ad
   Menoeceum* 125, p. 61.6 – 8
   Usener.

Index

Numbers following a colon refer to notes.

Ann Arbor Paperbacks